Steven Heller

The Picture Book Book

The Art of Seymour Chwast

gestalten

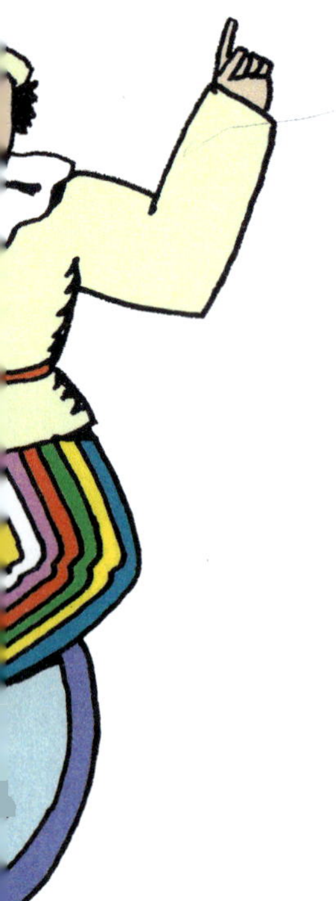

Steven Heller

The Picture Book Book

The Art of Seymour Chwast

Contents

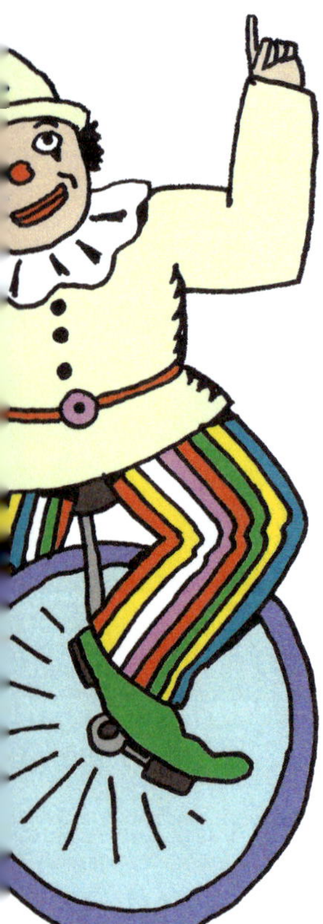

Books as Objects 116

Classics 142

How to Create a Children's Book 184

by Camille Murphy

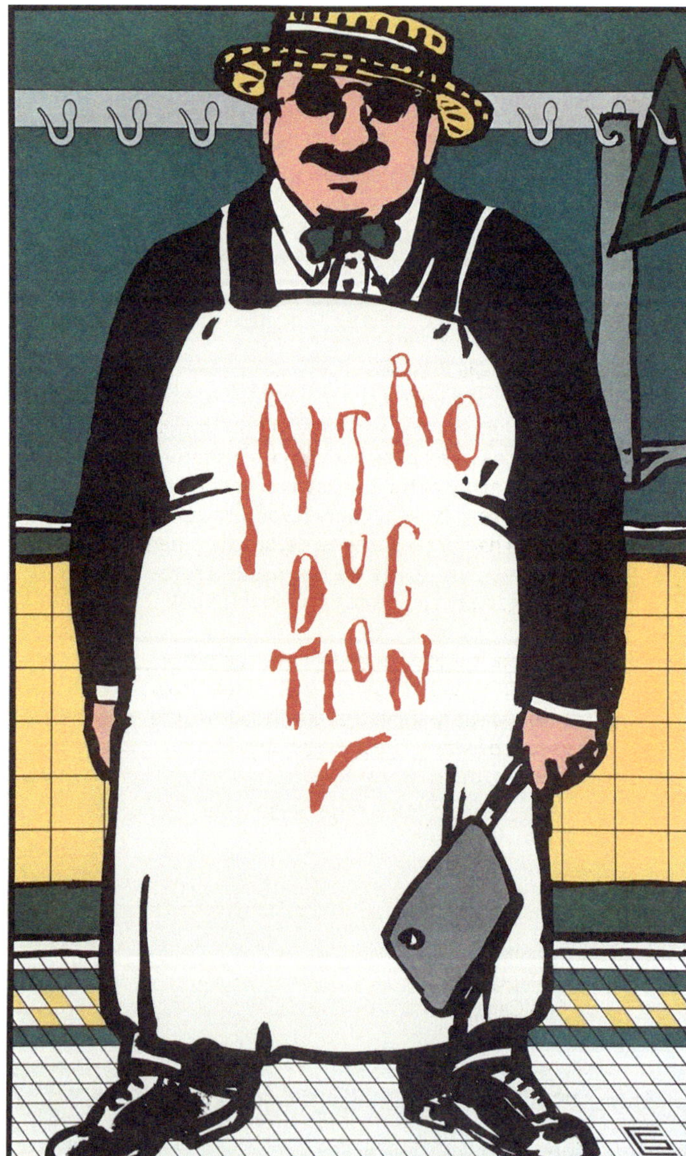
INTRO
DUC
TION

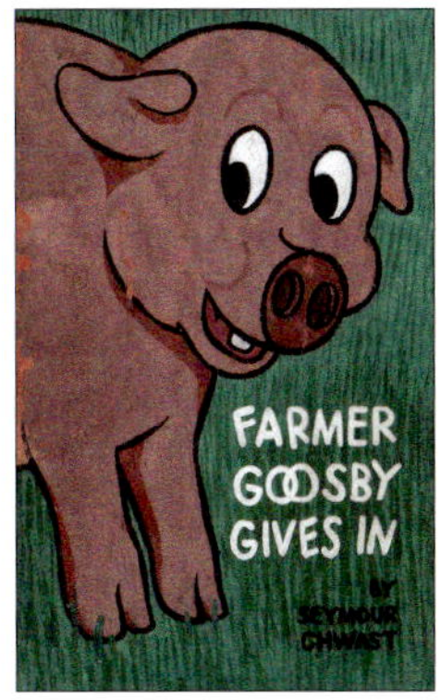

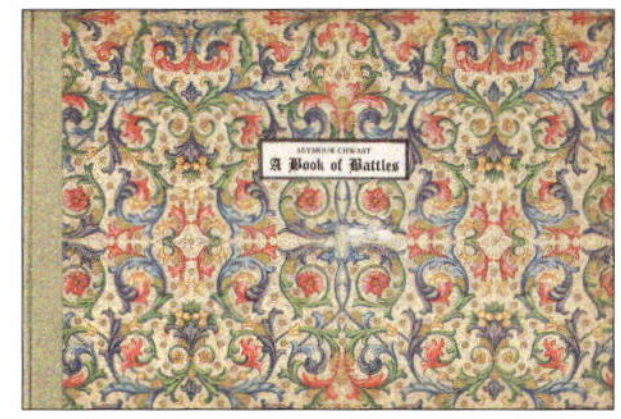

Seymour Chwast and I are best friends and collaborators. For four decades, I have written dozens of books, catalogs, articles, and essays with *and* about him, covering almost all the formal and conceptual aspects of his art and design, including metal sculptures of huge heads, chaotic military battles, extraordinary animals, large paintings of Mexican *lucha libre* wrestlers, and other flabbergasting experiments. You name it, I wrote something about it.

So, with all due modesty, I should know more about Chwast's work than almost anyone else—possibly even Chwast himself. But *The Picture Book Book* proves my claim is wrong. Until getting involved as the writer of this book I actually understood very little about Chwast's calling as a prolific children's book author and illustrator. Although I've seen many of the books herein (when my son was learning to read he kept a few favorites near his bed), until now I had not seen, no less read, all of them. A few that were unknown to me are unexpected revelations for their ingenuity and acuity; for me this book unearths a cache of lost treasures.

On the one hand, it is like hearing a never-before -released Beatles song. On the other, I ask myself: How could I have been so short-sighted as to virtually ignore his kid's books for so long. In my own defense, I had considered Chwast's "other" work—his posters, packages, magazines, record albums, book covers, jackets, and book illustrations for adult audiences, in short, a lifetime of most everything in his extensive archive—to be his *primary* oeuvre. Indeed, as an illustration and design authority, there was more than enough to sink my teeth into without addressing his kids' book legacy. It was best left to children's book experts, like Leonard Marcus, who in 2023 curated "Kid In A Candy Store," a retrospective exhibition of Chwast's collected books at the Eric Carle Museum of Picture Book Art in Amherst, Massachusetts. Paradoxically, I often described Chwast's métier as blending that of a child's play with mature concepts and visual/verbal linguistics. After investing more time with his children's books, it becomes crystal clear that the same sophistication is the foundation for everything he does. This eureka moment is to newly appreciate what is as plain as the nose on his face (and mine): namely, that the 40 children's books he has created comprise a significant part of his lifelong output (not counting the dozen that were never published) and represent a parallel career in their own right.

Chwast's own baby steps at making books for a younger audience manifested in the paste-up for *Farmer Goosby Gives In*, which he produced at Abraham Lincoln High School in Brooklyn, NY, as a class assignment for legendary art teacher Leon Friend. A jolly cover—yet to evolve into a truly *Chwastian* style—featured a happy pig against a bright green background. It never saw the light, remaining but one of many speculative projects mentally filed away under "Finding My Voice." A few years passed before Chwast made another book, this time a limited edition of a non-children's book, *The Book of Battles*, with hand-colored woodcut illustrations.

In describing Chwast's children's work, Marcus—whose scholarship includes a book on Maurice Sendak, among other champions of the picture book genre—concurs with my conclusion about Chwast's "other" work: "[His] revolutionary contributions to the world of graphic design have overshadowed his equally impactful picture book career—until now. This is the first museum exhibition to focus on Chwast's books for children . . . Chwast approaches his books with the same inventive design, signature humor, and love of typography found in his commercial art. His illustrations are characterized by bold colors and a flat graphic style. He creates unexpected scenes and populates his stories with witty human, animal, and imaginary characters," adding, ..."many of Chwast's books play with format, encouraging readers to reimagine the traditional reading experience."

In addition to vitrines filled with his books, the exhibition featured a number of surprising environmental extras—veritable Easter eggs from Chwast's inexhaustible reaches—including large blowups of single-page illustrations of clowns and animals, and a flock of hand-cut birds perched on, and hanging off, a tight rope that crossed the gallery space. Such elements, like the books themselves, are never solely intended for Chwast's young audience and their parents, but for his own playful pleasure.

The work in *The Picture Book Book* reflects that same urge to entertain. Whatever Chwast produces must trigger as much excitement for the audience as it does for the artist, if not more. I really don't believe that Chwast would be the pioneering illustrator he is had he not had the freedom provided by his picture books to stimulate neurogenesis and cross-pollinate his imagination.

— Steven Heller

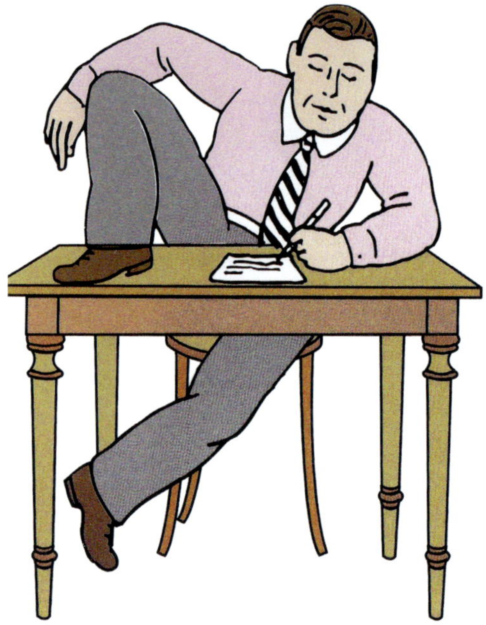

About Seymour

Seymour Chwast (pronounced Qwast *not* Shwast) brought a comical, vernacular sensibility to 20th-century American applied art and design. Along with unapologetic methods rooted in stylish vintage decorative traditions—notably Victorian, art nouveau, and art deco—he never slavishly *copied* the past. Instead, he synthesized, reinvented, and parodied it.

Chwast's art was postmodern long before the term was coined; yet it was resolutely modern in its rejection of the nostalgic and romantic representation that was popular in mainstream advertising and magazines at the time. Instead of prosaic and melodramatic tableaux, Chwast emphasized clever concepts. What makes the very best of his art so arresting, and so identifiable, is the tenacity of his *ideas*—simple, complex, rational, and absurd *ideas*. Droll humor and conceptual acuity were the foundations on which he built a visual language that advanced editorial illustration beyond pictorial mimicry of a sentence or headline. His images complimented and supplemented the words, giving them additional layers of meaning. What's more, Chwast is master of the visual pun, which enables him to manipulate pictorial concepts like a sculptor shapes soft clay.

He is also skilled at what standup comedians call the slow burn or double take; using commonplace things as foils for uncommon illusions, he twists imagery into double entendres. Chwast employs one of the most adaptable pictorial lexicons in the world. Yet when he repeats himself, as all artists do, he makes every effort to turn such repetition into something novel. Chwast is nothing if not novel (you can make book on that).

However, the big idea alone does not make art that shall be called "a Chwast." His ideas are routinely framed by means of playful stylistic conceits that, although varied, express his singular personality. Virtuosic drawing underpins almost everything he touches, but the results are never slick.

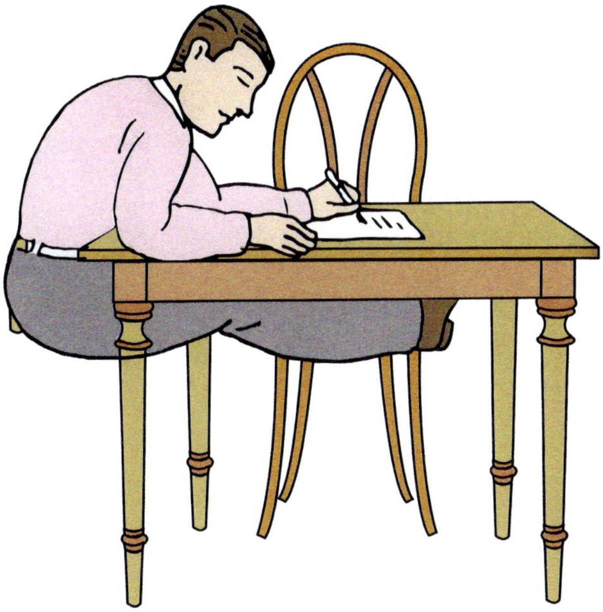

His finishes are often unfinished looking and not tethered to one particular method; his illustration ranges from gnarly to precise, from naive to sophisticated. He is versatile with media, including monoprint, collage, and montage; paint, ink, and charcoal; pencil, burin, and graver. Few are as flexible yet so consistent. Decades ago, he may have ended the brief revolutionary phase of his career (even Mao knew one cannot be a revolutionary forever), but judging from his output, Chwast is resilient and remains as restlessly motivated as ever.

Born to Polish immigrant parents in The Bronx, New York City, Chwast was—like so many first-generation Jewish children—given an aristocratic English surname as a first name (i.e., Milton, Murray, and Morris) and an unusual last name (which means "weed" in Polish). An only child, bright and inquisitive but painfully shy, he had few close friends; by way of compensation, drawing entered his life when he was seven. He attended WPA-sponsored art classes, which made him appreciative of the difference between "museum" and "commercial" art; he instinctively preferred billboards and advertisements to Picassos and Mondrians. Further influenced by Walt Disney, the Sunday comics, and serial movies, he developed a repertory of his own cartoon heroes, including Jim Lightning and Lucky Day, filling up various lined notebooks with their exploits. His mother and father (who divorced when Chwast was 16 years old), moved to Coney Island in the early '40s, where he was enrolled in Abraham Lincoln High School. What was outwardly a drab New York City public school for low- and lower-middle-class children was actually a pulsating heart of art and design. The school's art teacher, Leon Friend, changed Chwast's life.

At Lincoln, he was accepted as a member of the elite "Art Squad," a roving band of sign and poster artists. It was a spin-off of a graphic design class taught by Friend, through which Chwast learned to design typography, make stark graphic images, and tap the potential of commercial art as an expressive medium. Coauthor of a book titled *Graphic Design*, which wed practice to heretofore ignored history, Friend believed that there was no greater glory for a young artist than to have his work published in any public-facing venue, and he demanded that all his students enter every design competition. Chwast was a prodigious submitter, and at 16 his first illustration was published in the reader's column of *Seventeen* magazine (art directed by Cipe Pineles). Having tasted printer's ink, he took to it like a baby to mother's milk—or a vampire to fresh blood.

Early indoctrination into commercial art was total and unalterable. In 1948 (just as the Cold War was getting hotter), Chwast began the next stage of his education at New York's tuition-free Cooper Union along with Edward Sorel, Reynold Ruffins, and Milton Glaser, with whom he later joined forces to found Push Pin Studio. During those stimulating Cooper Union years, Chwast was profoundly inspired by the political graphics of Ben Shahn, Georg Grosz, Georges Rouault, and Honoré Daumier. The conceptual strength of these stylistically dissimilar, but spiritually kindred, critical commentators was reflected in his own penchant for expressive woodcuts. He was anti-bomb, anti-military, and pro-peace; as a member of SANE (National Committee for a Sane Nuclear Policy), Chwast repeatedly expressed concern for social commitment. As for his comic sensibility, his most direct antecedents were the masters of paradox and irony André François and Saul Steinberg. Chwast is nothing if not a practicing connoisseur of irony.

Cooper Union was tied to the then-fashionable abstract expressionist art canon at the same time that Chwast and his classmates were developing their proto-postmodern visual personas. His education was, therefore, as much rooted in the rejection of these abstract tendencies as the embrace of alternatives. Realizing that he couldn't (or wouldn't) paint in the proscribed manner pushed him into more comedic artistic realms and, subsequently, to commercial art. In their sophomore year, Chwast, Glaser, and Ruffins formed a small design studio called Design Plus. However, after completing two jobs, they summarily closed shop.

Upon graduating from Cooper Union, Chwast worked for a year in *The New York Times* promotion department where, under the tutelage of art director George Krikorian, he learned the principles of classical typography. He was

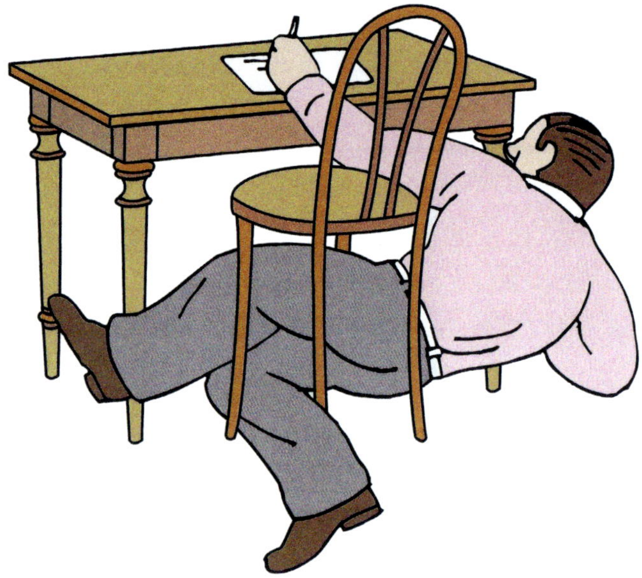

given some visible illustration work; however, a year was just about enough time to stay in *the The Times*, bullpen, so he left for greener pastures, bluer skies, and whiter whites (too bad he didn't know how good he had it). As it turned out, his subsequent jobs amounted to a string of failures, beginning with a layout job at *Esquire* magazine (from which he was fired because he was unable to render good preparatory comprehensives) and ending with a wretched stint in Condé Nast's art department.

In desperation he turned to freelancing. Together with Ruffins and Sorel, he produced a promotional publication designed to show prospective clients that ideas were as central to design and illustration as was emphasis on technique. The document turned into a semi-regular mailer the group called the *Push Pin Almanack*, inspired by the *Old Farmer's Almanac*. Each issue included drawings, texts, and bits of trivia on specific almanac themes. At the time there were a few other studios issuing regular promotion pieces, but none so ambitious or inventive as the *Almanack*, which brought in enough freelance work that Seymour, Sorel, and Glaser decided to form a studio, which they christened Push Pin. Seymour credits Glaser for realizing that a full-fledged studio had greater business and creative potential than going their individual ways.

Starting a design studio in 1954 was about as easy as printing a business card and renting office space. Push Pin's rent was low and a pay phone served all their telecommunications needs. Illustration assignments for educational slide shows and renderings for package design proposals provided respectable cash flow. After salaries were paid to an assistant and a secretary, each studio member earned a whopping $25 a week.

Push Pin fostered an adventurously eclectic aesthetic that revived Victorian, art nouveau, and art deco (Chwast dubbed this his "Roxy Style"). The studio created contemporary contexts for older graphic methods, foreshadowing the revivalism of the early '80s. Chwast collected varied historical styles, drawing nourishment and then discarded them as was his wont. He said he gave up woodcuts in the '60s because the German expressionist technique had lost its vigor. What's more, given Push Pin's sampler of styles, clients were asking for certain looks and moods, with Chwast trying to fulfill this need while tapping into his own inclinations.

What became known as the Push Pin Style—an eclectic mélange of illustration and design—derived, according to Chwast, not from forced imposition of a "look" but from the requisites of each assignment. It was his goal to state a client's message and identity in personal ways yet with as public and engaging vocabularies as possible. Although Chwast explains that he and the studio as a whole were swept along with the "pop art thing" of the '60s—bright colors and stylized outline drawings—such a statement should not diminish the significance of his own innovations.

A historic exhibition in 1970 at the Louvre's Musée des Arts Décoratifs, in Paris, underscored the inevitable canonization of Push Pin and Chwast's accession into the pantheon of great illustrators. It marked the first time an American design studio had been honored by such a prestigious (and foreign) cultural center. French critics applauded Push Pin for its nonconformity, and some even voiced surprise that such work would be supported by a capitalist system. The show traveled throughout Europe and to Brazil and cemented the Push Pin Style; Chwast's work had more visibility than ever.

Glaser left Push Pin in 1975 to explore different media and métiers, ending their 20-year collaboration. But Chwast felt no need to abandon the studio. He continued as Push Pin's director. He also continued publishing on a regular basis the highly popular, though occasional, *Push Pin Graphic*, which evolved directly from the *Push Pin Almanack* and subsequently became *Push Pin Monthly Graphic*, a thematic showcase of Push Pin's art and ideas. Thematic issues, including Mothers, The Condensed History of the World, Crime and Food, New Jersey, and The Chicken, served as outlets for Chwast's creative obsessions as well as a showcase for other members of the new Push Pin Studio. More than a decade after the *Graphic* folded, Chwast started *The Nose*,

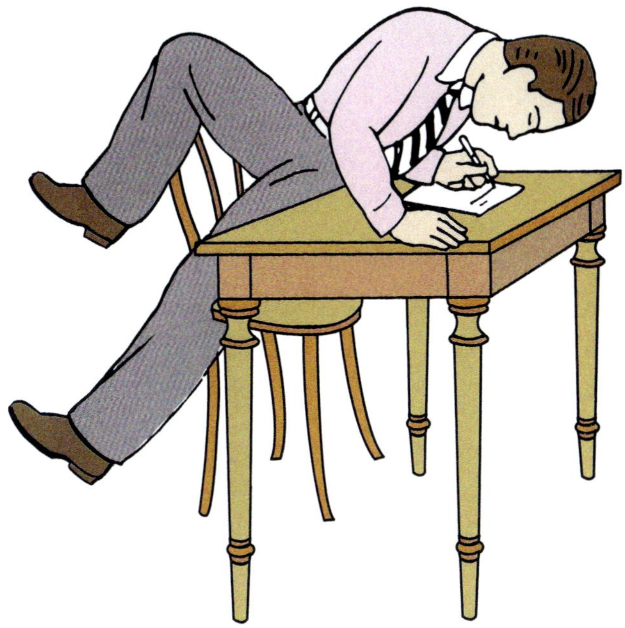

a quarterly *Festschrift* devoted to ideas on politics, society, and culture. Chwast also began something of a poster renaissance with projects for *Forbes* magazine and Mobil. During this time, Push Pin Press was founded as a means to package books that appealed to Chwast's sense of playfulness. In fact, the second stage of Chwast's career as a solo act, so to speak, was consumed with an insatiable desire to play . . . and so he did.

Chwast appears laid-back to a fault, a deception he has successfully cultivated as part of his mild-mannered, absent-minded image. In fact, he is a tireless worker and a ceaseless producer of quantity and quality. To understand what makes him tick, useful references are the comic strips, comic books, and animated films that made such a strong impression on him throughout his life. In addition to his formal art and design education, he learned some key lessons from the likes of *Mutt and Jeff* and *Bringing up Father*, *Krazy Kat* and *Dick Tracy*, among others. These strips taught him gesture, expression, and timing—traits that Chwast controls with exceptional facility yet minimalist means. It is therefore not surprising that his current drawings (and particularly his metal sculptures) have what he calls "traces of comic strip iconography." He reflexively borrows from the comic to tell narrative stories that cannot be told in one image. "Single image illustrations can tell stories too, but in a different way," he says. "My work usually combines metaphorical messages using the visual language. A strip can tell more with its possibility of a beginning and end or before and after."

Chwast is a peripatetic stylist, moving from one pictorial mode to another when either the mood or manuscript requires it. He has mastered various media like an actor inhabits different roles. Metal became his favored ersatz canvas. Cutting, sculpting, and painting on sheet metal gives him the physicality and scale that brings his two-dimensional ideas to three-dimensional life. What started out as cutting and bolting galvanized metal to replicate favorite toys (including tin cars and motorcycles) grew into an obsessive, if not dangerous métier that induced many cuts. Metal was once what separated his muse-inspired art from his commercial endeavors, but over time the boundaries blurred.

After a few years his art-making shifted again. He started painting battle scenes—or rather, "battle patterns"—on 8 × 9 ft (2.5 × 2.75 m) canvases, each one a jumble of tanks, soldiers, planes, and other materiel, as though a child might have scribbled them. He chose models for this cannon fodder from early 20th century tin toys that doubtless were ubiquitous in some young boys' toy boxes. The paintings, rendered in an obsessively naive manner, suggest the faceless, mechanistic, inhumanity of war; akin to wallpaper, they comment on how dangerous it is that, in many parts of the world, war has become little more than a backdrop.

For over seven decades, Chwast has unpretentiously contributed to visual culture. Unpretentious, because anyone who knows him will attest that he just tirelessly does his "jobs" with no other ambition than to *make* them. Sometimes they are just fine, but sometimes they are masterpieces of visual erudition. When his monograph, *Seymour Chwast: The Left-Handed Designer* (Harry N. Abrams), was published in 1985, it might have marked the pinnacle of his career. But in the years since its publication, Chwast has filled another volume and could easily fill more.

It may seem trite to call Chwast a consummate artist. Yet he is consumed by art. Chwast is his art; he is what he makes. His hands are always covered with ink; his clothes are stained with paint; his hair is speckled with pigment. There isn't a day when he doesn't create something. His collected physical work would easily fill a sizeable warehouse (or cruise ship); his editorial illustrations (before digital files) alone number in the thousands. He has designed and illustrated over 40 children's books. And after all this, he continues to generate witty, beautiful work for all ages. In the pantheon of American (nay, world) illustration, he stands, albeit slightly shorter and a little more rumpled, along with N.C. Wyeth, J.C. Leyendecker, and Norman Rockwell—and he's not through yet.

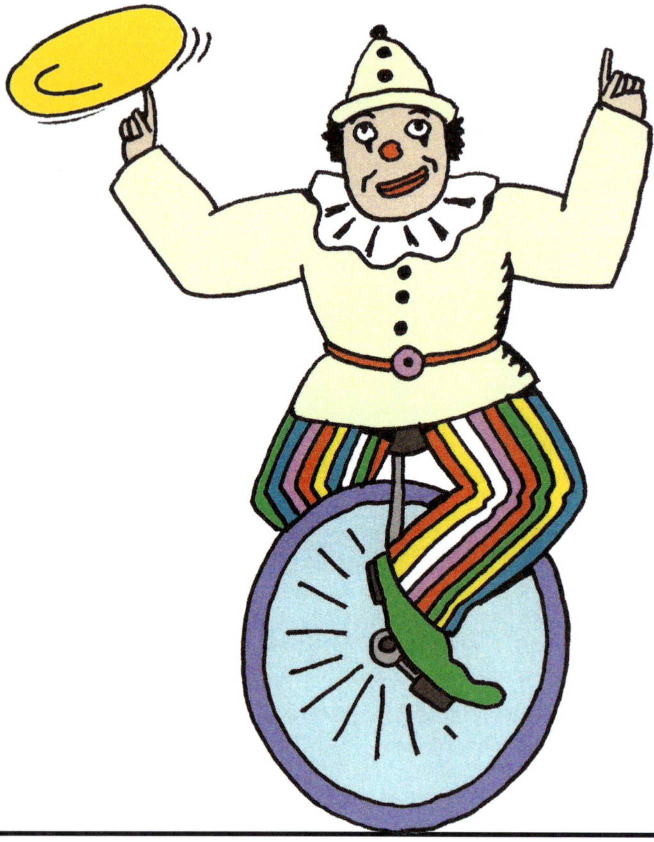

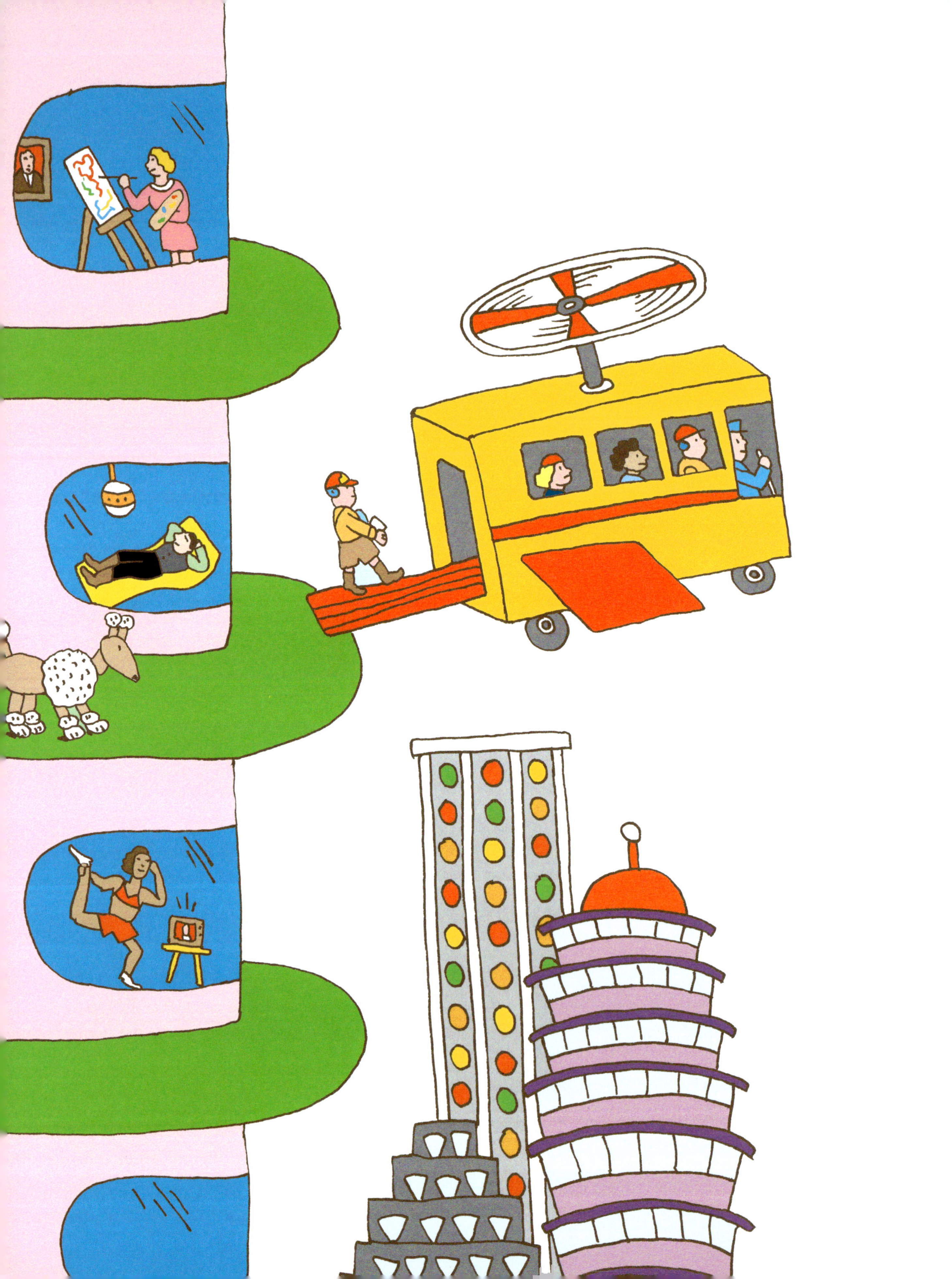

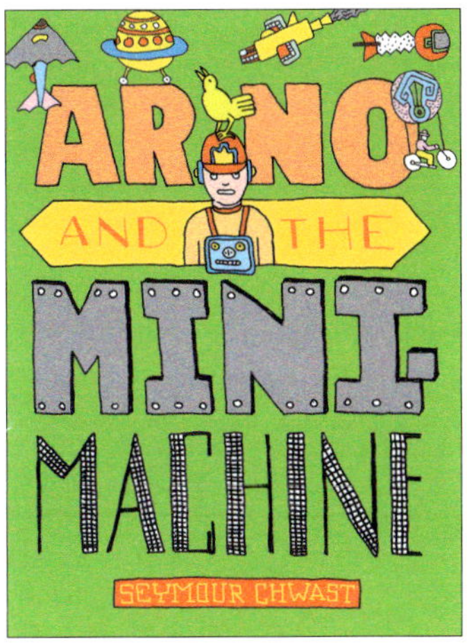

Arno and the Mini-Machine, by Seymour Chwast, 2019, 9" x 12" (22.9 × 30.5 cm), 32 pages.

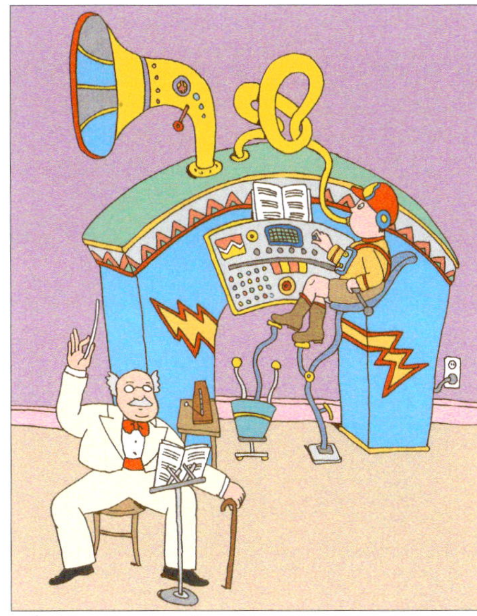

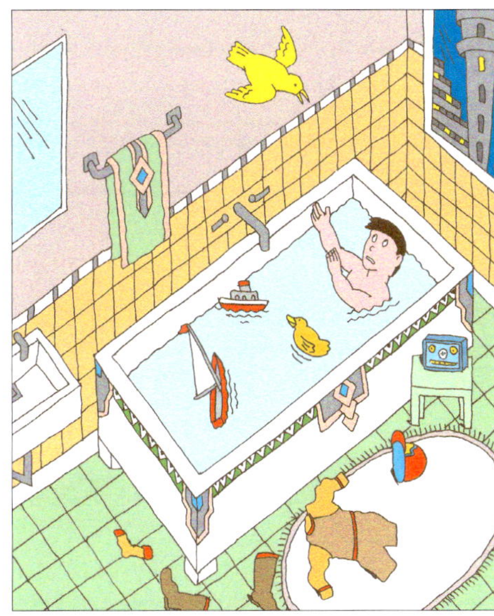

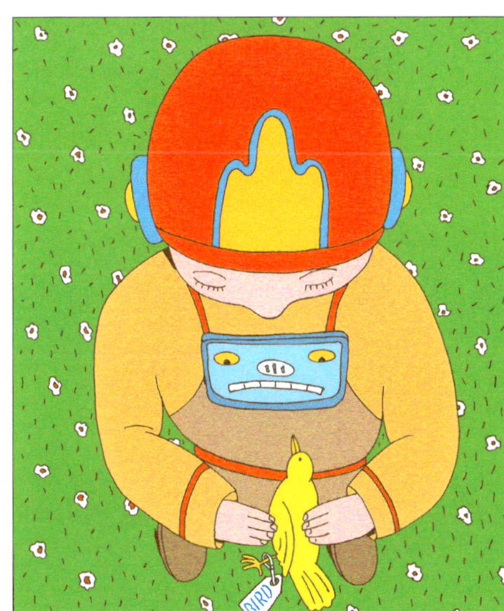

Arno and the Mini-Machine

This story takes place on planet Earth 200 years in the future—a time when individual freedom has ceased to exist and conformity is controlled by personalized MiniMachines. Arno's MiniMachine is forever barking orders at him to "Eat your Instant Mealtime," "Wait for the school jet," "Go to your electric tuba lesson," and more. Instead, Arno defies the programmed MiniMachine to make his own freedom. Curiosity and a little yellow bird lead Arno off his pre-programmed track. "Go Back to Your Class!" squawks the alarmed MiniMachine. *Arno and the Mini-Machine* is Chwast's not-so-subtle protest against society's slavish infatuation with Artificial Intelligence, "smart" gadgets, and electronic devices.

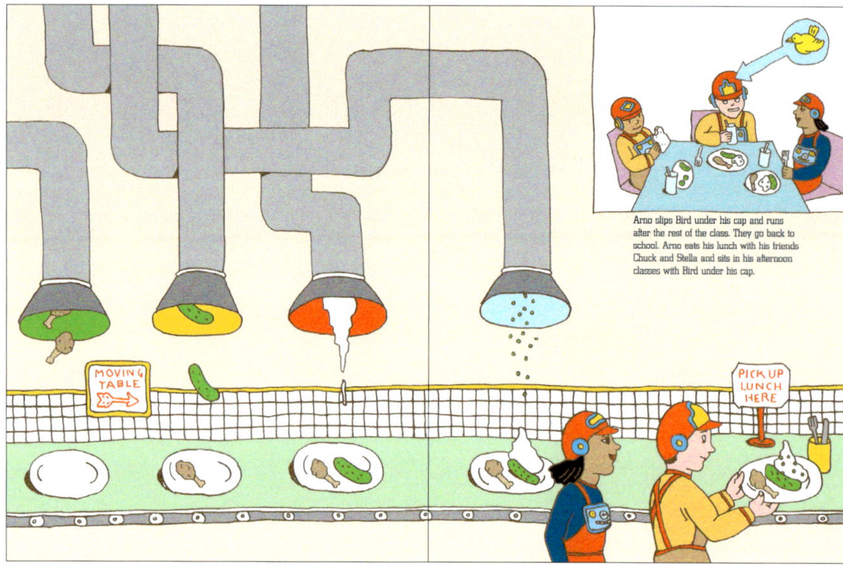
Arno slips Bird under his cap and runs after the rest of the class. They go back to school. Arno eats his lunch with his friends Chuck and Stella and sits in his afternoon classes with Bird under his cap.
MOVING TABLE
PICK UP LUNCH HERE

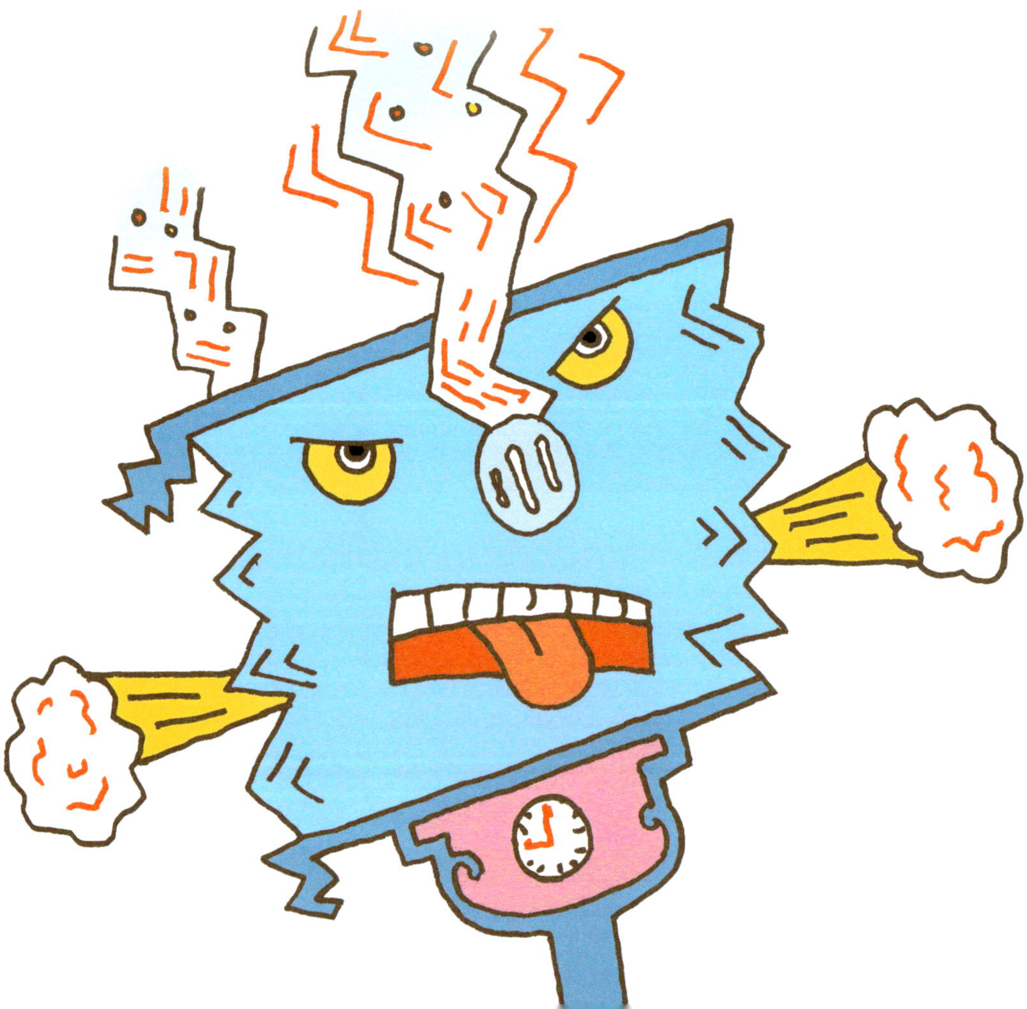

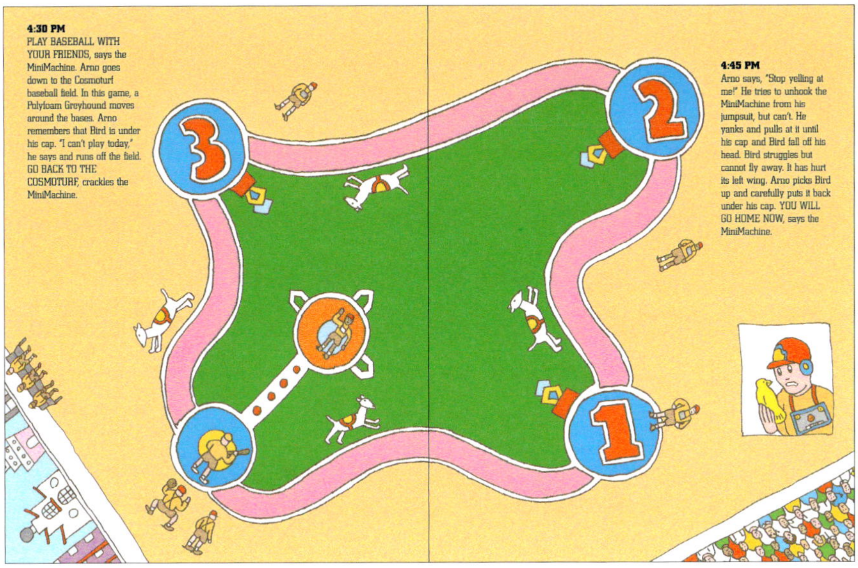
4:30 PM
PLAY BASEBALL WITH YOUR FRIENDS, says the MiniMachine. Arno goes down to the Cosmoturf baseball field. In this game, a Polyfoam Greyhound moves around the bases. Arno remembers that Bird is under his cap. "I can't play today," he says and runs off the field. GO BACK TO THE COSMOTURF, crackles the MiniMachine.
3
2
1
4:45 PM
Arno says, "Stop yelling at me!" He tries to unhook the MiniMachine from his jumpsuit, but can't. He yanks and pulls at it until his cap and Bird fall off his head. Bird struggles but cannot fly away. It has hurt its left wing. Arno picks Bird up and carefully puts it back under his cap. YOU WILL GO HOME NOW, says the MiniMachine.

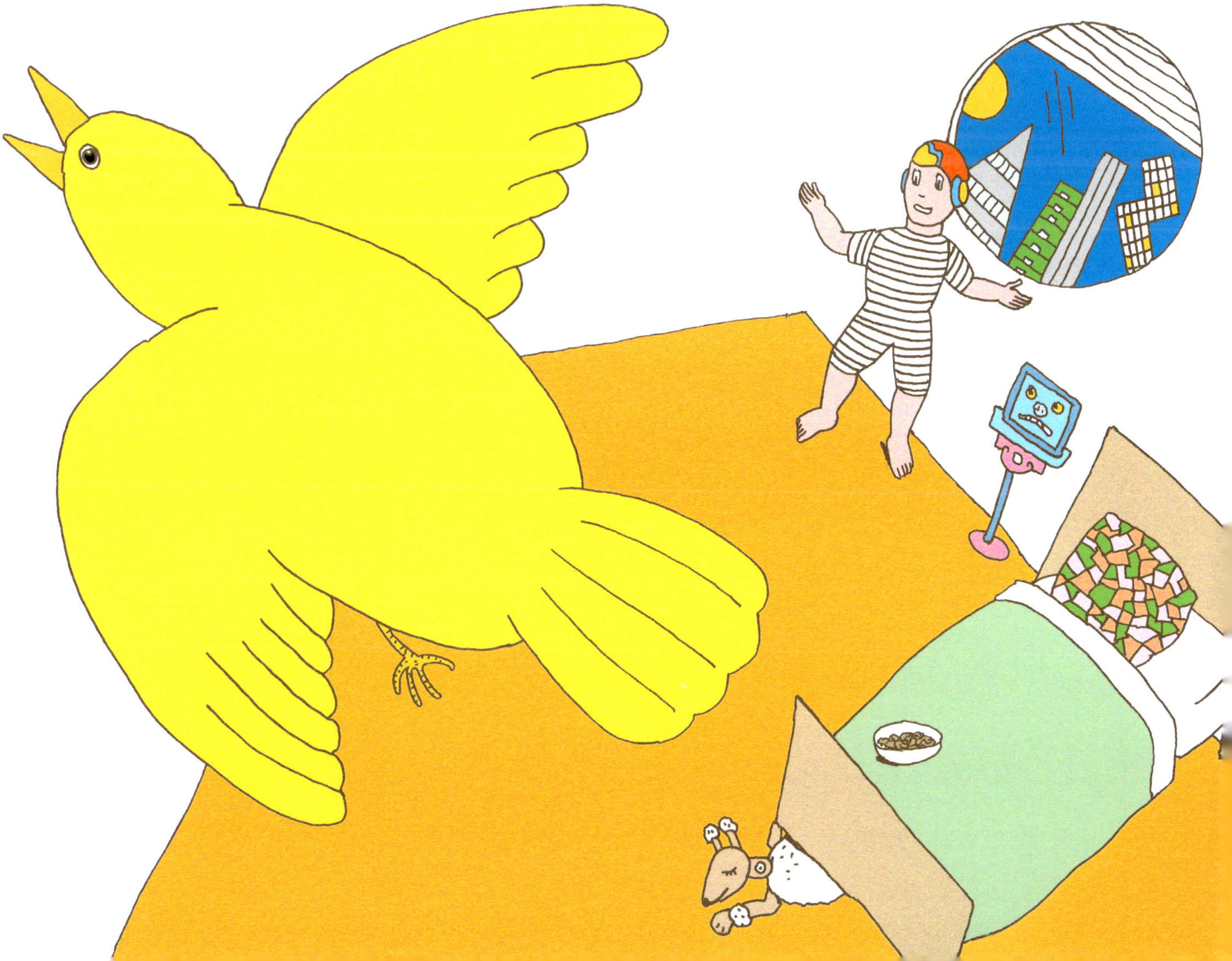

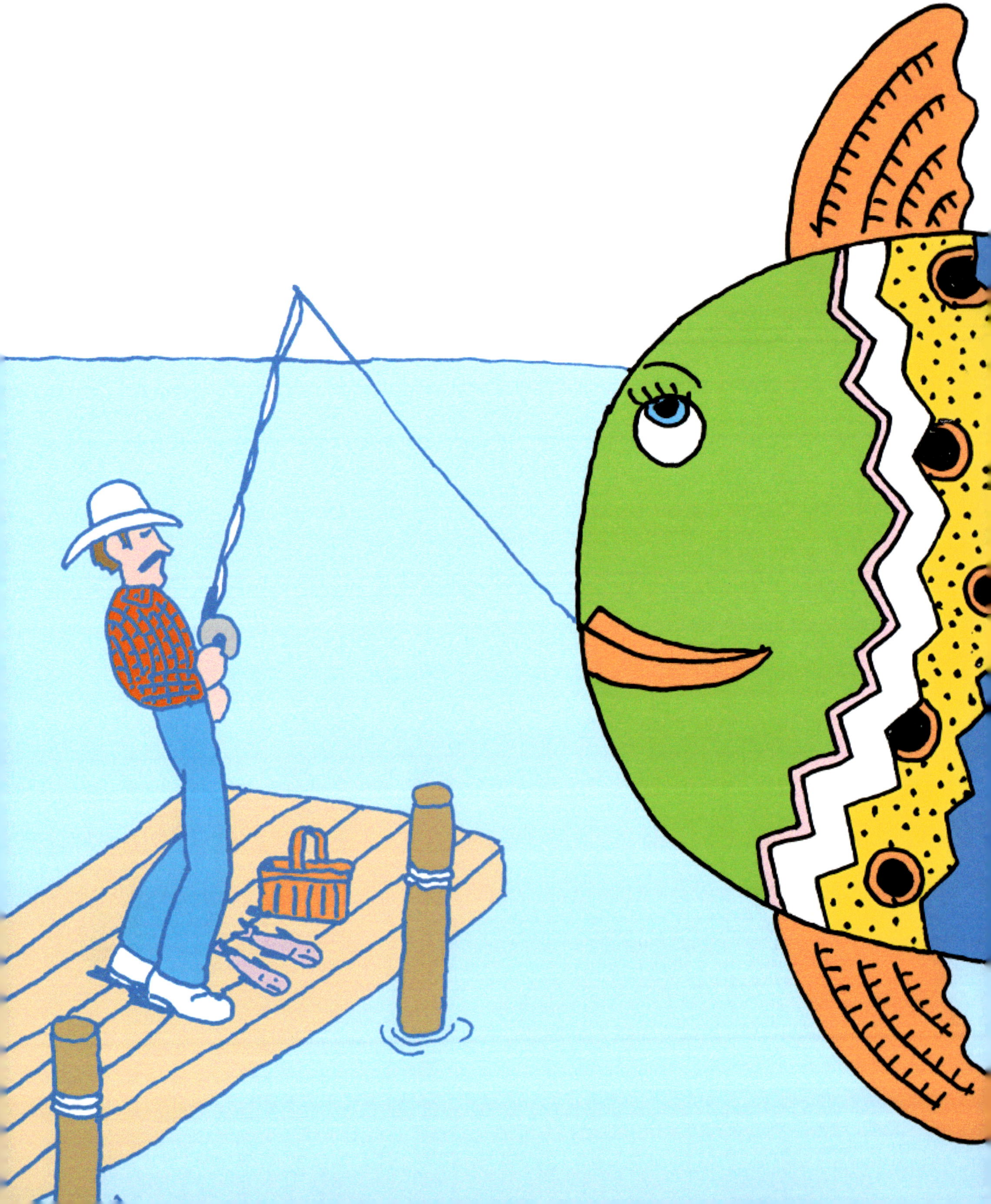

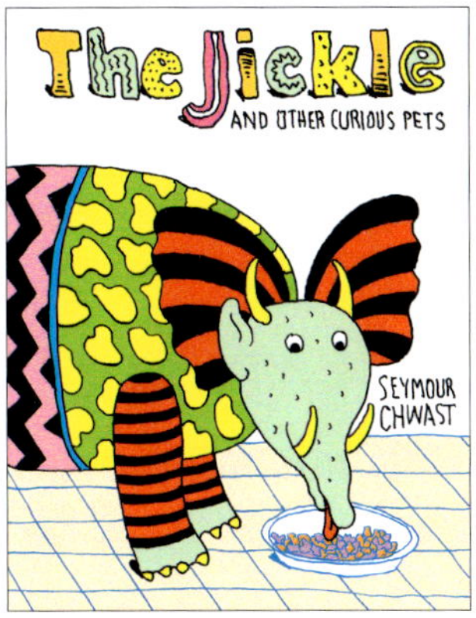

The Jickle and Other Curious Pets, by Seymour Chwast, 2017, 8.5" × 11" (21.5 × 28 cm), 32 pages.

The Jickle and Other Curious Pets

In a twist on the usually common act of visiting a pet store to find a loving pet for a family, in *The Jickle,* an unsuspecting family enters a world of colorful, unusual beasts. The pet shop is very odd, to say the least, and the family finds that each pet they select is somehow incompatible with its new surroundings. The Gruffin, for instance, has three gruesome heads that are continuously arguing with each other and never ever say "goodnight" to their owners. Chwast's imaginary menagerie derives from his personal passions for newspaper comics and art deco styling—and while the pets may be beautiful on the outside, they are difficult to live with inside the house.

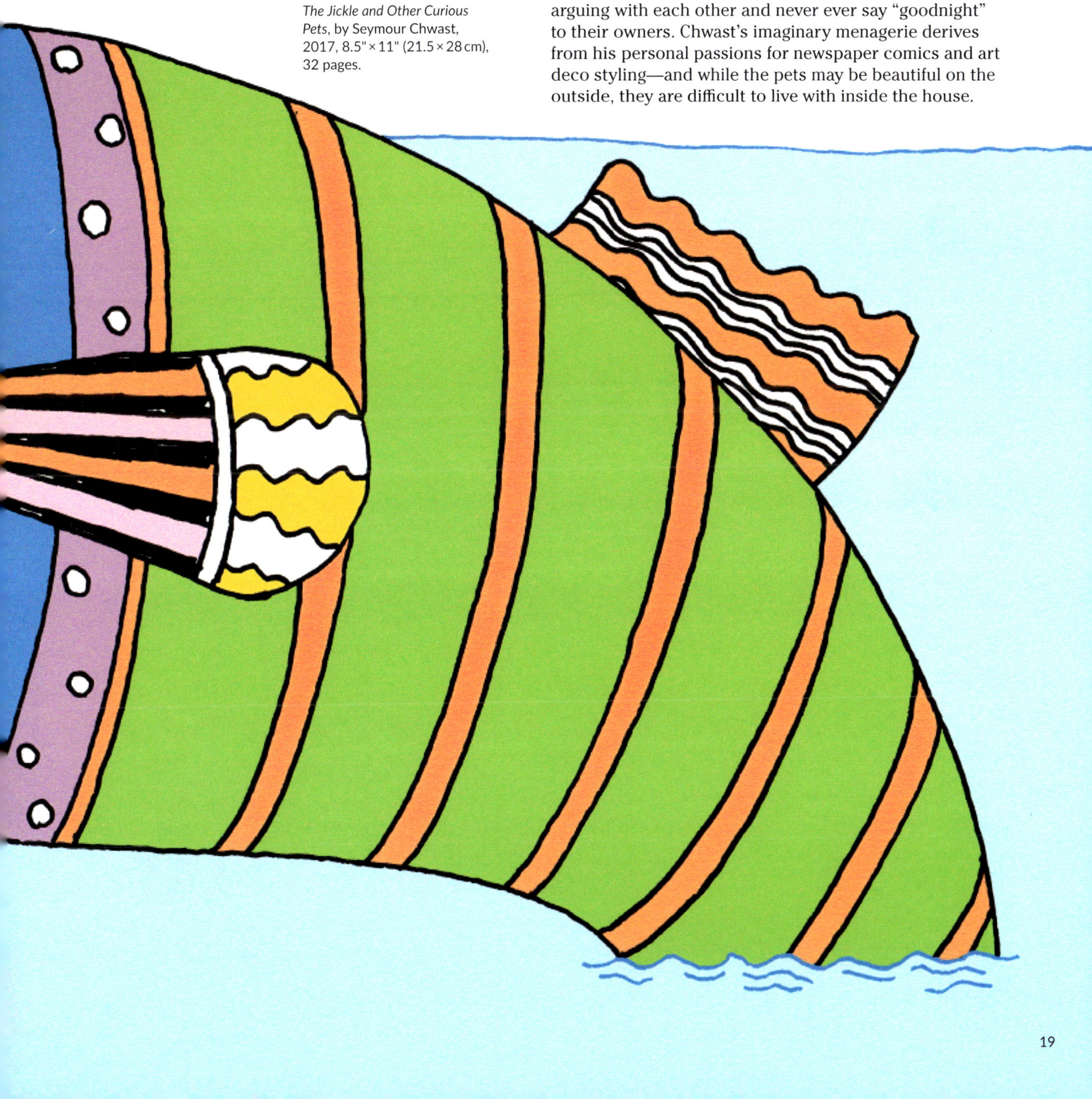

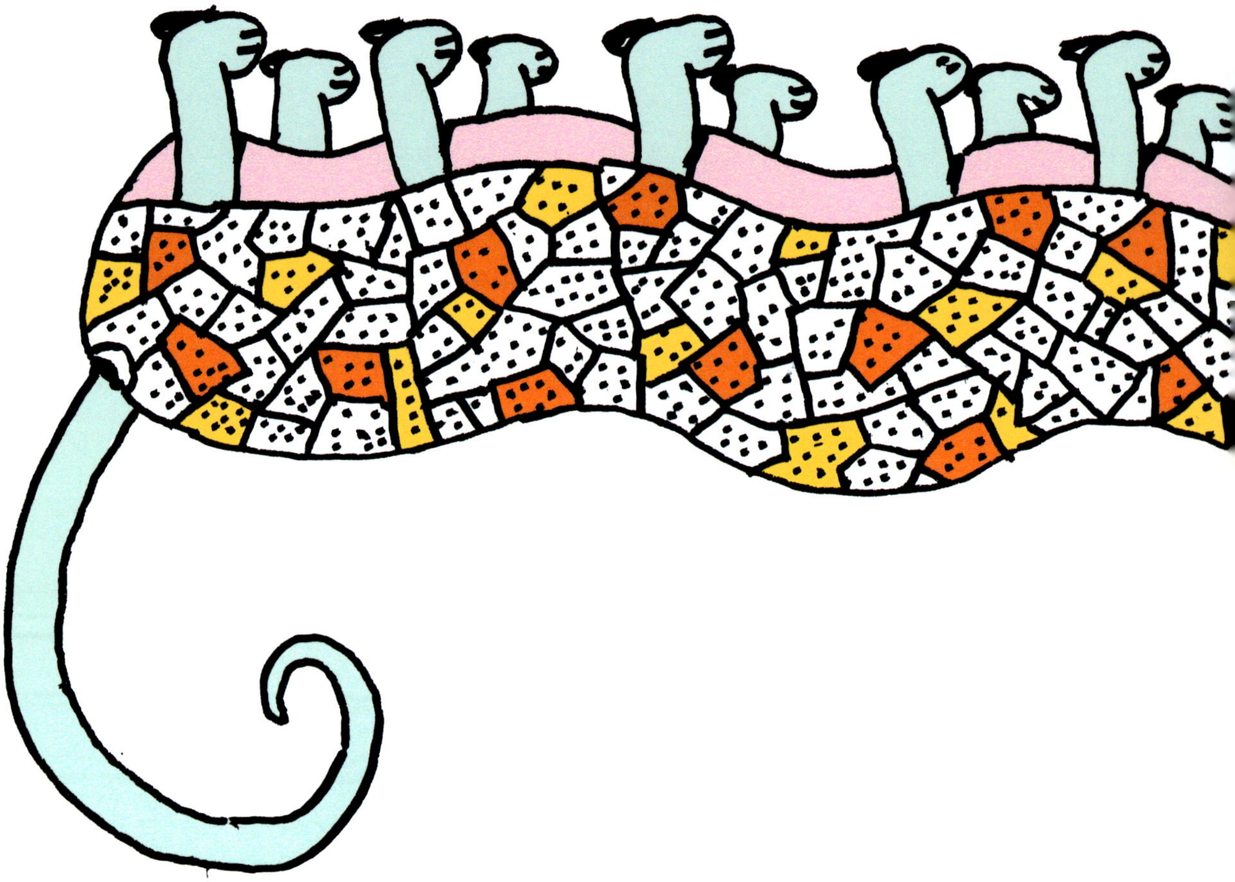

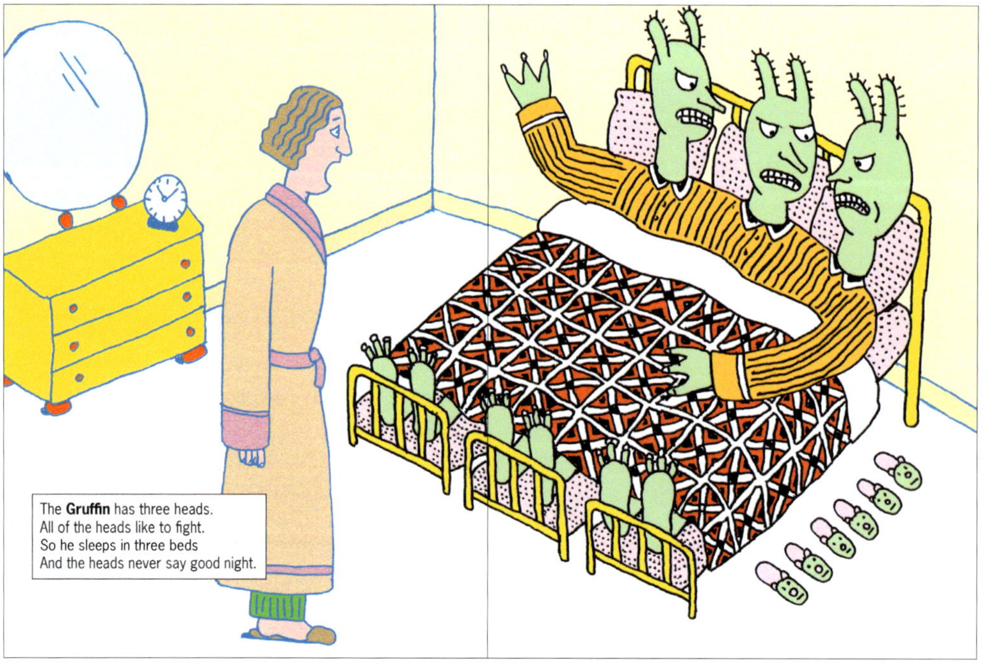

The **Gruffin** has three heads.
All of the heads like to fight.
So he sleeps in three beds
And the heads never say good night.

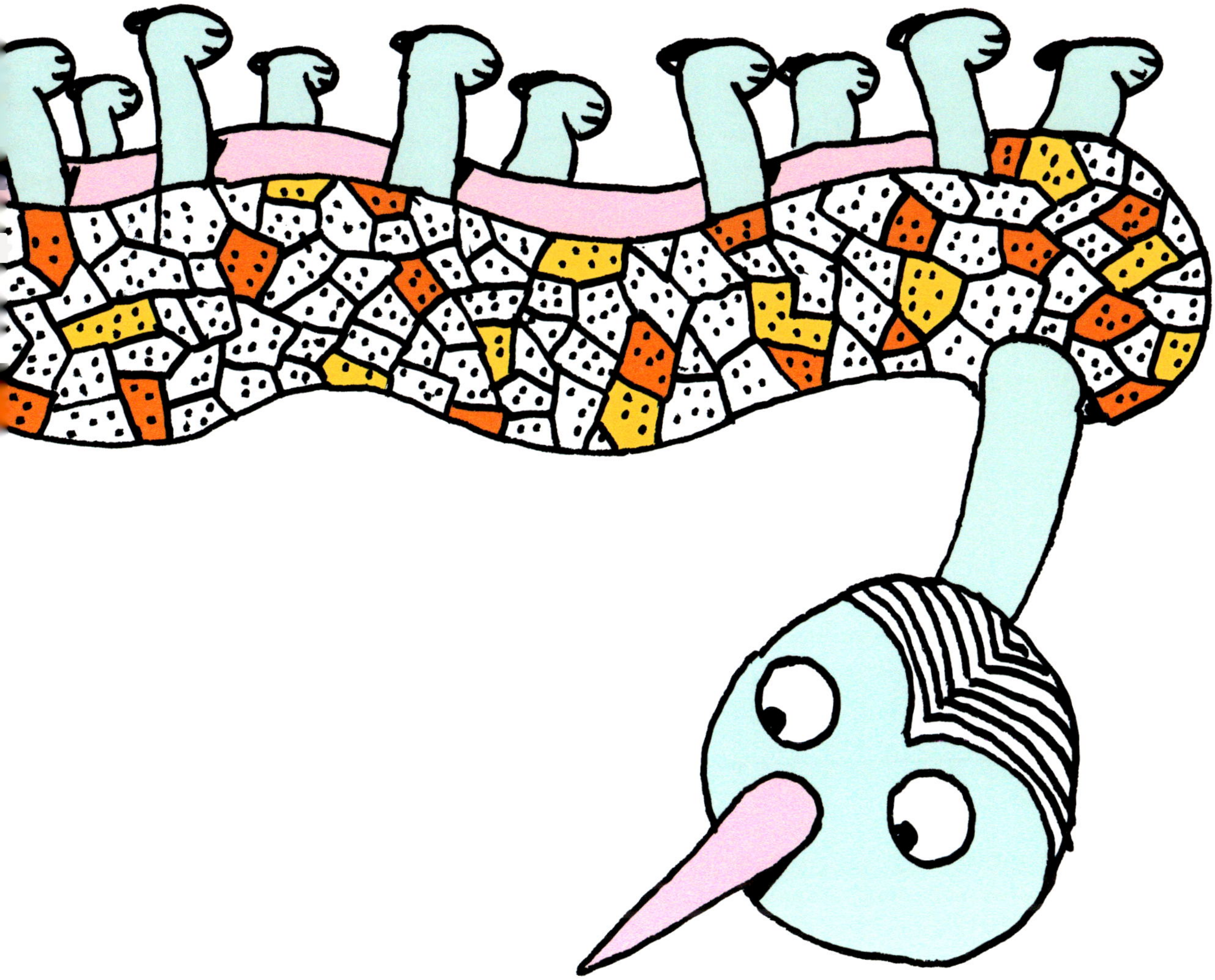

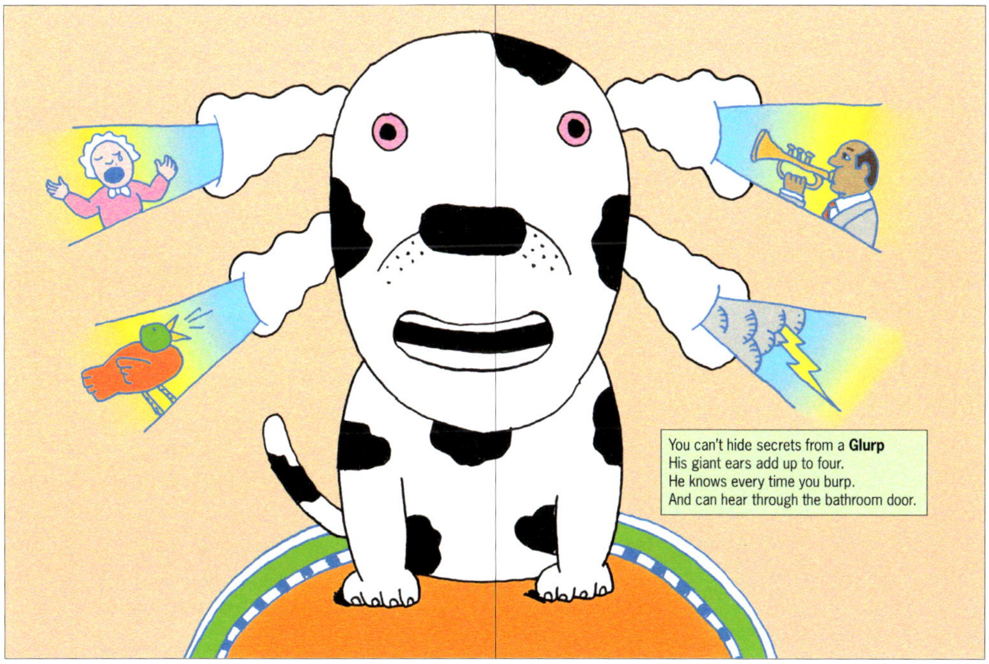
You can't hide secrets from a **Glurp**
His giant ears add up to four.
He knows every time you burp.
And can hear through the bathroom door.

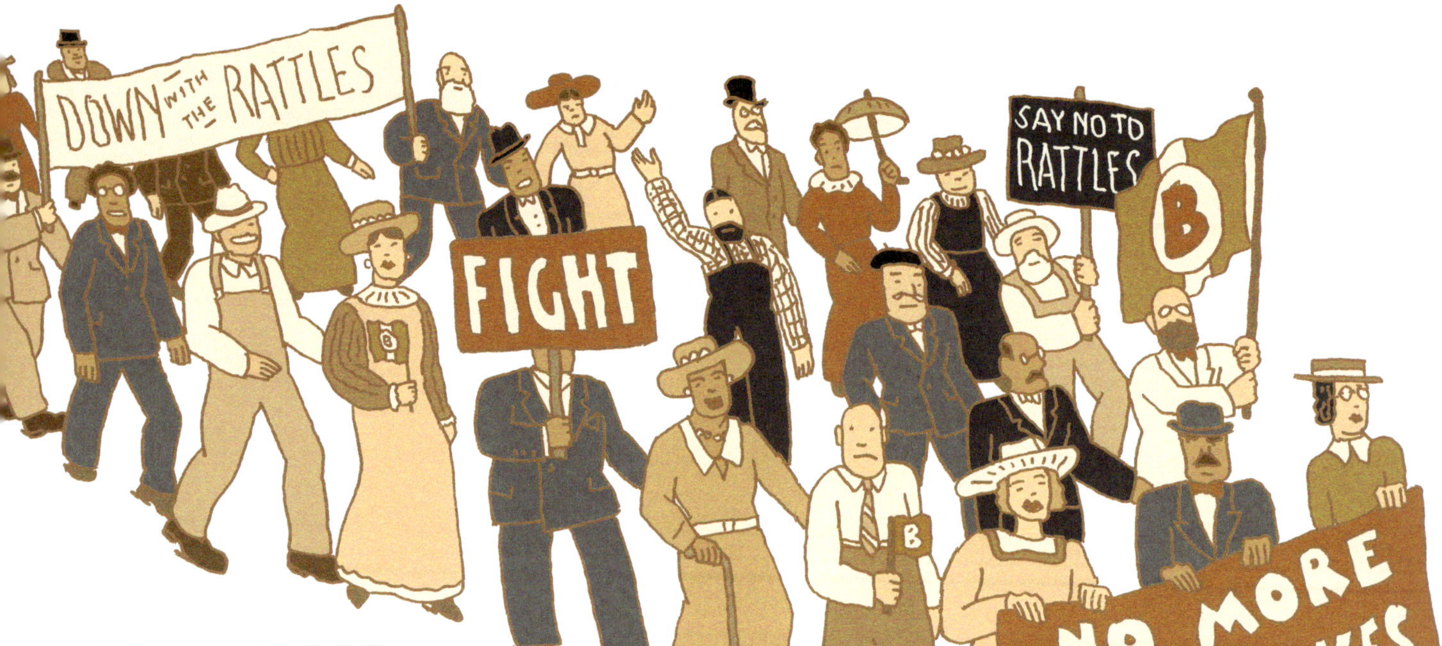

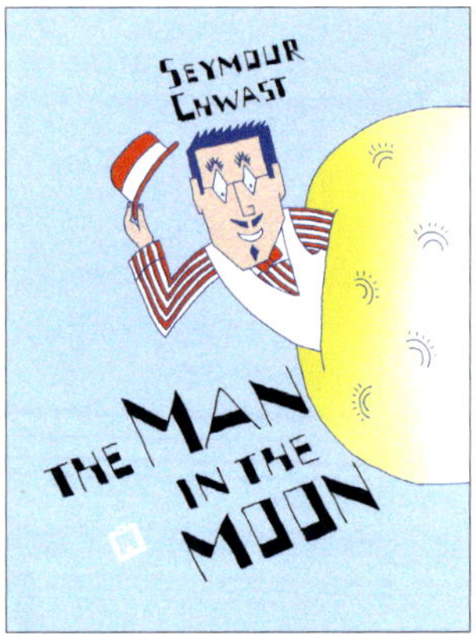

The Man in the Moon, by Seymour Chwast, 2019, 8.66" × 11.22" (22 × 28.5 cm), 32 pages.

The Man in the Moon

On Earth, the inhabitants from two neighboring mythical regions on the Island of Bamboo—the northern Biddles (fruit growers) and the Rattles (bakers)—are bitter enemies. Each blames every disaster on the other. Their soldiers face off and a battle seems imminent; the Man in the Moon sees everything from his place in the starry sky and has the perfect solution to end their strife. He will make an especially delicious fruit pie to avoid a war and restore peace. This is a book of nuanced agendas that combines Chwast's war against warfare with his interest in ending strife through resolution.

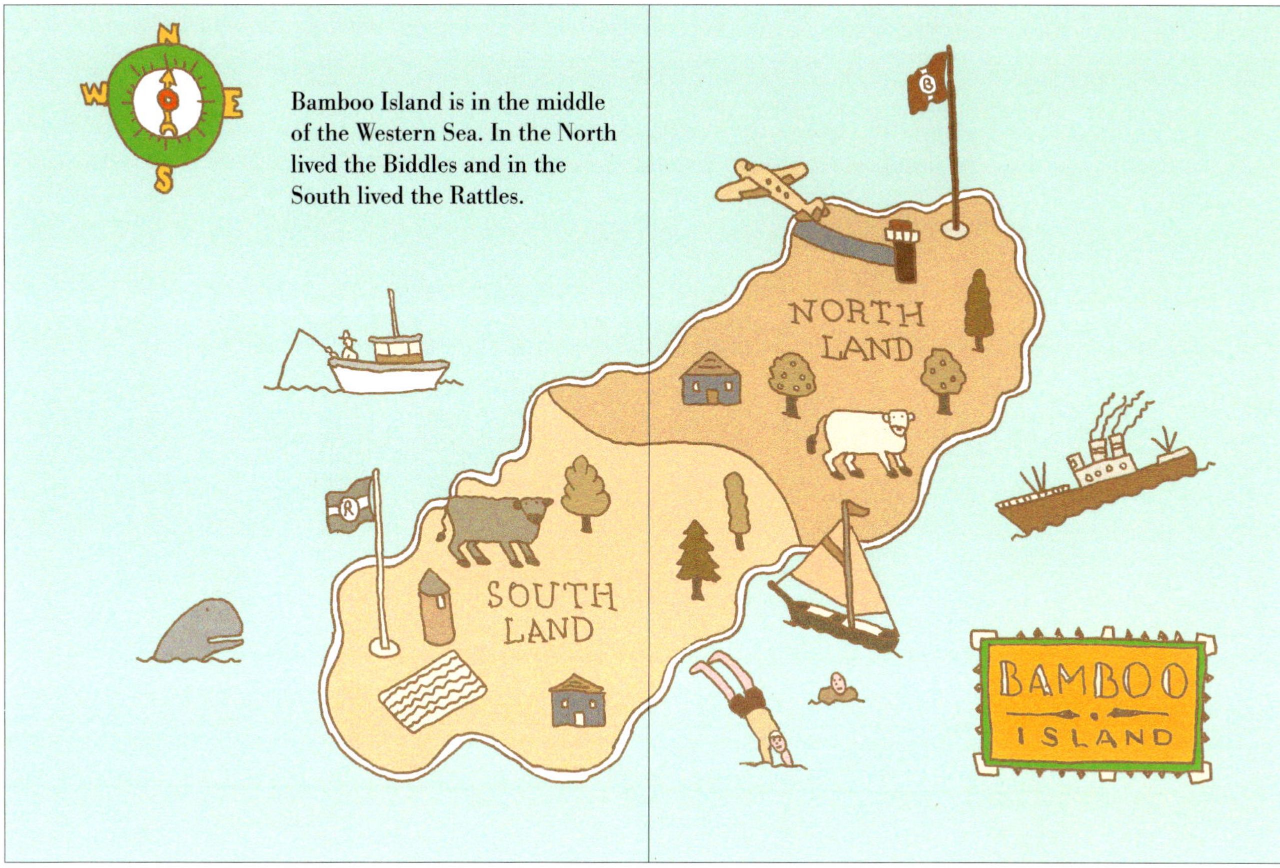

Bamboo Island is in the middle of the Western Sea. In the North lived the Biddles and in the South lived the Rattles.

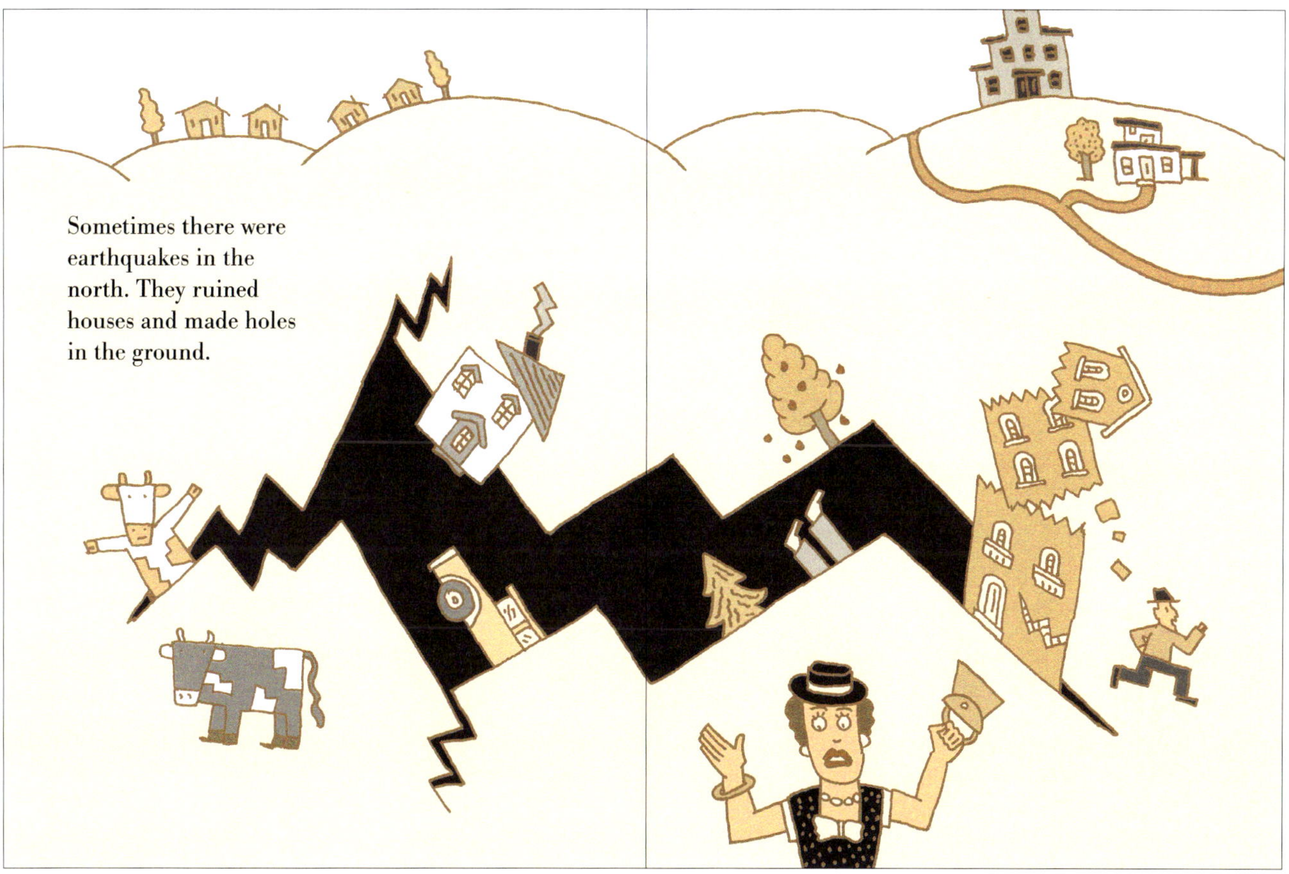

Sometimes there were earthquakes in the north. They ruined houses and made holes in the ground.

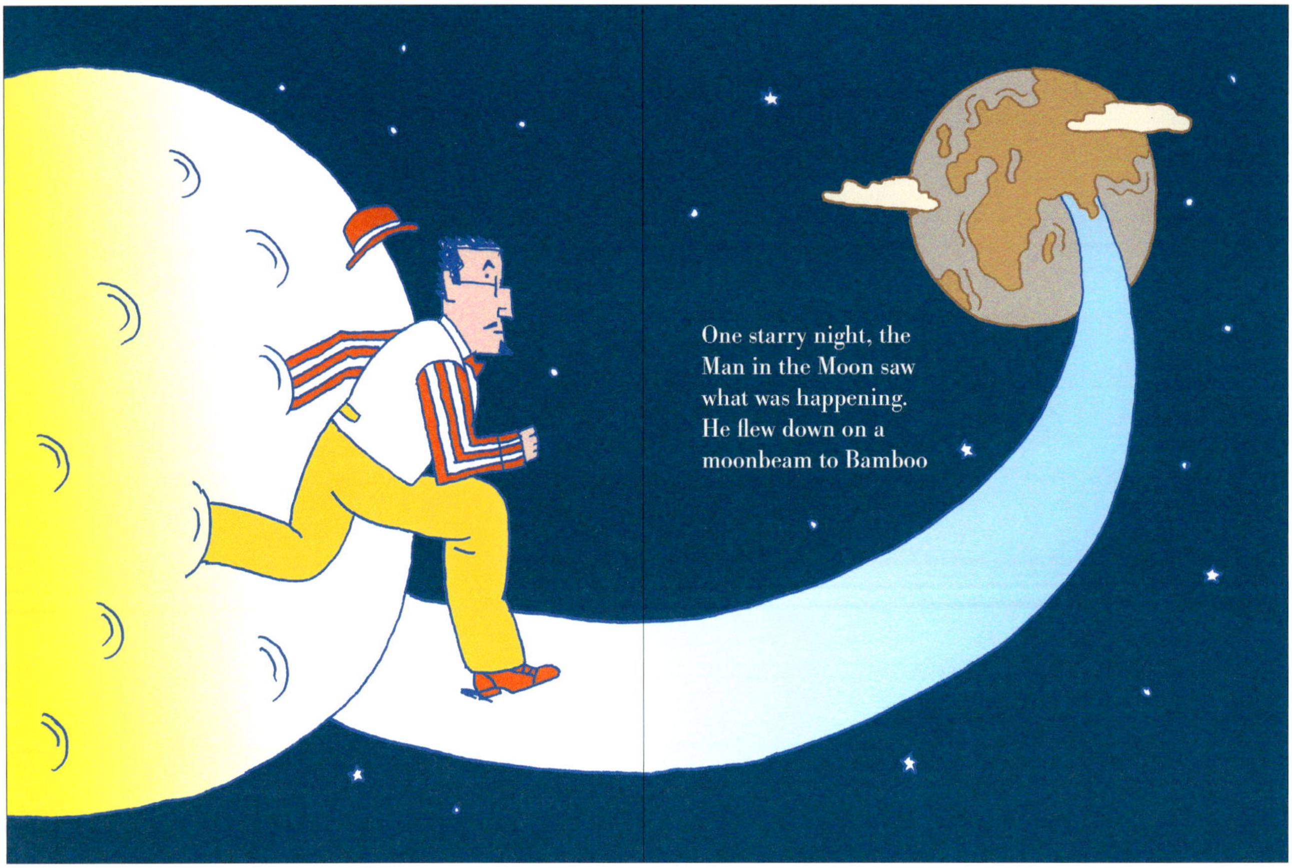

One starry night, the Man in the Moon saw what was happening. He flew down on a moonbeam to Bamboo

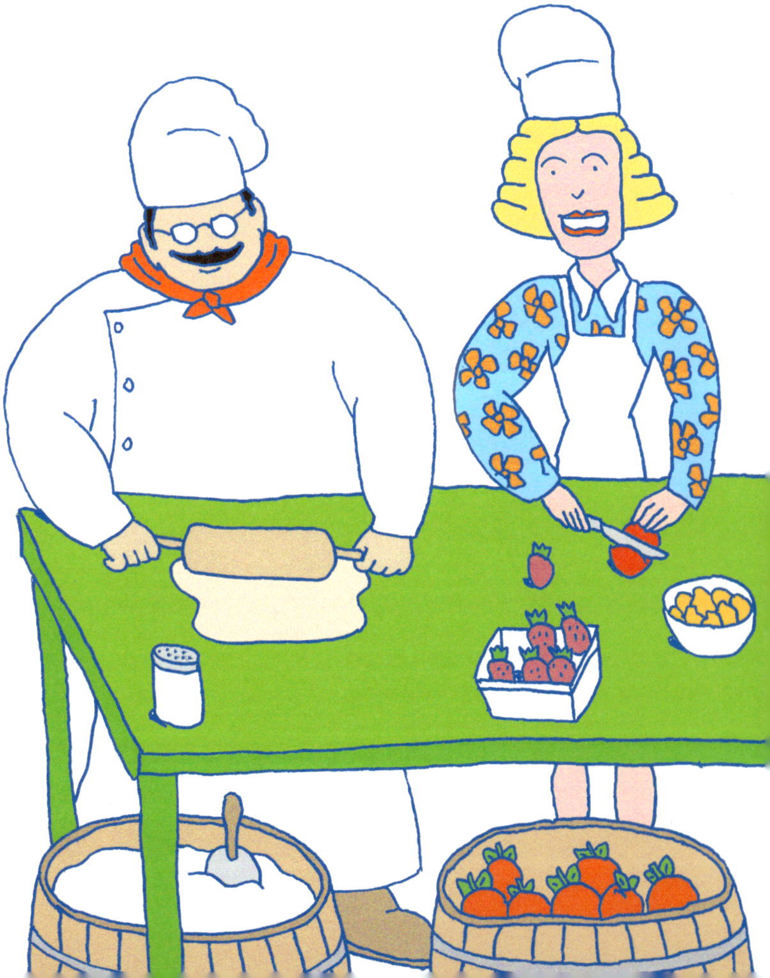

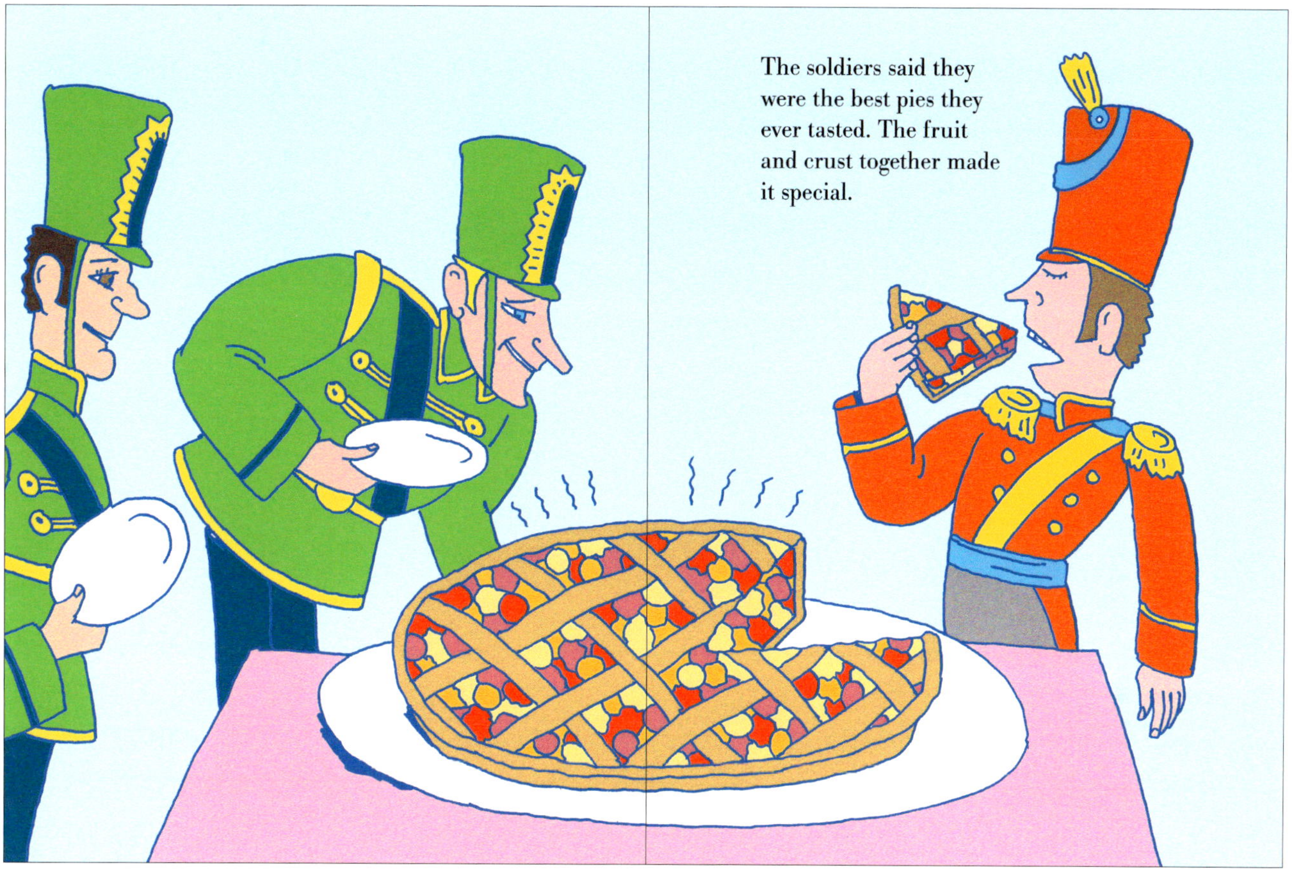

The soldiers said they were the best pies they ever tasted. The fruit and crust together made it special.

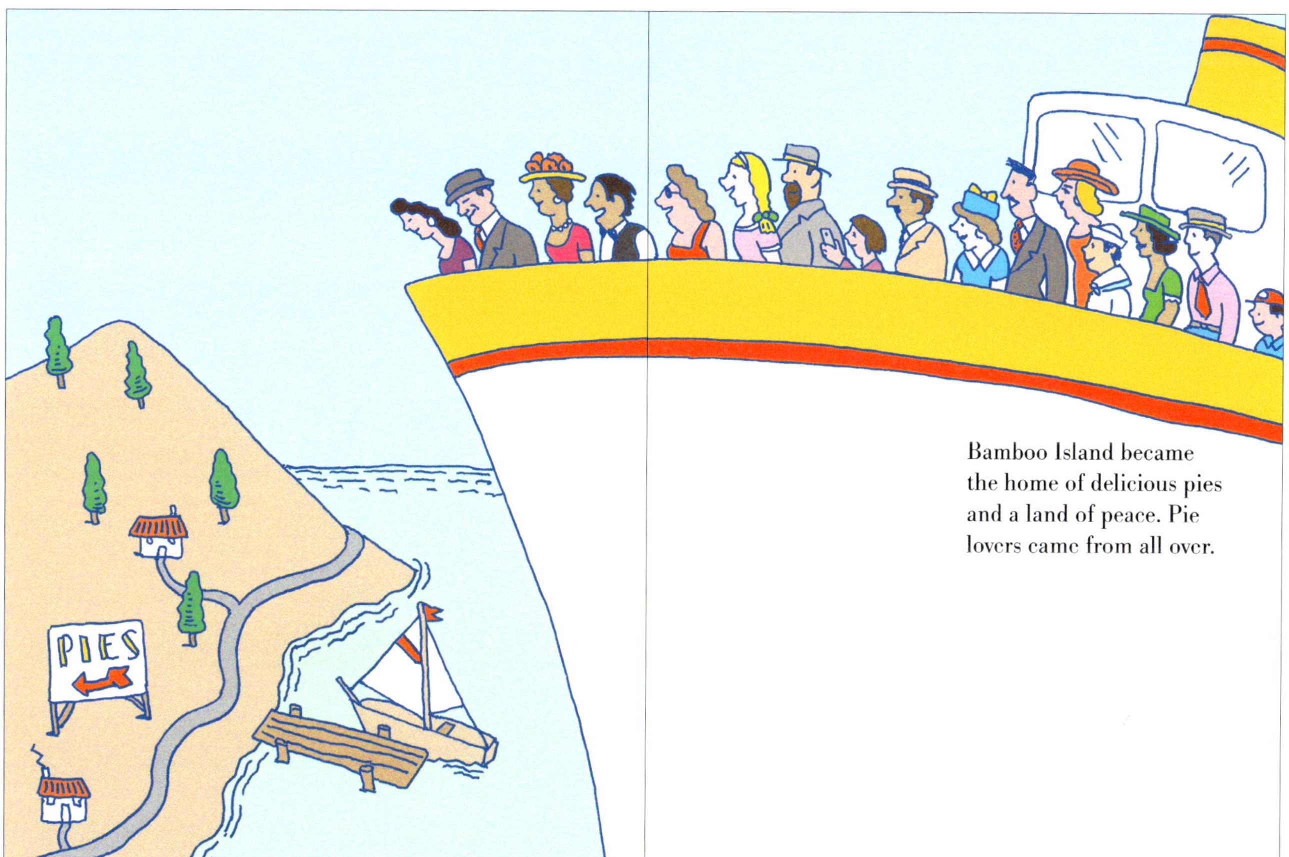

Bamboo Island became the home of delicious pies and a land of peace. Pie lovers came from all over.

Moonride

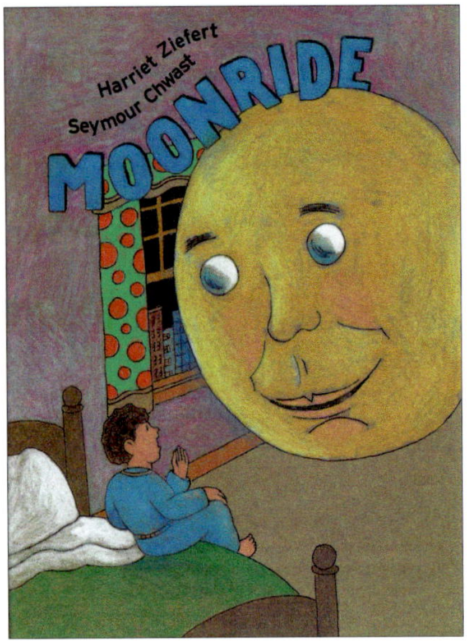

Moonride, by Harriet Ziefert, illustrated by Seymour Chwast, 2000, 9" × 11.75" (23 × 30 cm), 32 pages.

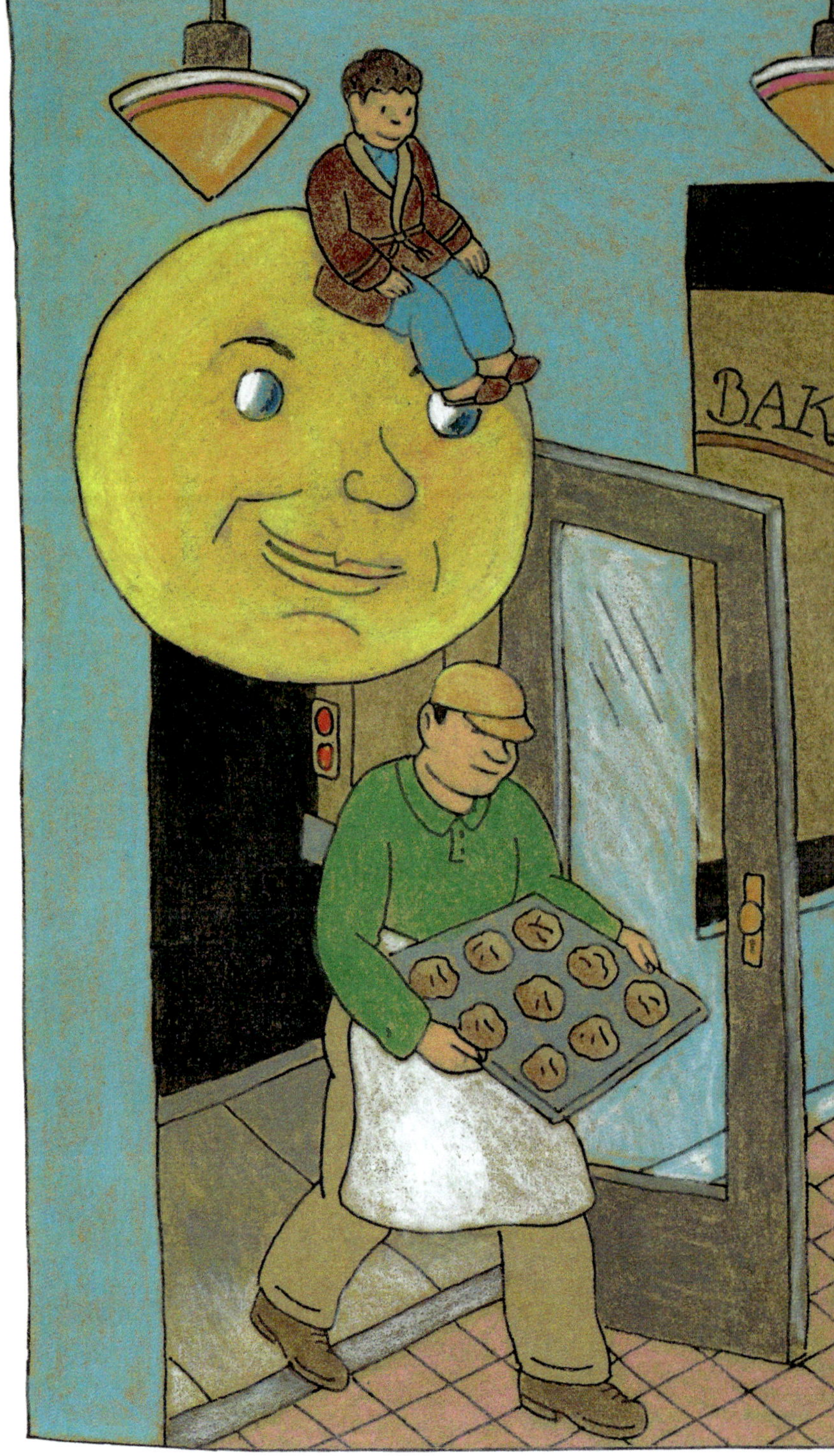

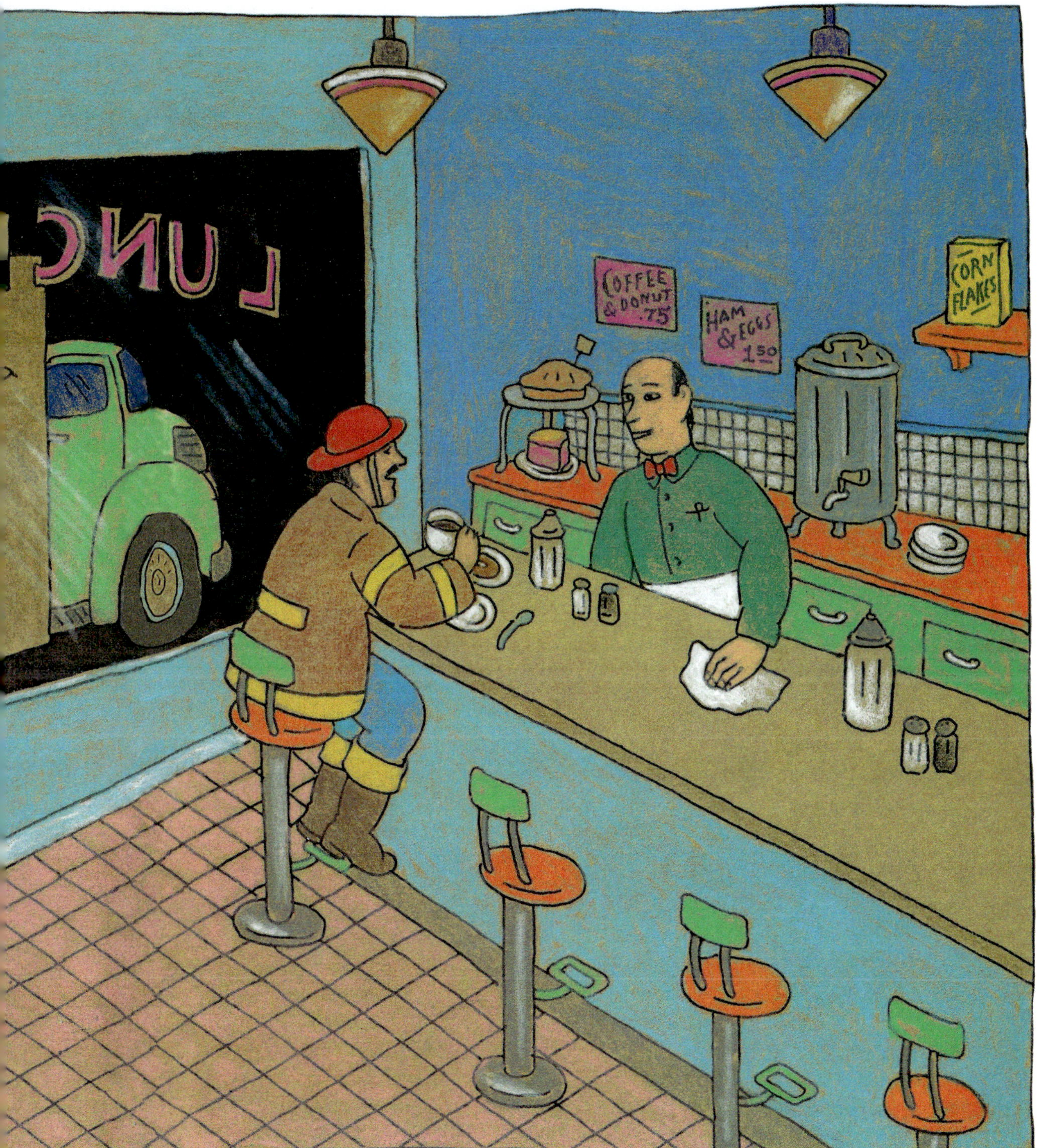

While the moon is waiting for a cup of coffee,
you may want to use the bathroom.

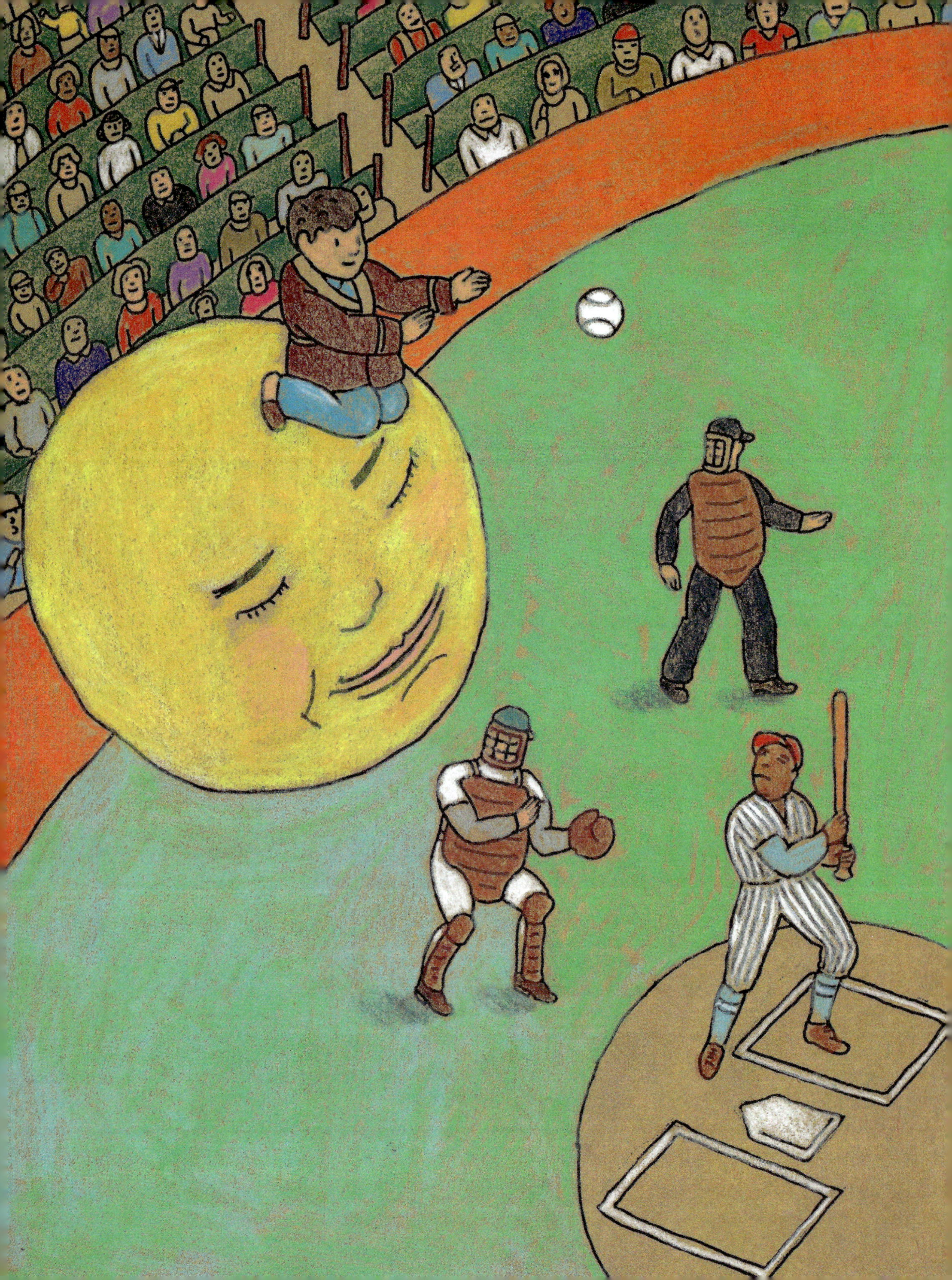

The moon is the perfect object out of which to create a compelling character. In *Moonride*, conceived with text by Harriet Ziefert, a full moon with a kind face offers to take a young boy on the ride of his life, guiding him through the exciting city where he lives. They fly over buildings and baseball games, and from atop the moon's head the boy sees wonderful things that happen at night in the city. The illustrations are rendered in acrylic and colored pencils on brown butcher paper, which is a more improvisational style than seen in most of Chwast's other children's books.

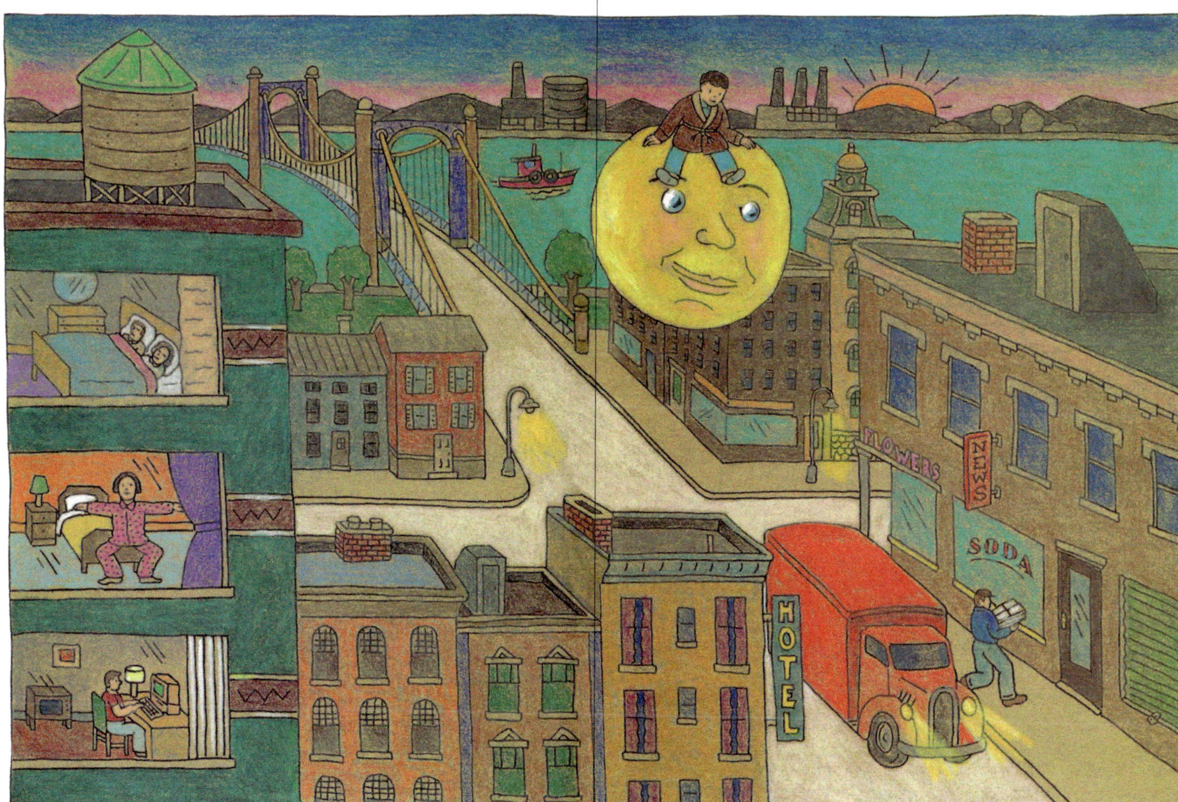

Don't ask "Are we there yet?" or "How much longer until I'm home?"

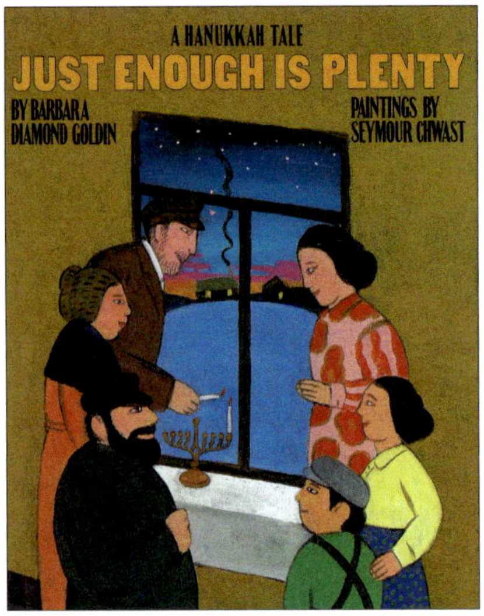

Just Enough is Plenty, A Hanukkah Tale, by Barbara Diamond Goldin, illustrated by Seymour Chwast, 1988, 7.25" × 9" (18.5 × 23 cm), 32 pages.

Just Enough is Plenty

Chwast is accustomed to creating absurd and surreal comic tableaux, but he is just as happy creating empathetic fictional characters. In *Just Enough is Plenty* by Barbara Diamond Goldin, he has illustrated a Hanukkah tale where the plot revolves around the idea that sharing a meager meal with a stranger at such an auspicious time will bring unintended rewards. Malka, the daughter of a poor tailor, is worried her family will not have enough food. Yet when a peddler comes to the door, he is invited to join their holiday celebration. On the first night of Hanukkah, the peddler entertains them with wonderful stories and songs. Before the family awakens the next morning, the stranger has gone, leaving behind unexpected gifts. Chwast painted his narrative illustrations using acrylic paint on canvas board, evoking the an innocence of East European folk art.

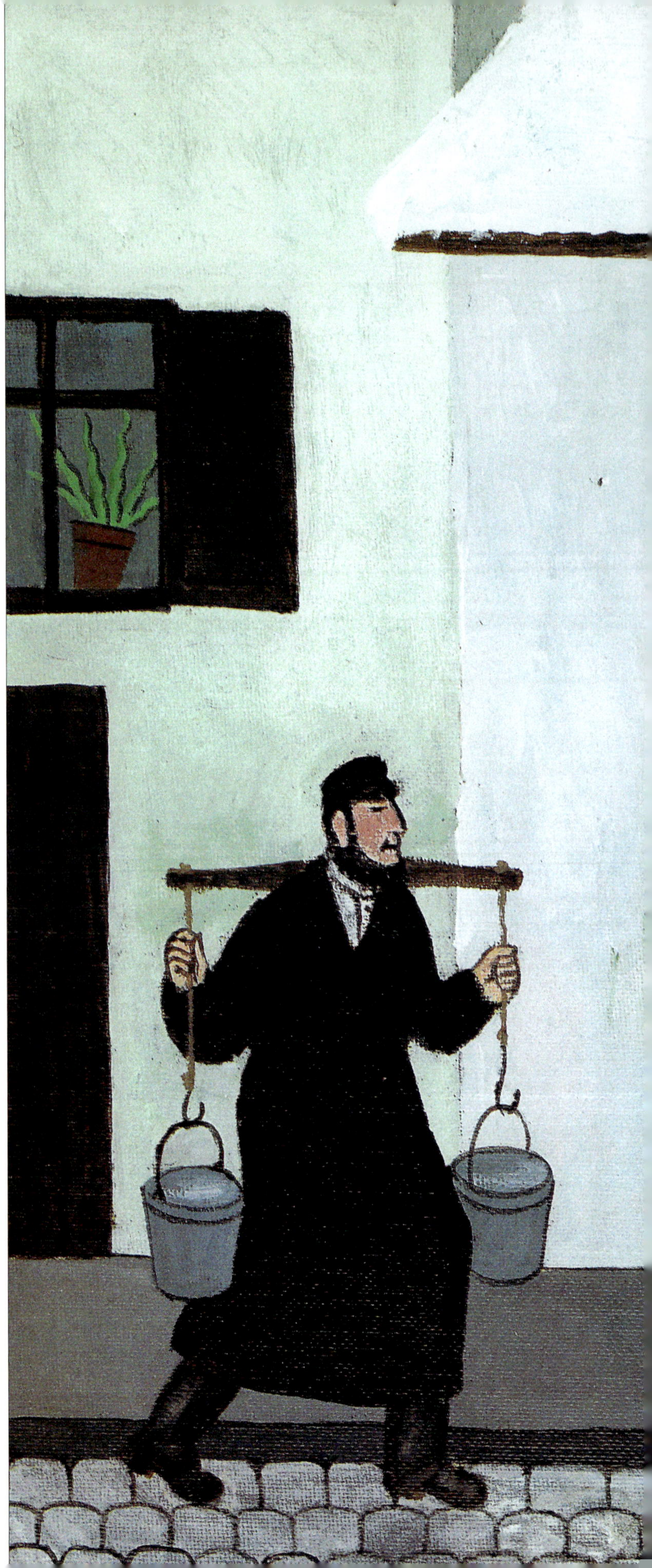

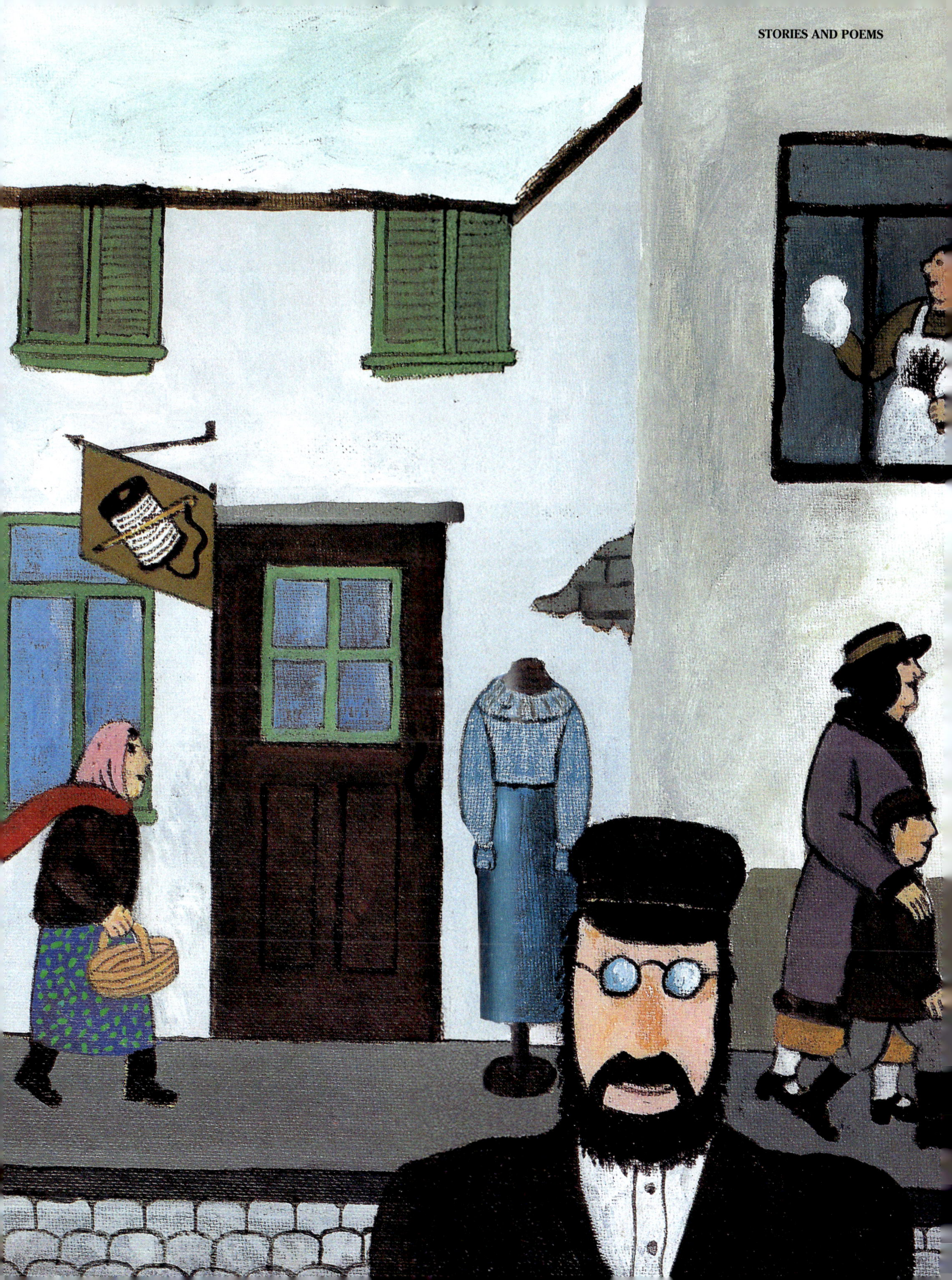

She raced into Papa's shop. "Mama sent me to buy more eggs."

"More eggs. More this, more that. Soon there will be no kopeks left. Not even one for Hanukkah money."

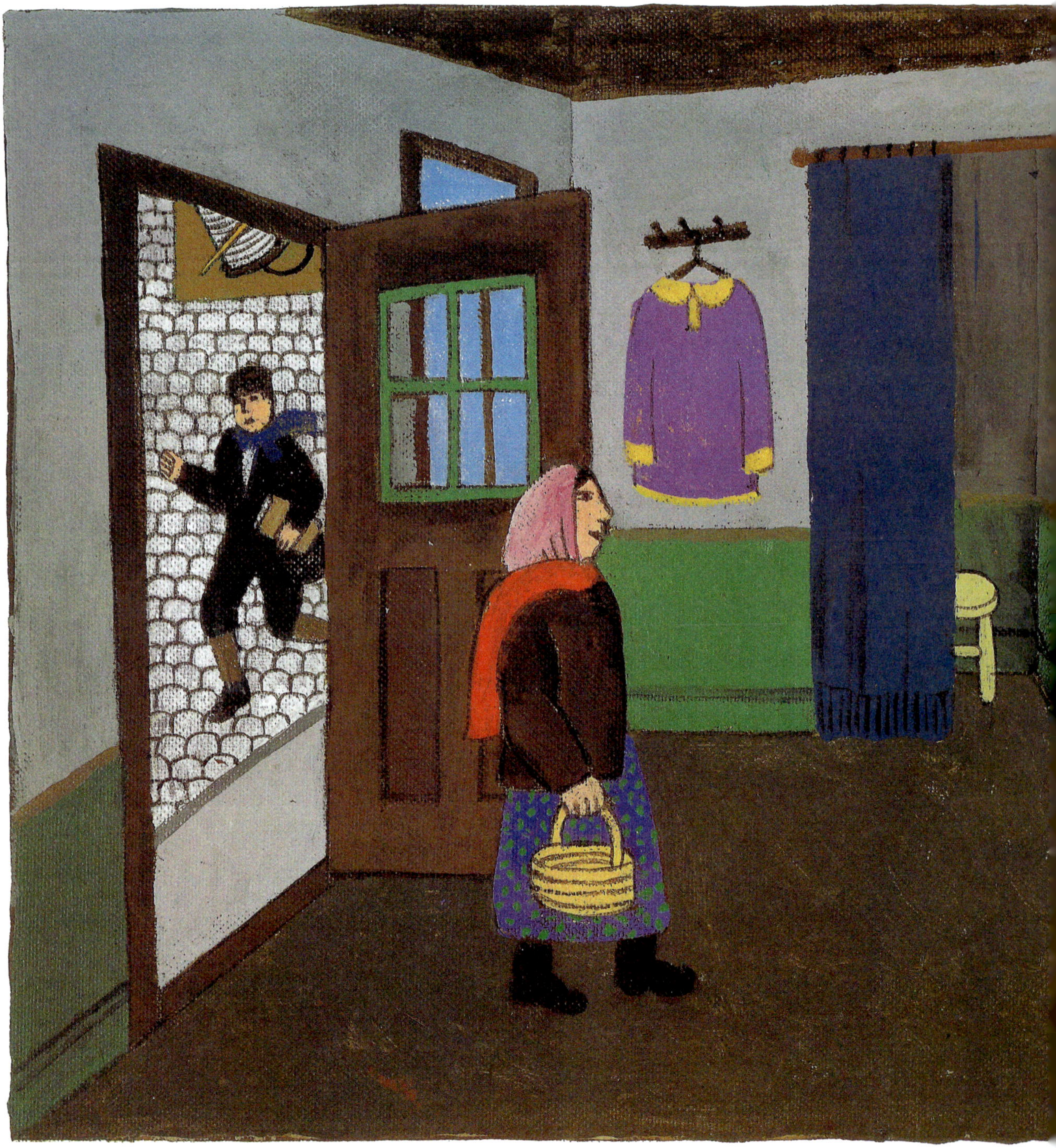

Malka stood still in the doorway. No Hanukkah money! Was Papa joking? How could she and Zalman play the dreidel game without even a kopek?

"Malka, don't just stand there. Here. Go buy the eggs," Papa said. "And quickly. Aunt Hindy and Uncle Shmuel will be here soon."

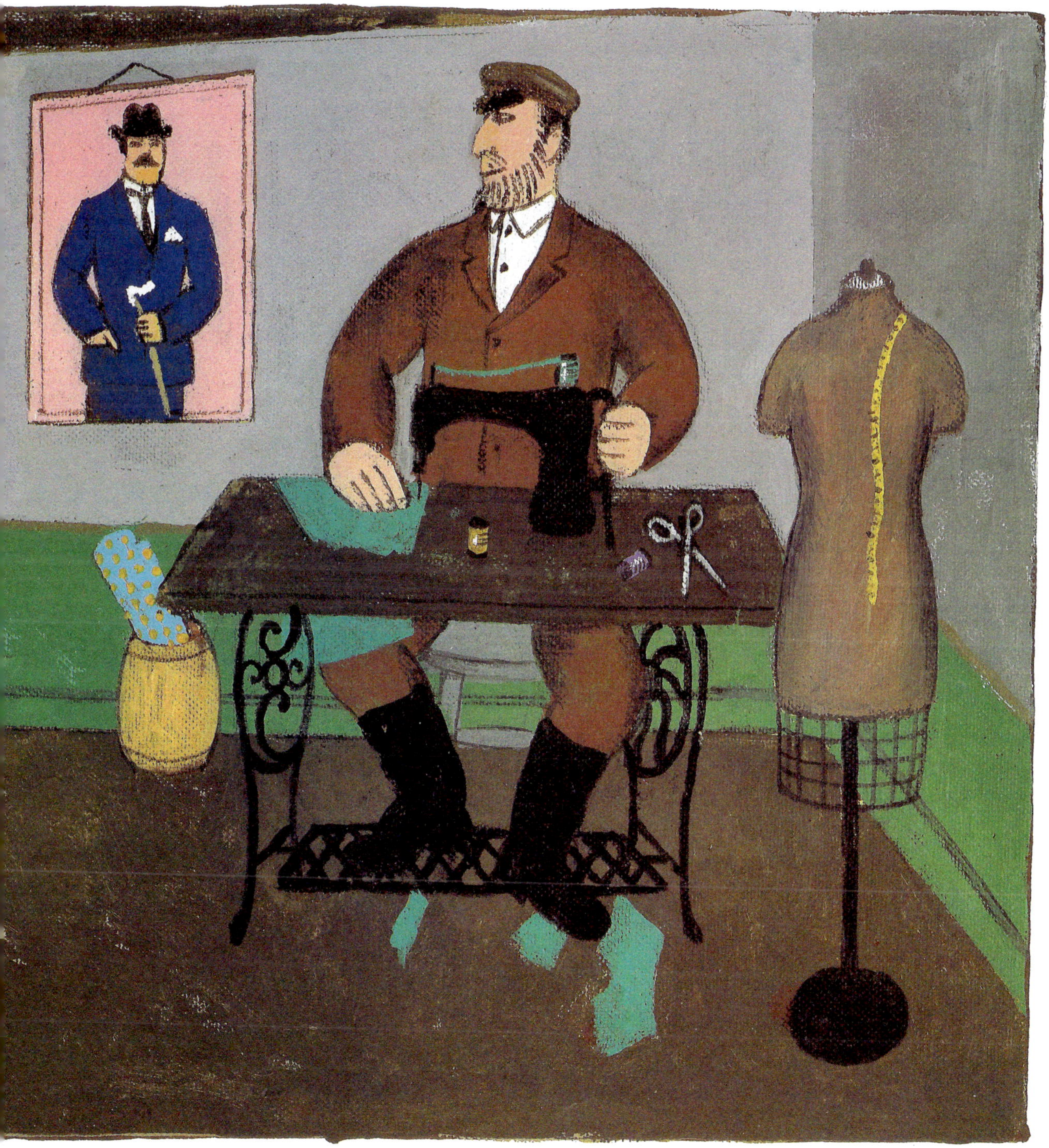

The Pancake King

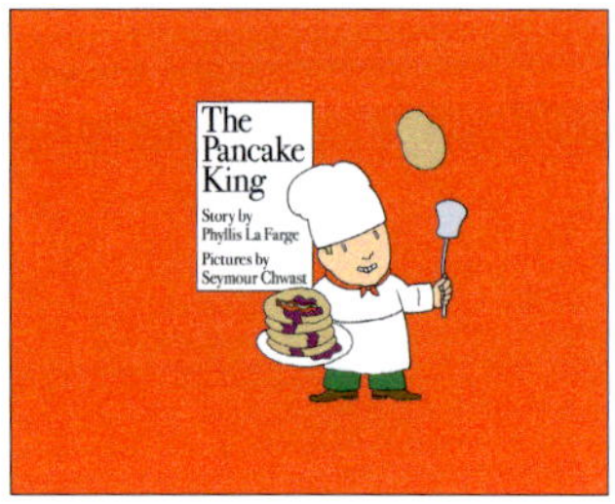

The Pancake King, by Phyllis La Farge, illustrated by Seymour Chwast, 1971, reprinted 2016, 9.25" × 12" (23.5 × 30.5 cm), 32 pages.

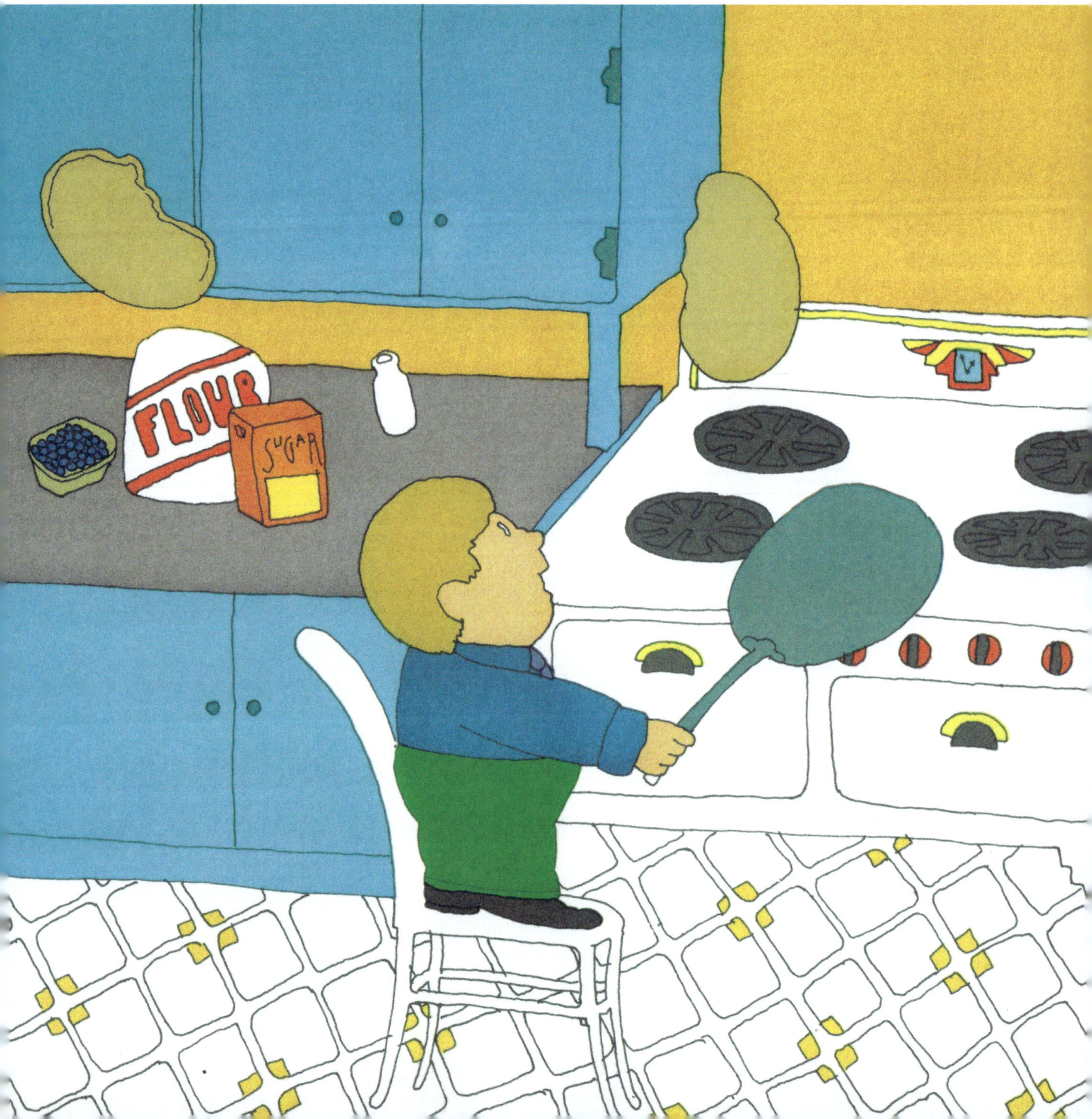

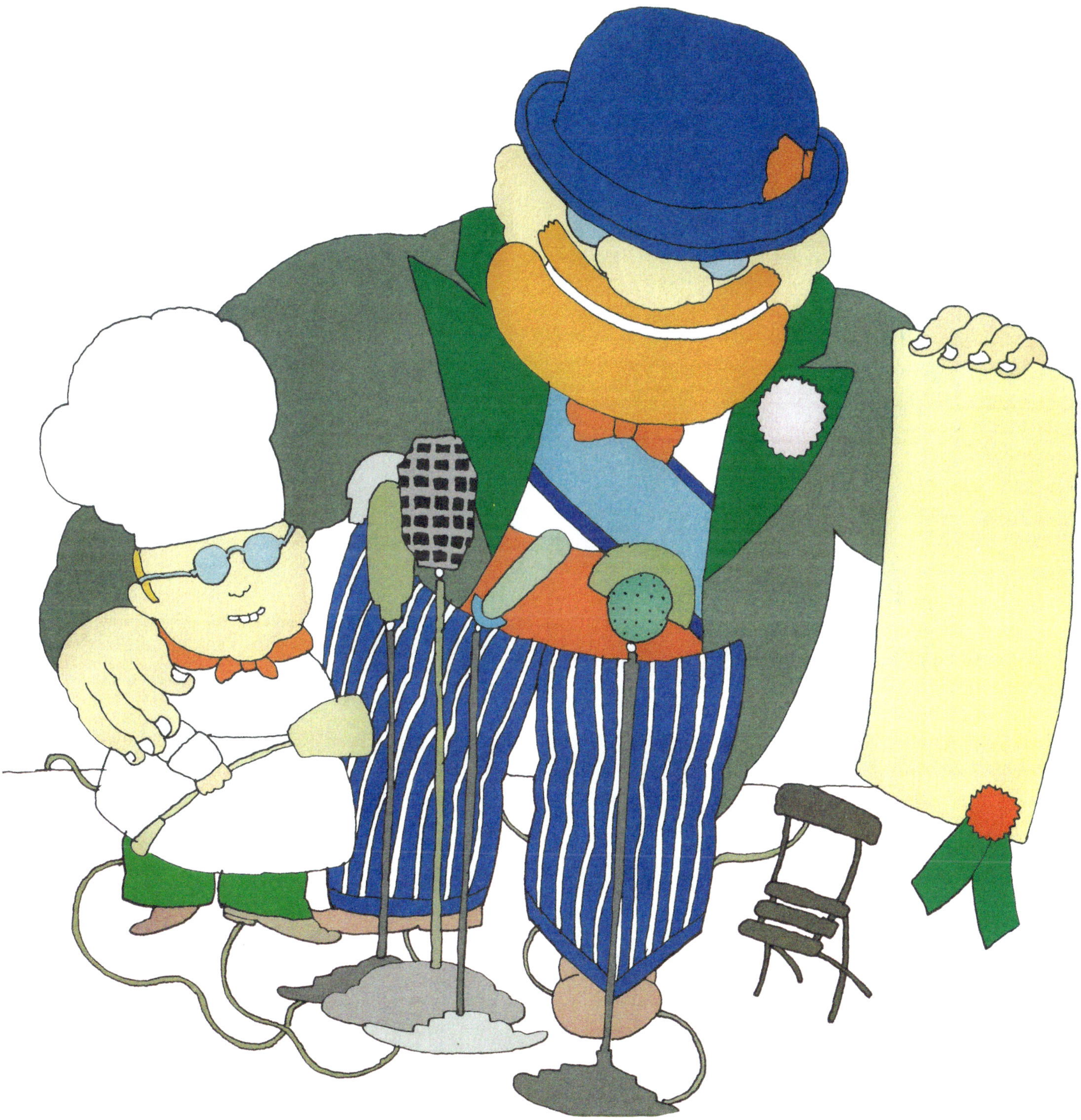

This saga of one Henry Edgewood, *The Pancake King* by Phyllis La Farge, is among Chwast's favorite children's books for its graphic economy and delightful characters. Henry has a compulsive passion for making pancakes. With the desire to satisfy others, he becomes America's Pancake King, and his delicacies are enjoyed by everyone, including the president of the United States. Henry is a sought-after celebrity but is soon overwhelmed by his pancake compulsion. Chwast employs his outline style, which is fluid and simple, with fills of adhesive sheets of flat and vibrating color called Cell-o-tac. This style imbues the art with a psychedelic look. Chwast sometimes uses a wide-angle perspective to make Henry appear small in relation to his surroundings as his reputation grows. As he becomes discontented with his fame, he attempts to return to being a normal kid. The book ends with Henry's Famous Pancake Recipe for readers to make their own pancakes.

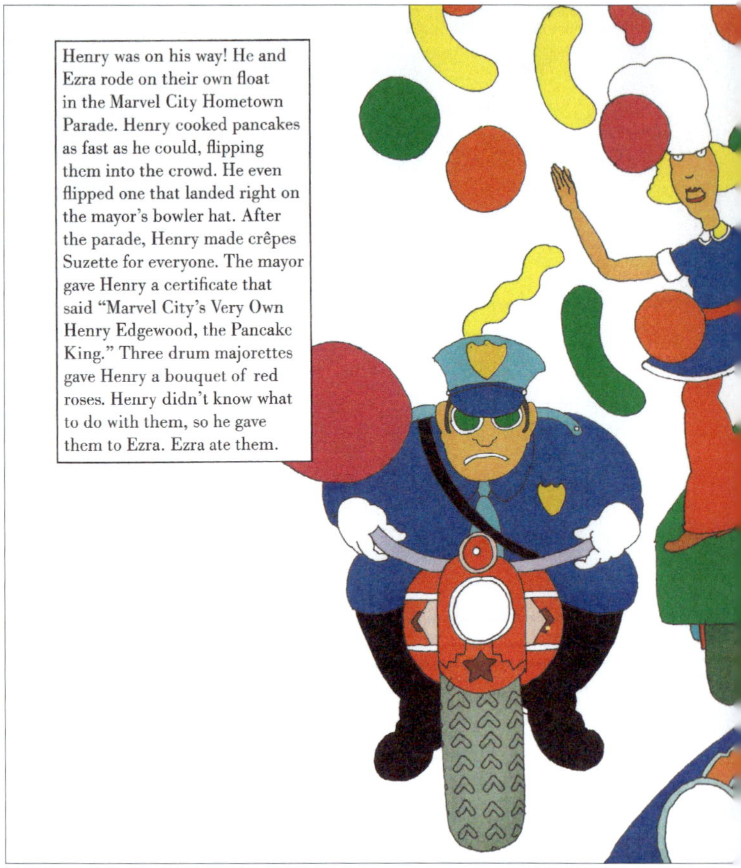

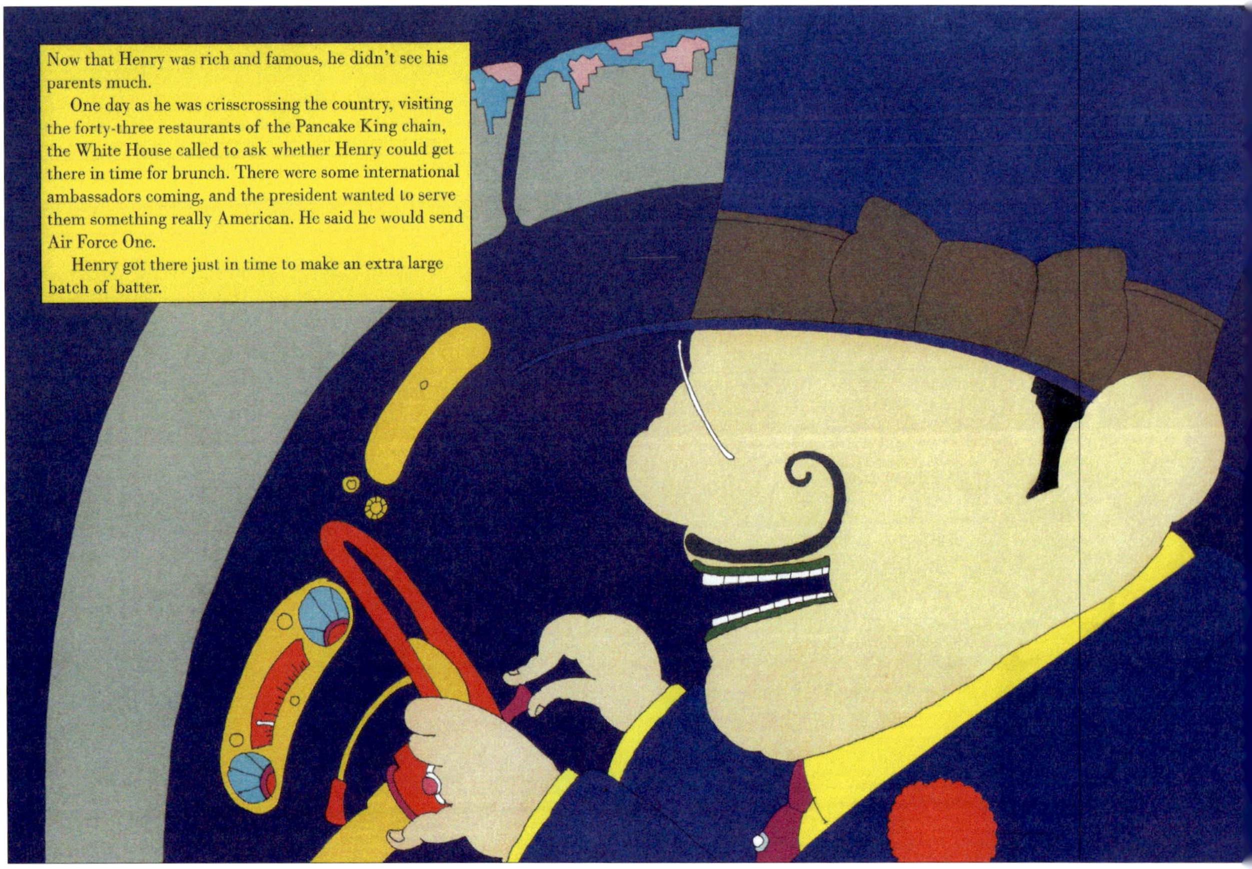

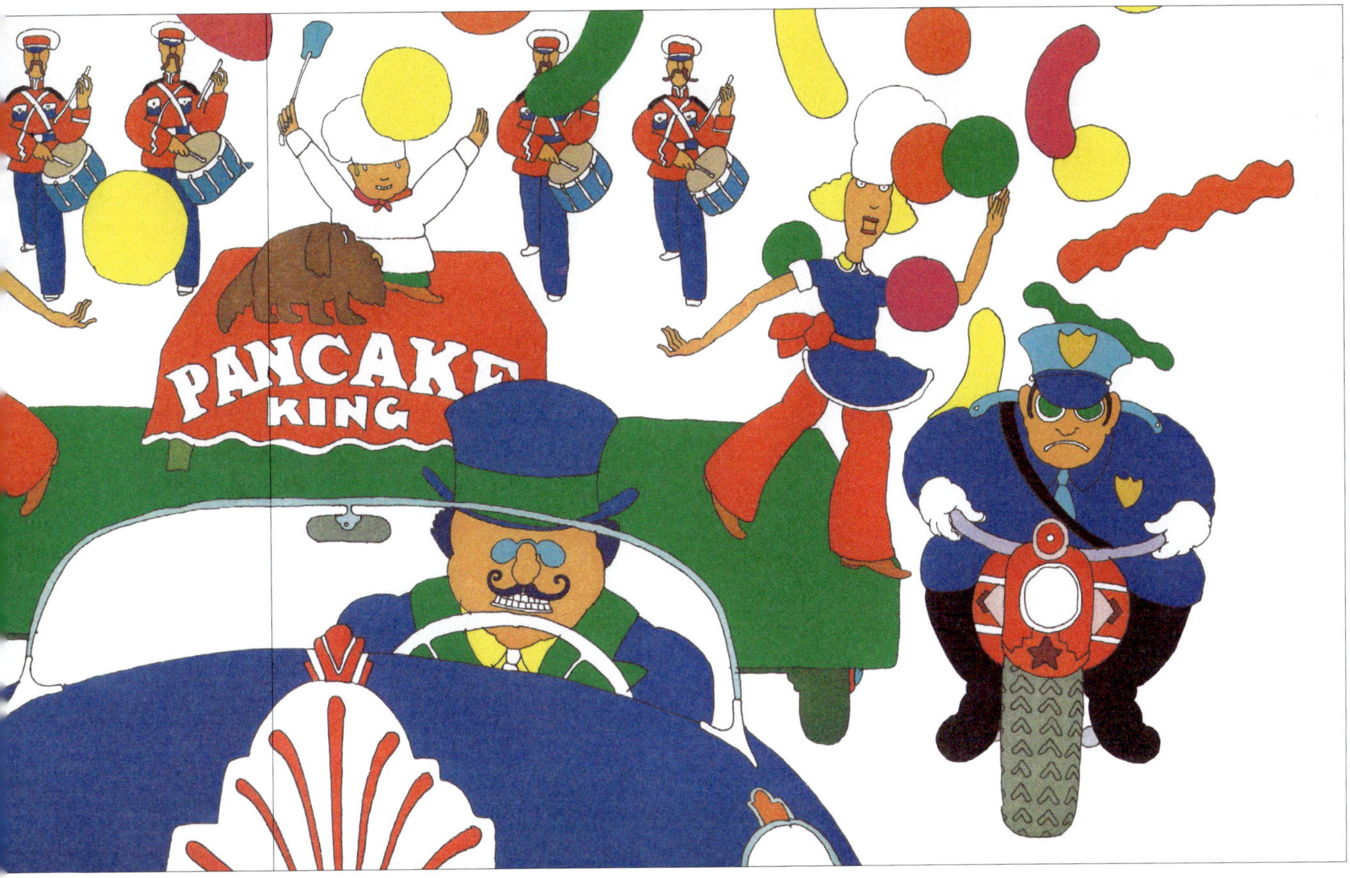
PANCAKE
KING

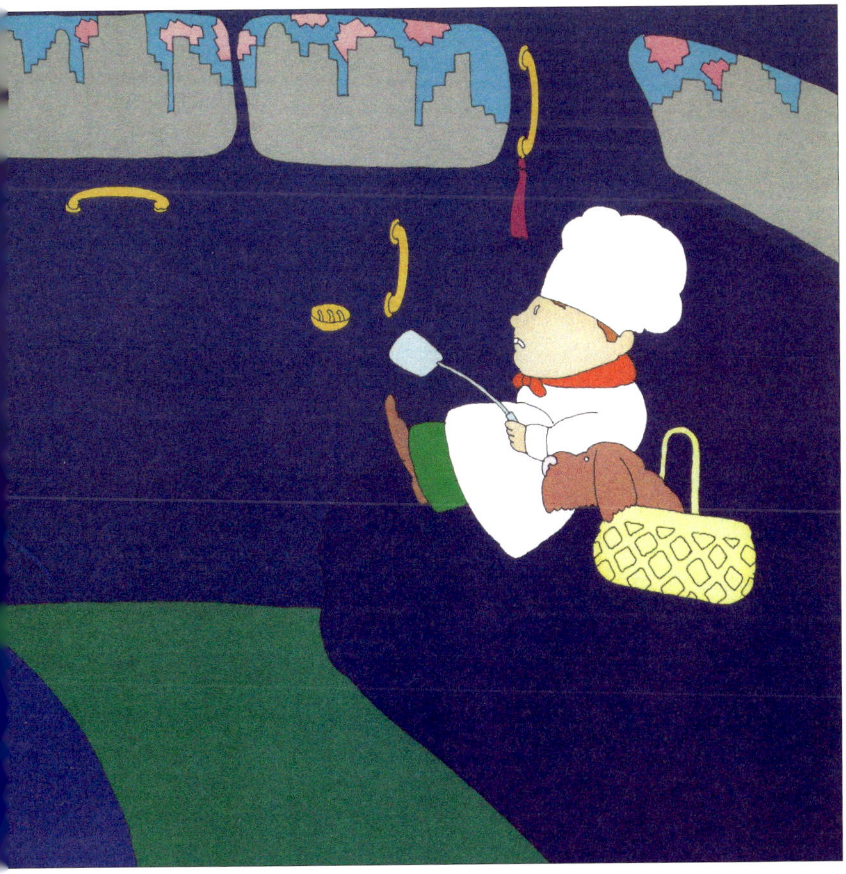

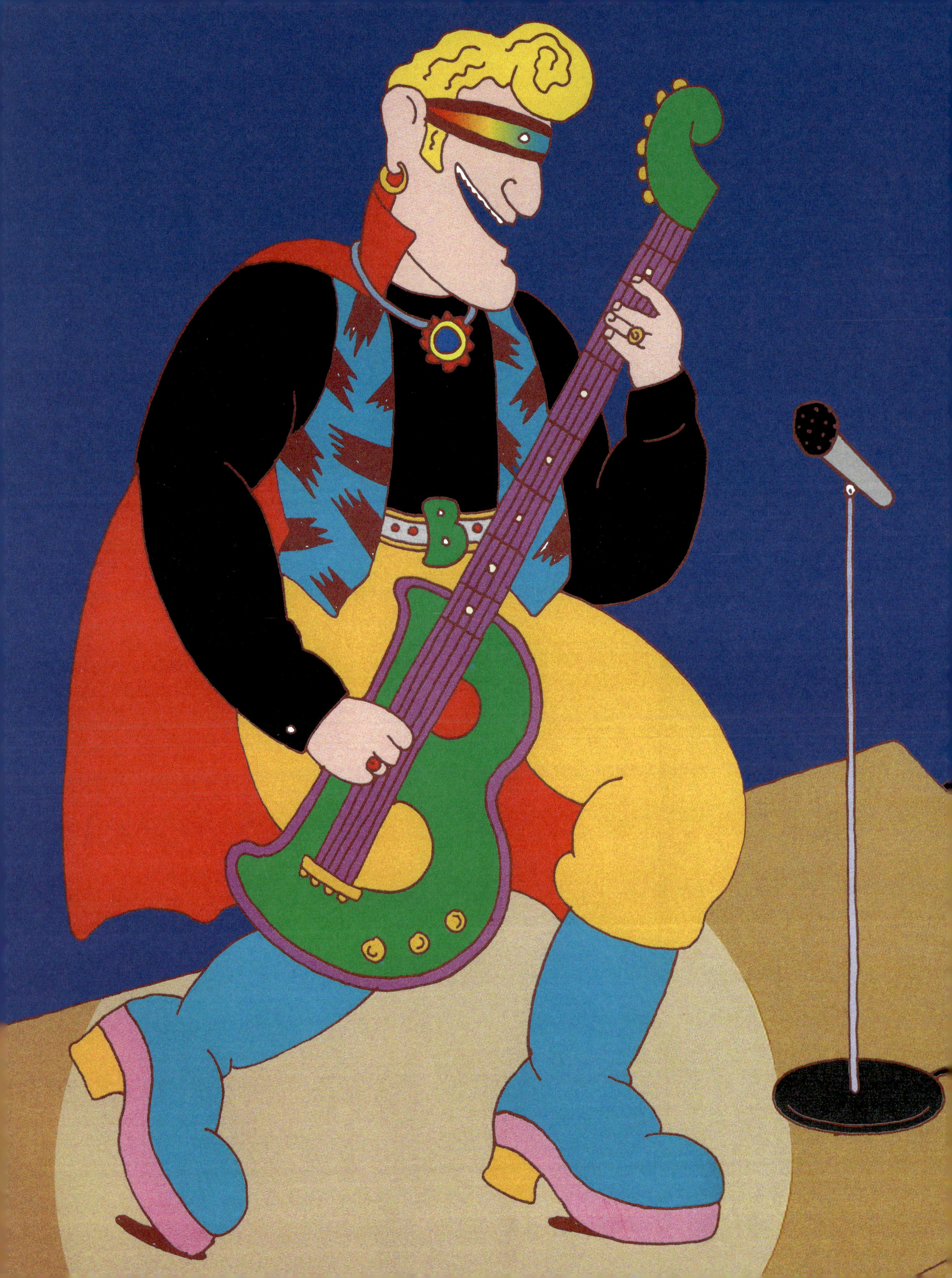
B

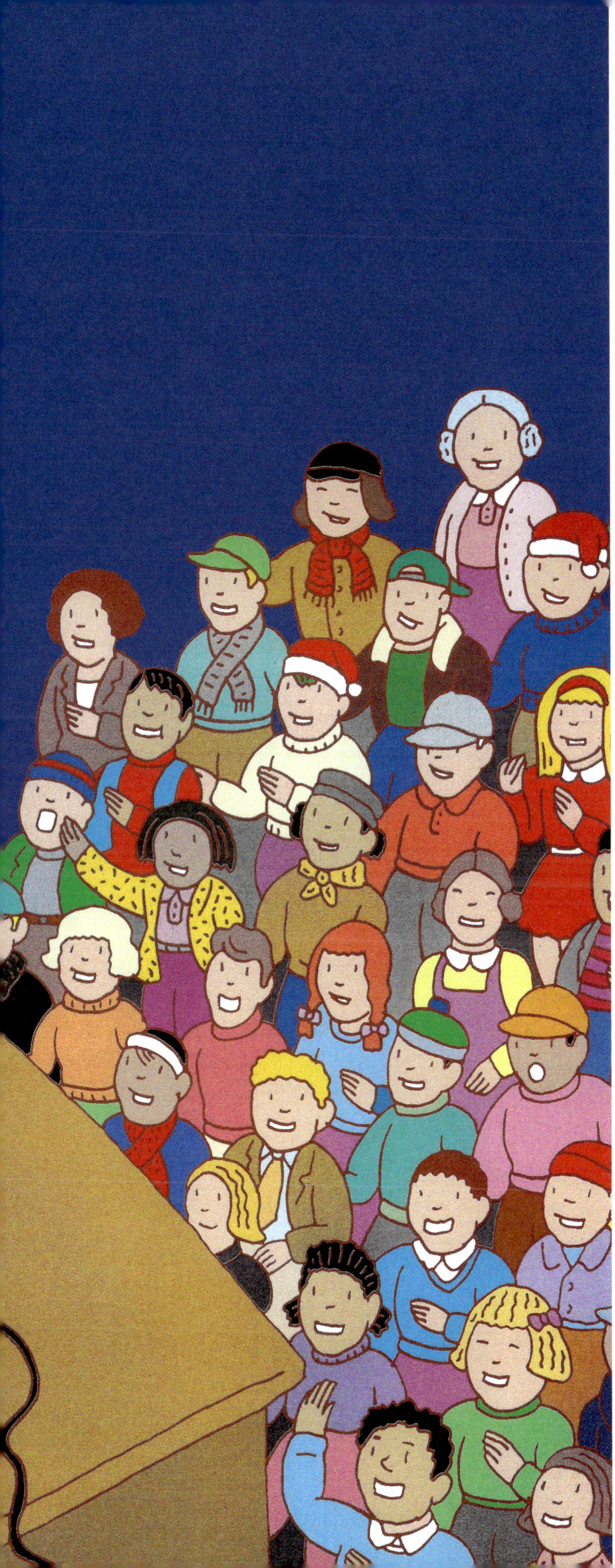

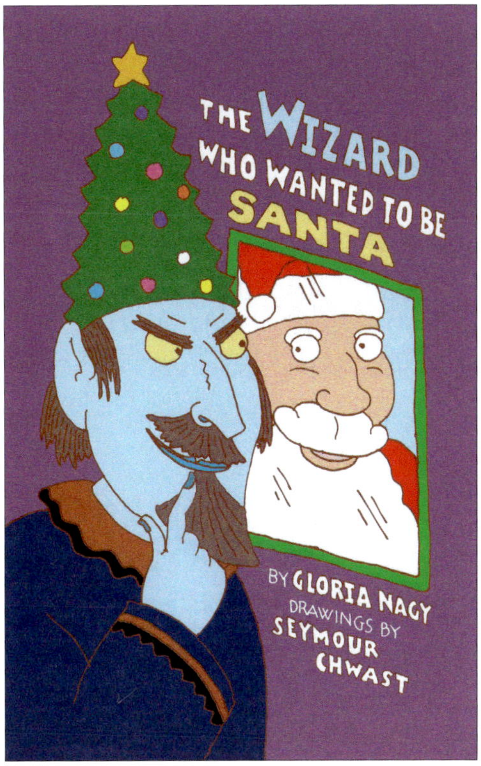

The Wizard Who Wanted to Be Santa, by Gloria Nagy, illustrated by Seymour Chwast, 2000, 8" × 12.25" (20.25 × 31 cm), 48 pages.

The Wizard Who Wanted to Be Santa

Underpinning *The Wizard Who Wanted to Be Santa,* by Gloria Nagy, is an election for a new Santa to replace the tired old one. The election is decided by the winner of a speed race between Santa and an evil wizard named Beedlebas, who believes it is unfair for the old Saint Nick to forever keep the best job on the planet. Beedlebas drives a supercharged racing car and old Santa Claus is behind the reins of his famous, reindeer-powered sleigh. "A ballot was included at the end of the book that children could tear out and send in to vote," explains Chwast, who made the illustrations using pen on paper, scanning them into his computer and coloring them digitally in Adobe Illustrator.

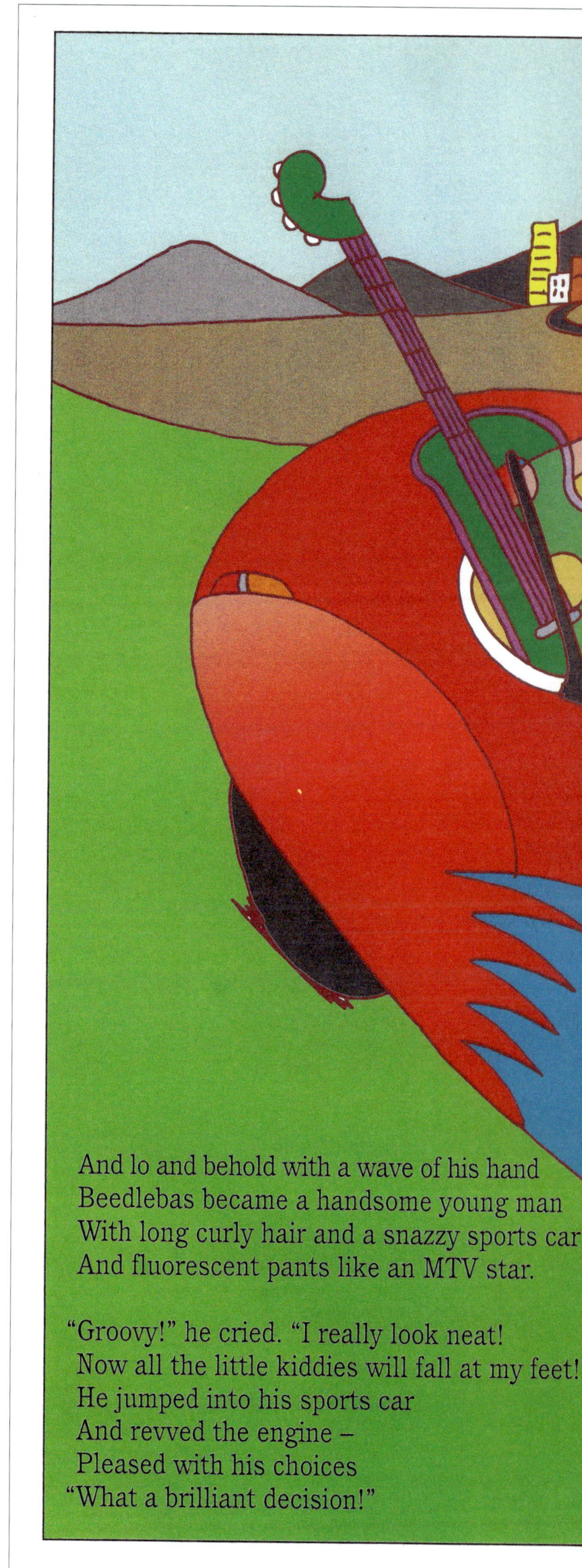

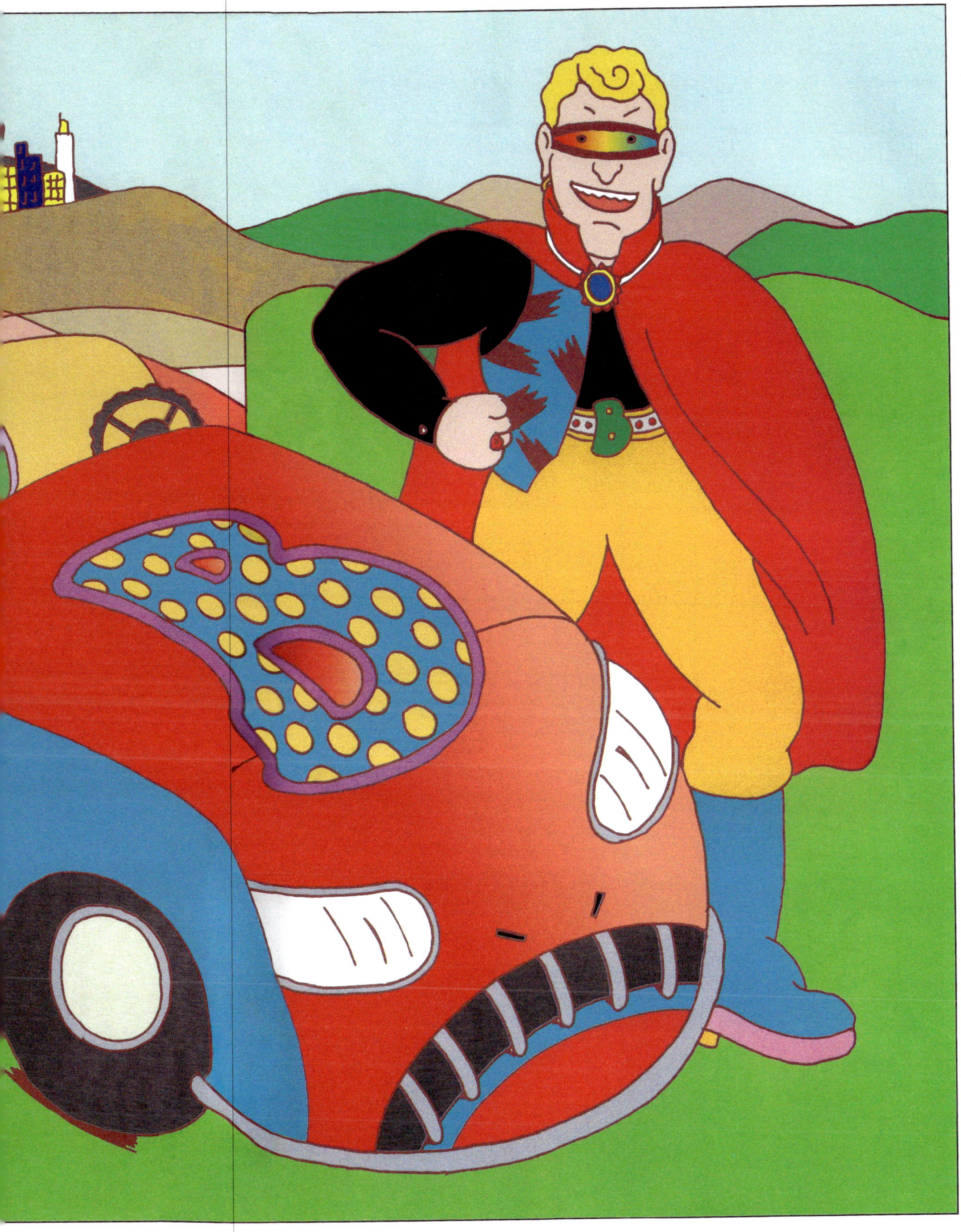

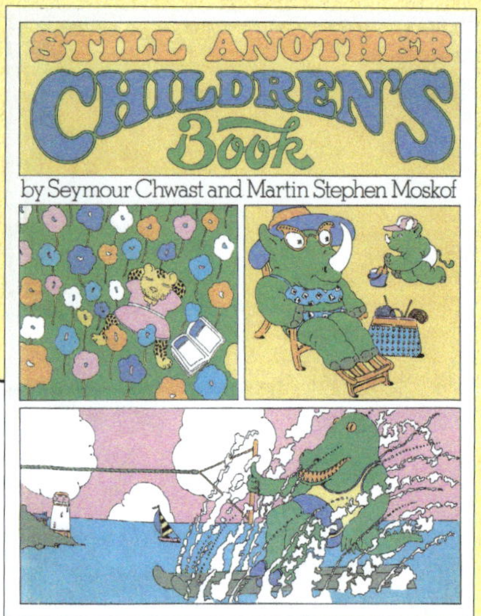

Still Another Children's Book, by Martin Stephen Moskof, illustrated by Seymour Chwast, 1972, 8" × 10" (20.25 × 25.5 cm), 40 pages.

Still Another Children's Book

This book was part of a series that also included *Still Another Number Book* and *Still Another Alphabet Book* (coauthored with Martin Stephen Moskof). "It was based on the idea that there exist consistent formulae for children's books," explains Chwast. "It's the only one in the series with a narrative story," he added. He included just enough detail in the story to give each animal among this ensemble cast of vacation-enjoying creatures its individual character.

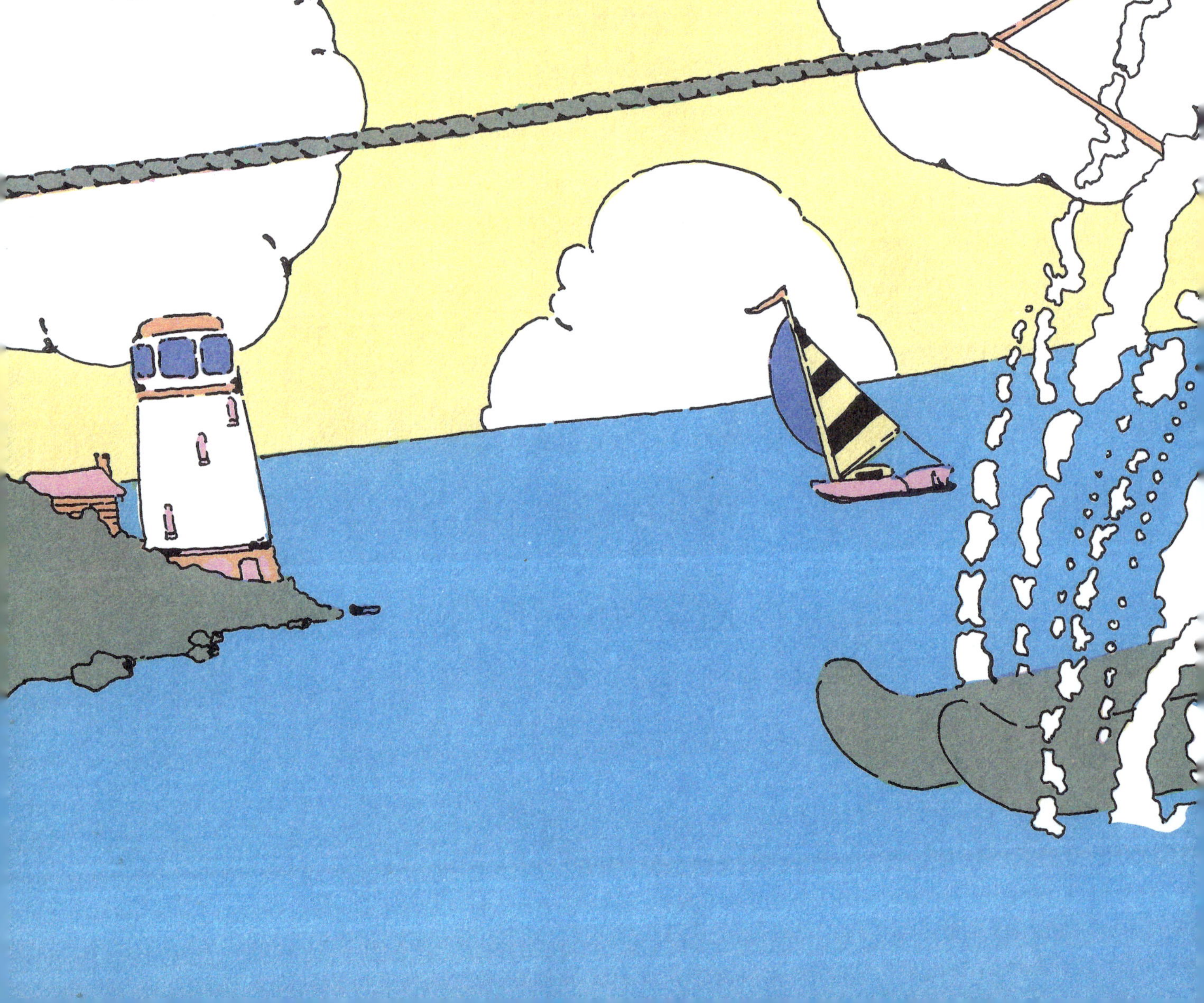

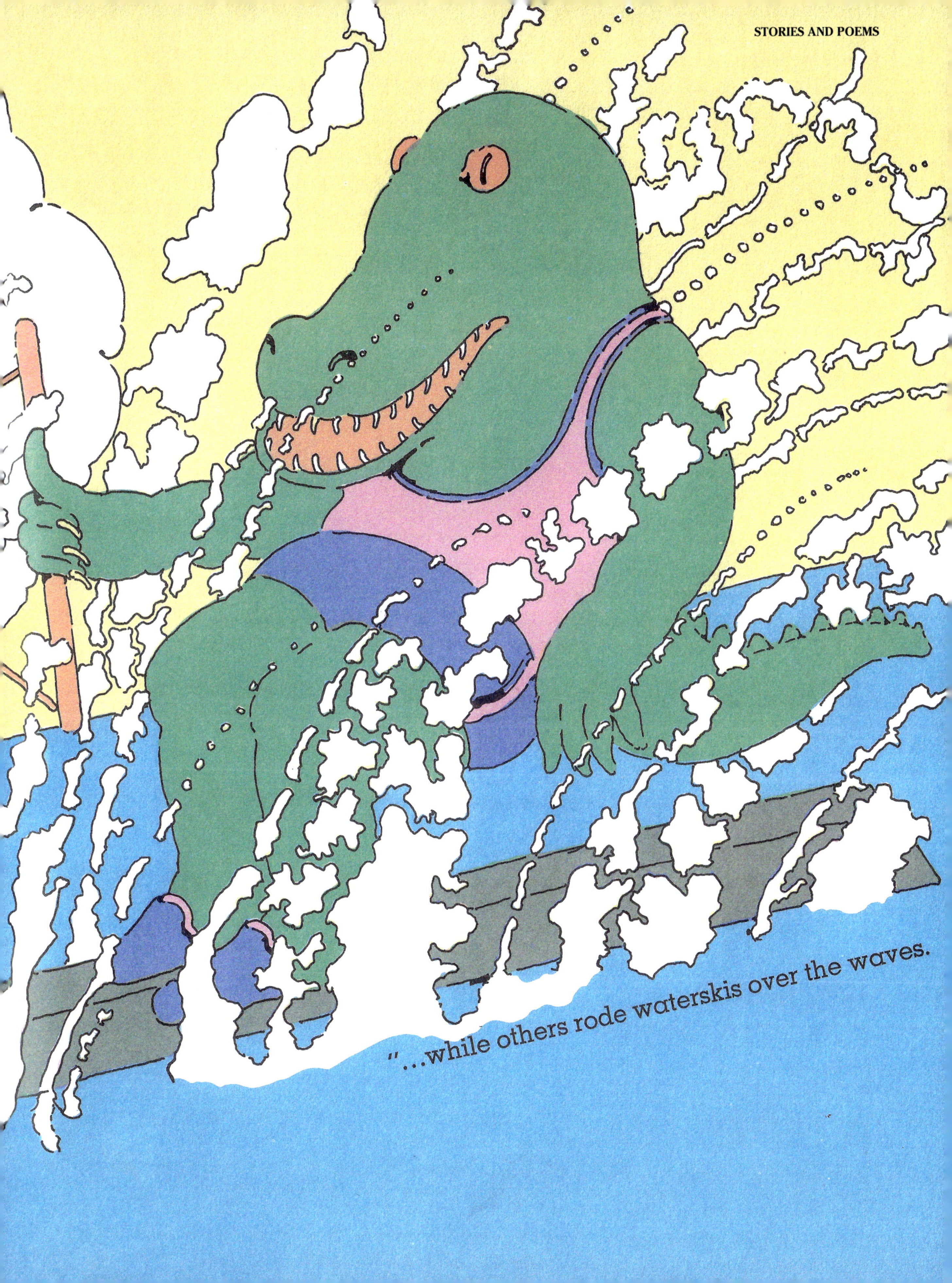

"...while others rode waterskis over the waves.

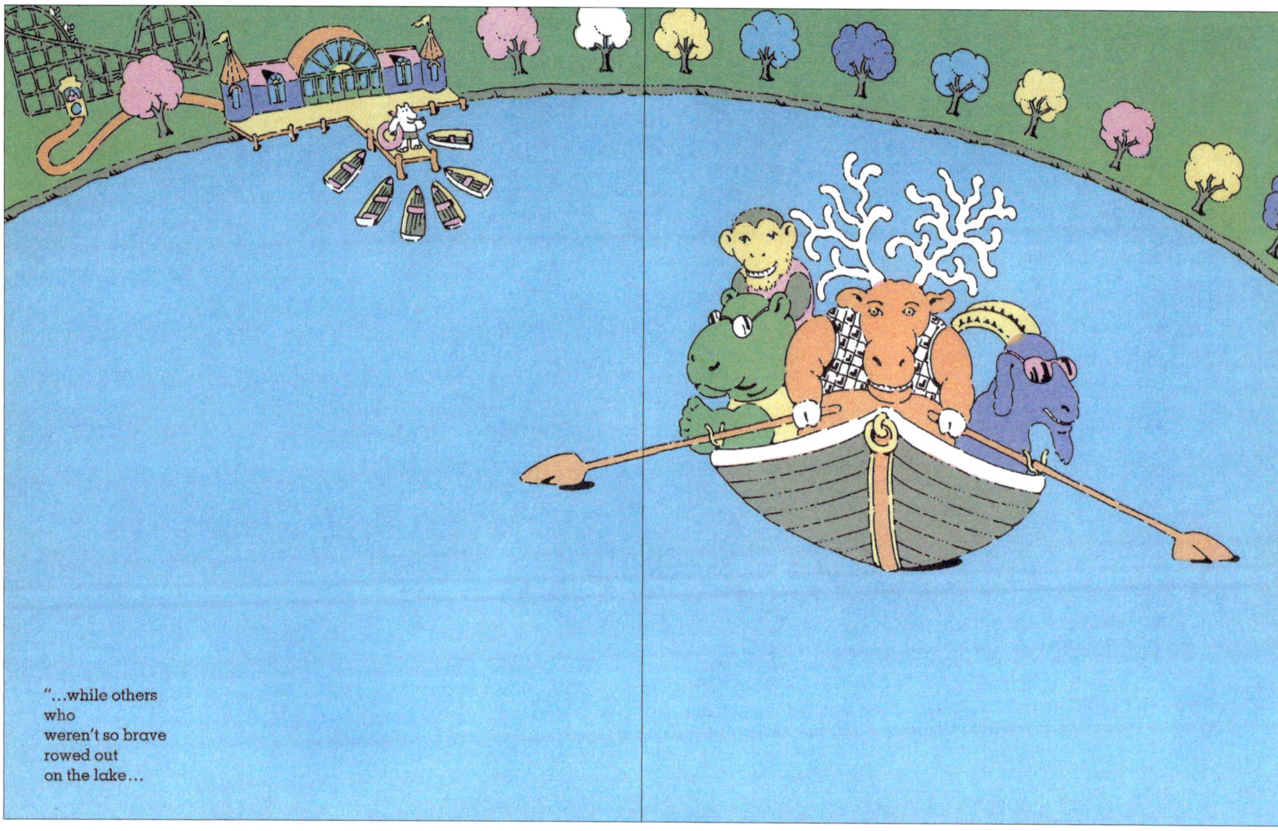

"...while others
who
weren't so brave
rowed out
on the lake...

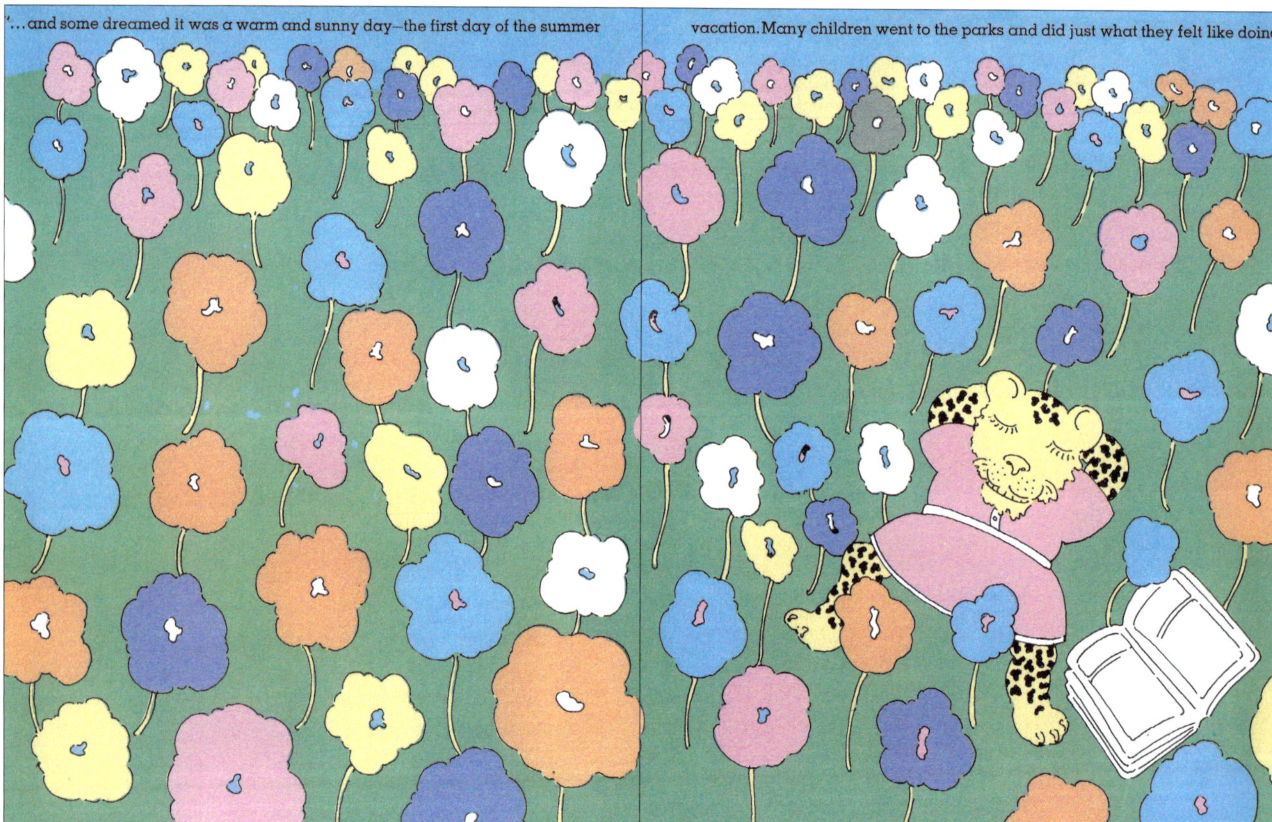

"...and some dreamed it was a warm and sunny day—the first day of the summer vacation. Many children went to the parks and did just what they felt like doing.

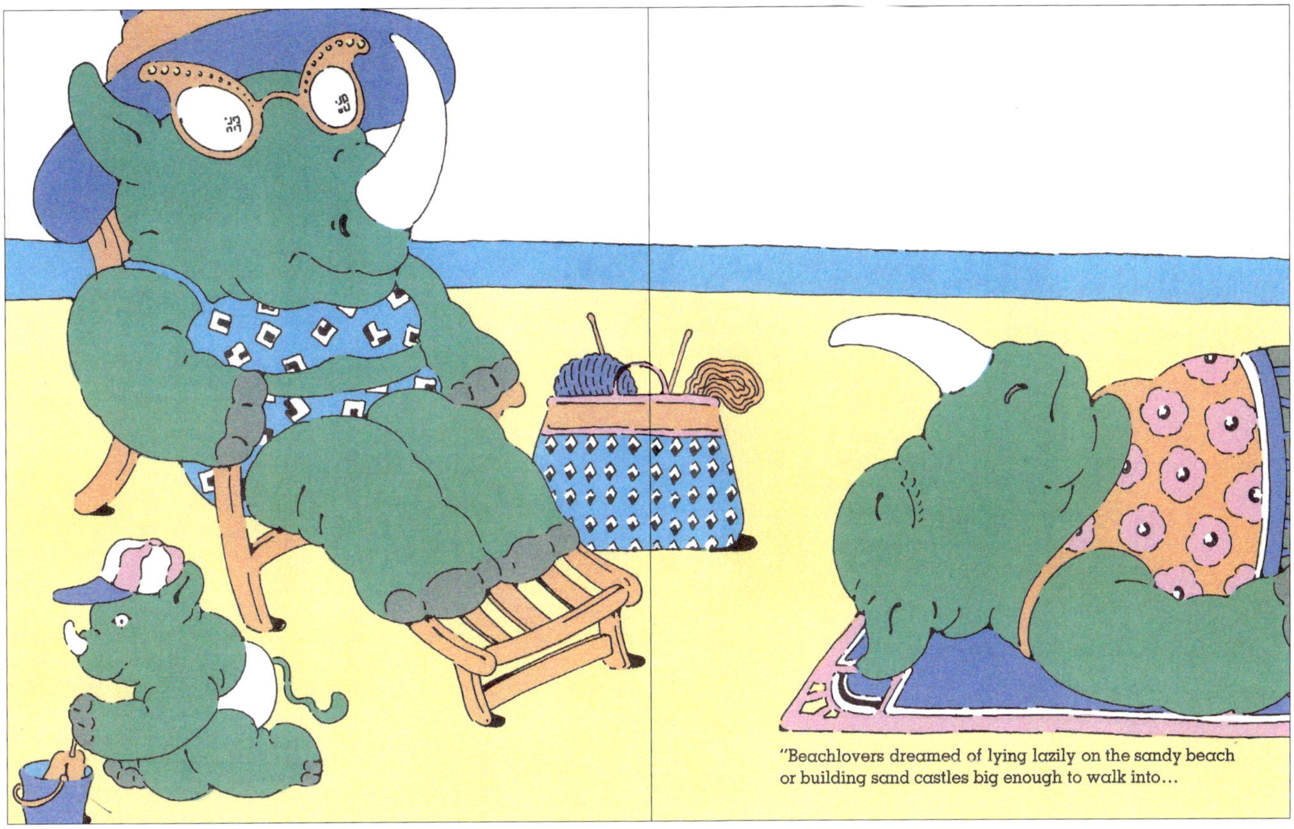
"Beachlovers dreamed of lying lazily on the sandy beach
or building sand castles big enough to walk into...

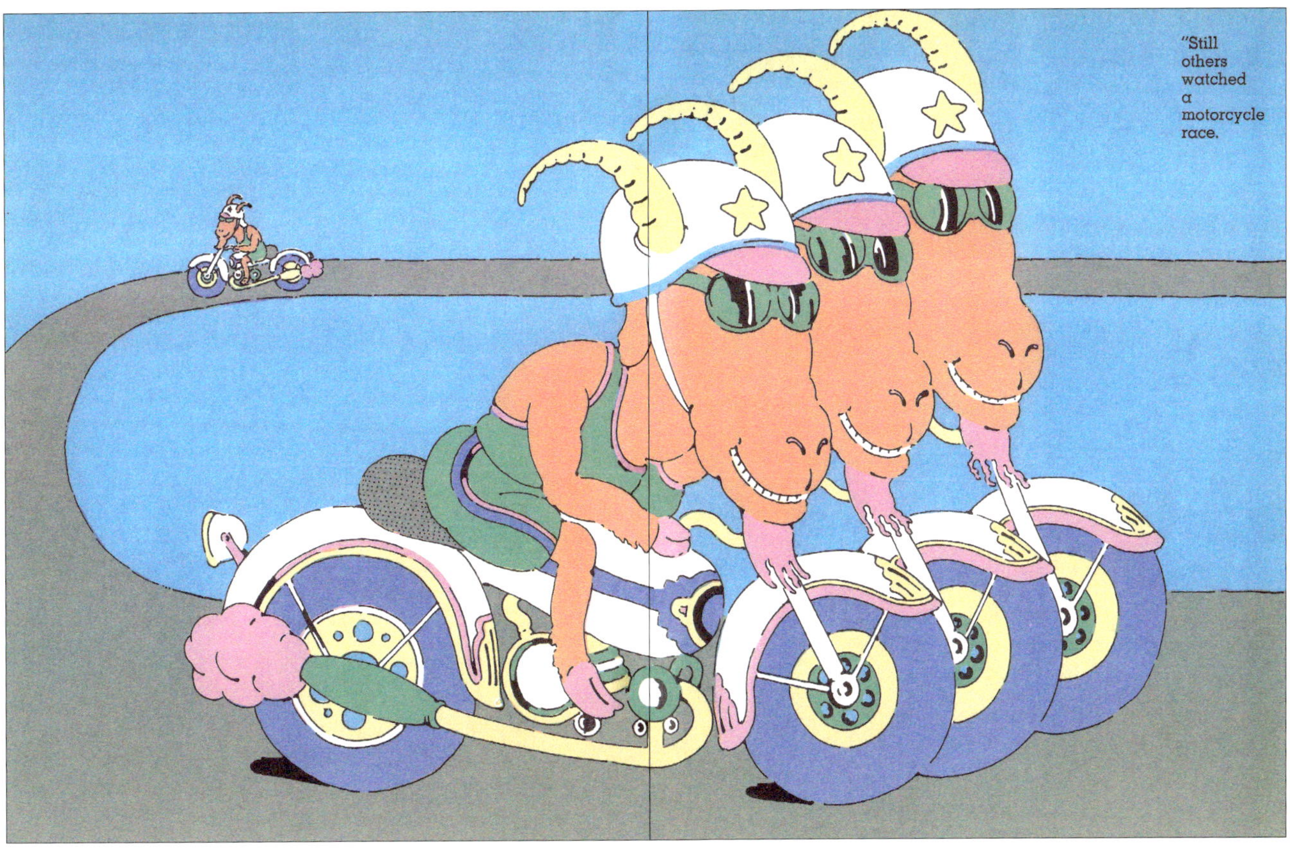
"Still
others
watched
a
motorcycle
race.

Sara's Granny and the Groodle

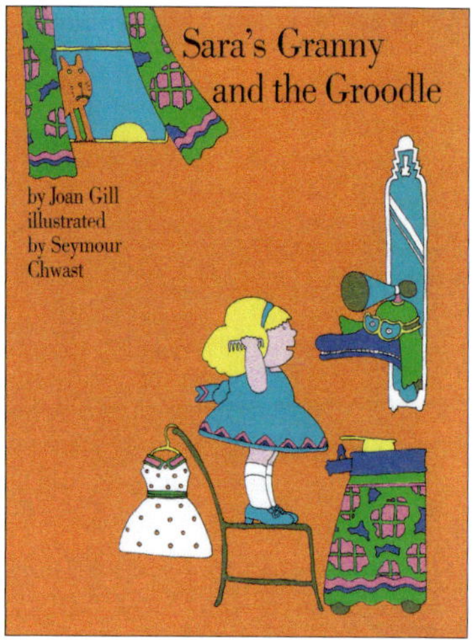

Sara's Granny and the Groodle, by Joan Gill, illustrated by Seymour Chwast, 1969, 8.5" × 11" (21.5 × 28 cm), 32 pages.

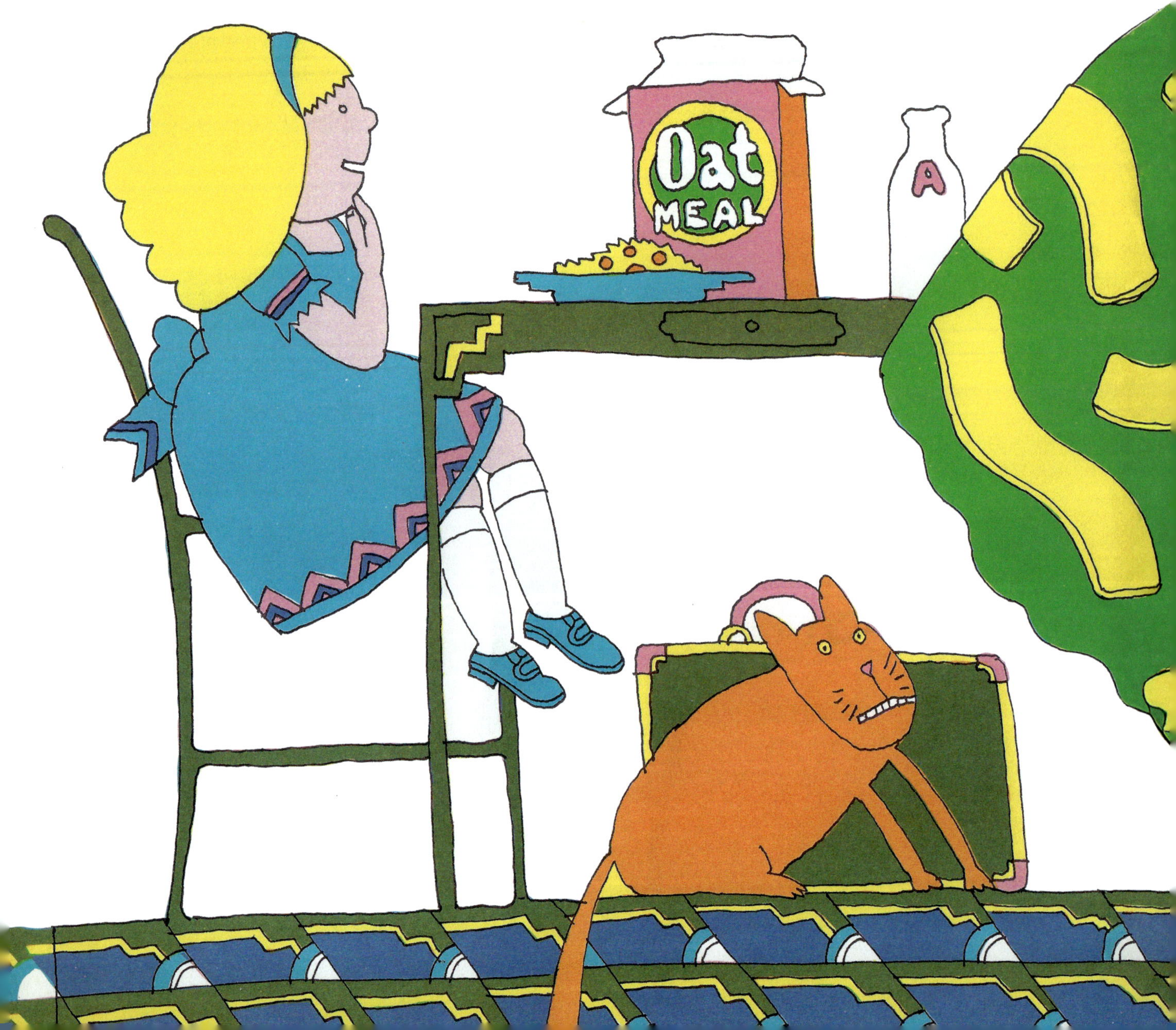

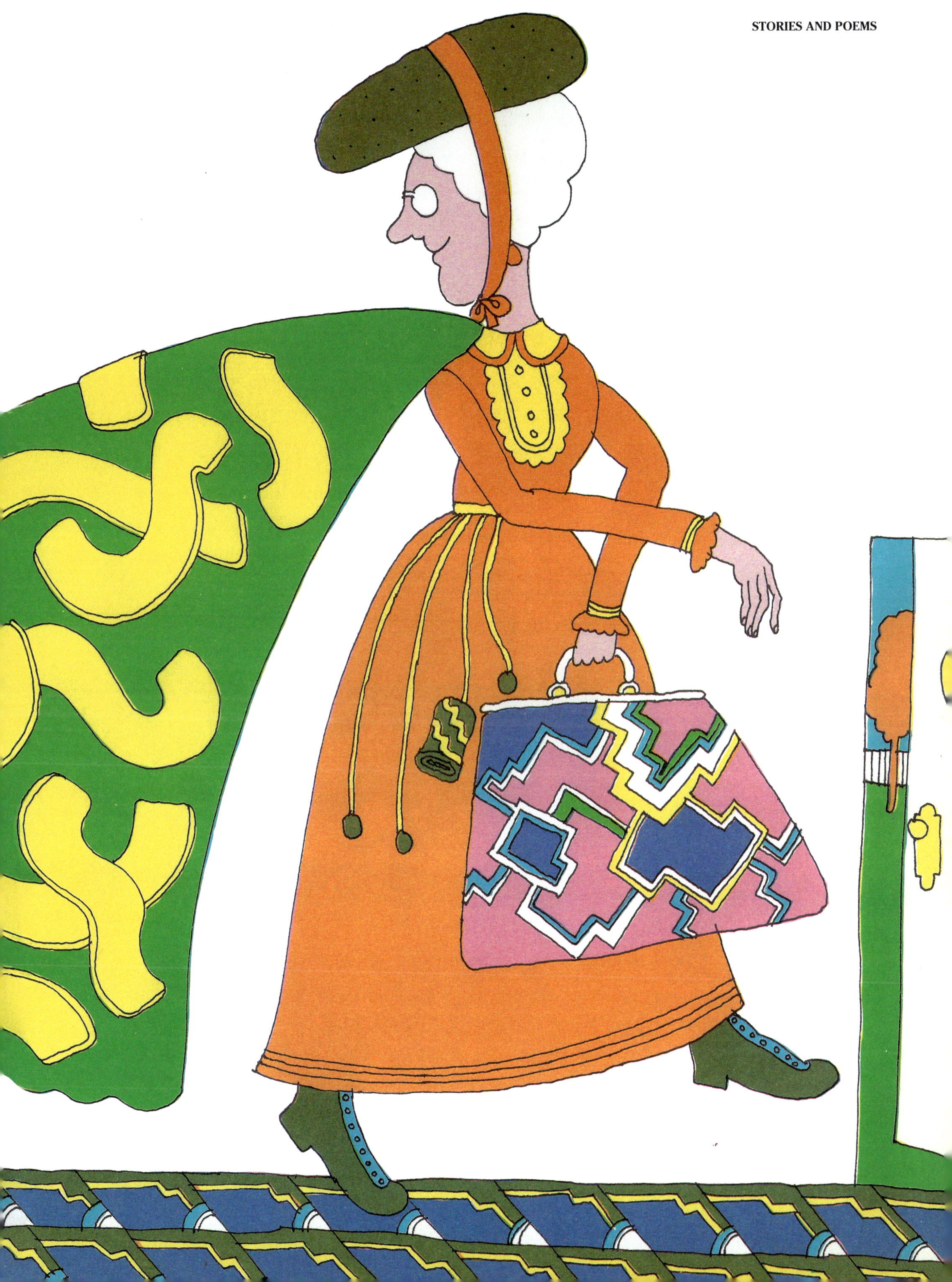

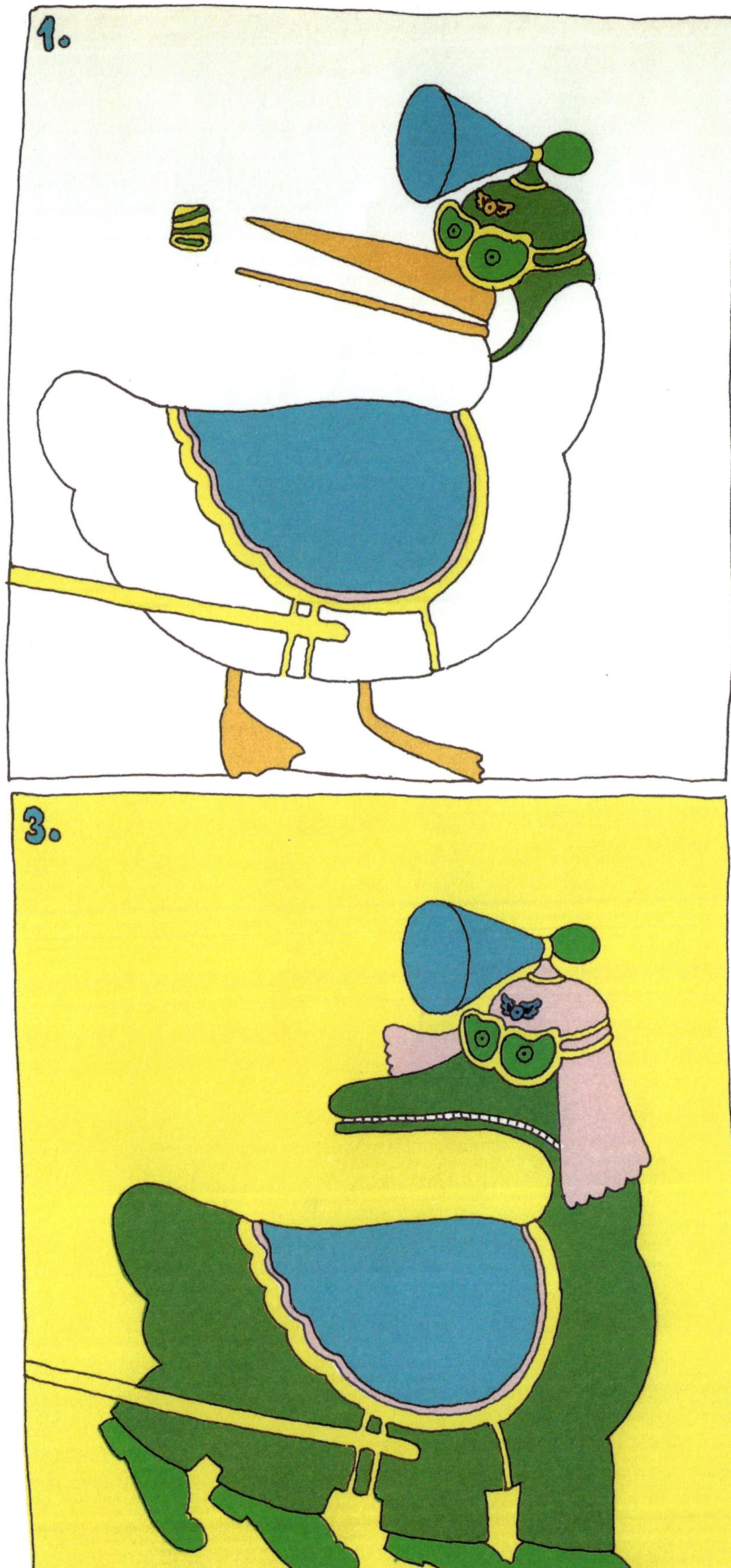
1.
3.

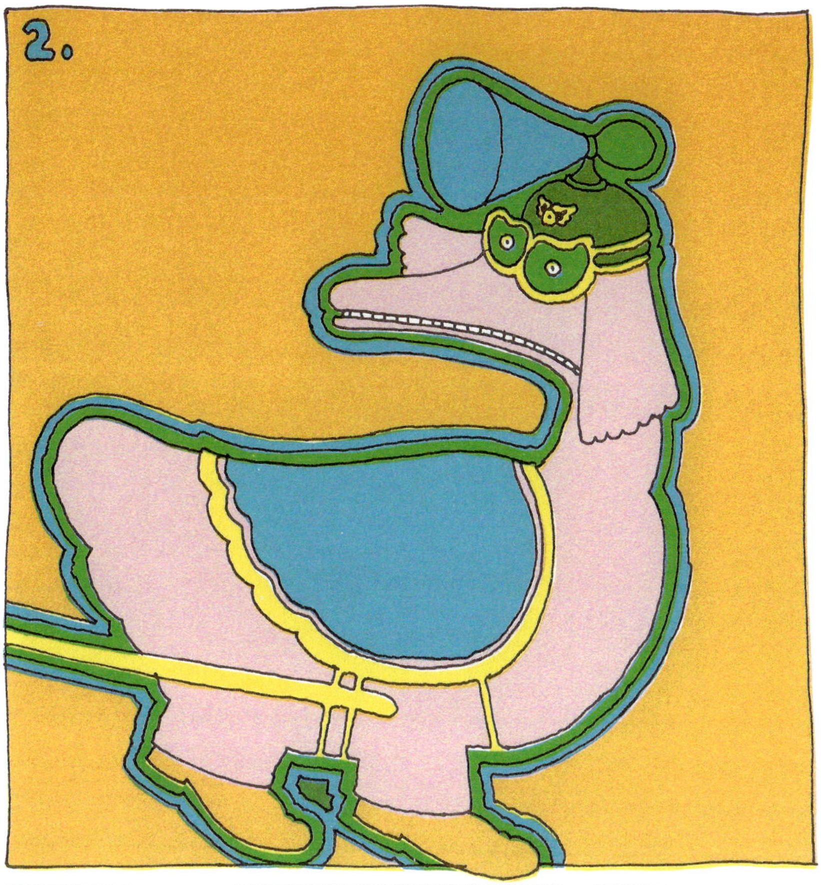

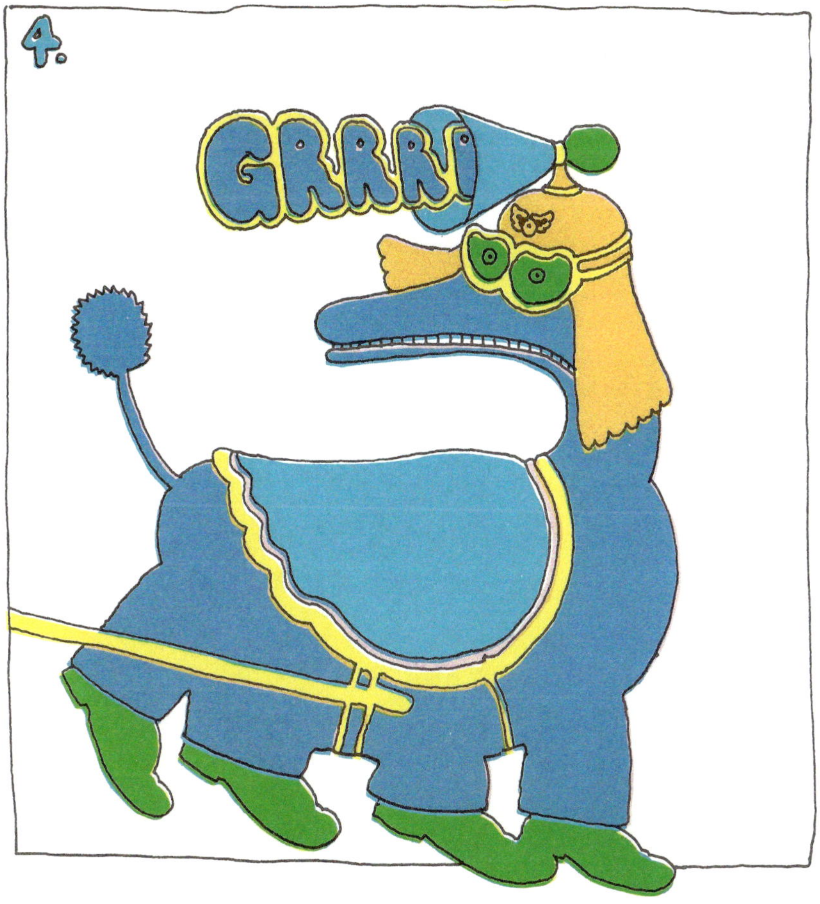

Like *The Pancake King, Sara's Granny and the Groodle,* by Joan Gill, is visually powerful owing to the graphic simplicity of the characters and the intensity of Chwast's favorite decorative art and design elements. The images present Sara on a wild ride on a chariot pulled by a Groodle, a cross between a goose and a poodle (or whatever the young reader imagines a Groodle to be). Chwast says, "Everyone should have a lively granny like Sara's." Not only was it lots of fun to invent the mythical Groodle, but the book was named the *New York Times,* Best Illustrated Children's Book of the Year in 1969.

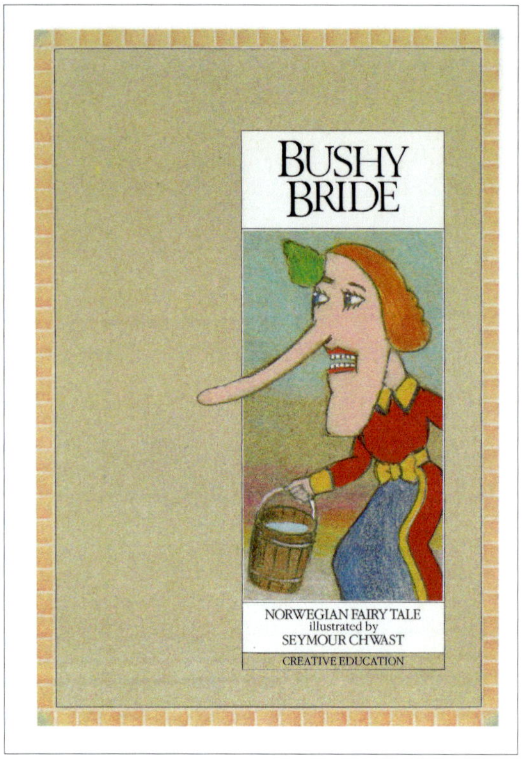

Bushy Bride, Norwegian Fairy Tale, illustrated by Seymour Chwast, art direction by Rita Marshall, 1983, 6.25" × 8.75" (16 × 22.25 cm), 32 pages.

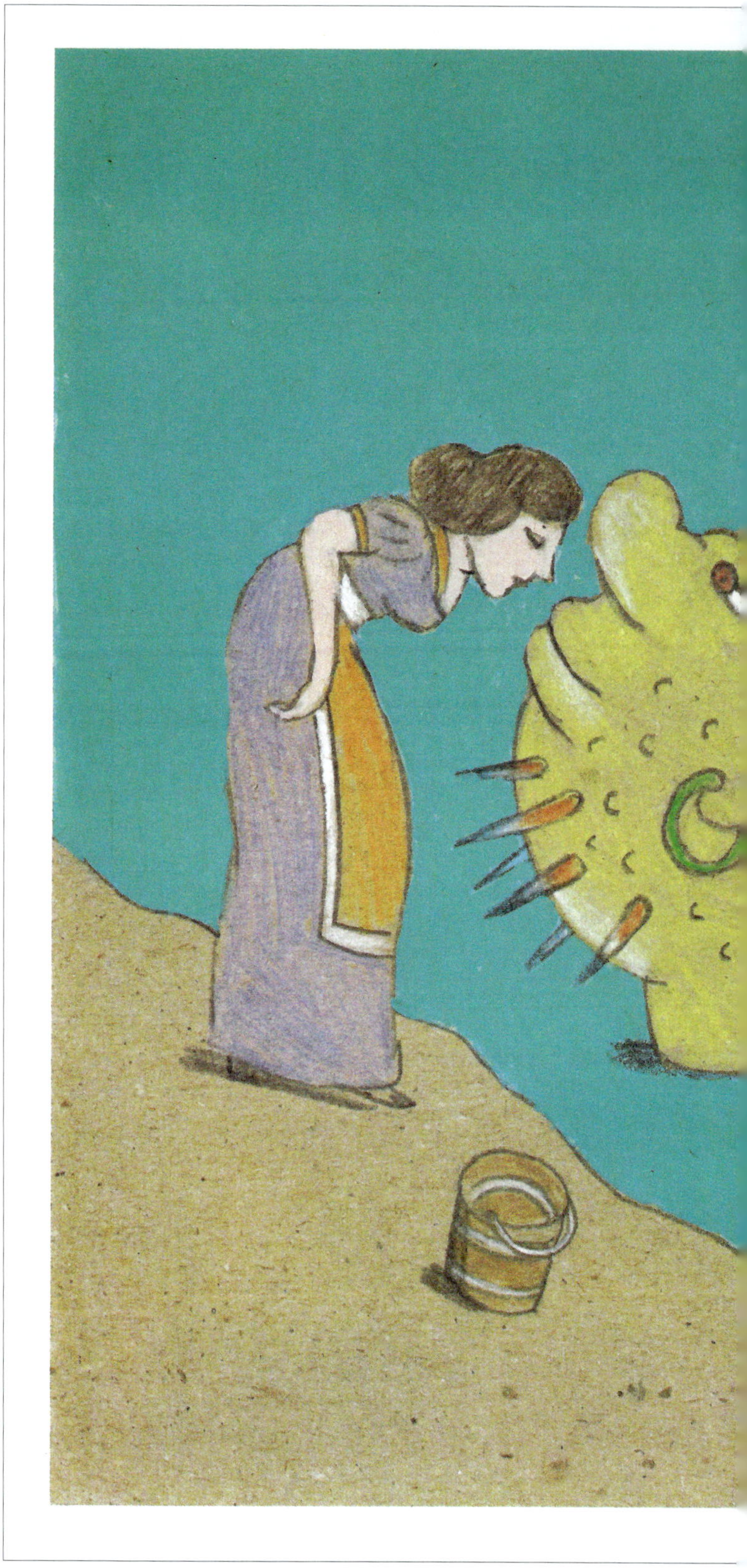

Bushy Bride

In this mid-19th-century Norwegian fairy tale, deception and greed are familiar themes. In the manner of Disney's *Cinderella*, a stereotypically cruel stepmother mistreats her stepdaughter. One day, the stepmother sends her to fetch water at a stream where the stepdaughter finds three monstrous heads have arisen from under the water; they demand that the stepdaughter wash, groom, and kiss each of them. She obeys and, surprisingly the heads reward her by making the young girl more beautiful than she already is. Later, she attracts the eye of a king, who is somehow deceived into believing the girl's ugly stepsister is the one he is promised to marry. When he learns that the beautiful stepdaughter is his true bride, he makes sure the imposter and her deceitful mother are thrown into a snake pit. Chwast captures the beauty and brutality with nuanced wit and colored pencil.

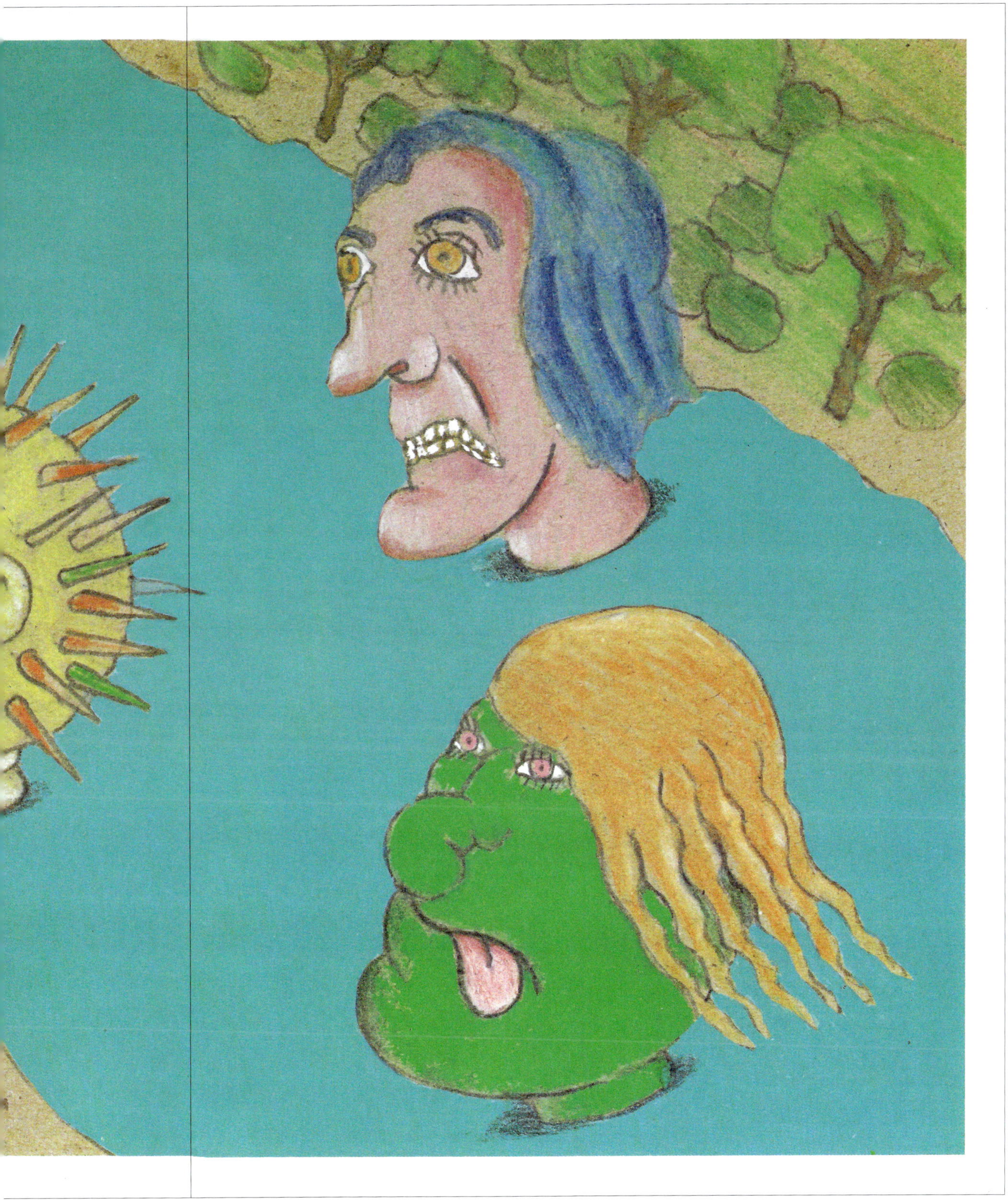

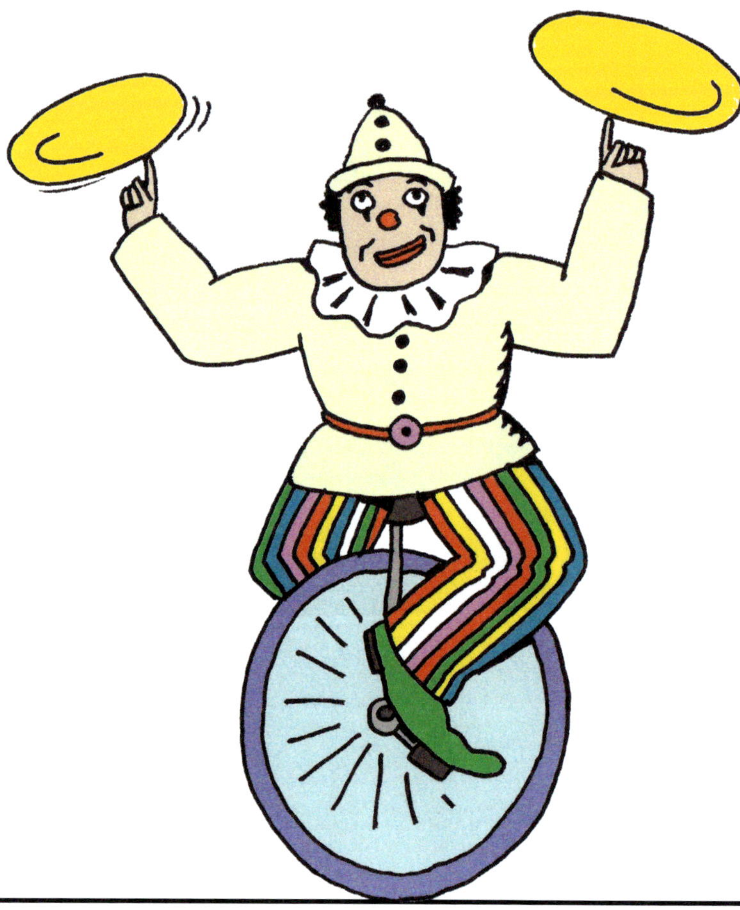

Get Dressed!

For this book, Chwast is delightfully playful as designer and illustrator. He has conceived a book with a book jacket that opens from the middle like an actual piece of clothing. "The spreads explore what you would wear for all occasions, whether in the dead of winter or in the summer on the beach," he says with a smile. Inside, he has cast a menagerie of funny species waiting to get dressed in their appropriate costumes. The illustrations were drawn with pencil on paper, scanned into a computer, and then digitally colored in Adobe Photoshop.

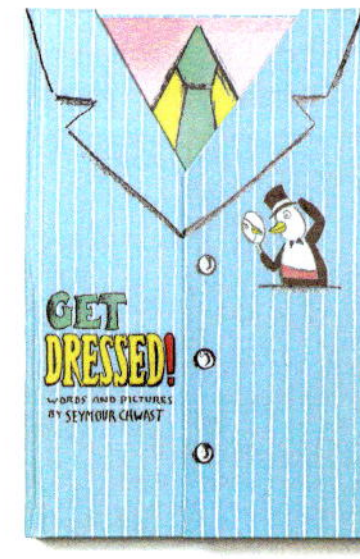

Get Dressed!, by Seymour Chwast, 2012, 6.5" × 9.75" (16.5 × 24.75), 18 pages plus flaps.

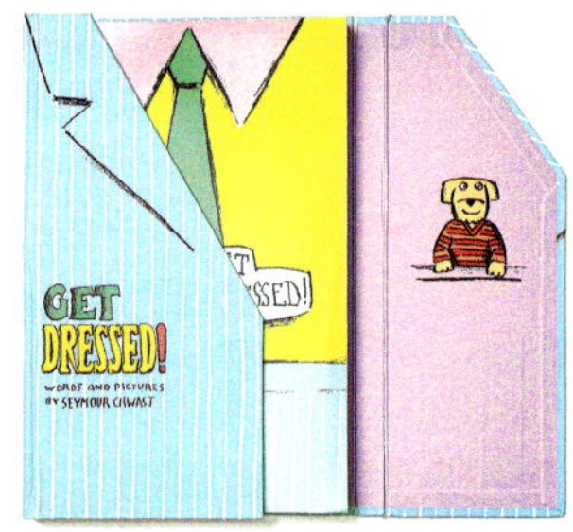

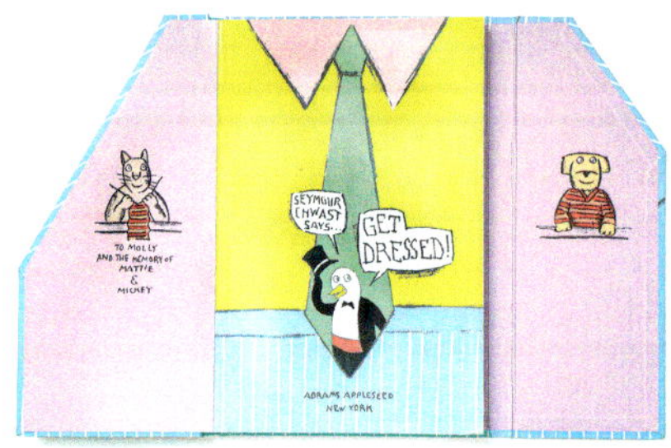

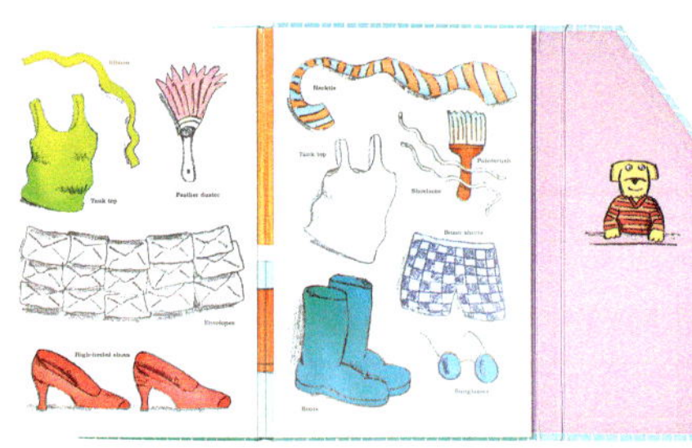

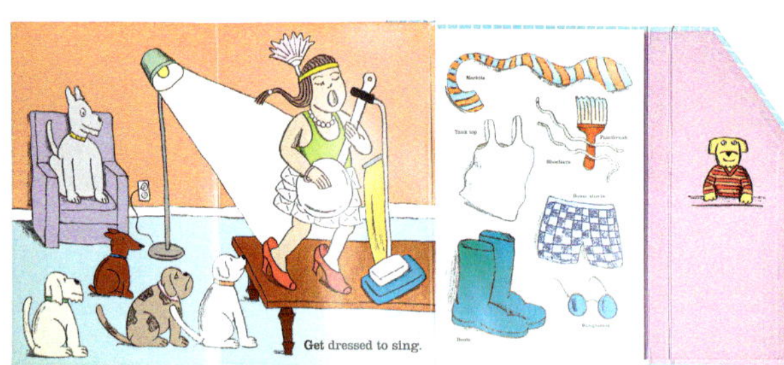

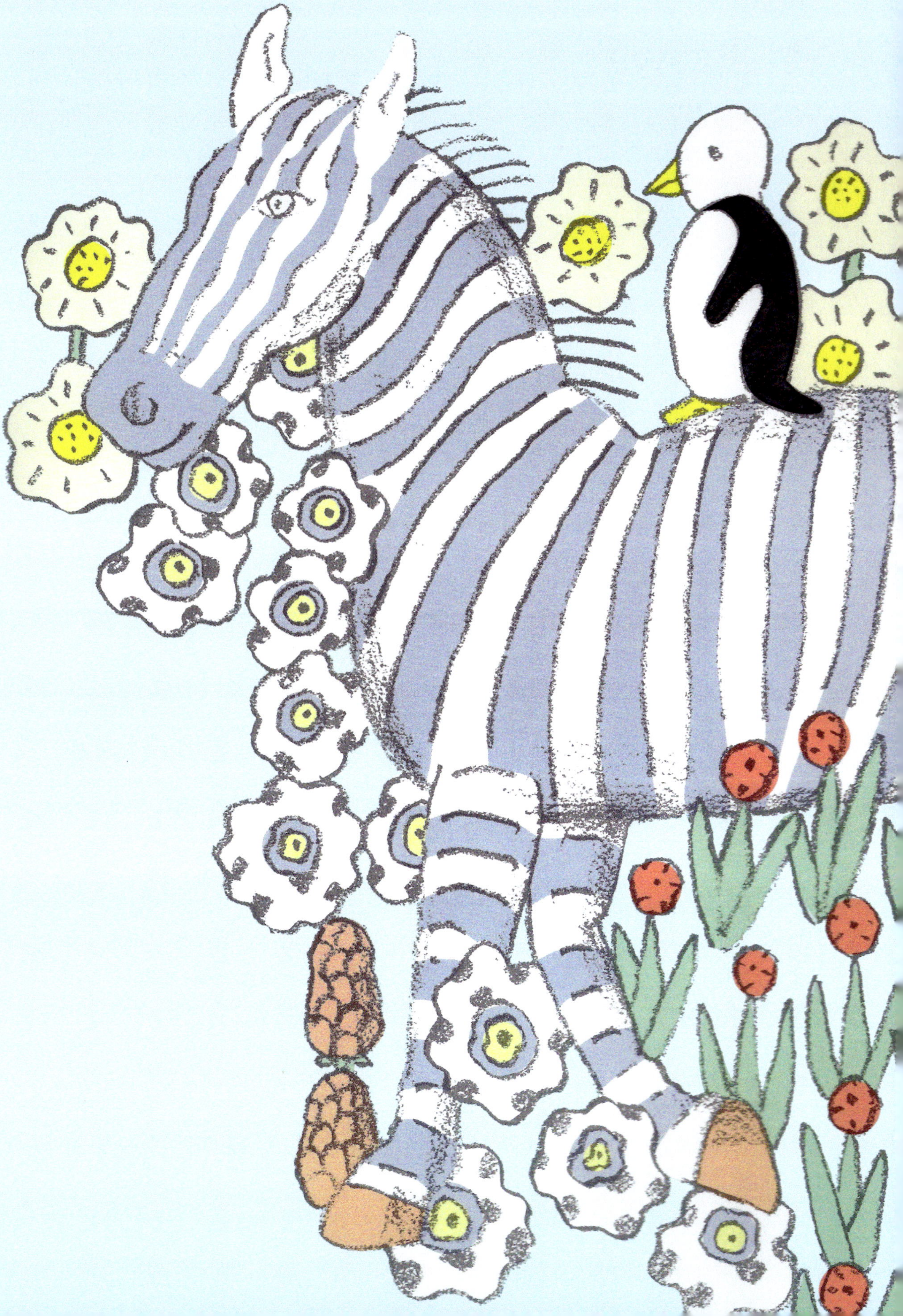

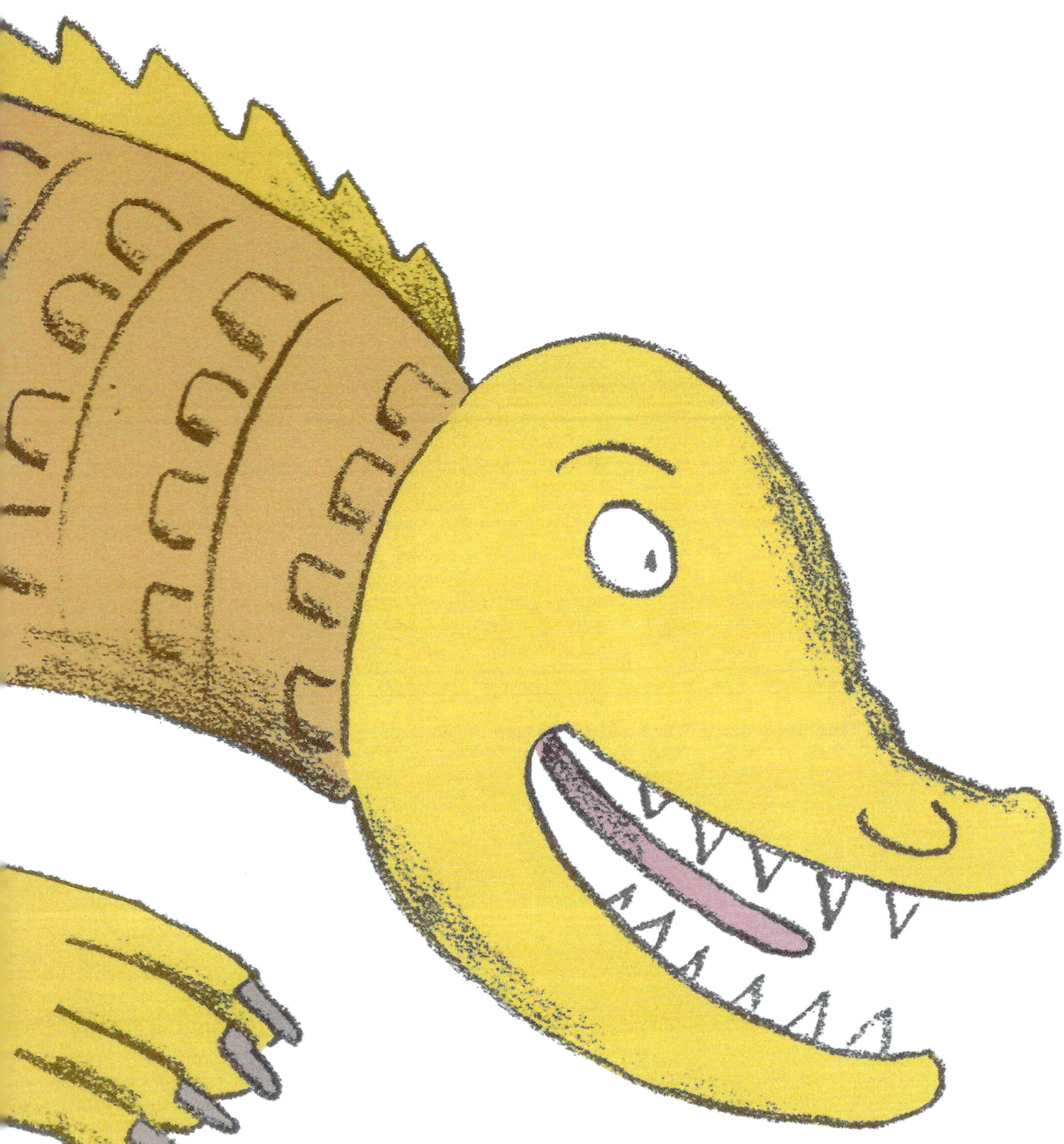

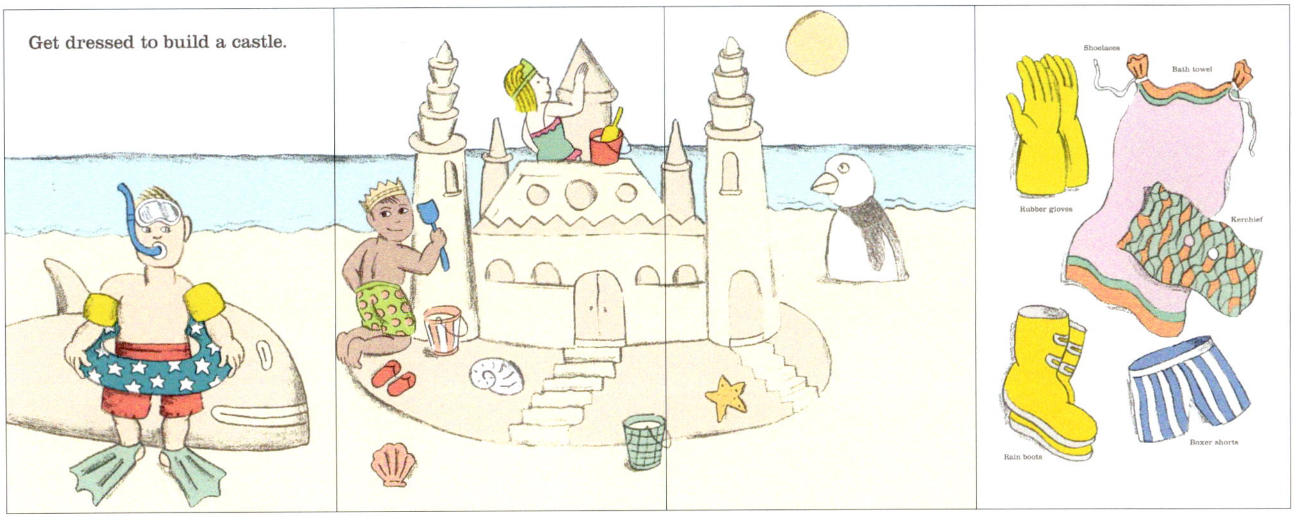
Get dressed to build a castle.
Shoelaces
Bath towel
Rubber gloves
Kerchief
Rain boots
Boxer shorts

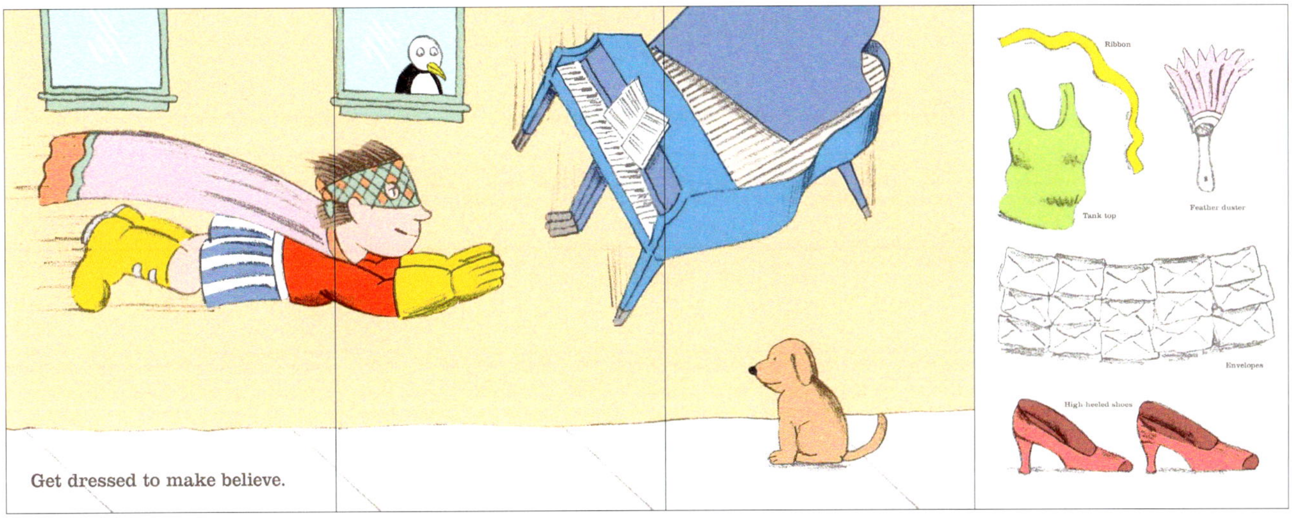
Ribbon
Tank top
Feather duster
Envelopes
High-heeled shoes
Get dressed to make believe.

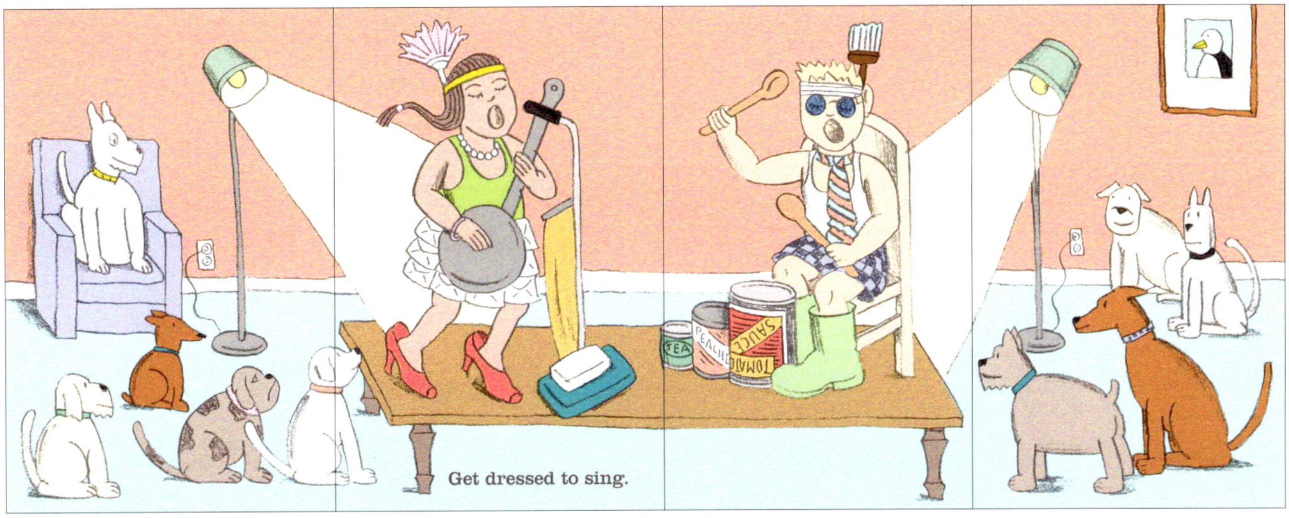
TEA
PEACH
SAUCE
TOMATO
Get dressed to sing.

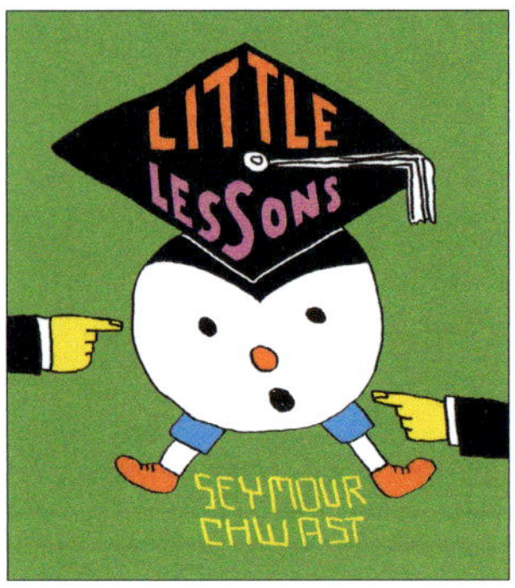

Little Lessons, by Seymour Chwast, 2023, 6.75" × 7.81" (17.25 × 19.75 cm), 40 pages.

Little Lessons

This collection of commonplace mottos and rules to live by is no joke. *Little Lessons* is, however, a very fun way to learn (or be reminded of) certain truths. Rendered in Chwast's late-career, progressively simpler linear style and complimented by his sketchy lettering technique, this handbook of maxims and aphorisms gives new meaning to old apothegms and proverbs.

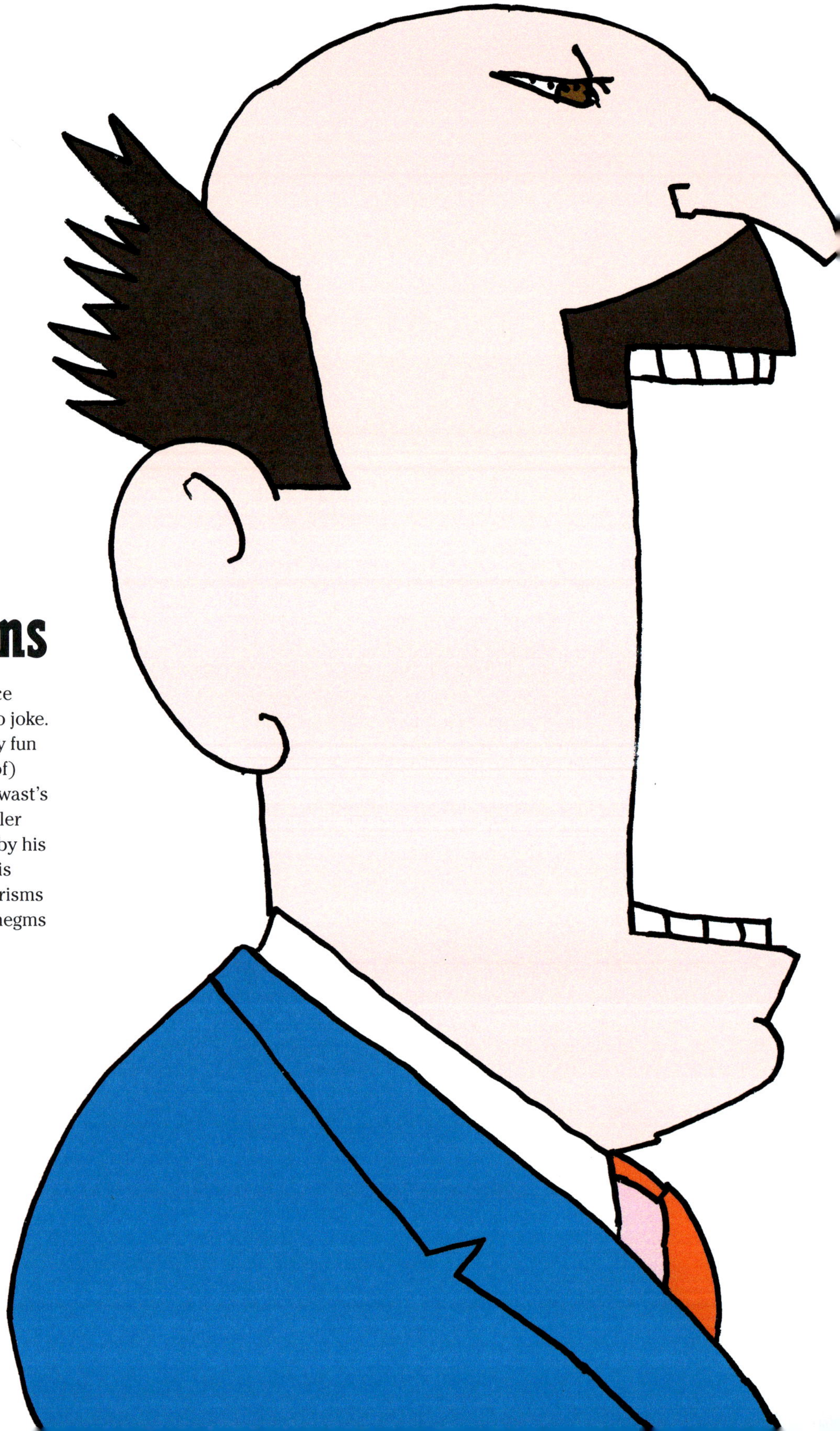

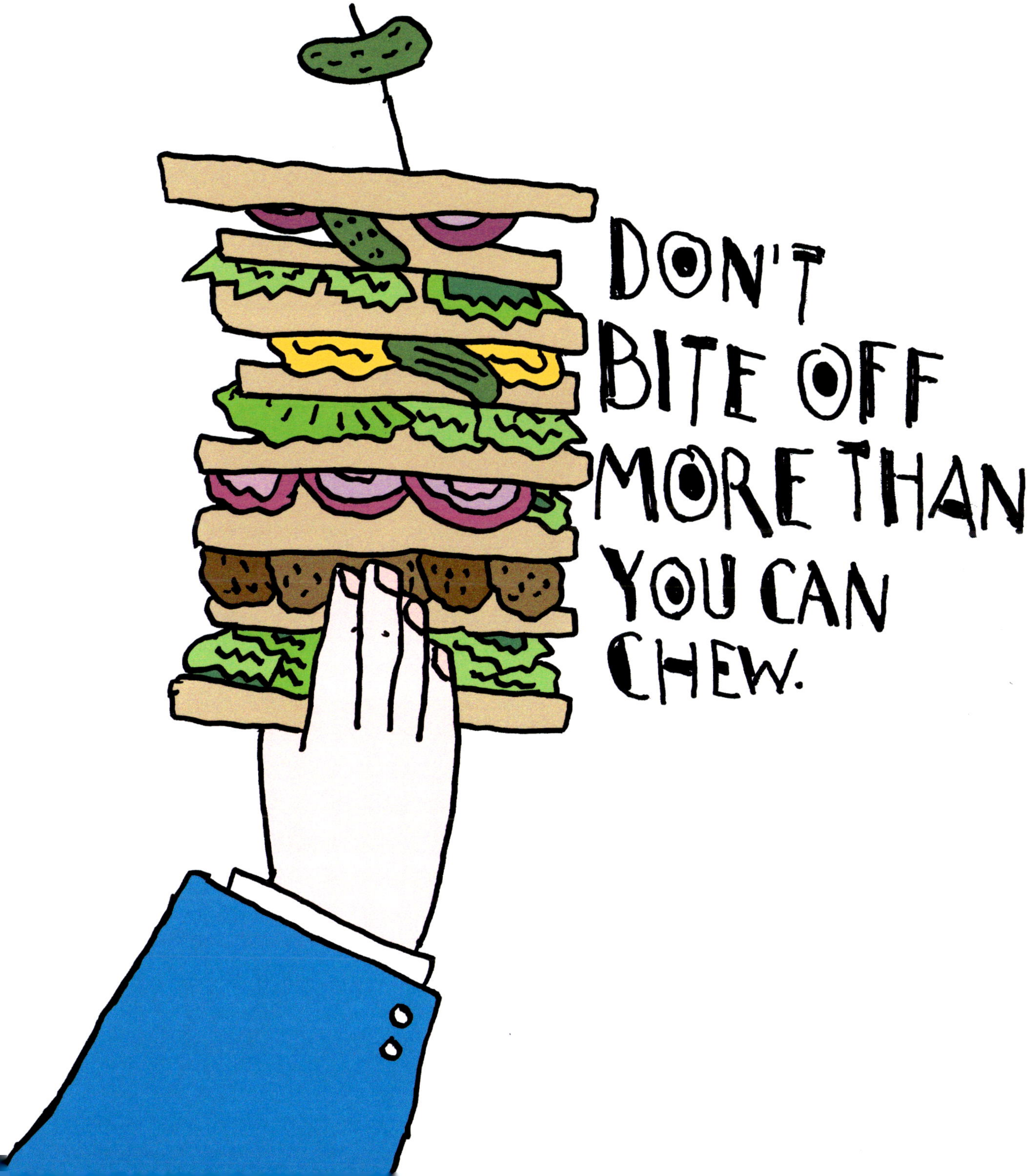
DON'T
BITE OFF
MORE THAN
YOU CAN
CHEW.

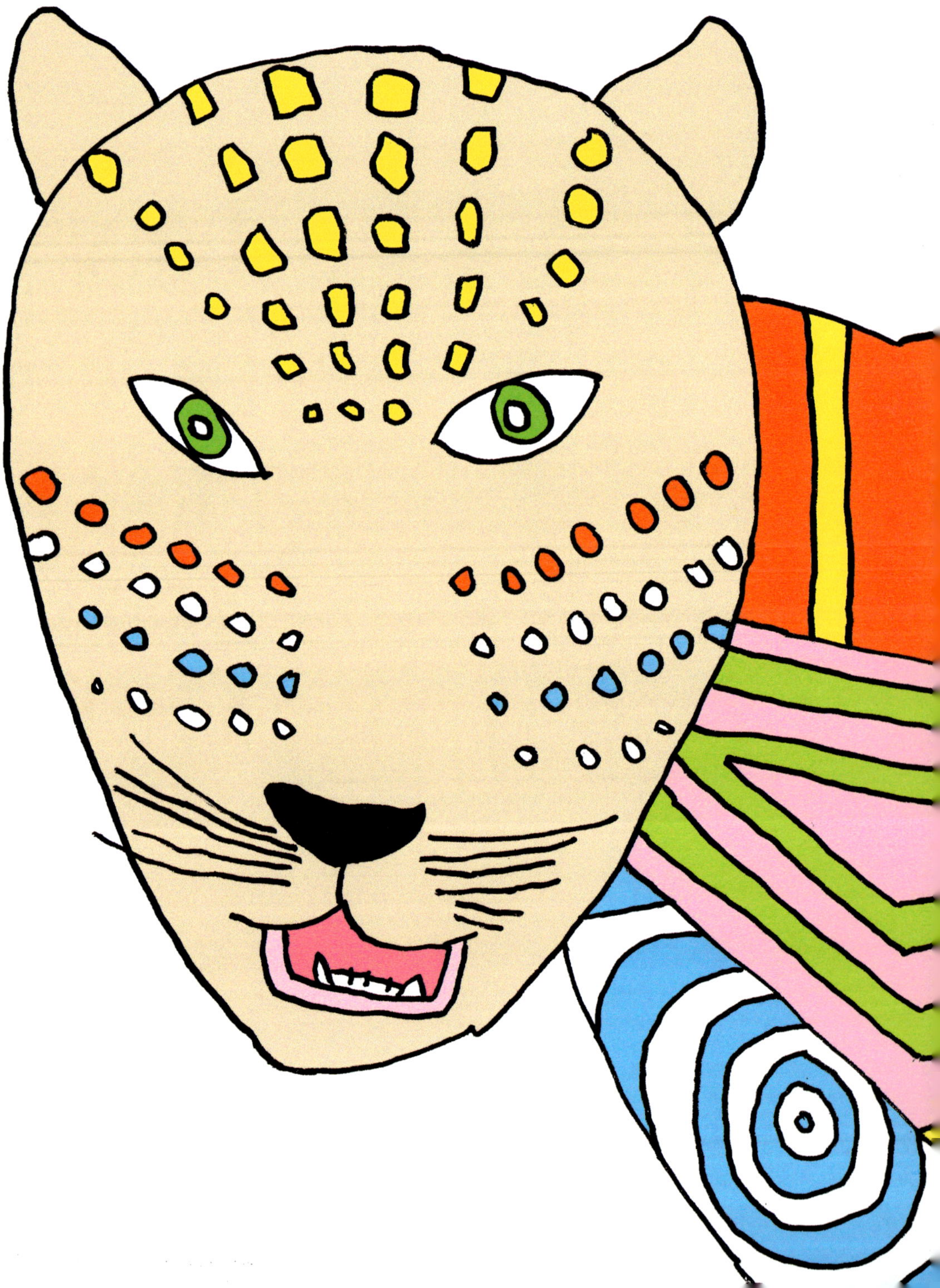

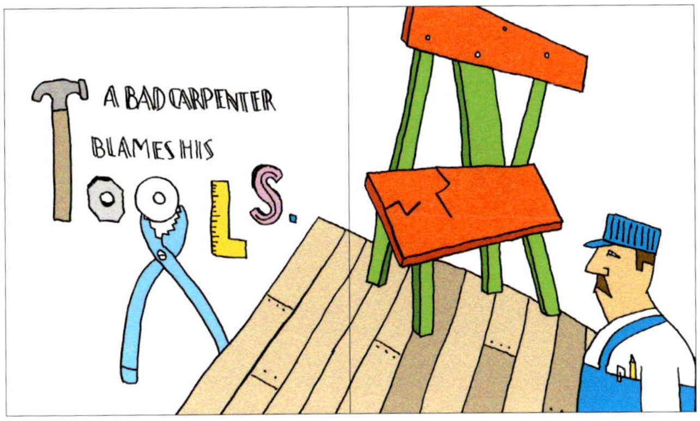
A BAD CARPENTER
BLAMES HIS
TOOLS.

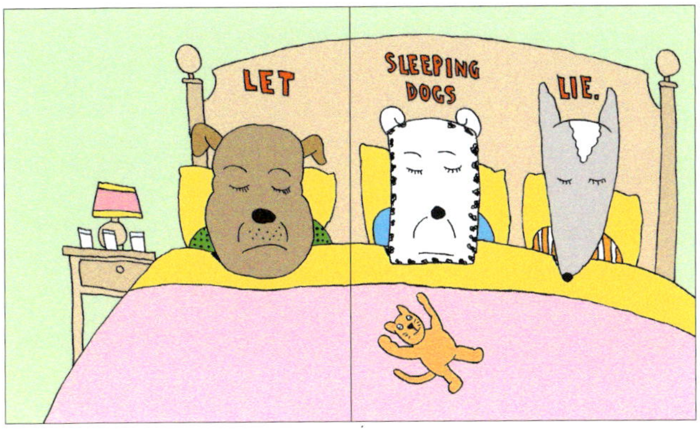
LET
SLEEPING DOGS
LIE.

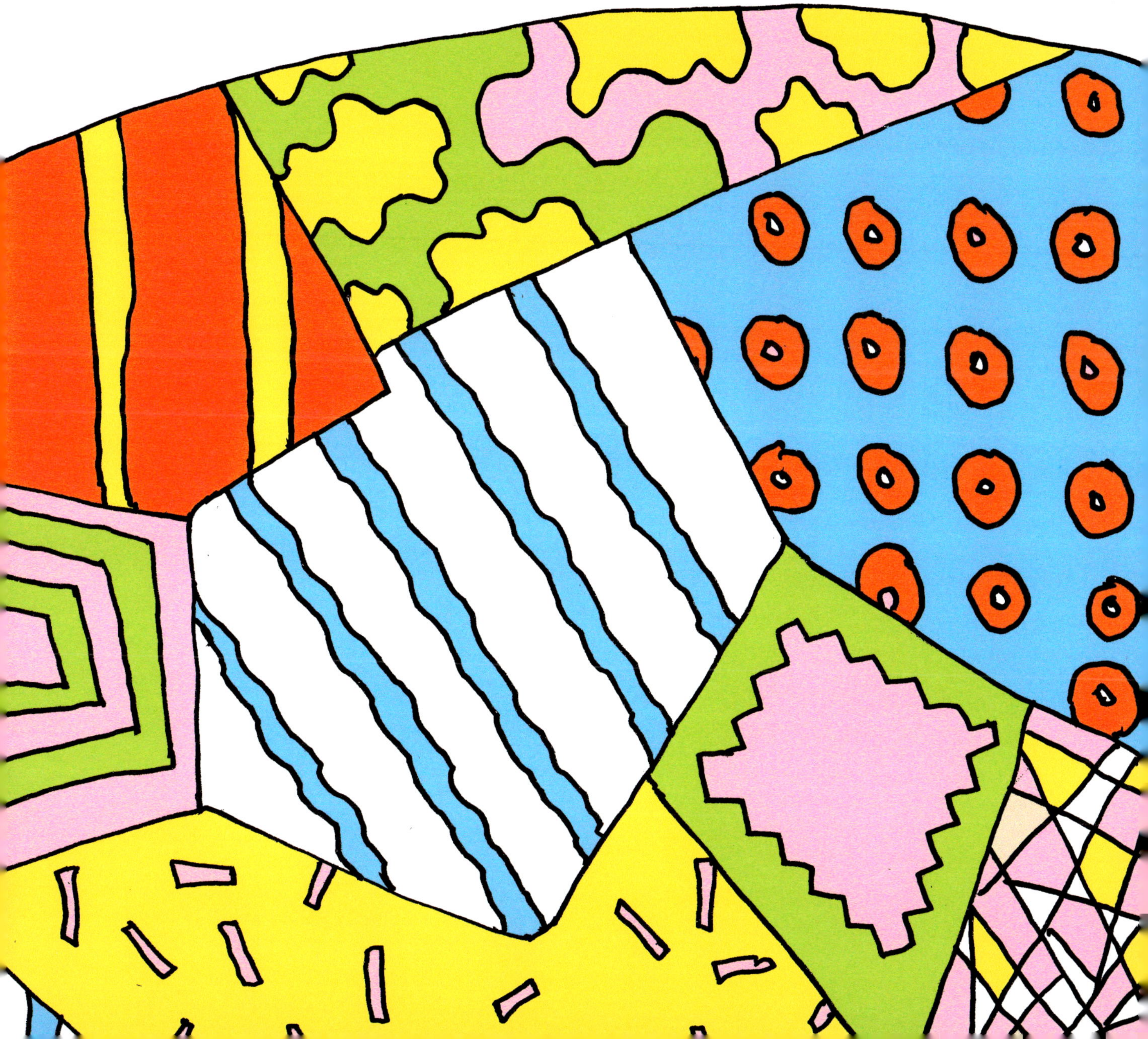

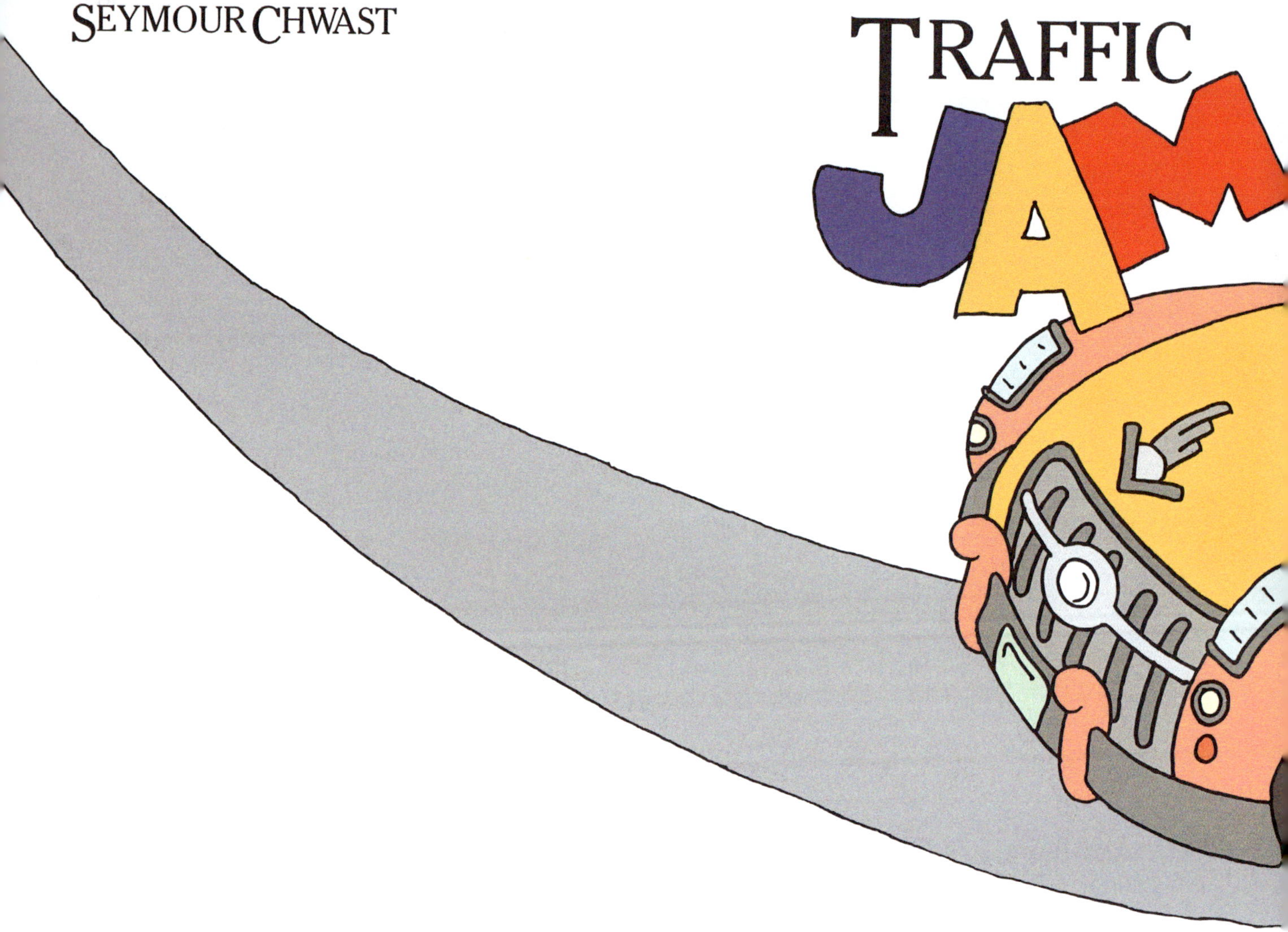

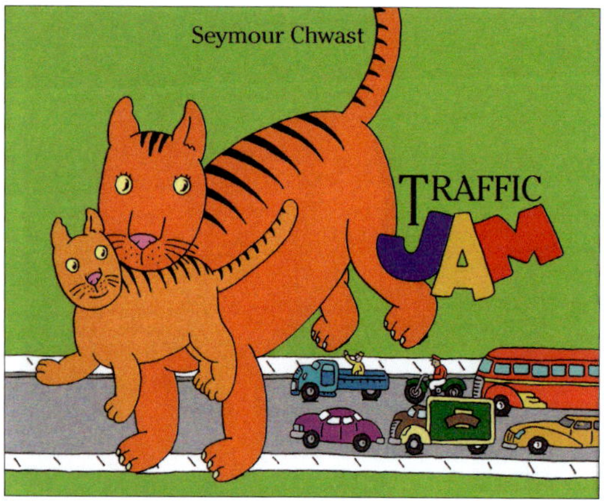

Traffic Jam, by Seymour Chwast, 1999,
8.25" × 10.25" (21 × 26 cm), 32 pages.

Traffic Jam

A cat and her kitten cause a major traffic jam when they cross a busy urban thoroughfare. The streets are in a congested mess and Chwast visually surveys the disgruntled drivers and befuddled passengers as they express their annoyance. In a school bus, one student confides to another, “I hope we never get to school,” while a girl tells a friend, “I hate the boys in my class.”

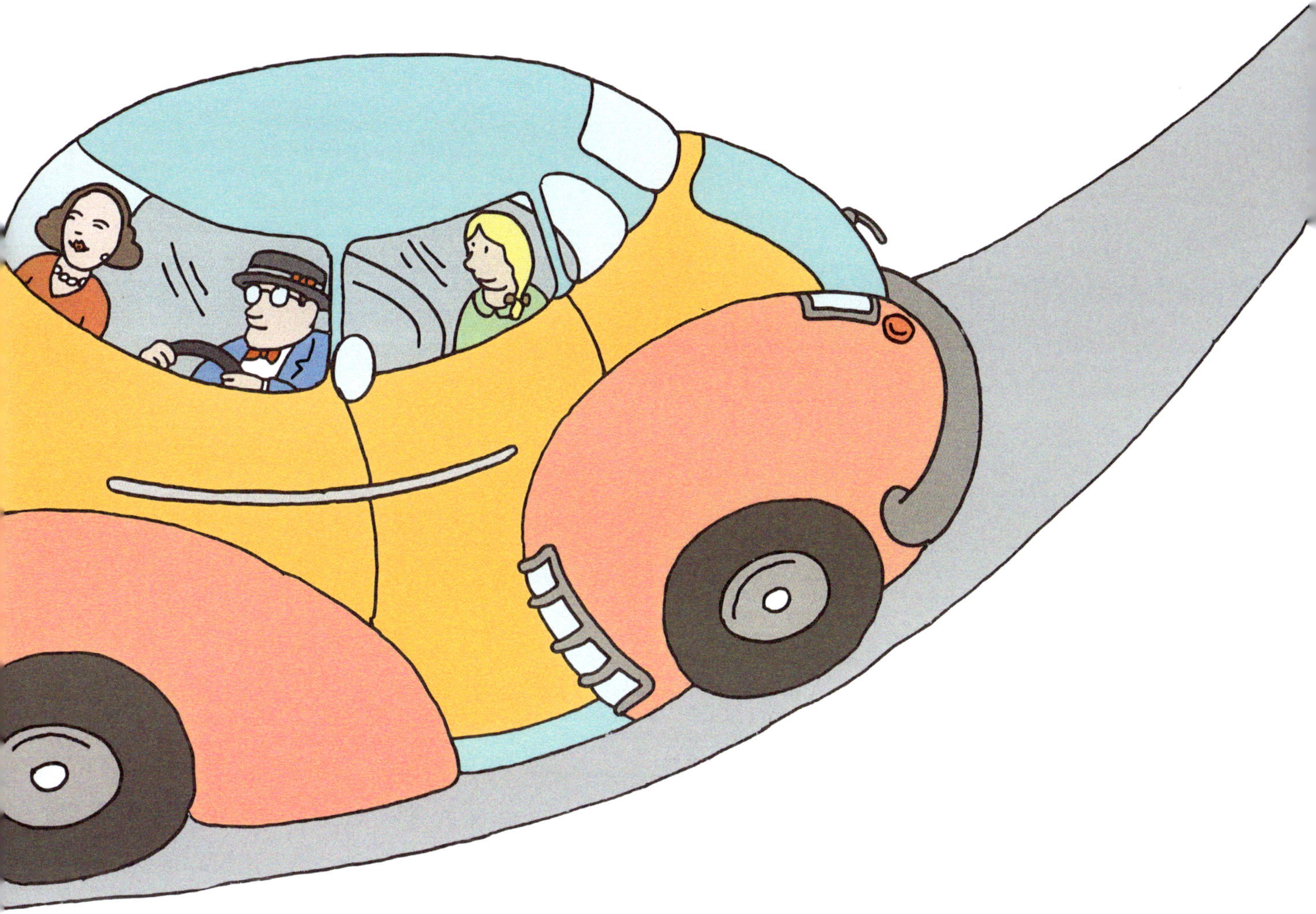

The streets are filled with brightly-colored illustrations of Chwastian characters—a race-car driver, bus driver, motorcycle policeman, three clowns, three firemen, two burly truck drivers menacingly clenching their fists, and a guitar-playing hippie—all waiting restlessly for the traffic to move. Chwast's proudest part of the book is a page that unfolds into six panels showing all of the cars, trucks, buses, and passersby who are delayed by the kitty. As for Chwast's rationale for this book, he says, "I live in New York and I love cats. What else do you have to say?"

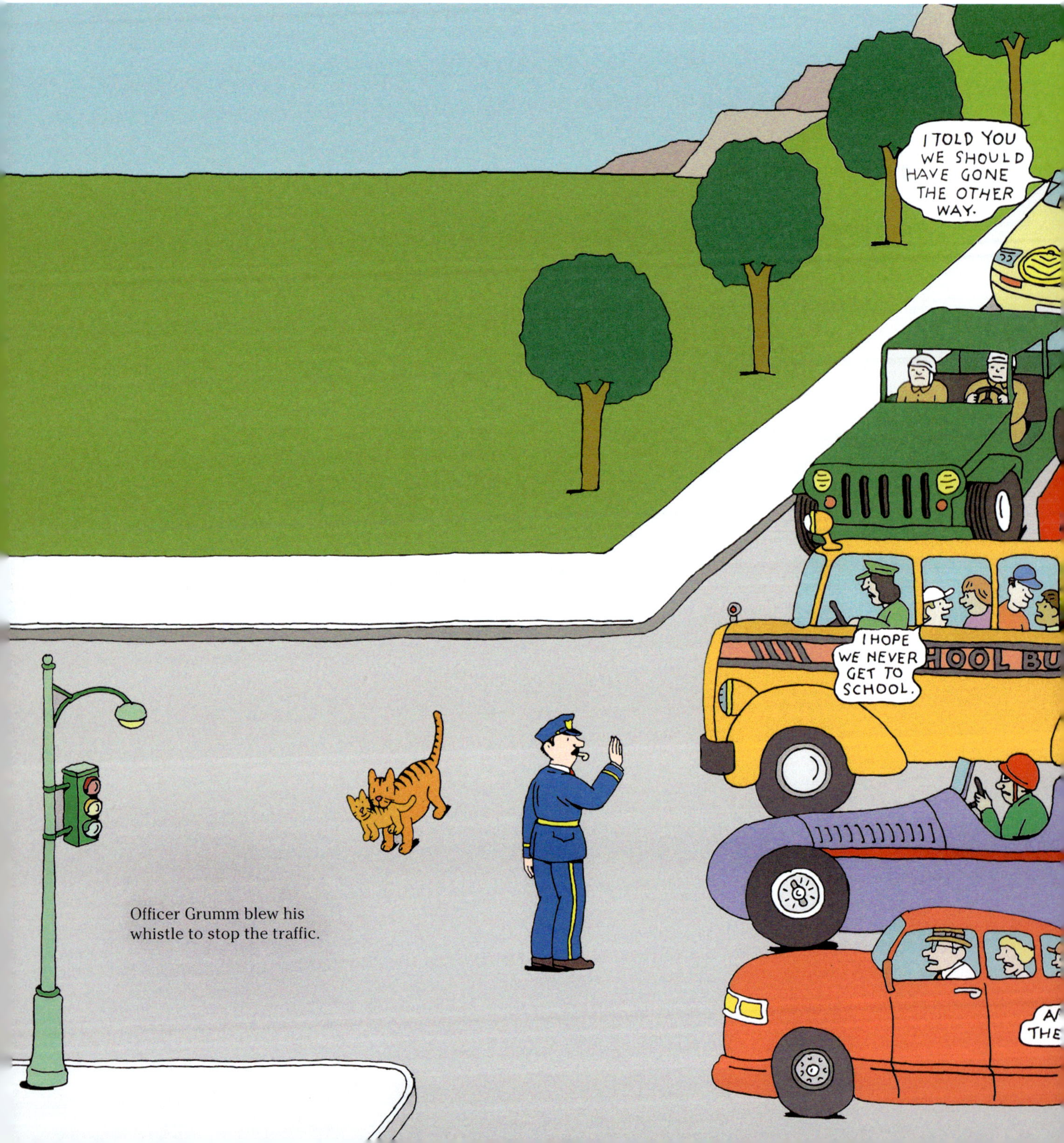

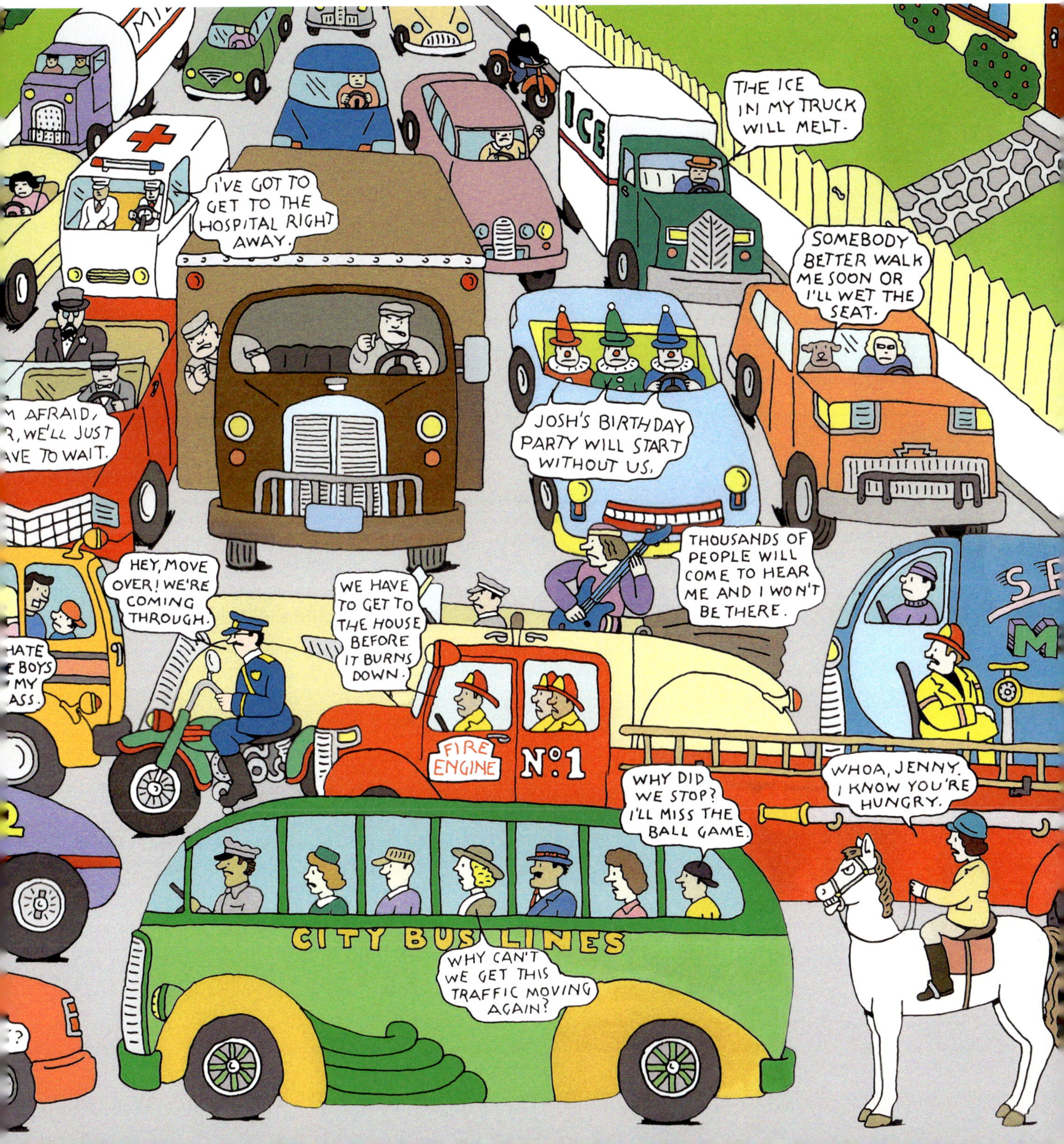
ICE
THE ICE IN MY TRUCK WILL MELT.
I'VE GOT TO GET TO THE HOSPITAL RIGHT AWAY.
SOMEBODY BETTER WALK ME SOON OR I'LL WET THE SEAT.
JOSH'S BIRTHDAY PARTY WILL START WITHOUT US.
THOUSANDS OF PEOPLE WILL COME TO HEAR ME AND I WON'T BE THERE.
HEY, MOVE OVER! WE'RE COMING THROUGH.
WE HAVE TO GET TO THE HOUSE BEFORE IT BURNS DOWN.
FIRE ENGINE
N°1
WHY DID WE STOP? I'LL MISS THE BALL GAME.
WHOA, JENNY. I KNOW YOU'RE HUNGRY.
CITY BUS LINES
WHY CAN'T WE GET THIS TRAFFIC MOVING AGAIN?

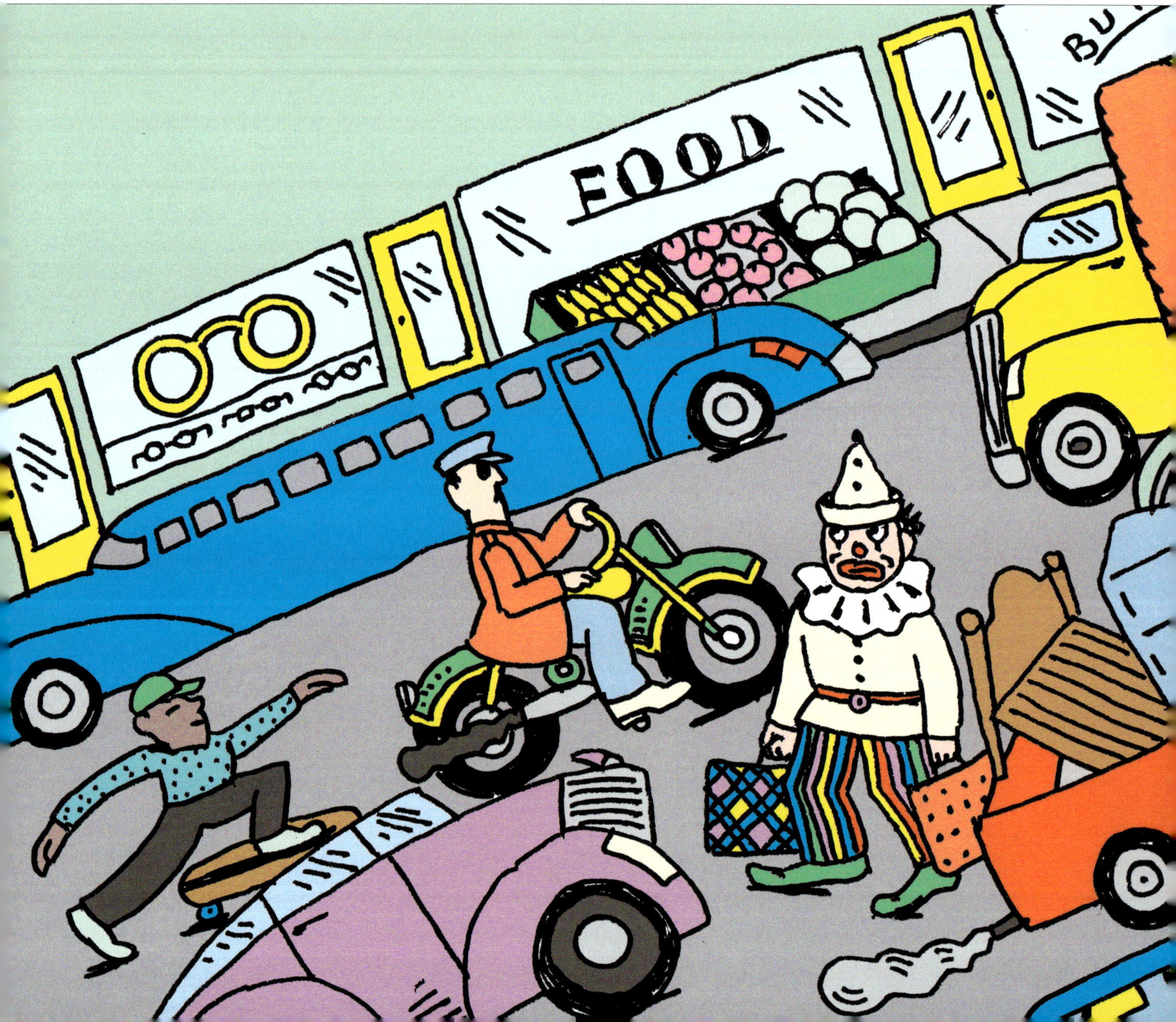
FOOD

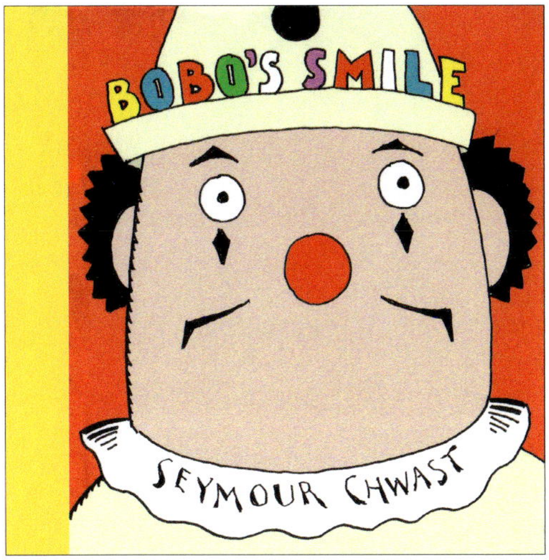

Bobo's Smile, by Seymour Chwast, 2012, 8.5" × 8.5" (21.5 × 21.5 cm), 32 pages.

Bobo's Smile

Bobo is an unhappy clown. Of course, this defeats the entire purpose of being in the clown profession. He tries to cure his congenital despair by traveling to exciting places around the world via plane, submarine, and gondola, among other modes of transport. In the end, he finds that his true joy is playing with the children back at home. The drawings are colorful and perky—the perfect counterpoint to Bobo's sad demeaner. "The fact is I *like* clowns," Chwast says, "I've illustrated many of them."

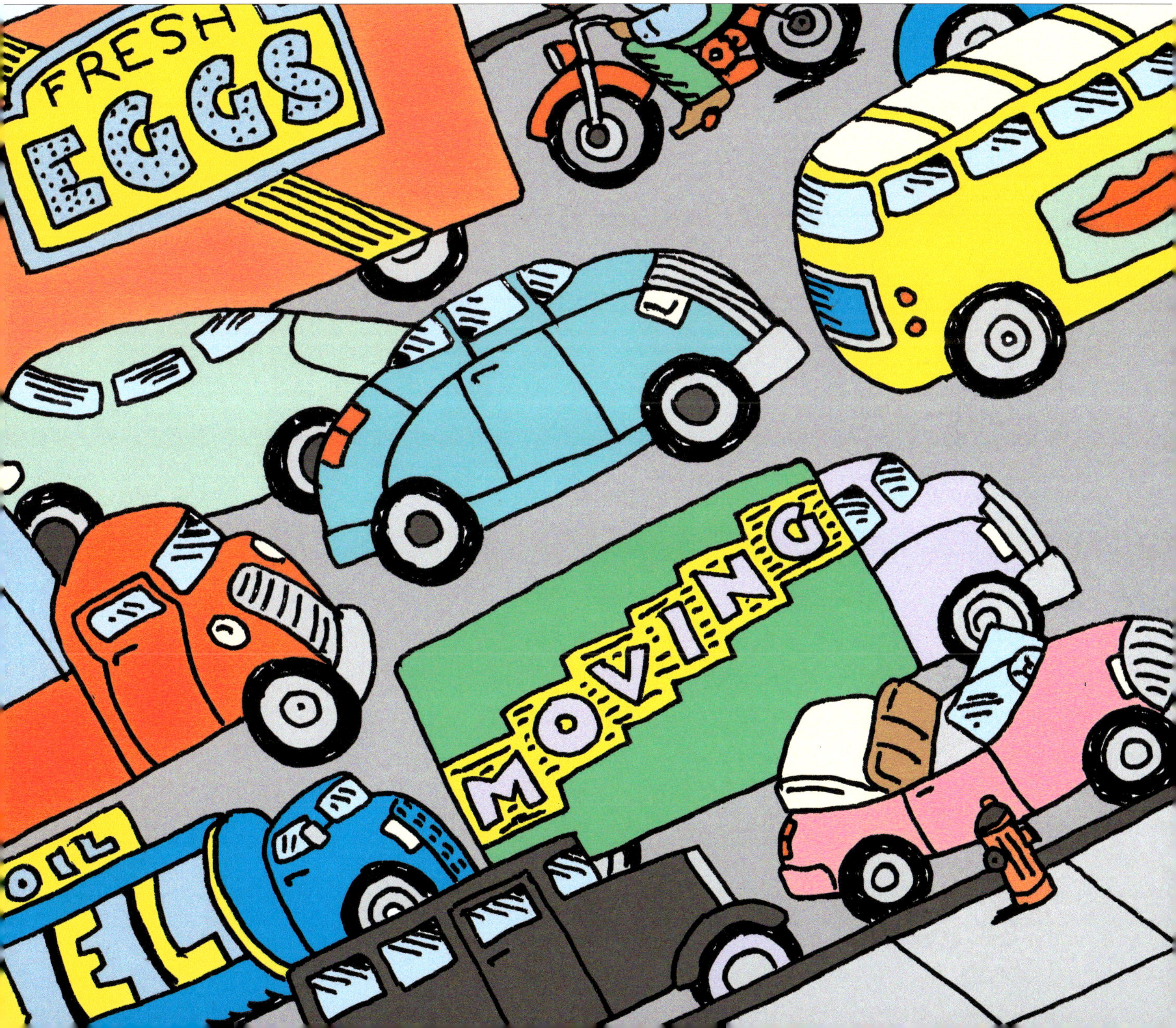

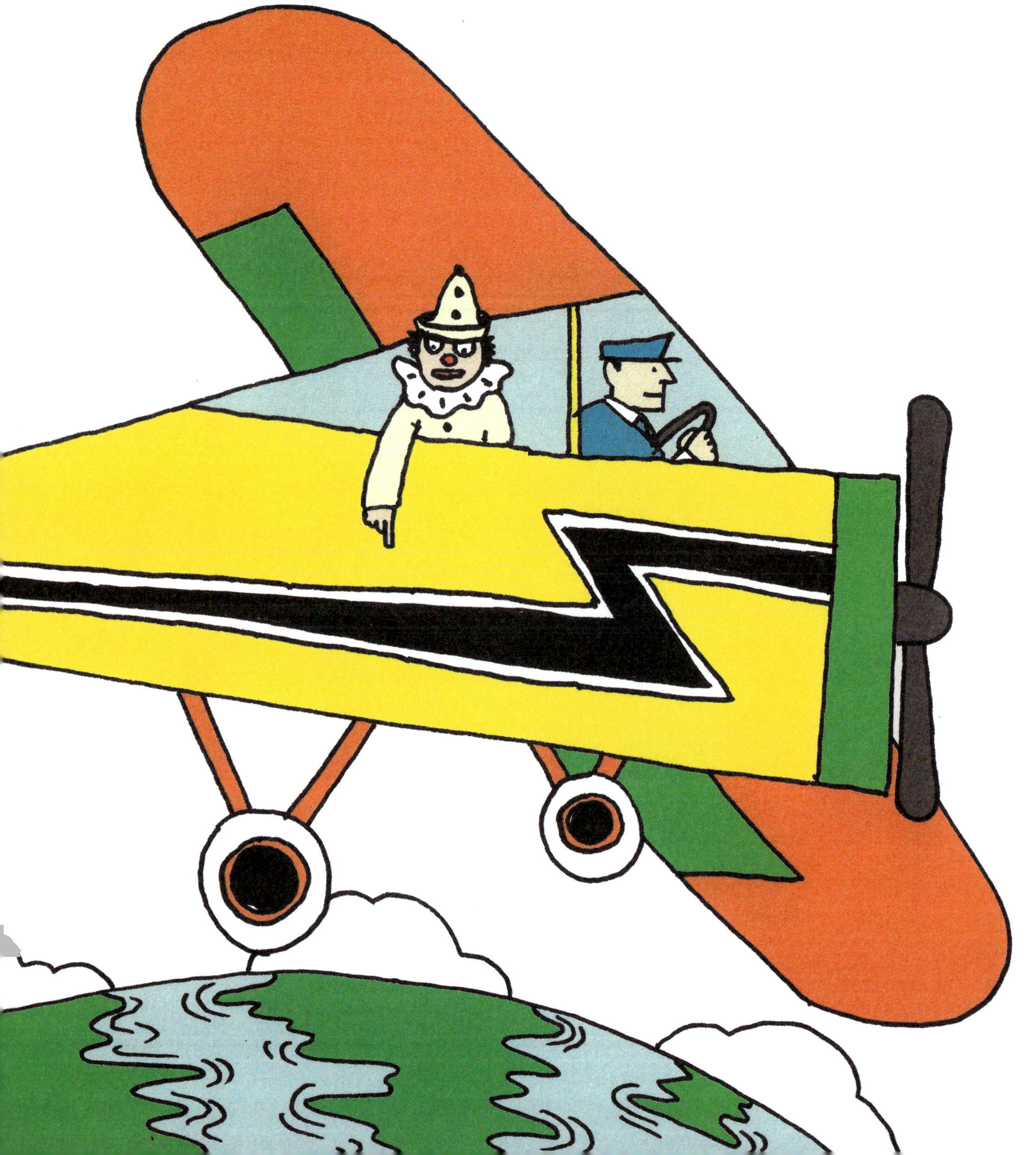

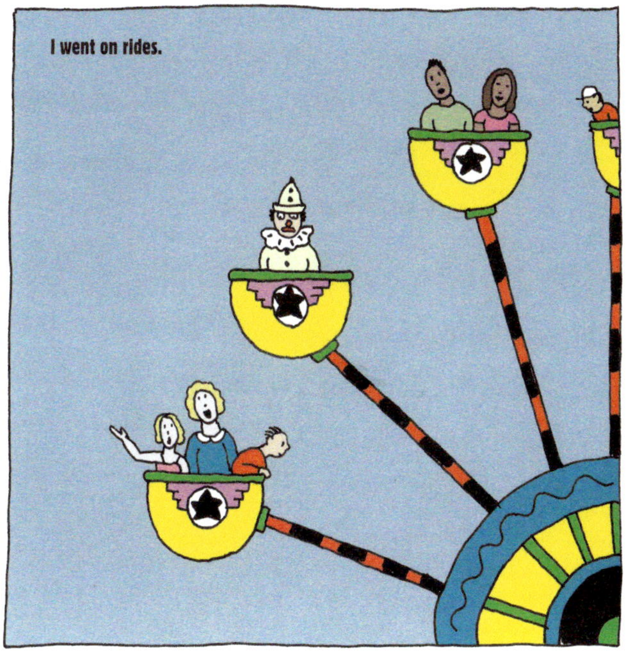
I went on rides.

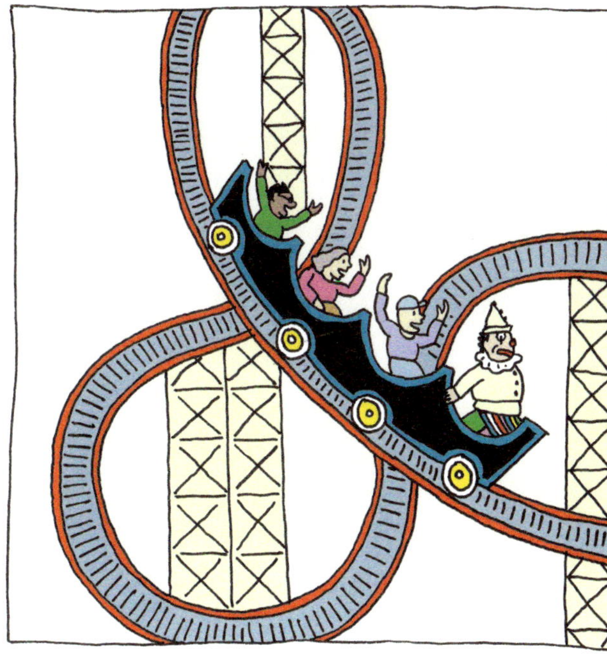

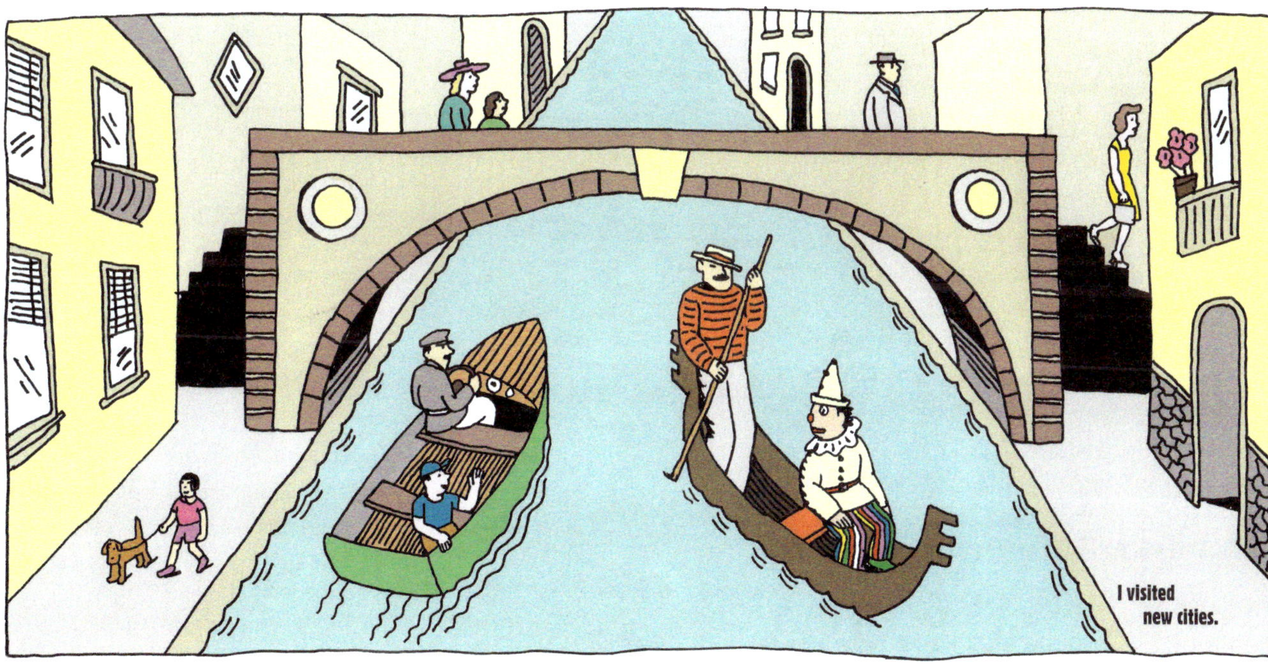
I visited
new cities.

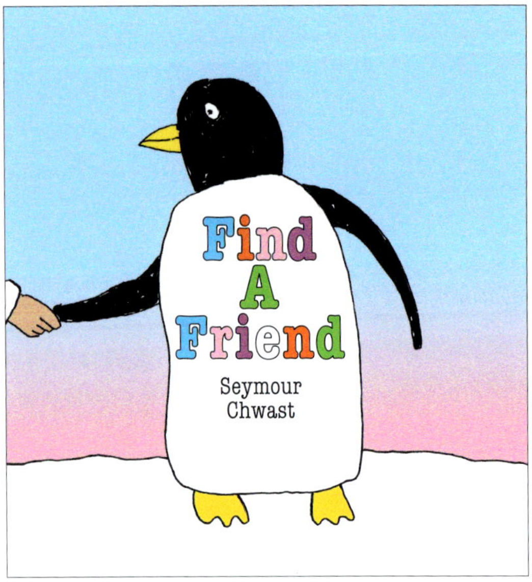

Find a Friend, by Seymour Chwast, 2023,
8.31" × 8.31" (21 × 21 cm), 48 pages.

Find a Friend

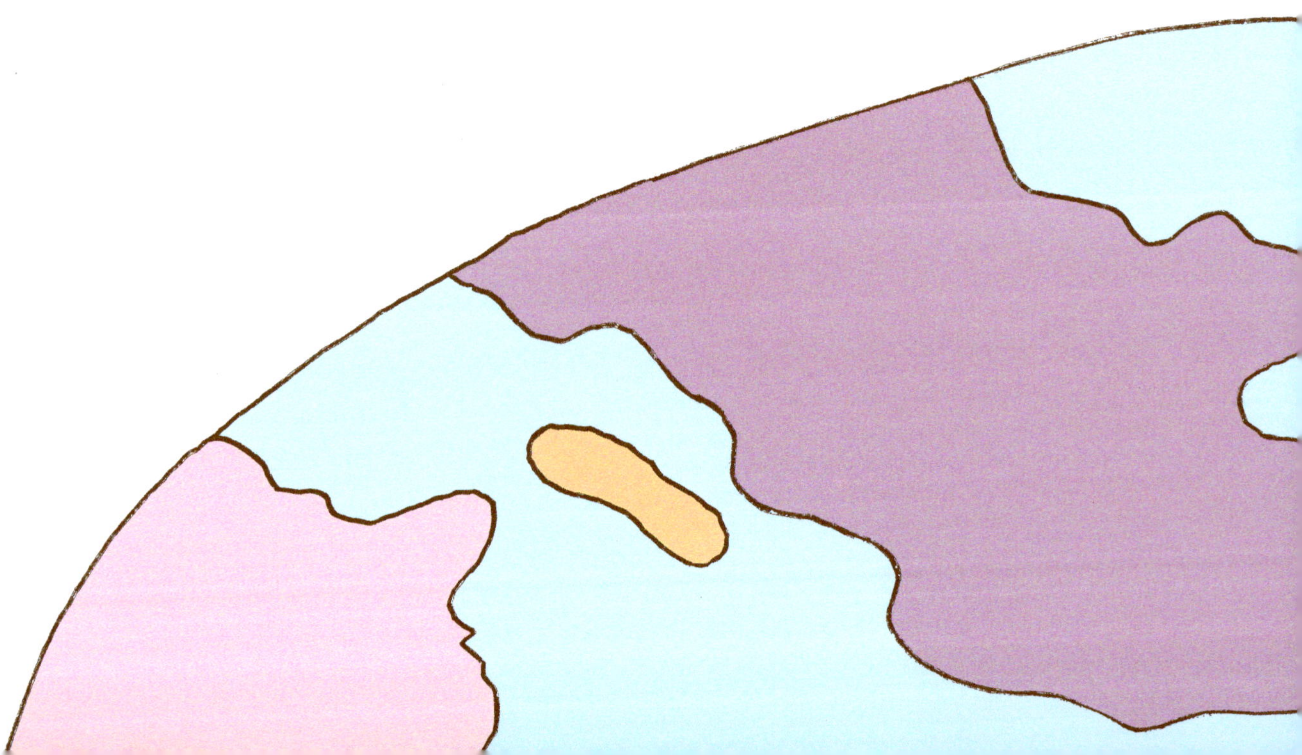

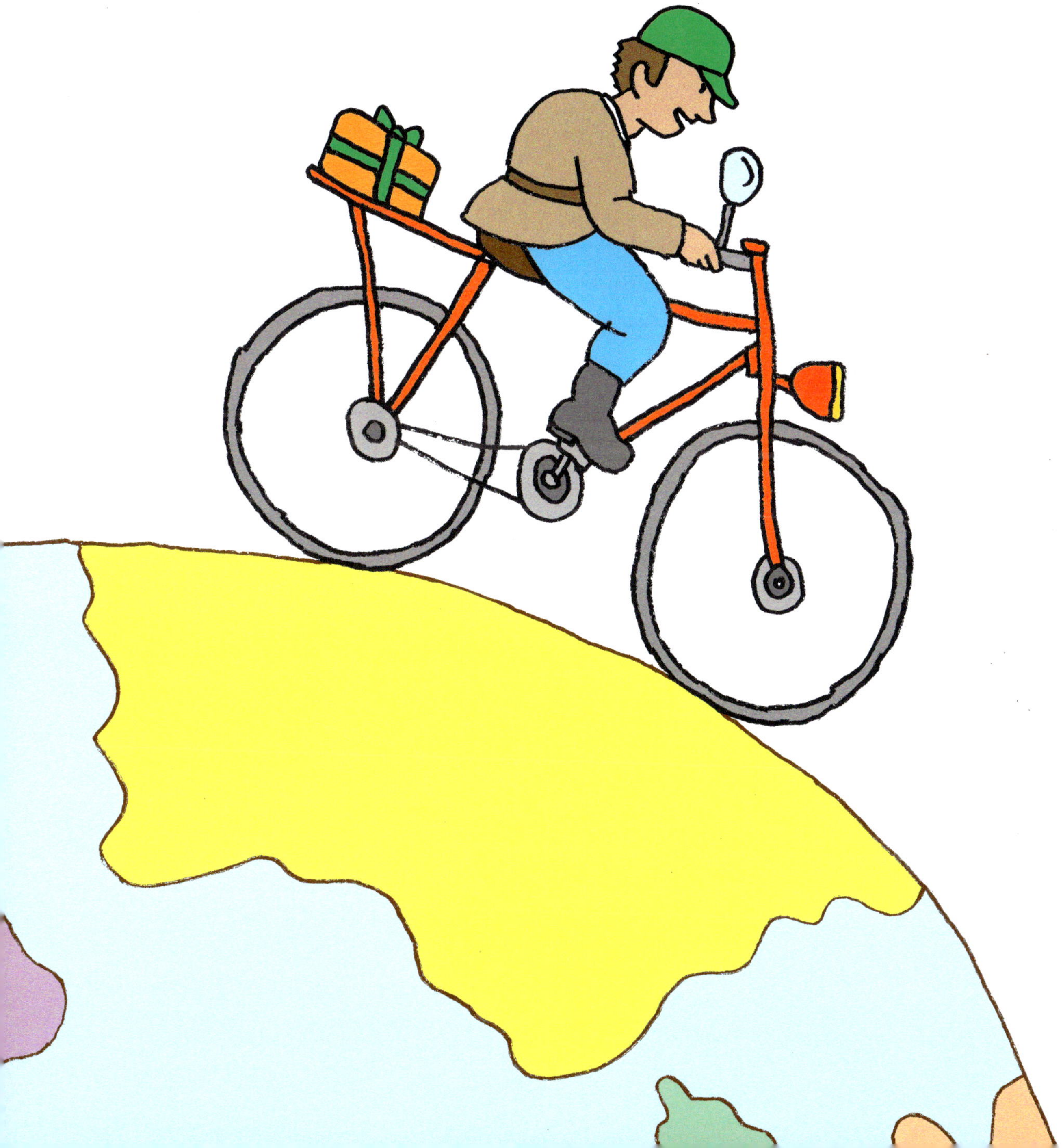

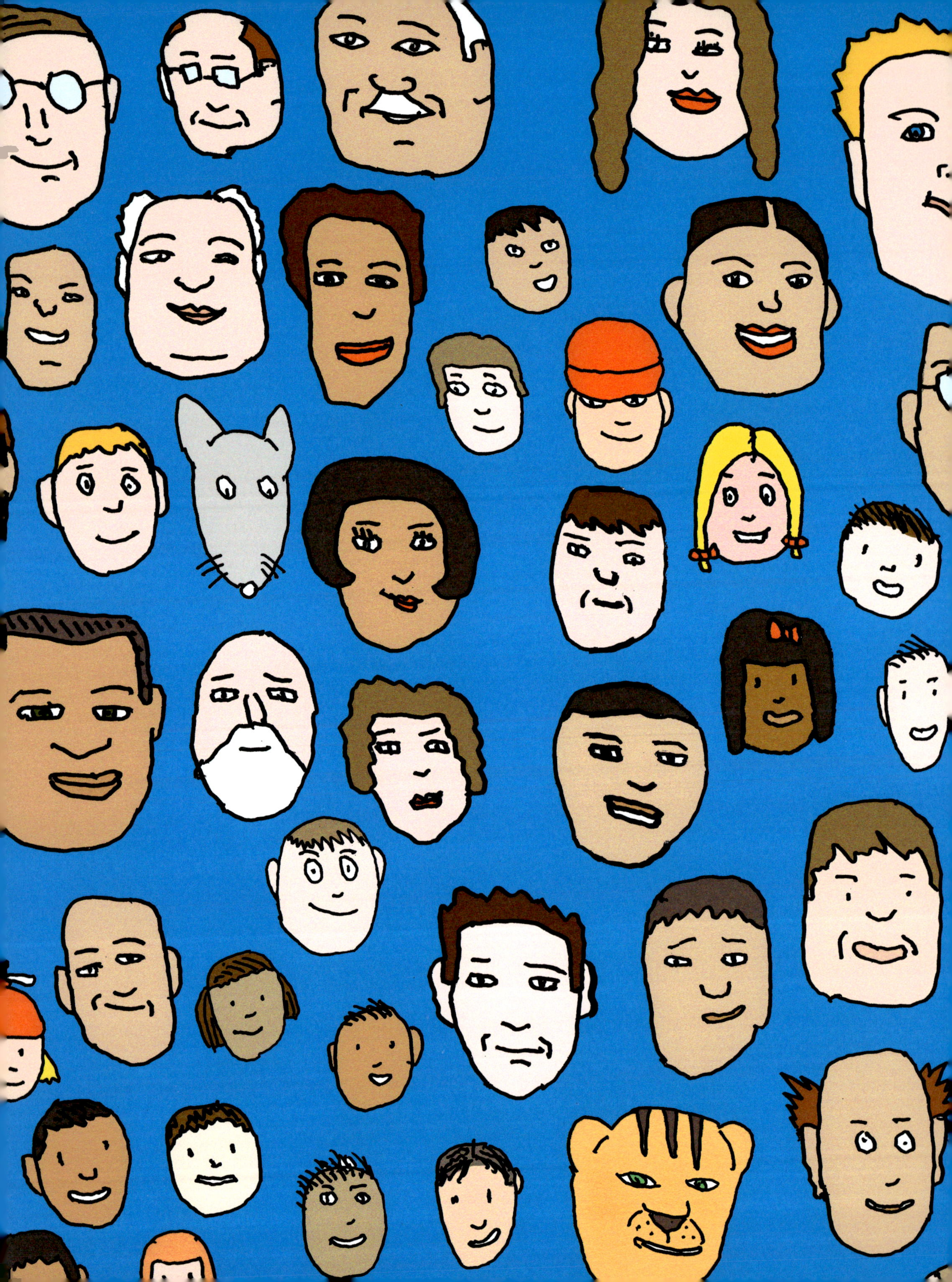

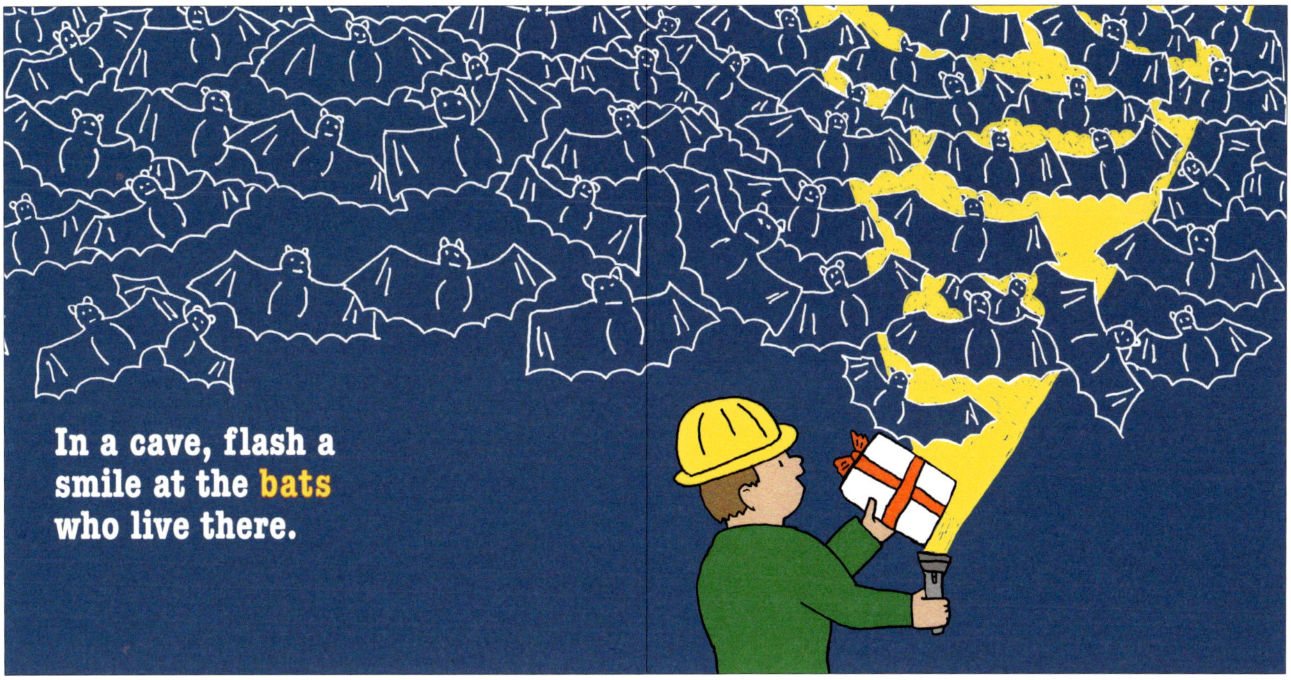

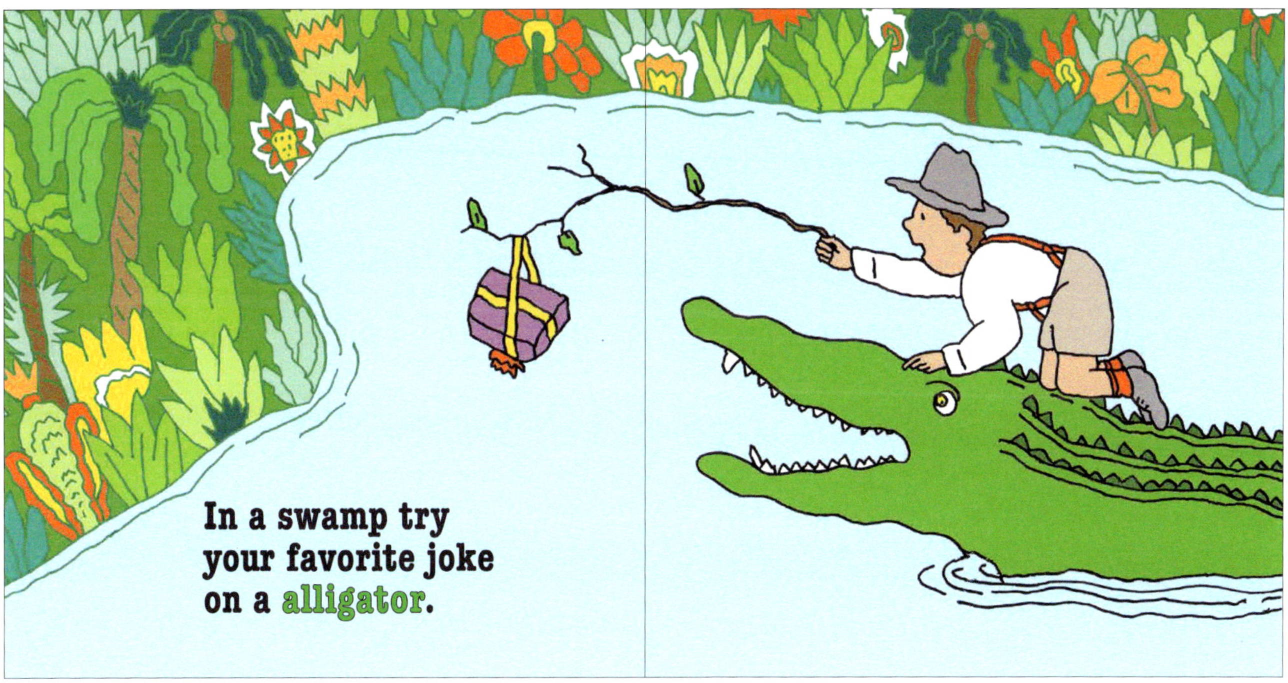

Many of Chwast's stories involve a quest to locate some missing thing—be it a person, place, or object—that, when found, brings great happiness to an often lonely main character. Perhaps they are reflections of Chwast, who was himself a the only child of divorced parents and always on the move. The moral of this book, he says, is that "you can find a friend anywhere" just by being available to them. In the short and long run, every creature wants a companion with whom to share their lives.

Harry's Bath

"Harry, are you in the tub yet?"
called Harry's mother
from downstairs.

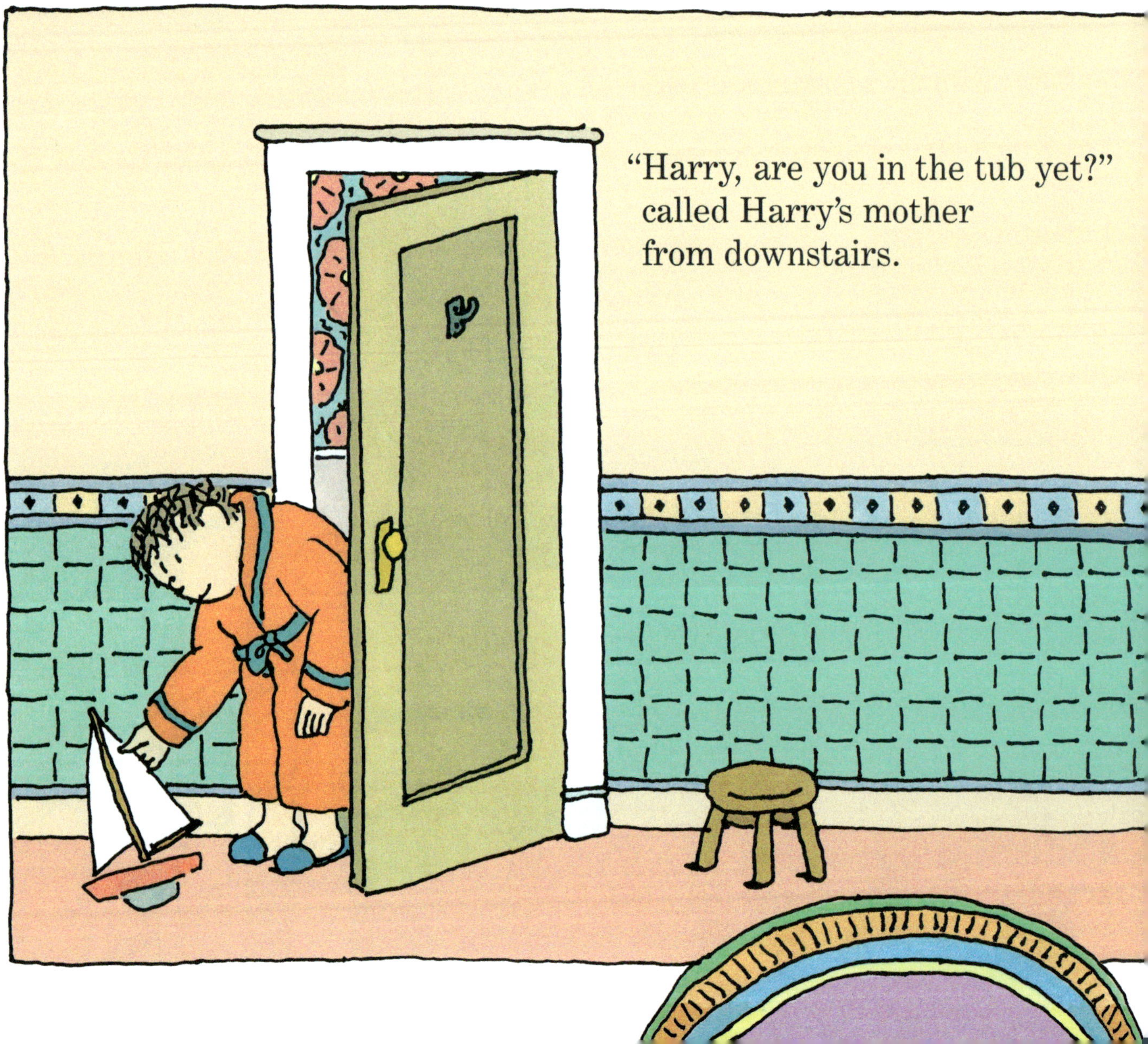

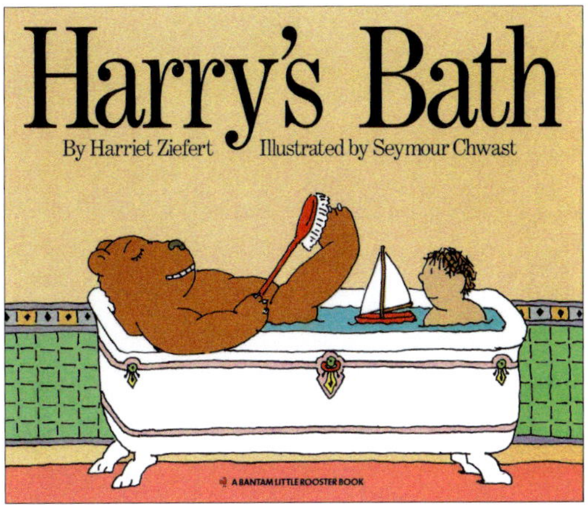

Harry's Bath, by Harriet Ziefert, illustrated by Seymour Chwast, 1990, 8" × 9" (20.25 × 23 cm), 32 pages.

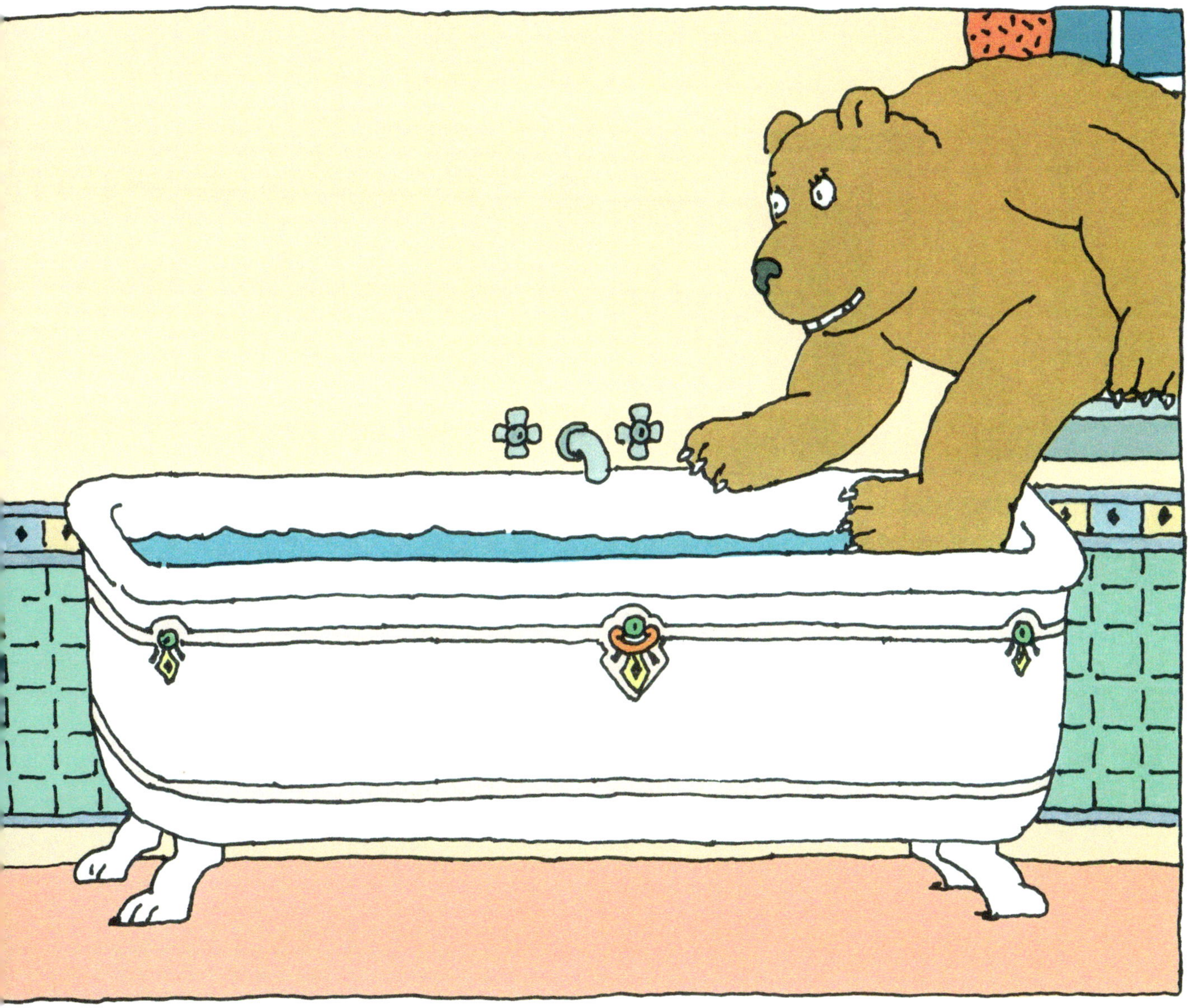

This book was written by Harriet Ziefert about a young boy called Harry. "I read the text and I immediately liked it," Chwast says about Harry's travails as he tries to obey his mother's command to take a bath but is involuntarily hindered by unwanted visitors. Chwast says he knew he could do some funny spreads of hapless Harry coping with the perplexing intrusions by beasts of all kinds that fill up the tub. Chwast employed his signature linear outline style filled in with flat color in scenes featuring art deco elements, including the bathroom tiles, bath rugs, and a classic clawfoot bathtub.

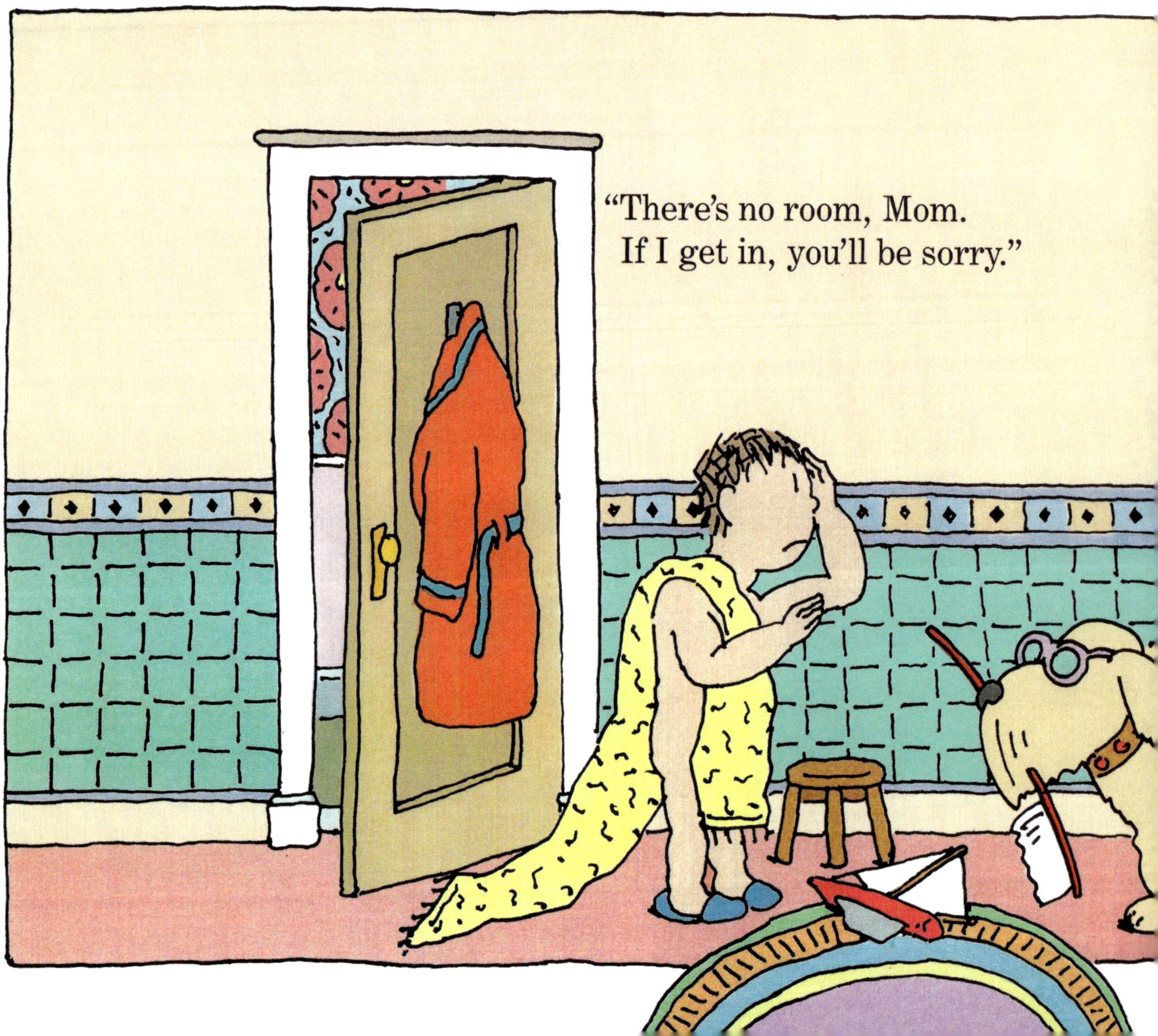

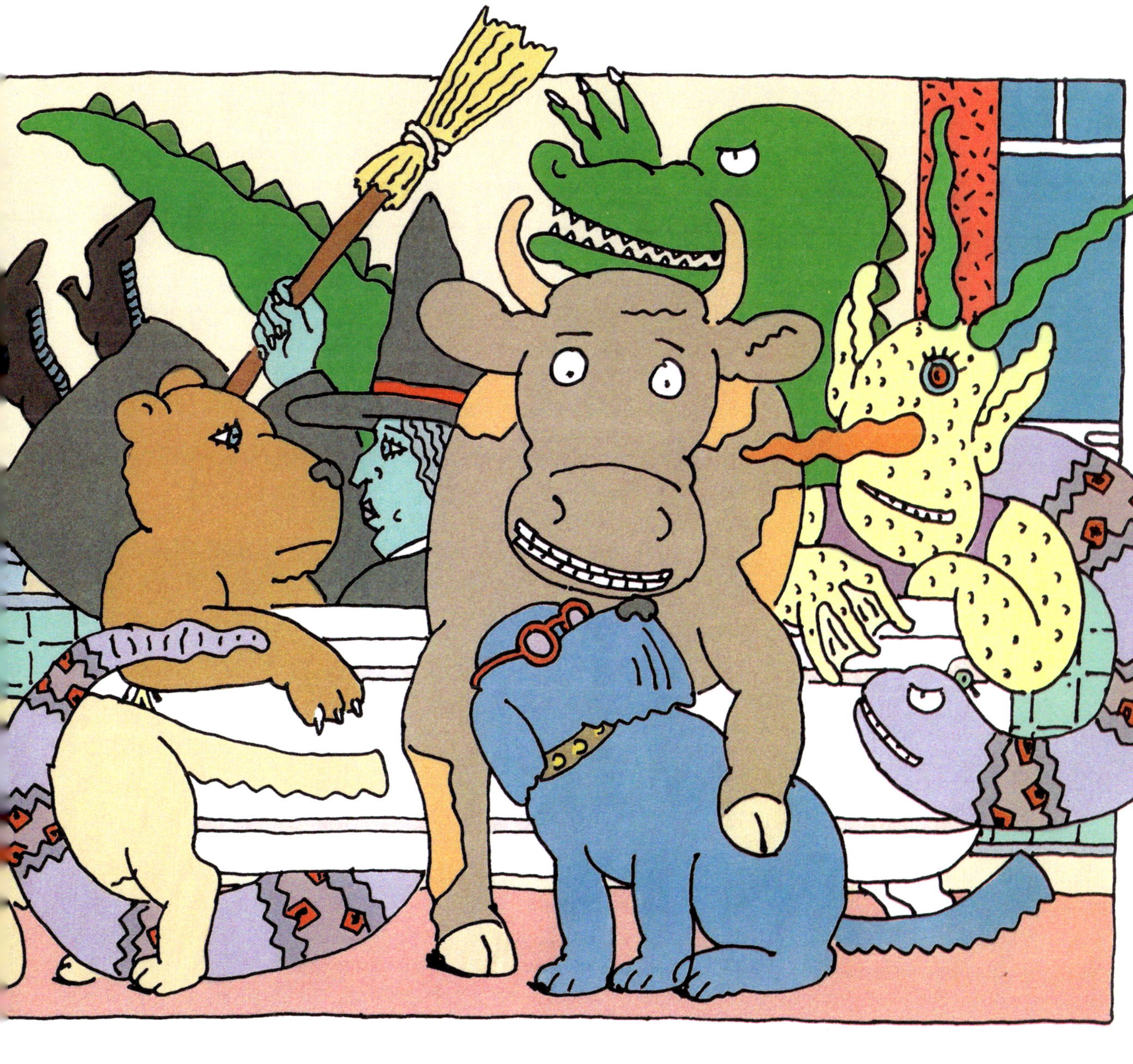

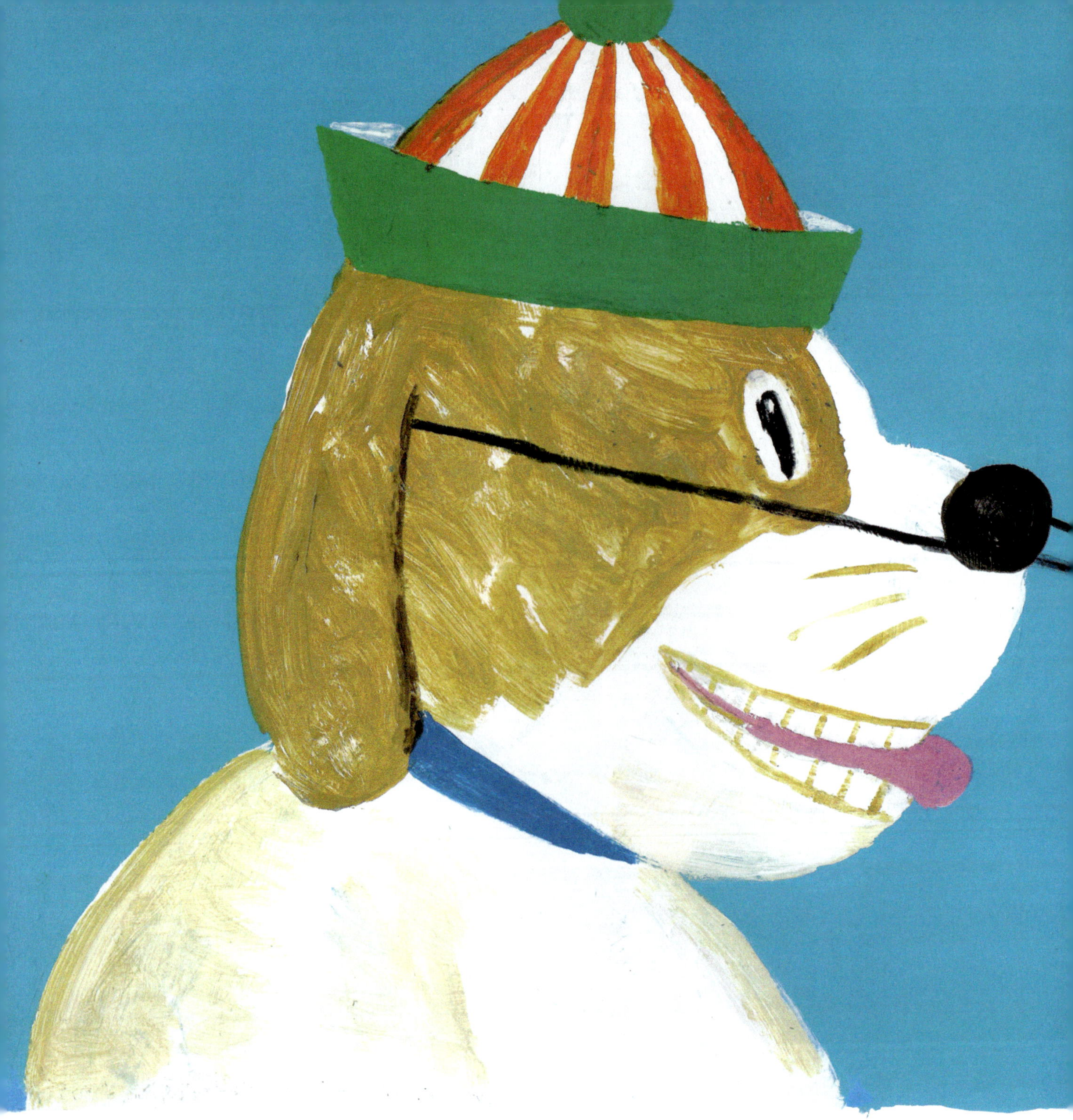

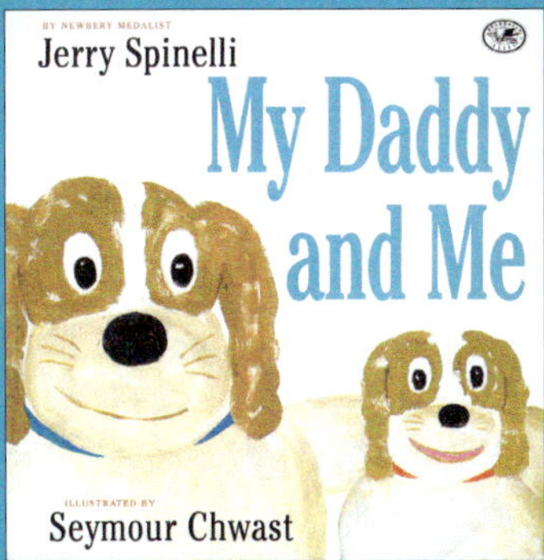

My Daddy and Me, by Jerry Spinelli, illustrated by Seymour Chwast, 2006, 10" × 10" (25.5 × 25.5), 40 pages.

My daddy should be a clown.
When he puts on his funny face,
it's like having my very own circus!
He walks like a penguin
and talks like a duck.
I pull on his nose
and tickle his toes—
and he does the same to me!

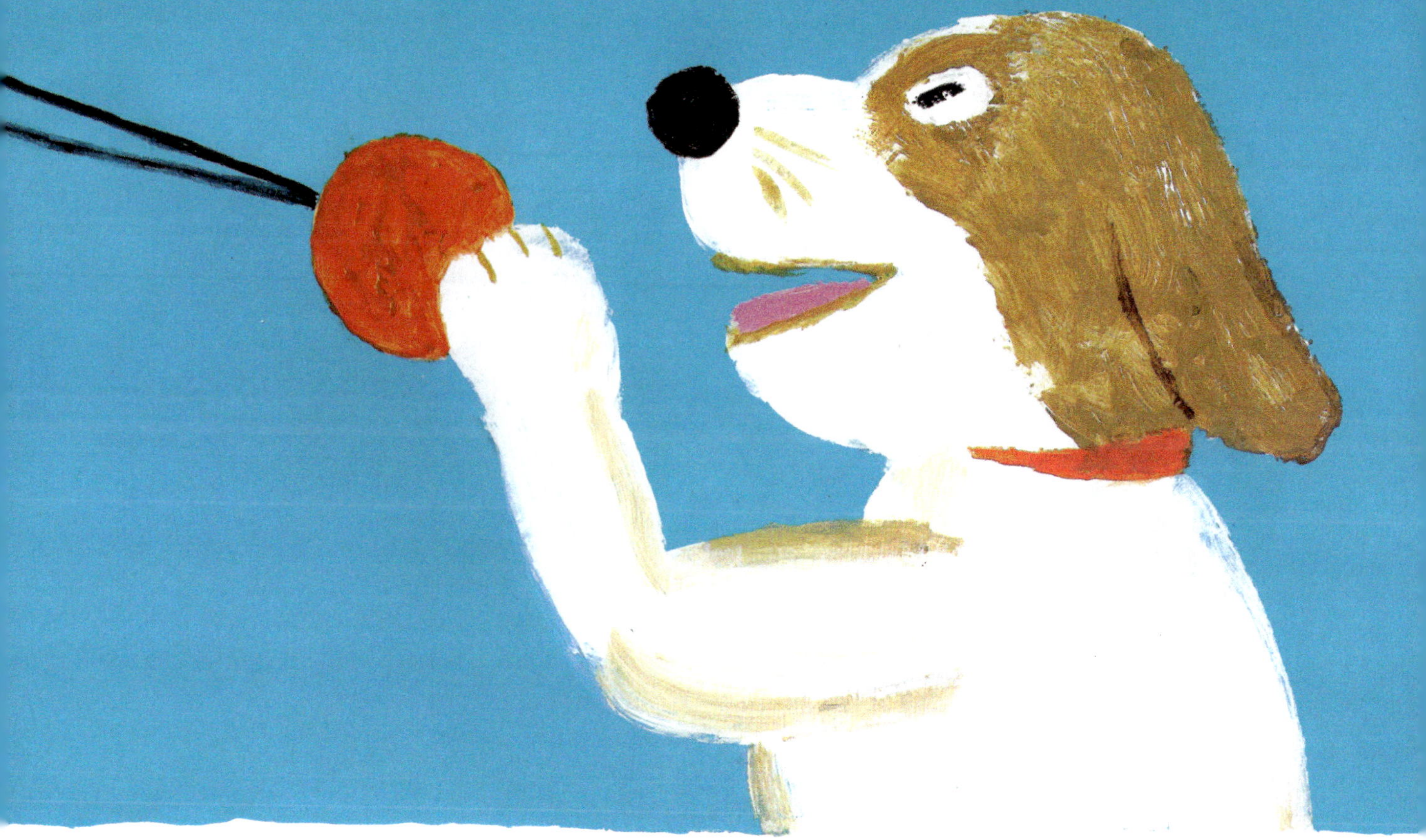

My Daddy and Me

With words by Jerry Spinelli, this book was an opportunity for Chwast to alter his usual picture book methodology, changing from pen and ink to paint. Instead of having contained outlines, these pictures are looser and more improvisational. The characters, Daddy and Me, express their playful energy through the fluidity of Chwast's brushstrokes.

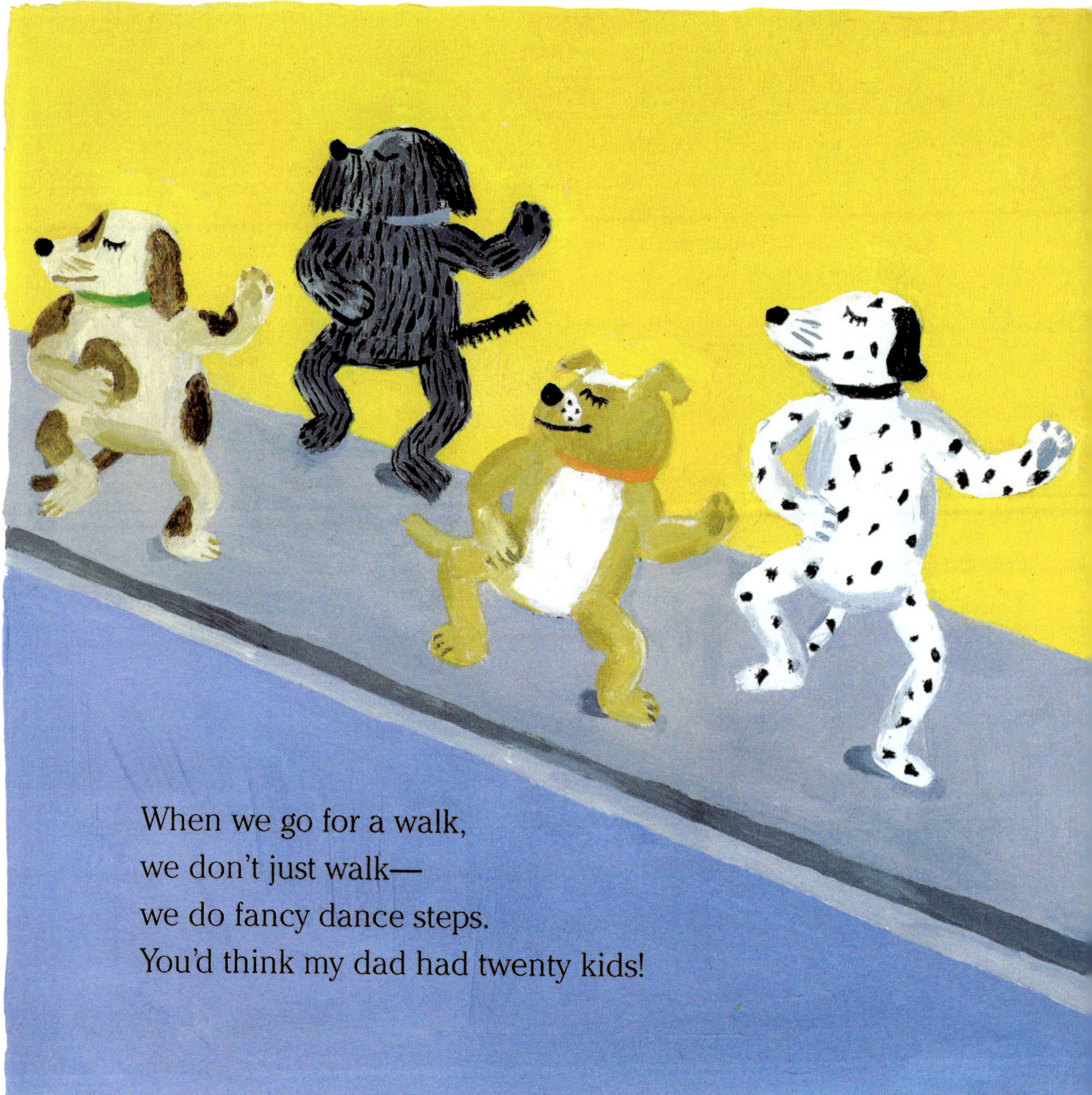

When we go for a walk,
we don't just walk—
we do fancy dance steps.
You'd think my dad had twenty kids!

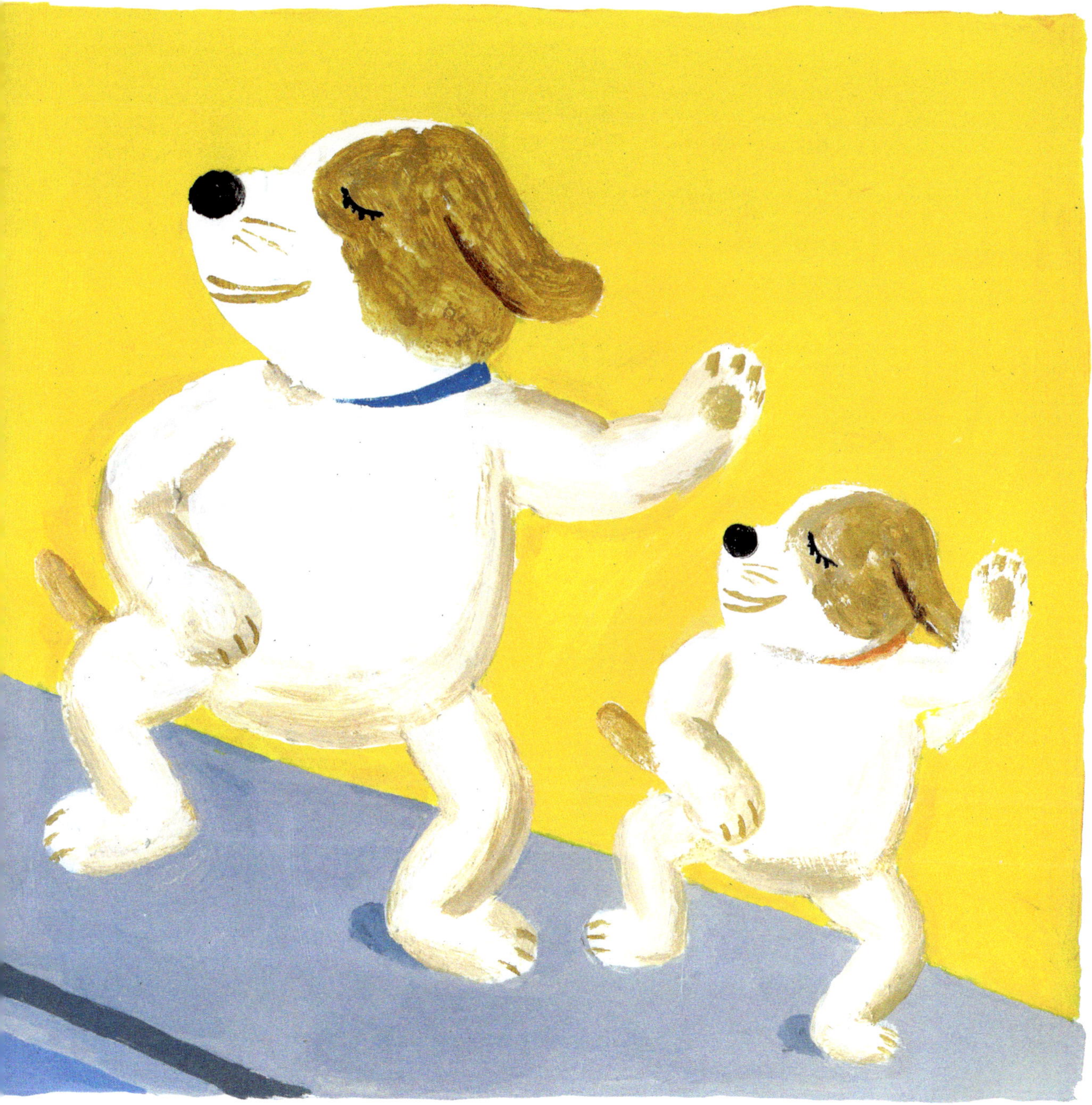

Harry, I Need You!

Chwast enjoys creating challenging situations in which his main character is called upon to be the unwitting hero. Here, Harry imagines that his mother, who has asked for him to help her with a problem in the kitchen, is in some kind of real danger. He imagines a robot on an unannounced visit, aliens invading Earth, firemen rushing in to put out a fire, and maybe even a flood from an overflowing sink. With humor, Chwast fantasizes these calamities, the way a child might do when called upon to do a common household chore.

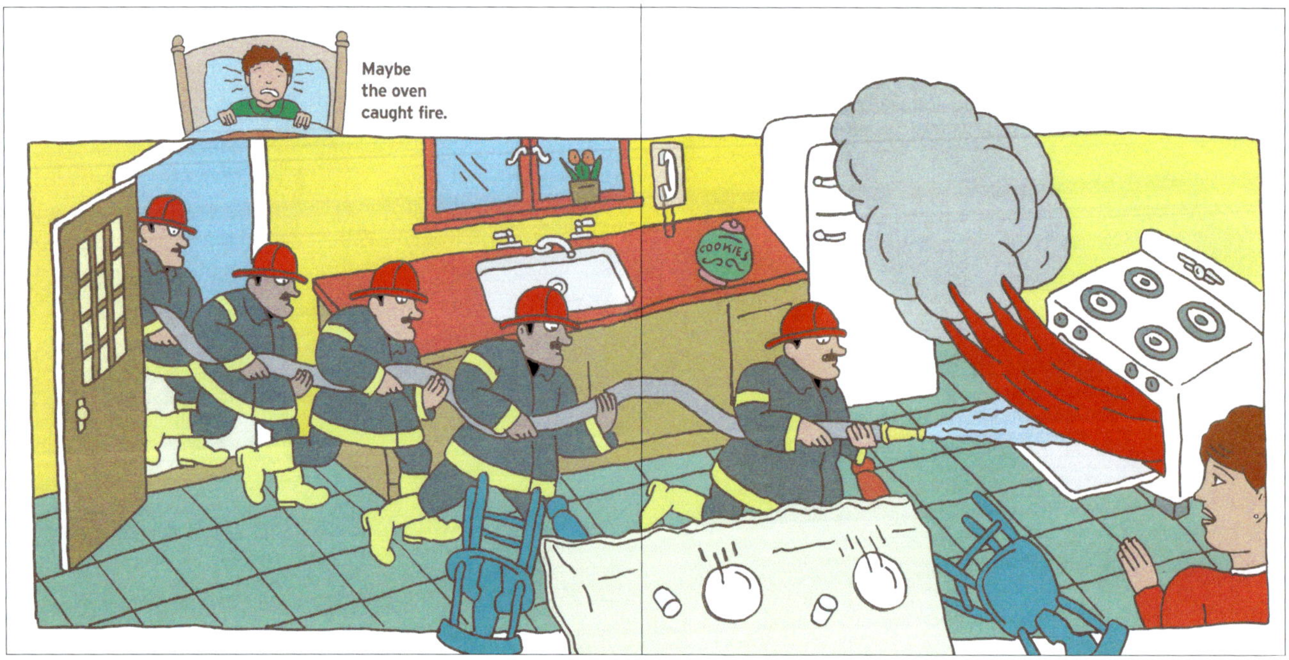

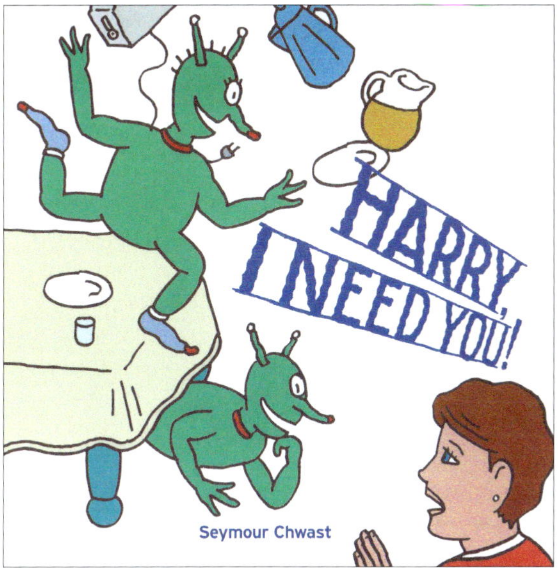

Harry, I Need You!, by Harriet Ziefert, illustrated by Seymour Chwast, 2002, 9.5" × 9.5" (24.25 × 24.25 cm), 32 pages.

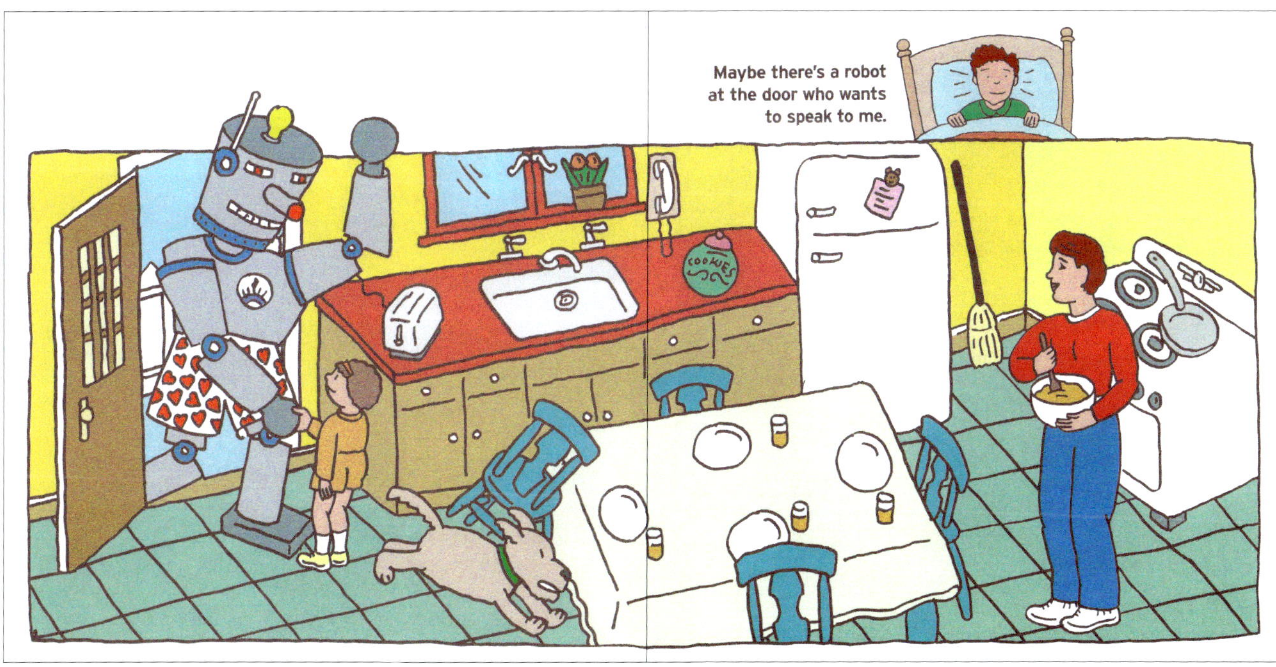

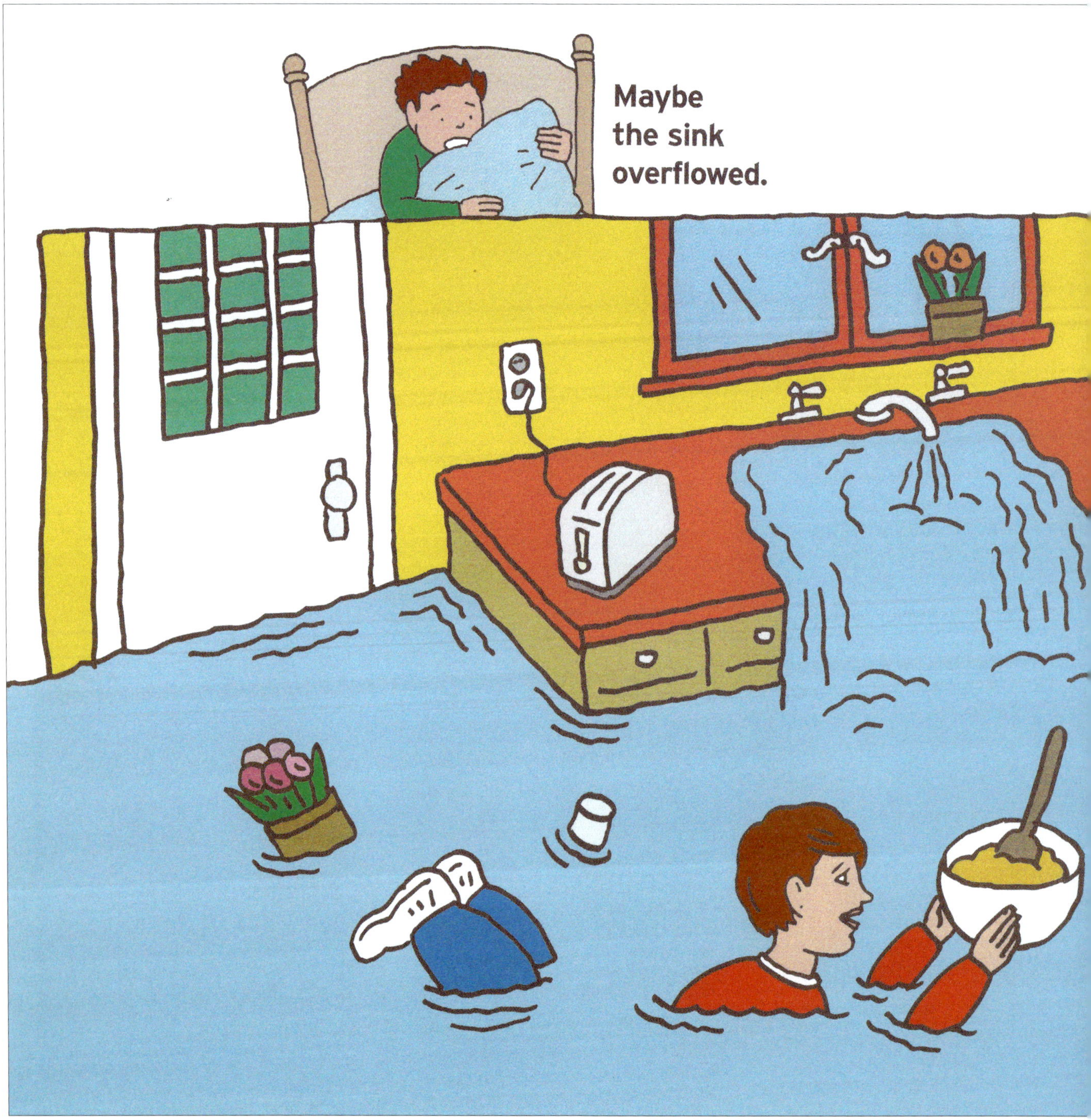
Maybe
the sink
overflowed.

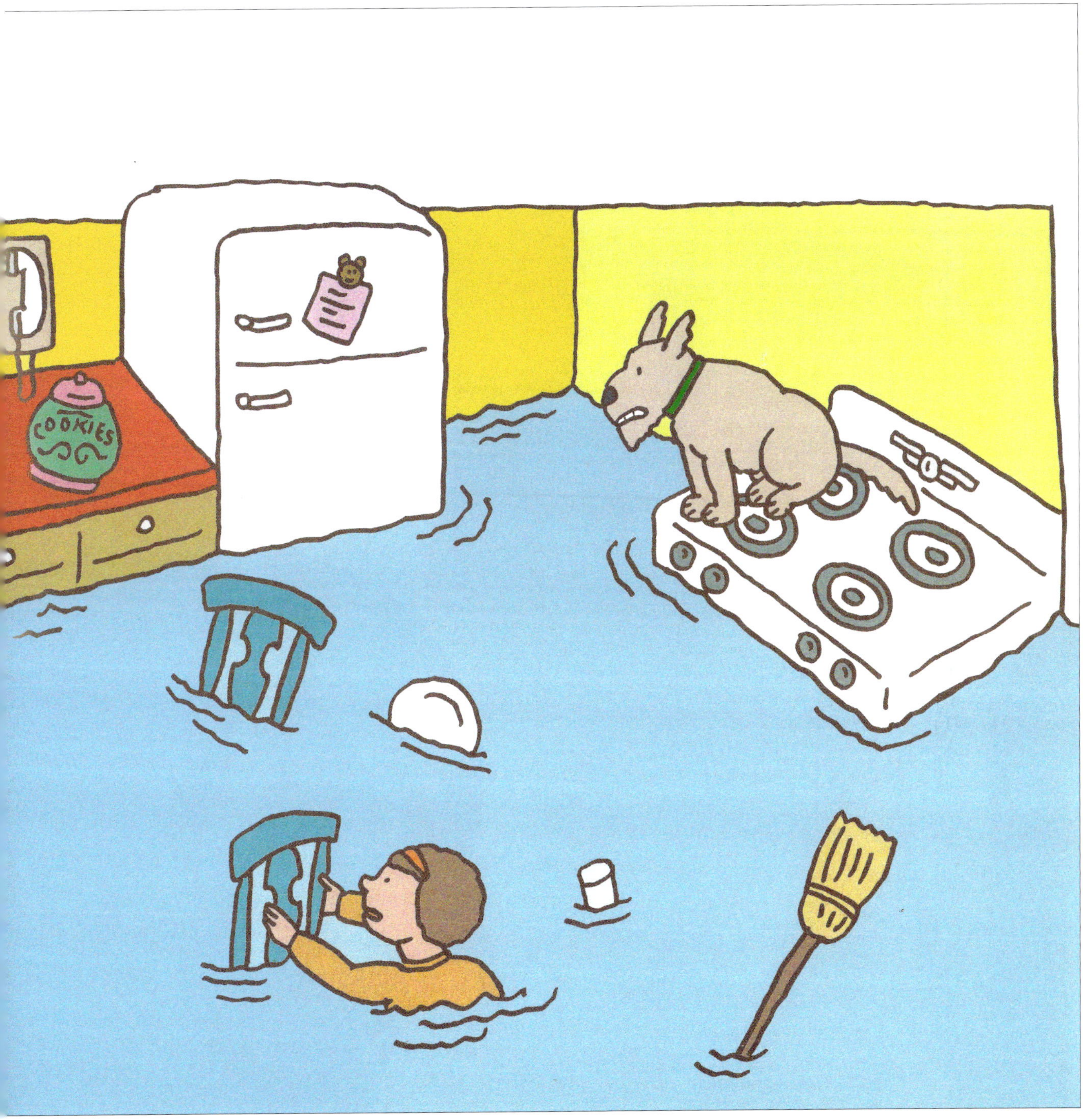
COOKIES

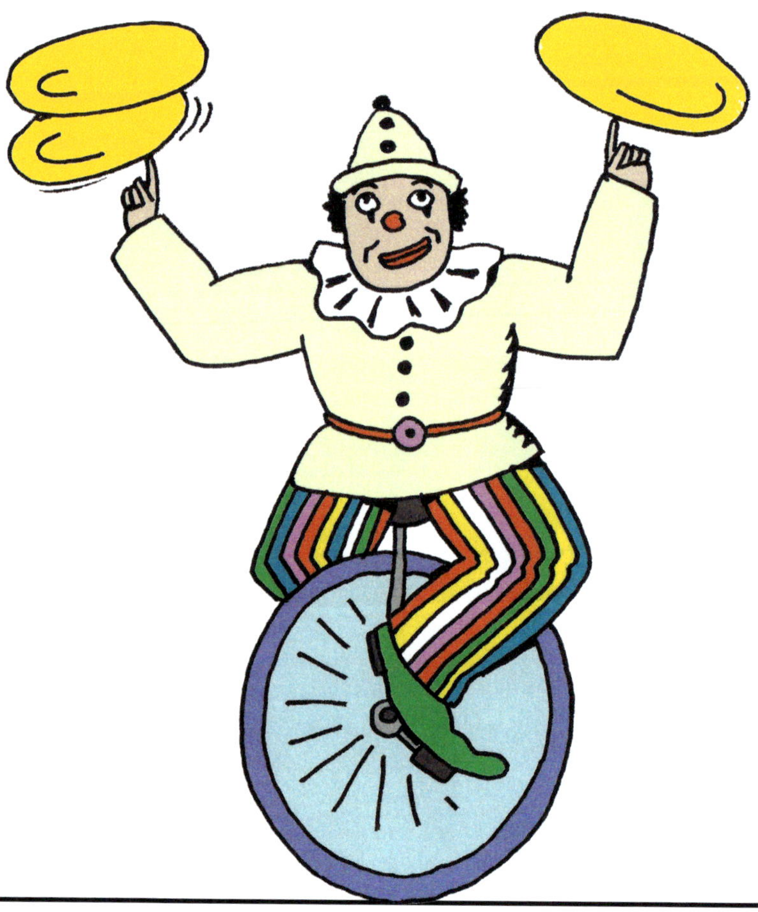

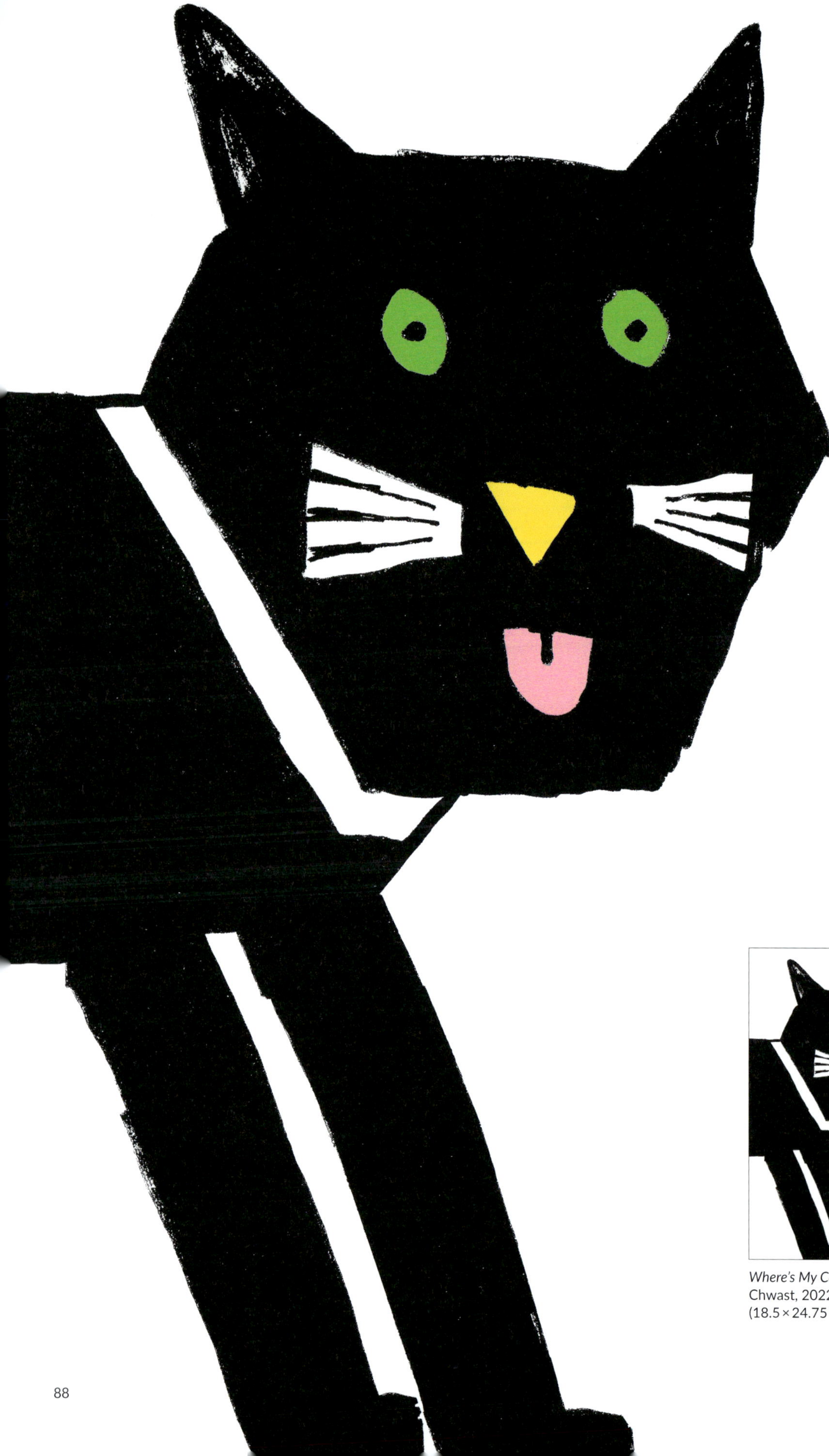

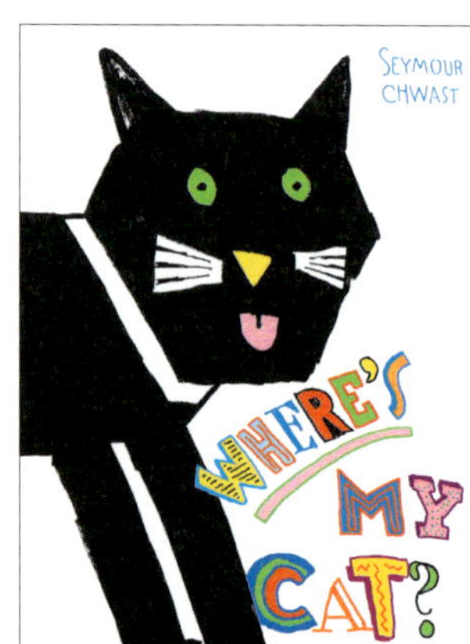

Where's My Cat?, by Seymour Chwast, 2022, 7.32" × 9.76" (18.5 × 24.75 cm), 48 pages.

Where's My Cat?

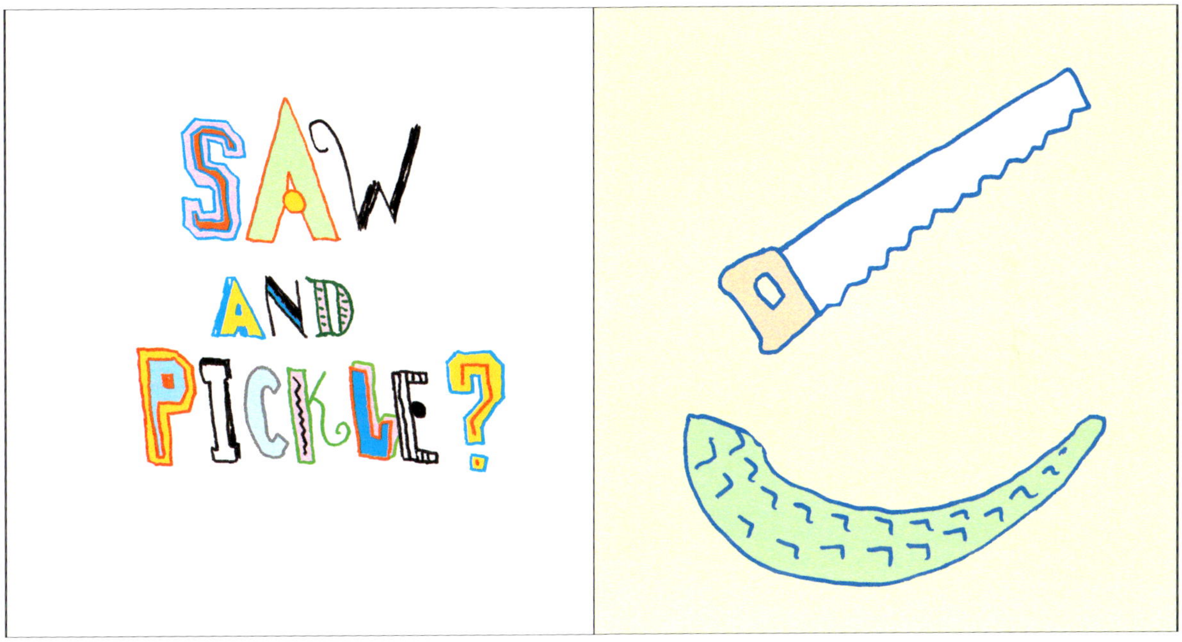

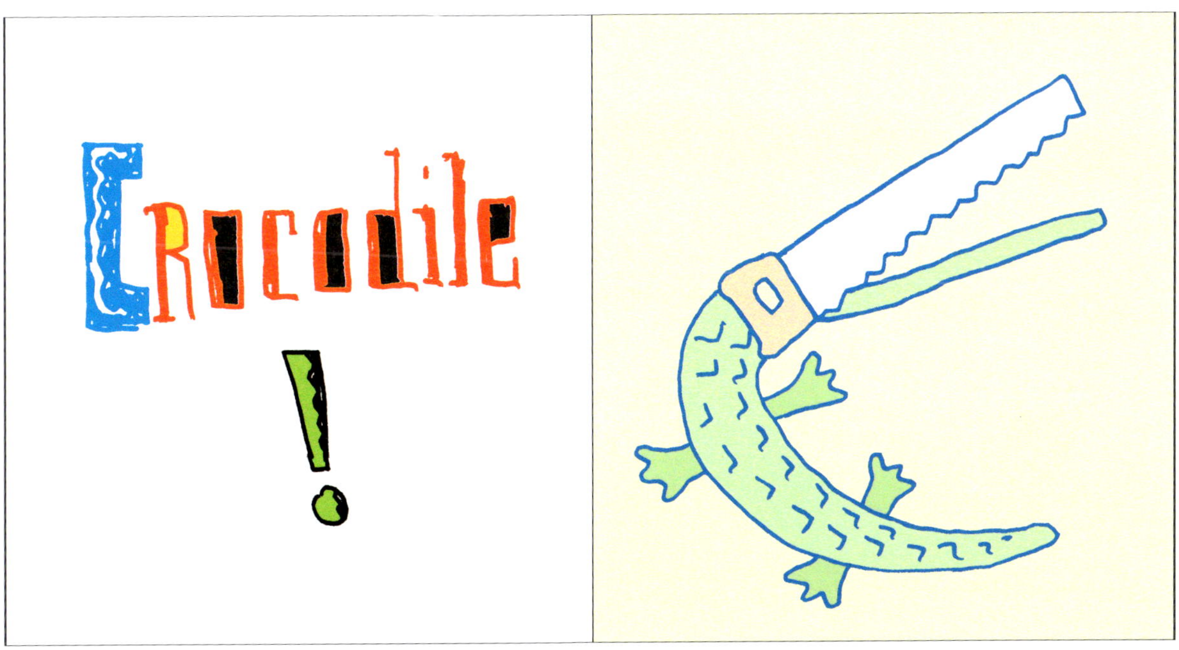

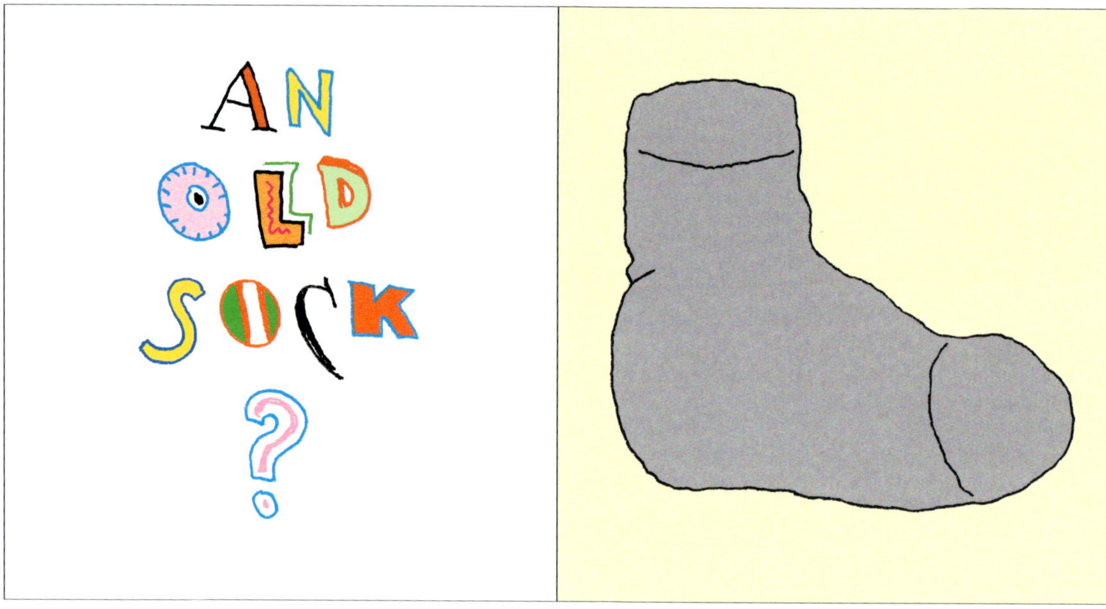
AN OLD SOCK ?

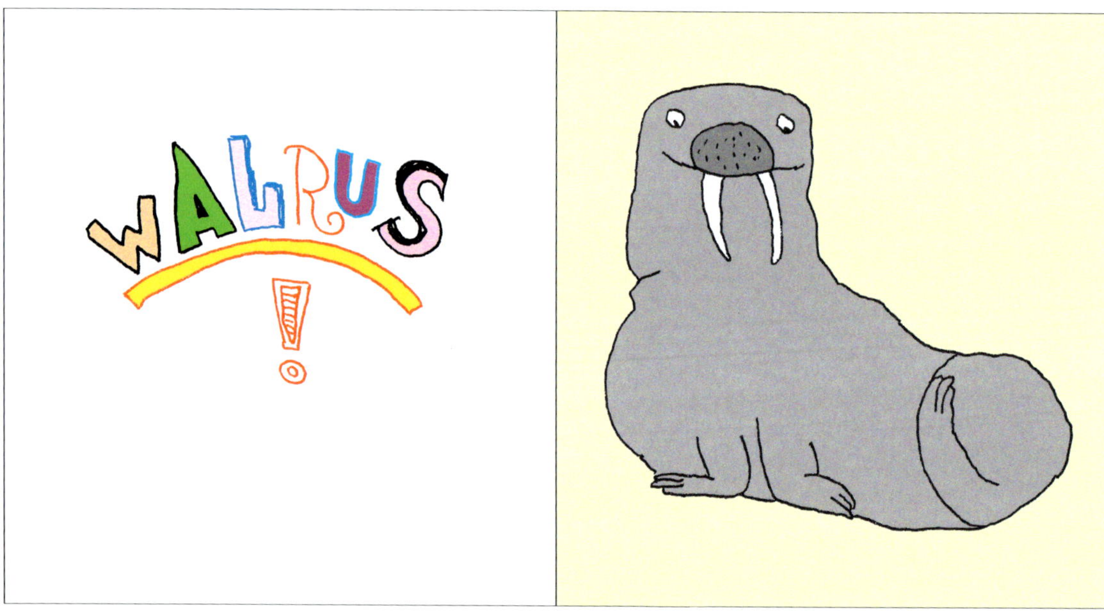
WALRUS !

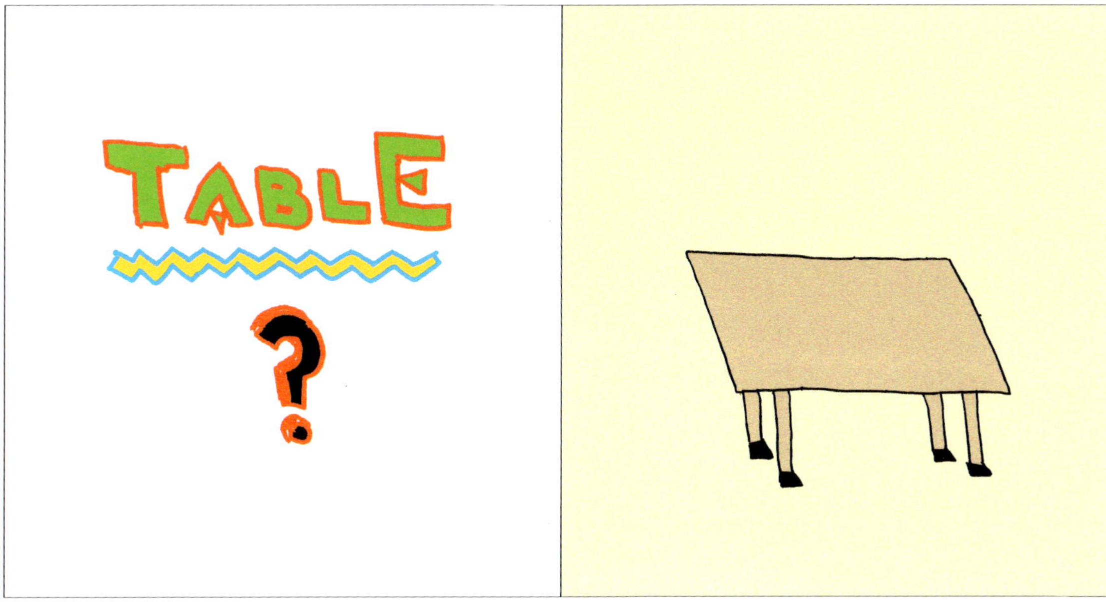

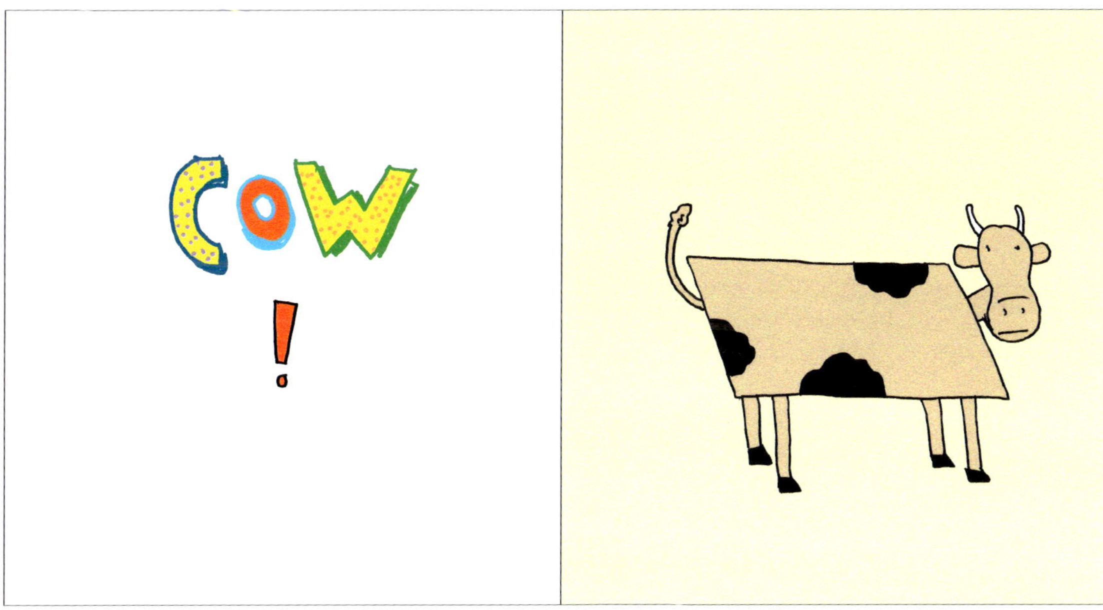

Cats play a big role in Chwast's art. "They are immensely satisfying to draw," he says. The cat of this title only makes a cameo as part of a larger collection of visual riddles. "It's a puzzle where the reader has to solve a visual problem," Chwast explains. "I was interested in an idea where inanimate objects become animate ones with some minimal drawing. The reader is fooled until the page is turned." Among the joyful elements here are Chwast's customized illuminated letters used on the cover and the clues inside the book. The colors and shapes are designed to make the reader happy, too.

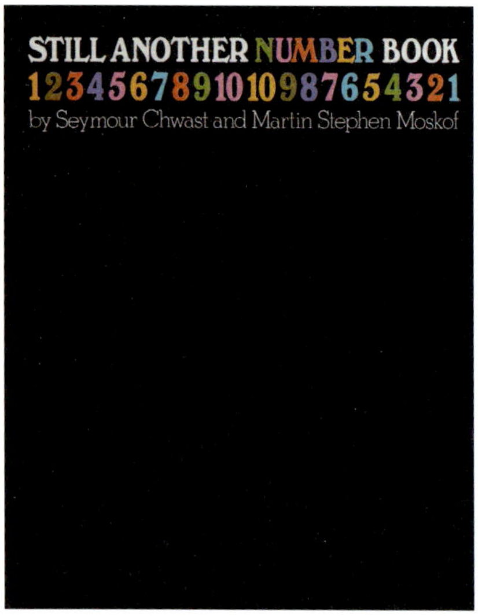

Still Another Number Book, by Martin Stephen Moskof and Seymour Chwast, 1972, 8" × 10" (20.25 × 25.5 cm), 64 pages.

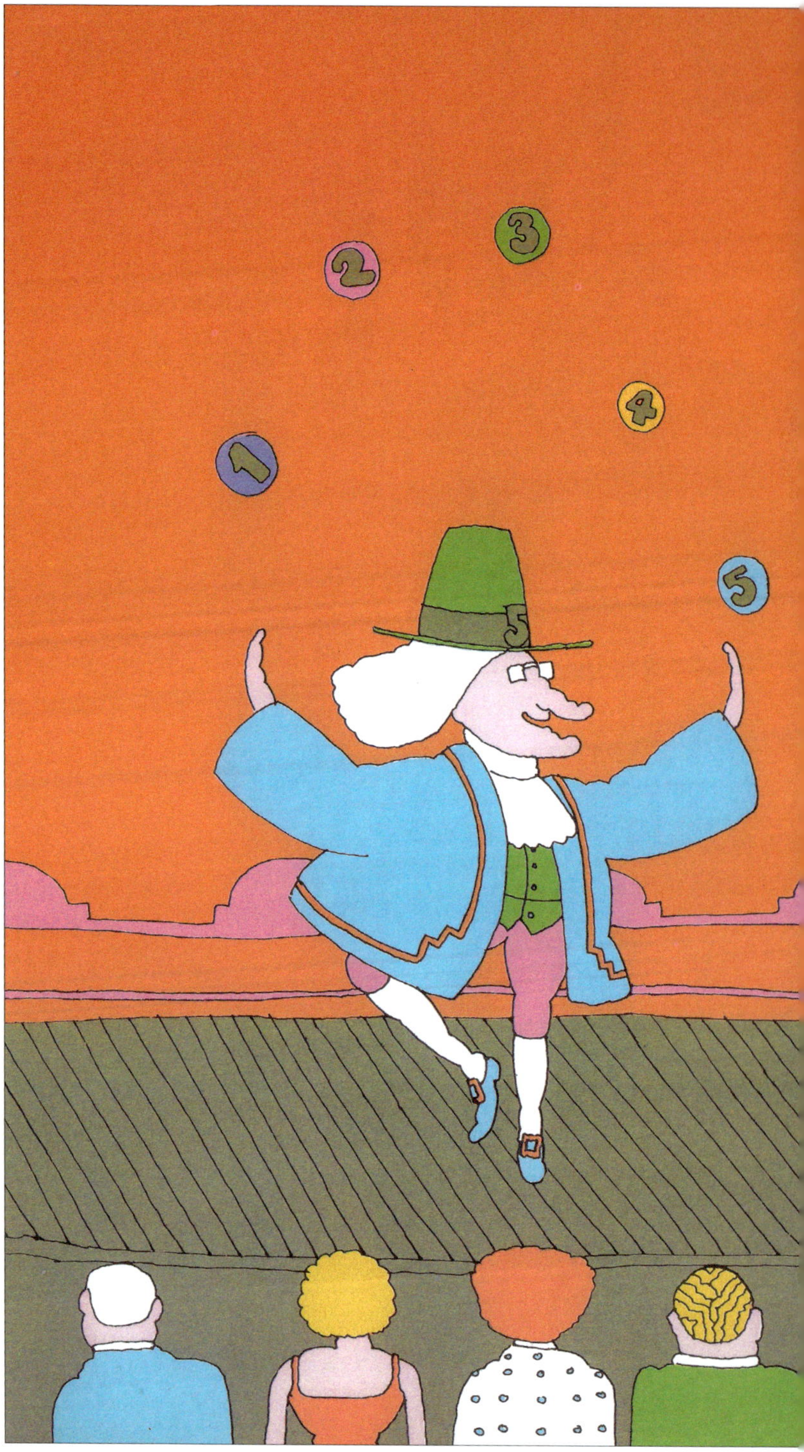

Still Another Number Book

Created in collaboration with writer Martin Stephen Moskof, this title riffs on the fact that dozens of "number books" have been published already. The drawings are surreal in the juxtaposition of odd elements that, when seen from particular perspectives, reveal surprising numerical combinations. Chwast employs his black ink outline method to fashion a carnivalesque amalgam of comic characters doing normal and extraordinary things.

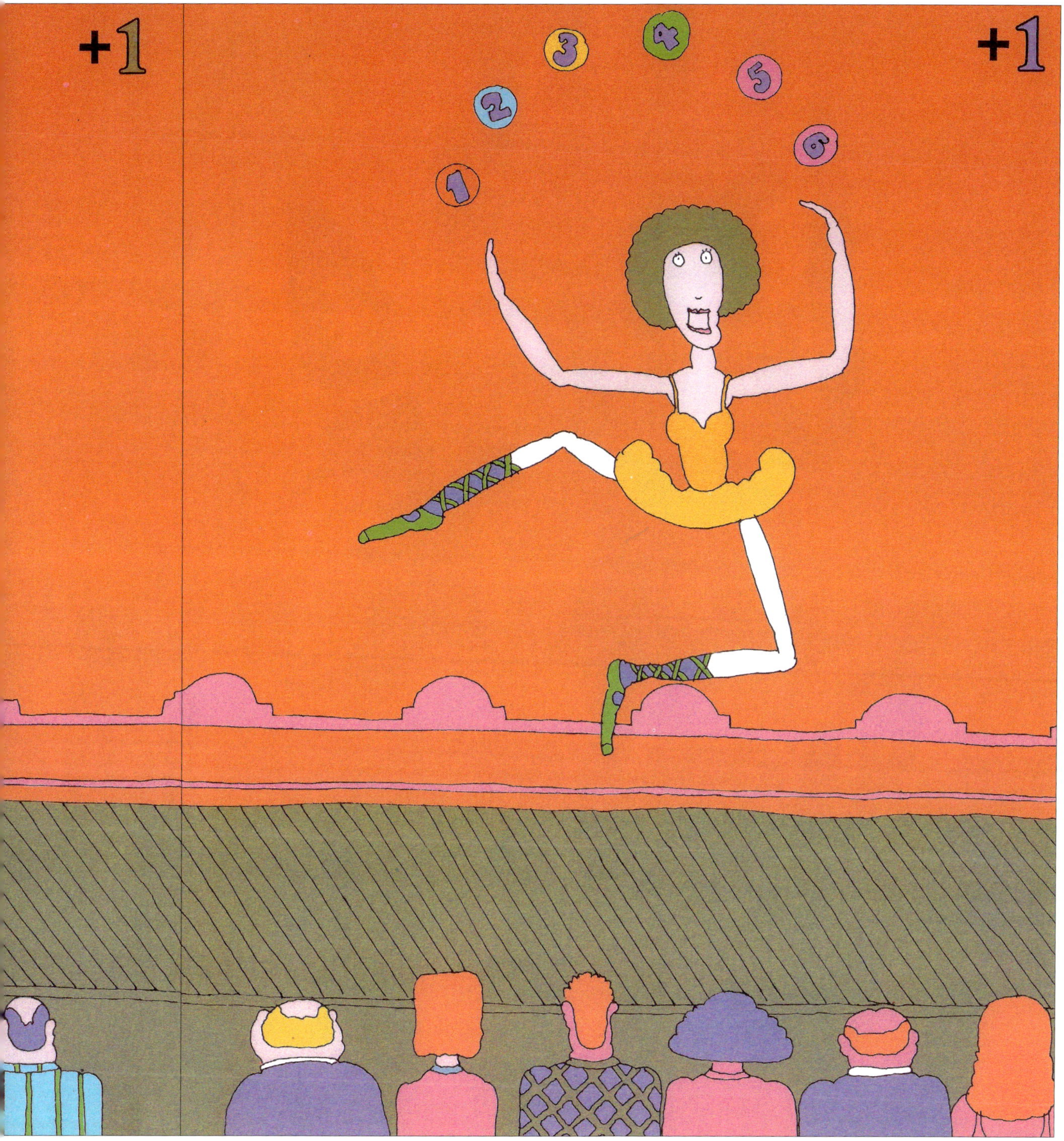
+1
+1

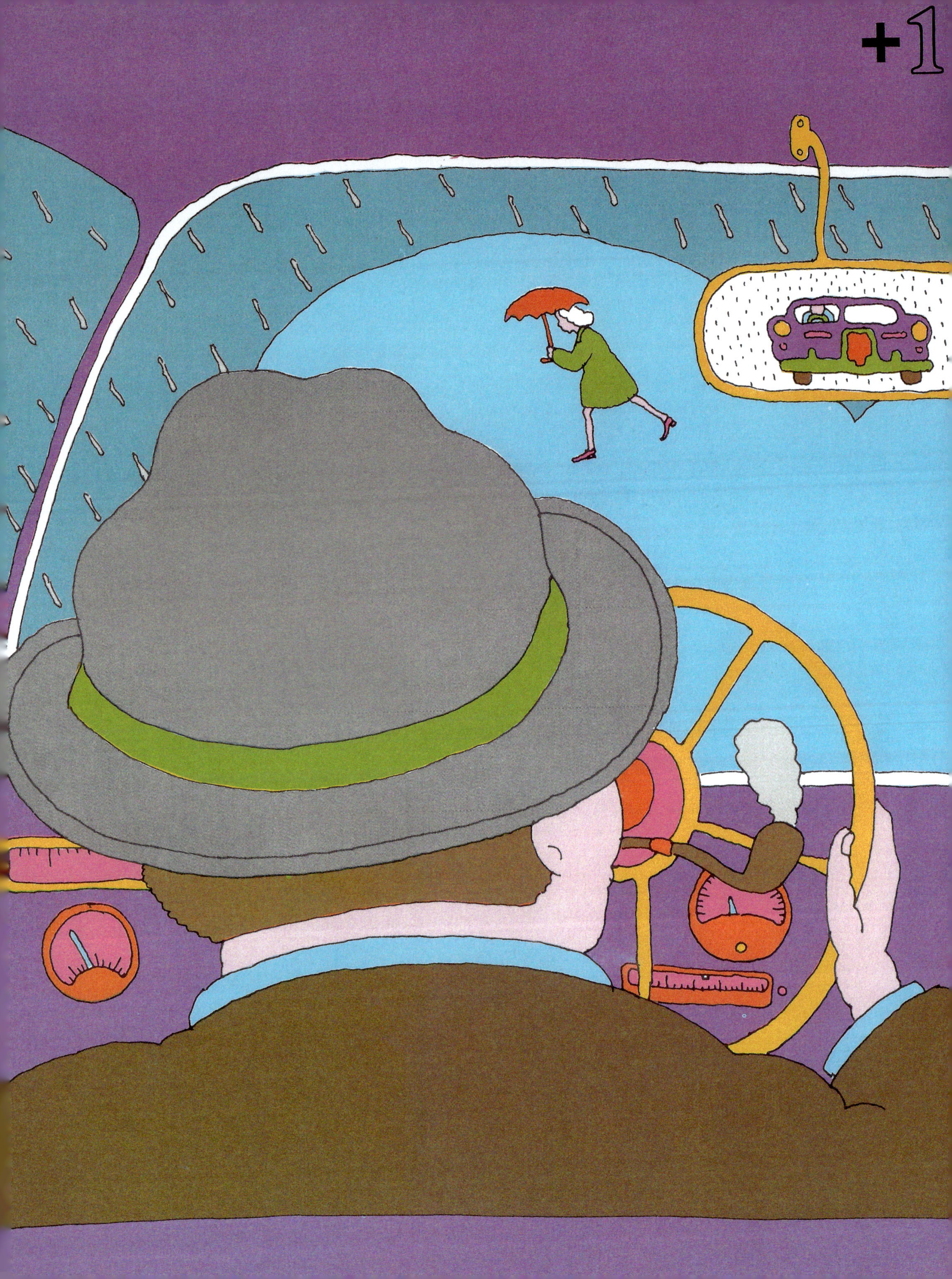
+1

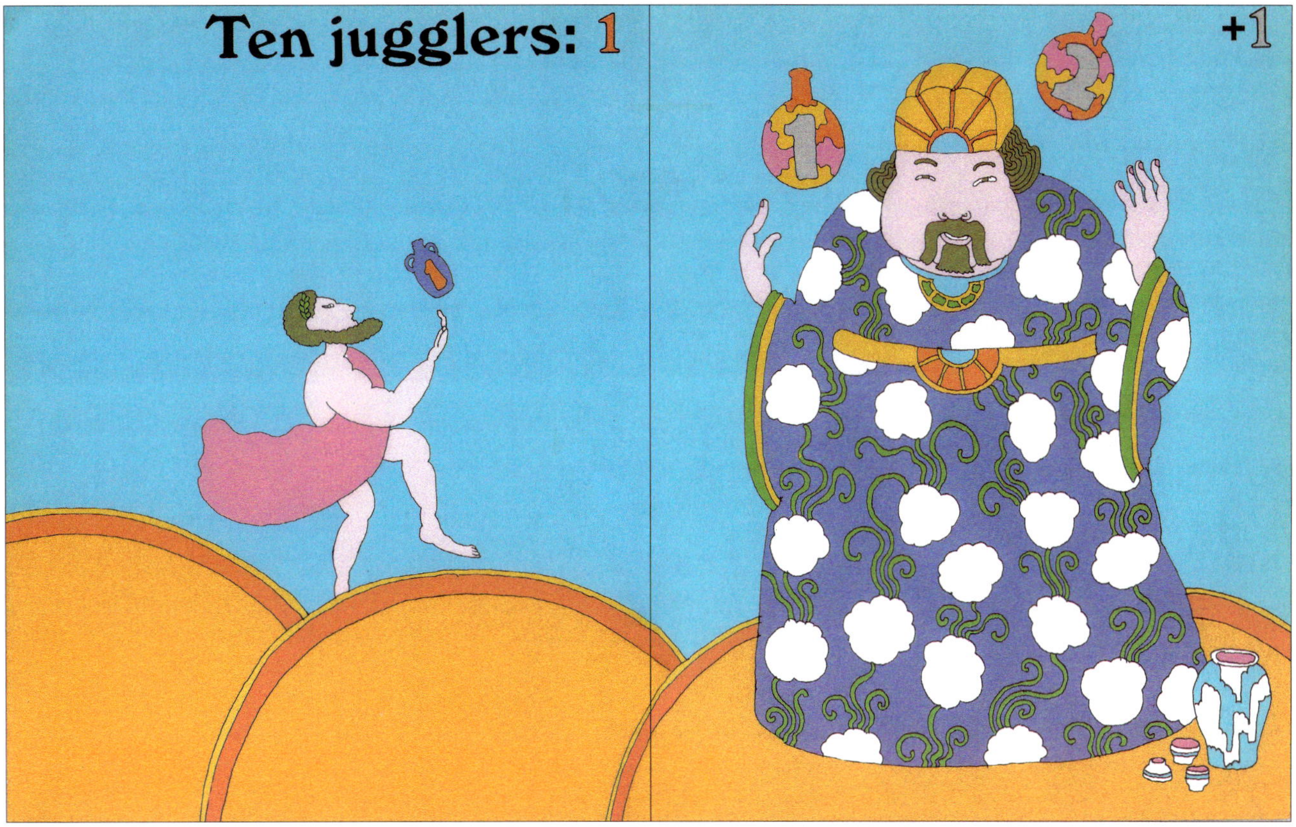
Ten jugglers: 1
+1
1
2

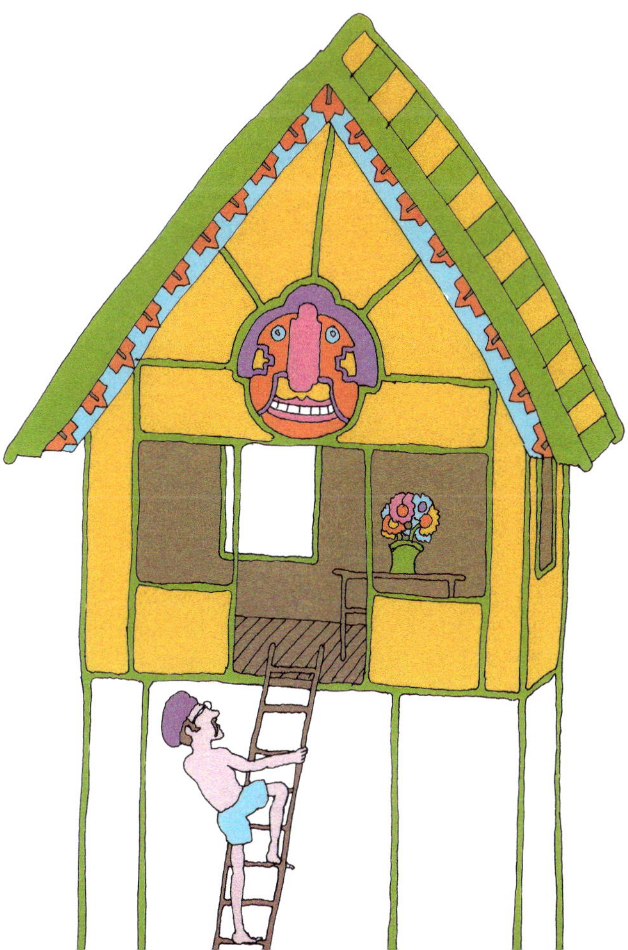

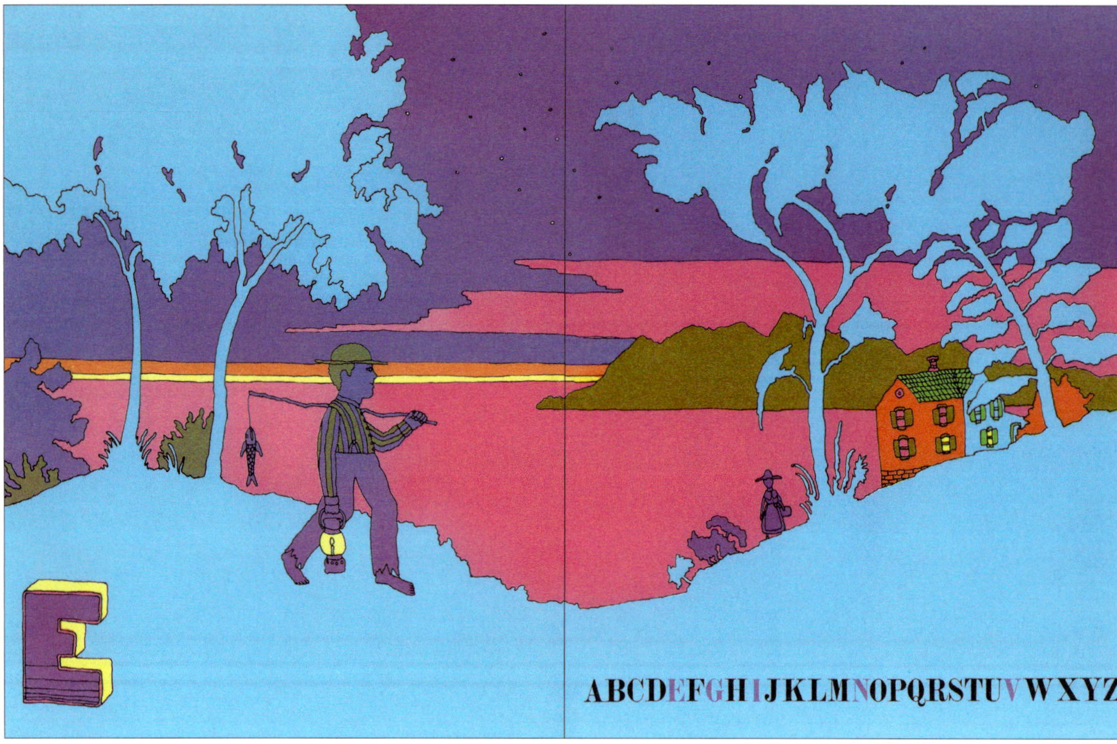

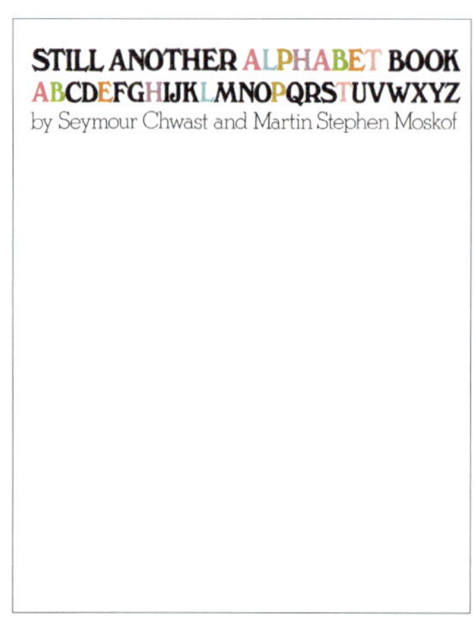

Still Another Alphabet Book, by Martin Stephen Moskof and Seymour Chwast, 1969, 8" × 10" (20.25 × 25.5 cm), 64 pages.

Still Another Alphabet Book

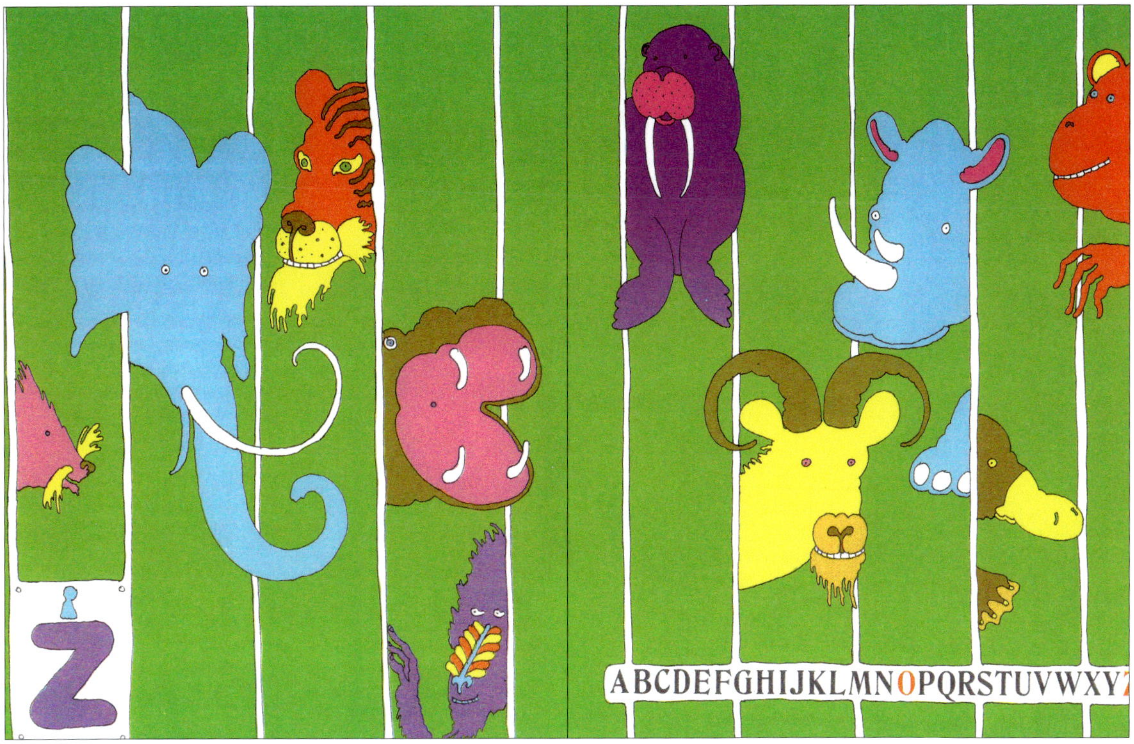

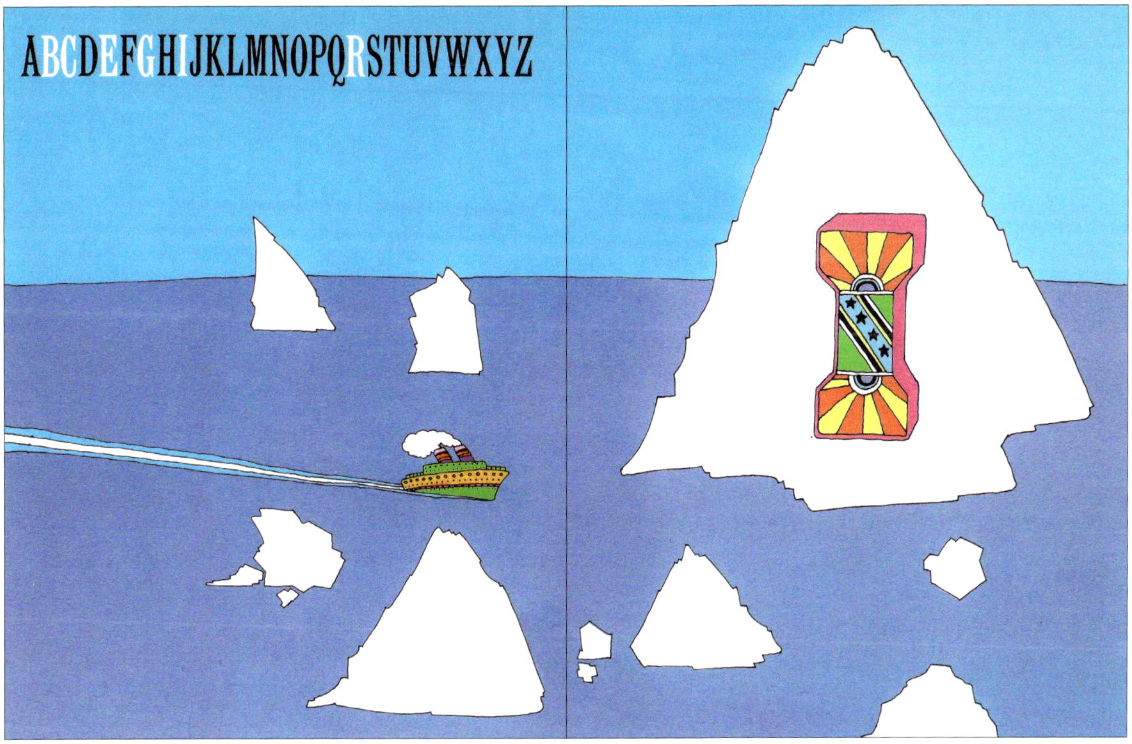

It can be fun to find letters in places where they are ordinarily absent—so much so that Moskof and Chwast used this conceit for this puzzle book. Chwast takes pleasure in hiding letters just about everywhere. His colorful, art nouveau–esque and comic book decorative approaches both enhance and impede finding the missing letters. But how does it work? Letters highlighted at the top of a page spell out the description of an illustration below. For example, S N A K and E are highlighted on one page, helping the reader to learn to spell SNAKE. The illustration features other elements that start with an S: S for swan, S for stones, and S for street, for example, providing more things for the reader to find. While some letters, like the S, are vivid, it is very difficult to locate the elusive Z.

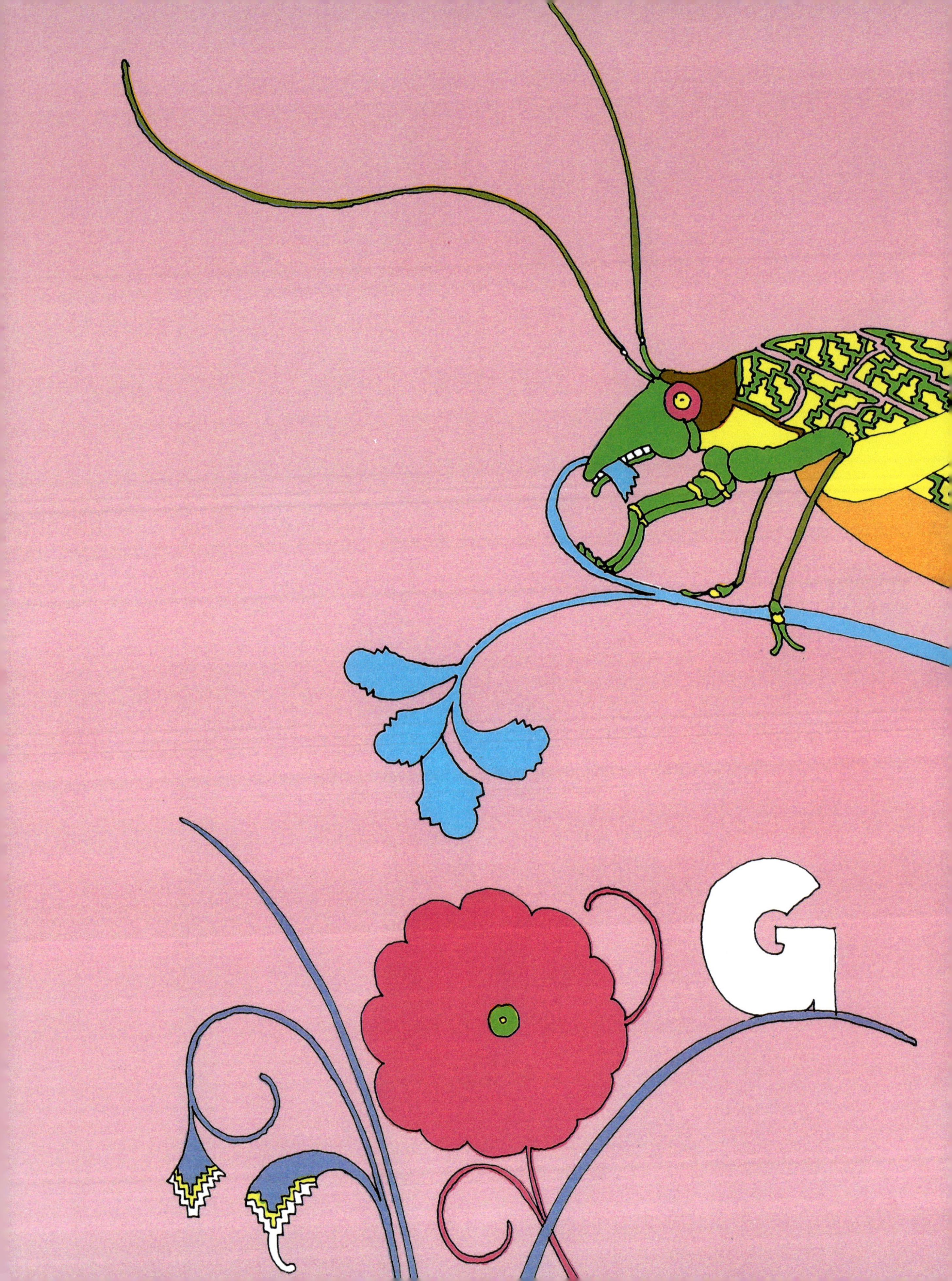
G

ABCDEFGHIJKLMNOPQRSTUVWXYZ

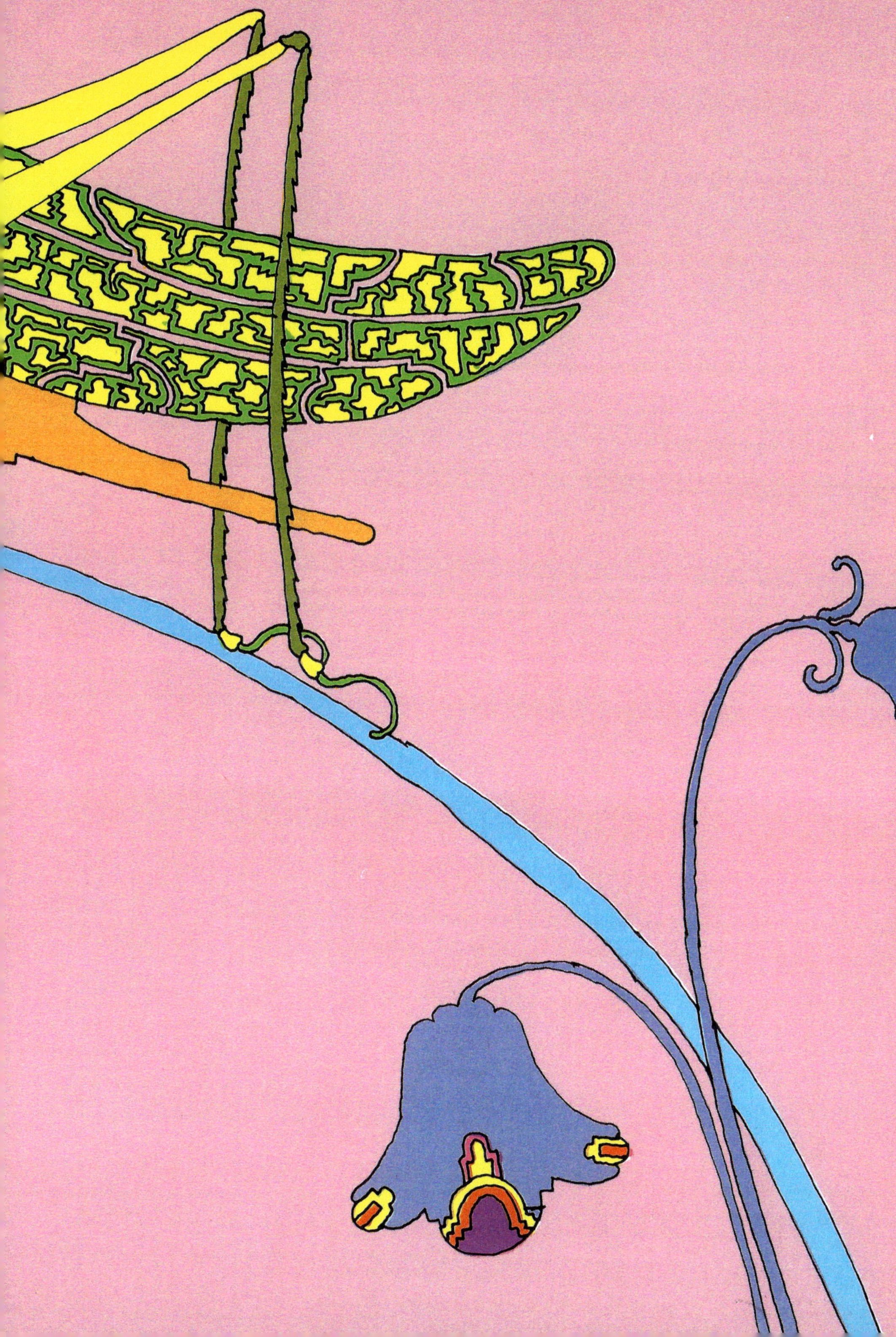

Find your G.

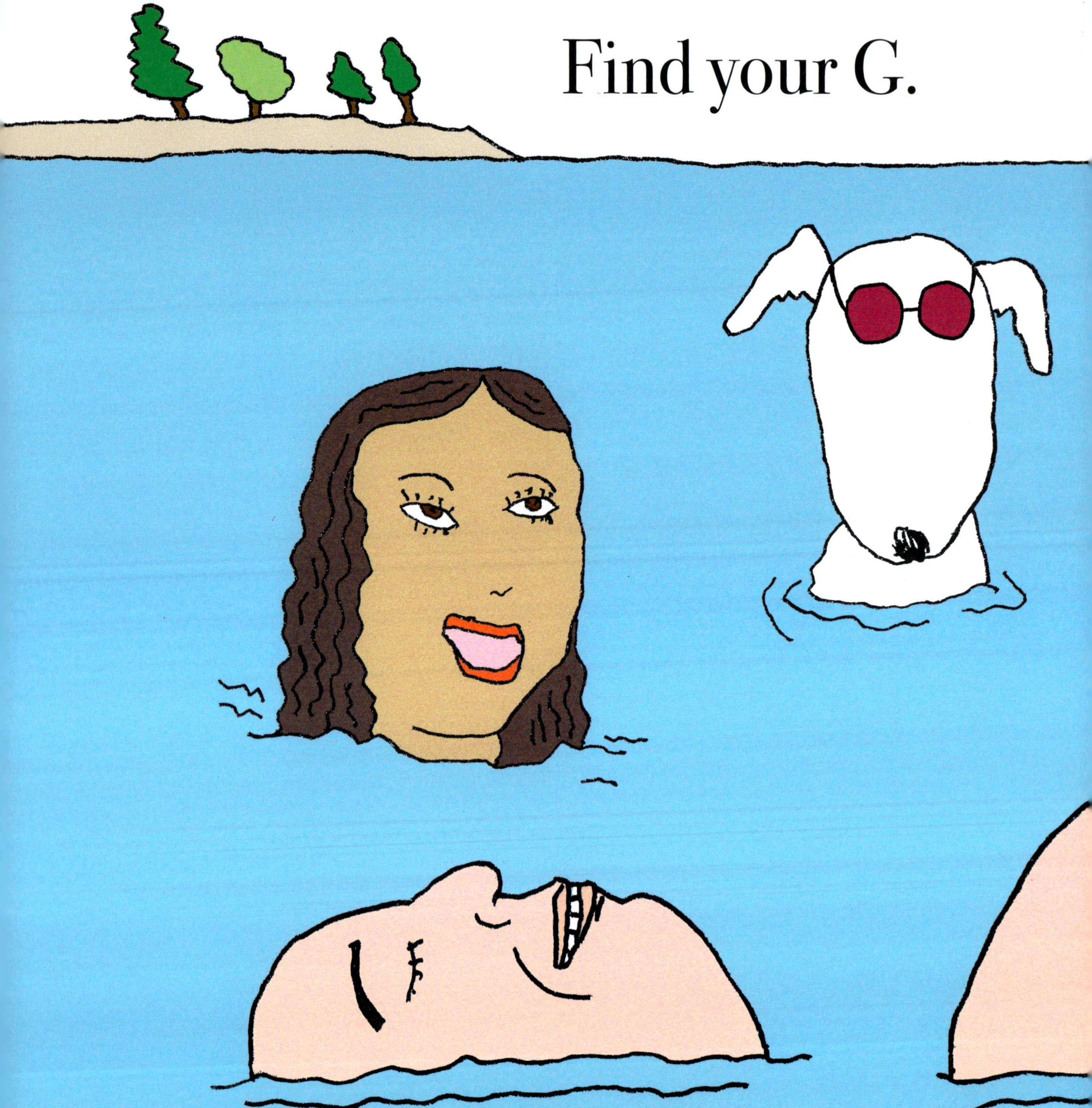

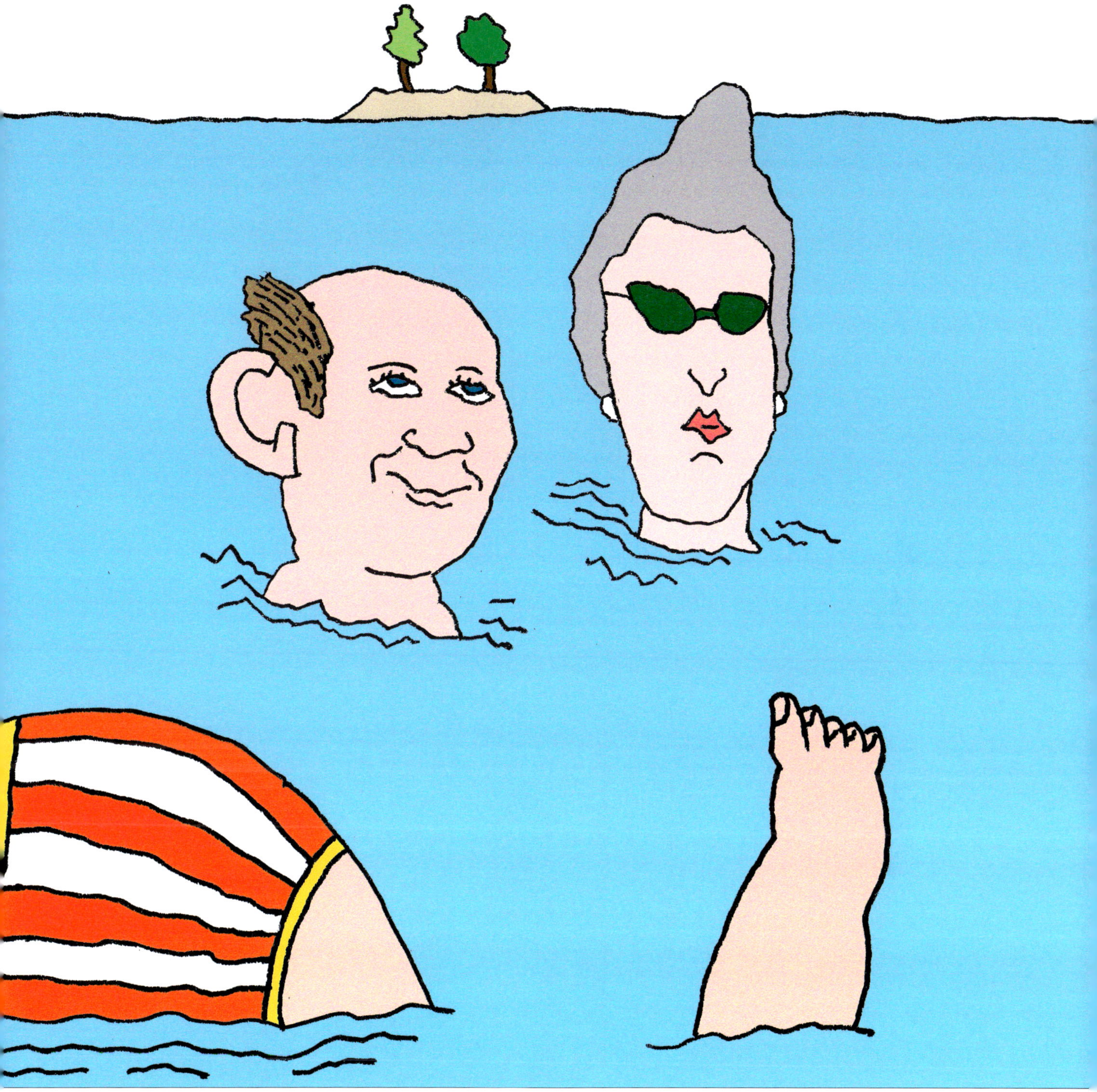

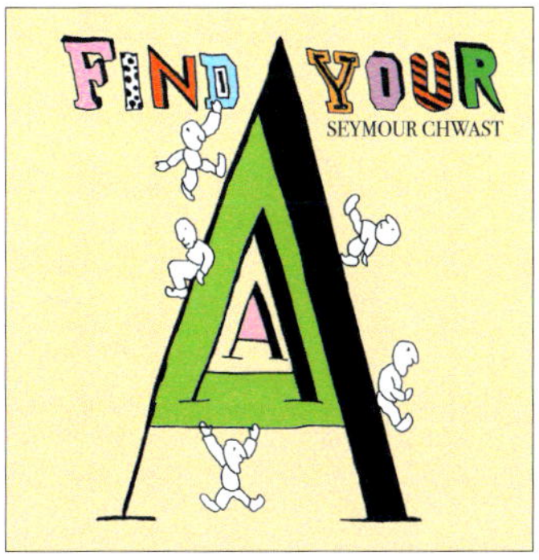

Find Your A

Find Your A, by Seymour Chwast, 2022, 10.3" × 10.45" (26.25 × 26.5 cm), 48 pages.

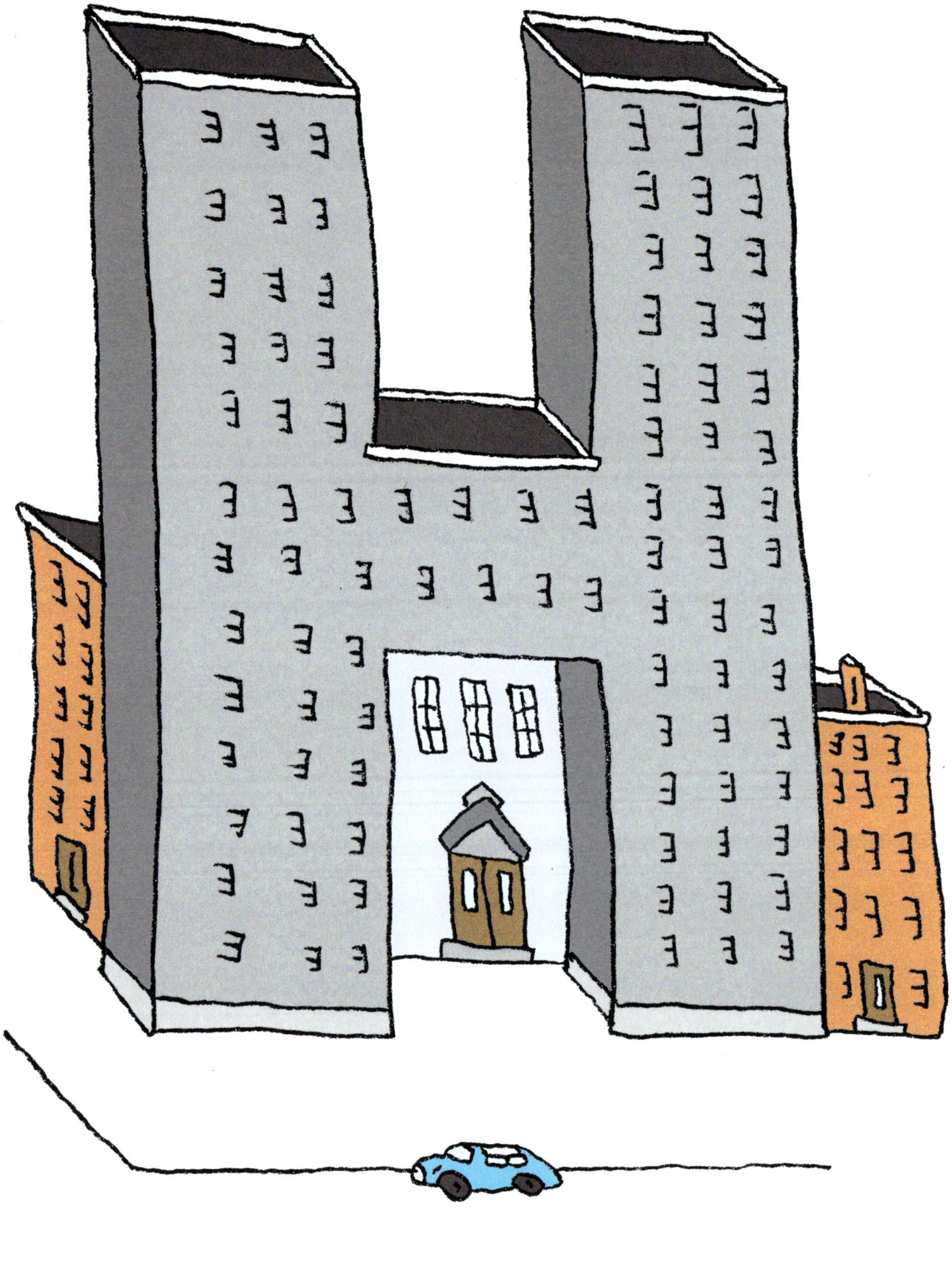

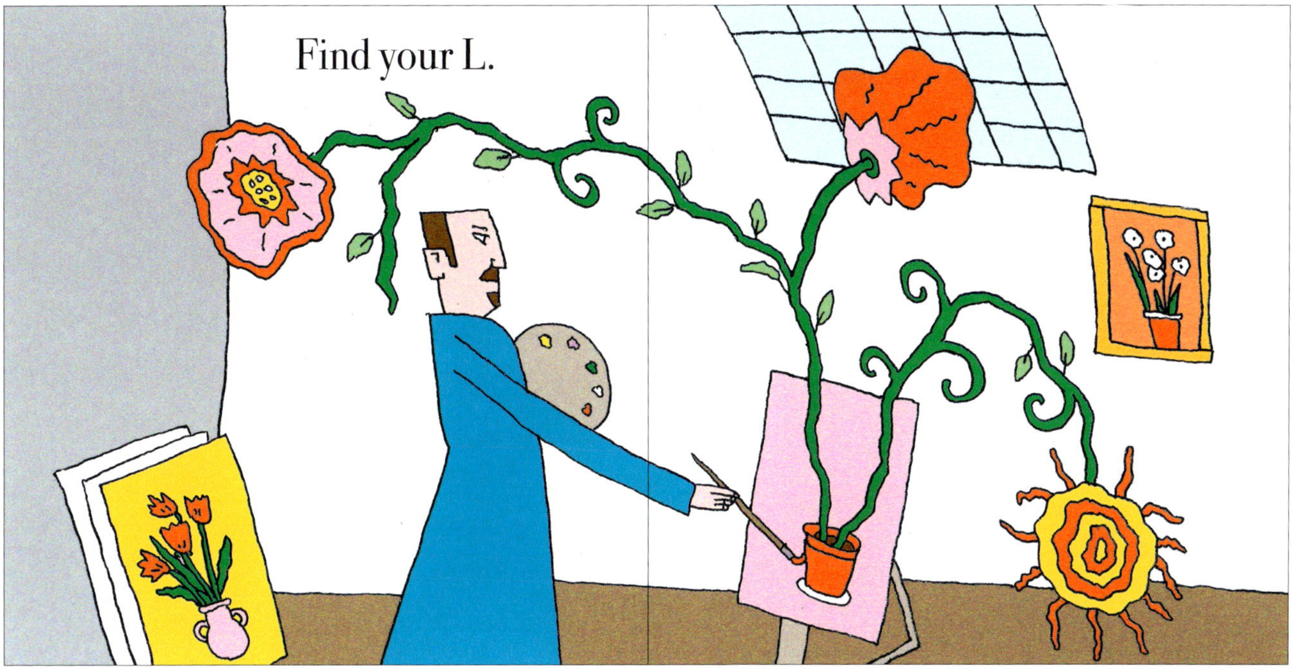

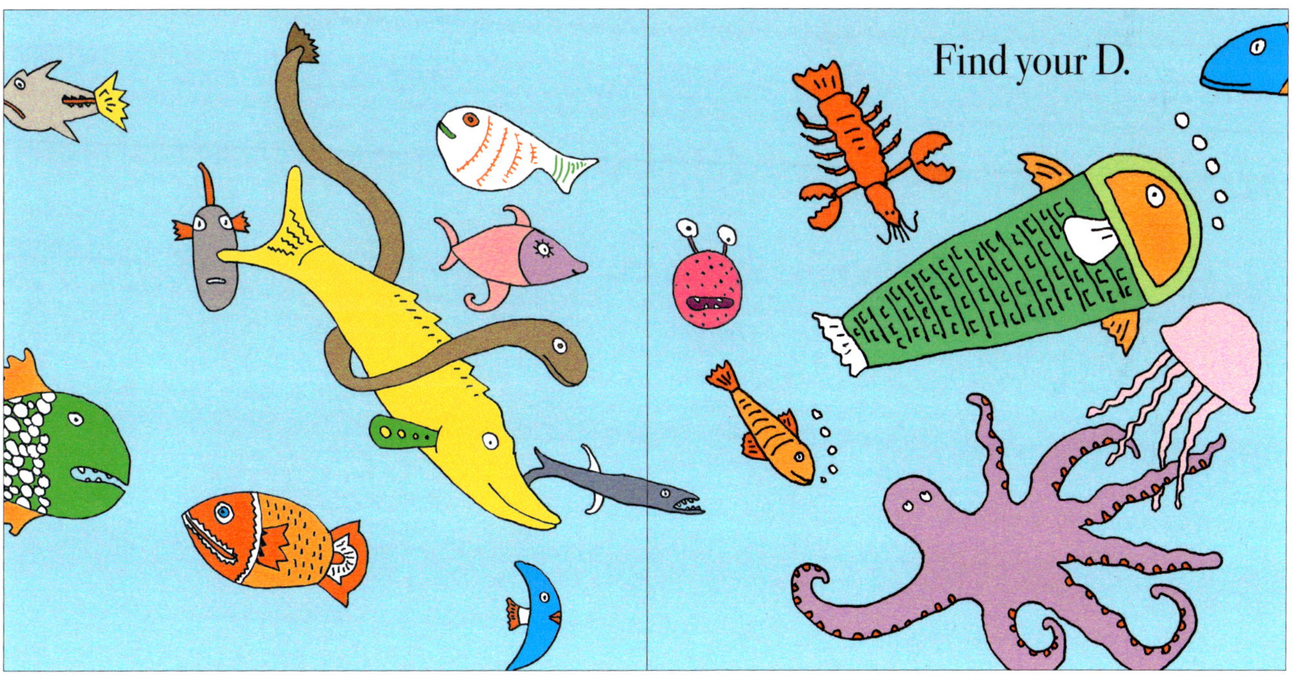

This book, written and illustrated by Chwast, is a tour de force of visual puns. It may seem to repeat concepts from the *Still Another...* series, but the rendering of the heavier line and aggressive tone of the illustrations distinguishes this alphabet book from Chwast's others. Some letters are easy to find, such as a swimmer's G-shaped ear or an H-shaped building, but others are slyly difficult. "Finding L is the best one and it's the hardest I think," Chwast snickers.

The Alphabet Parade

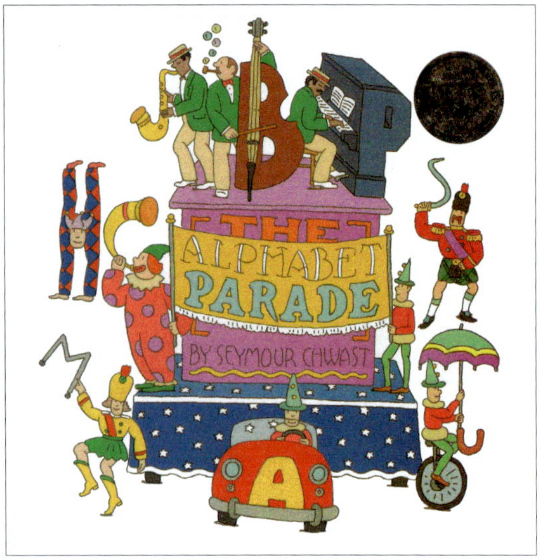

The Alphabet Parade, by Seymour Chwast, 1991, 10" × 10" (25.5 × 25.5 cm), 32 pages.

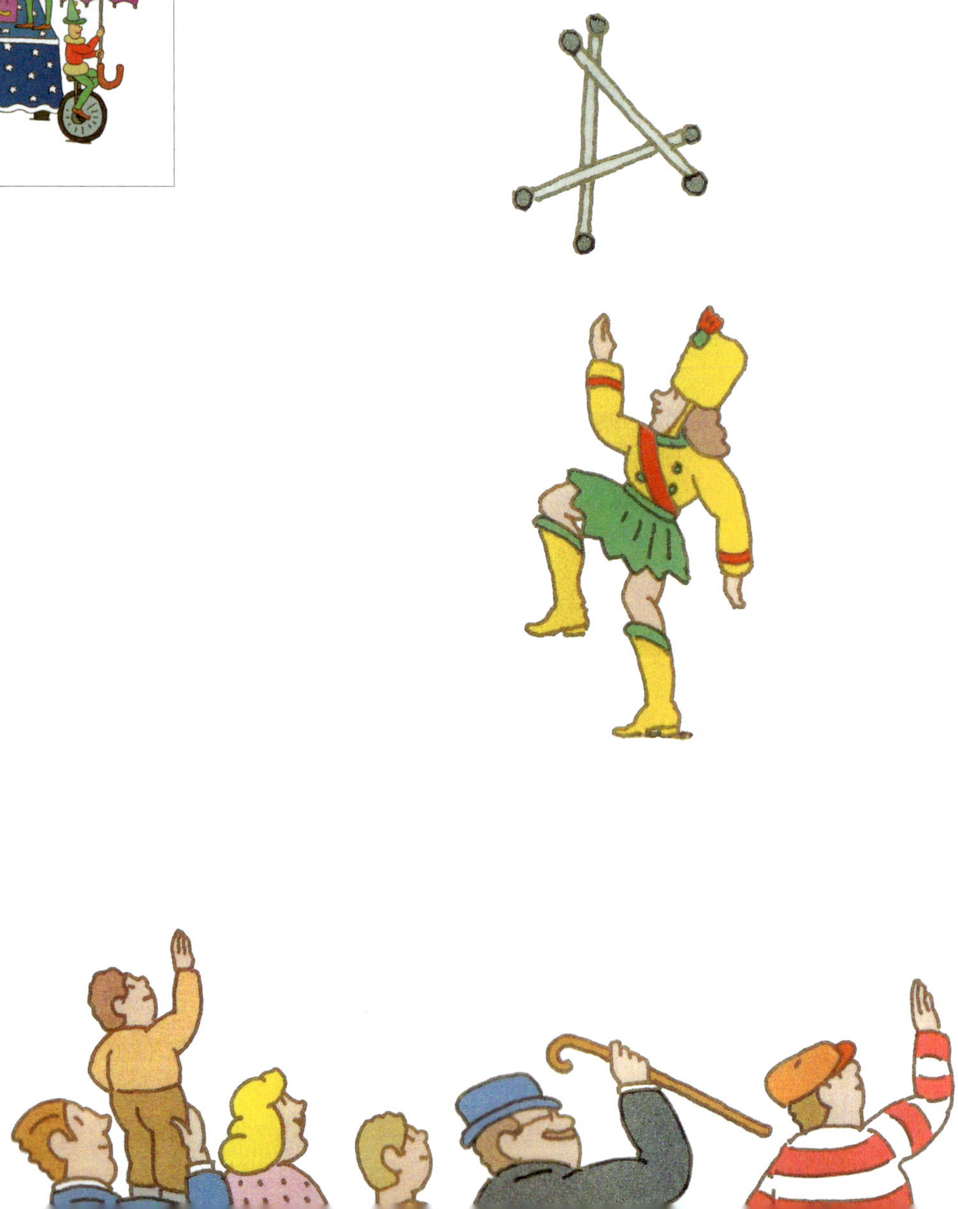

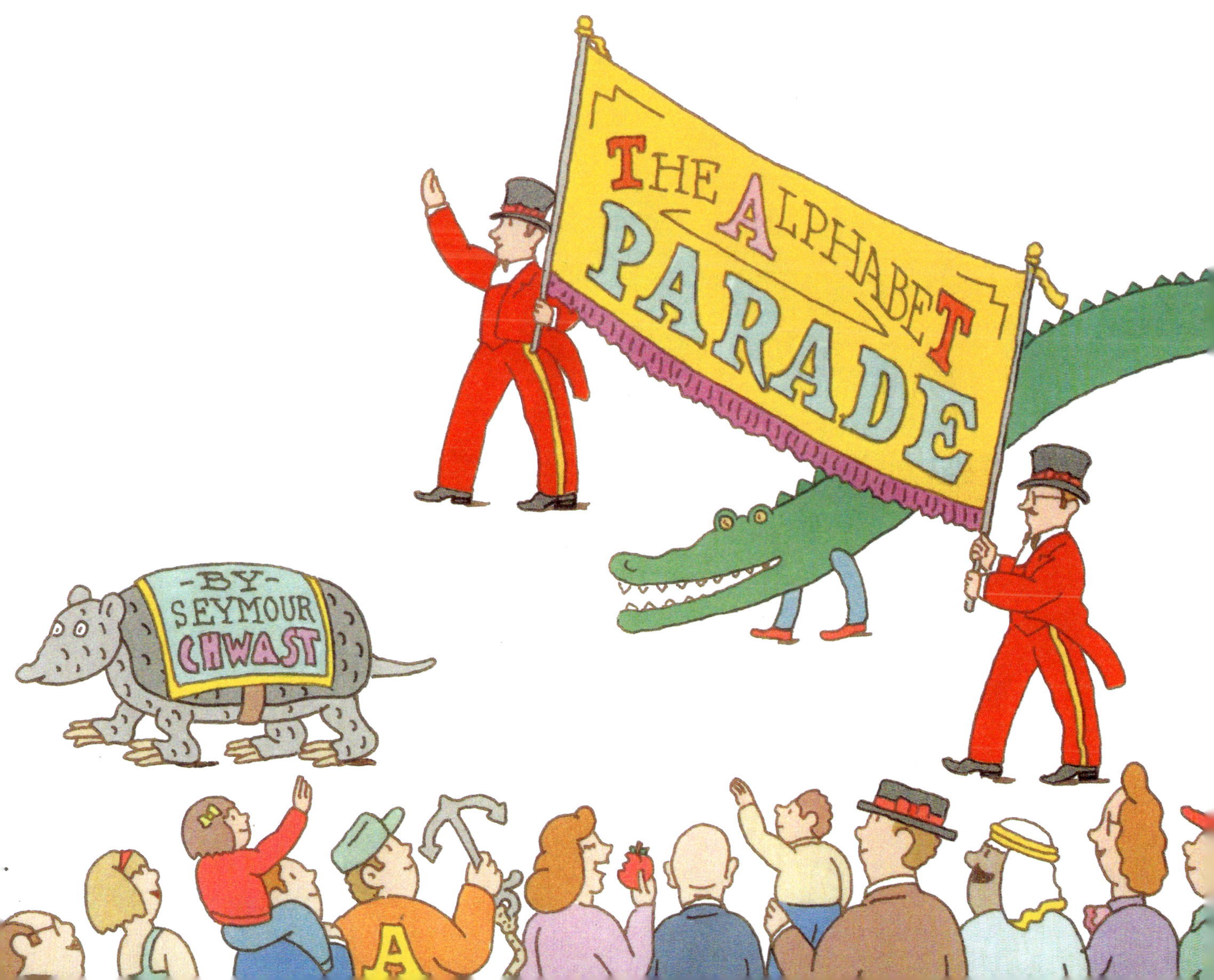
THE ALPHABET PARADE
-BY-
SEYMOUR
CHWAST

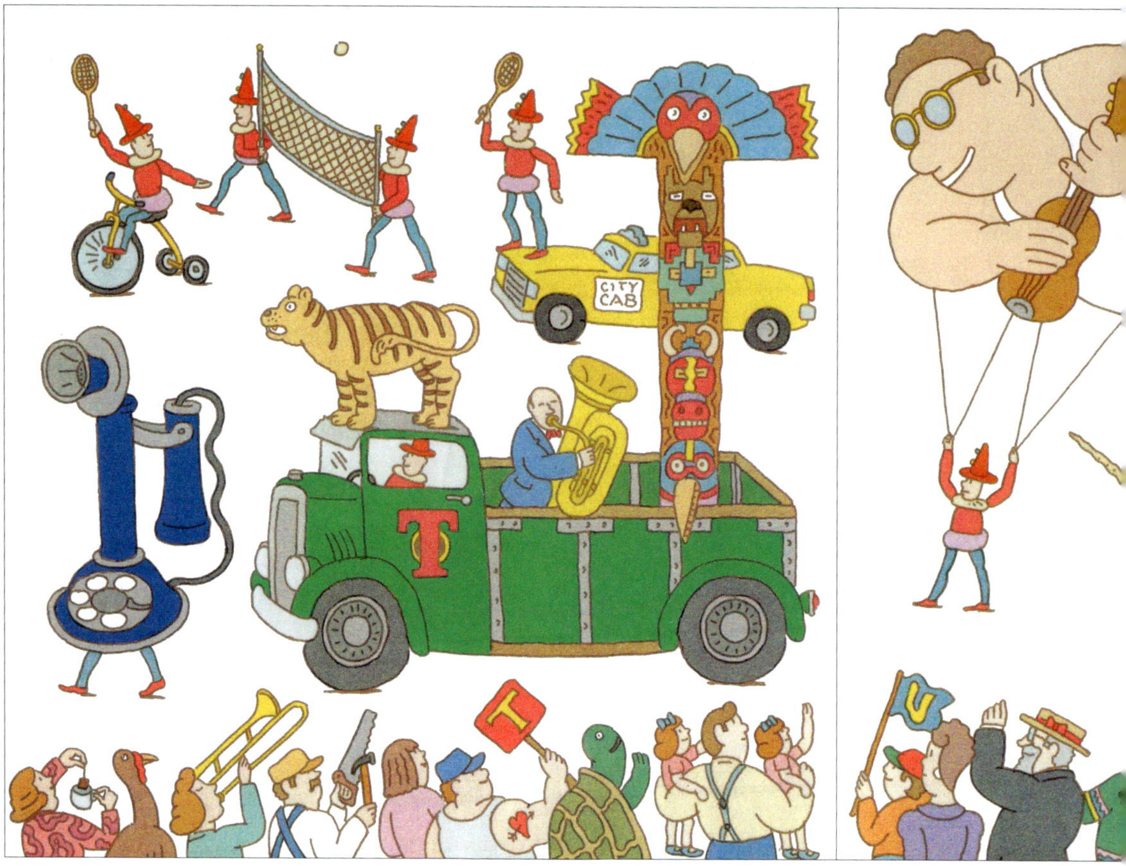
CITY
CAB
T
T
U
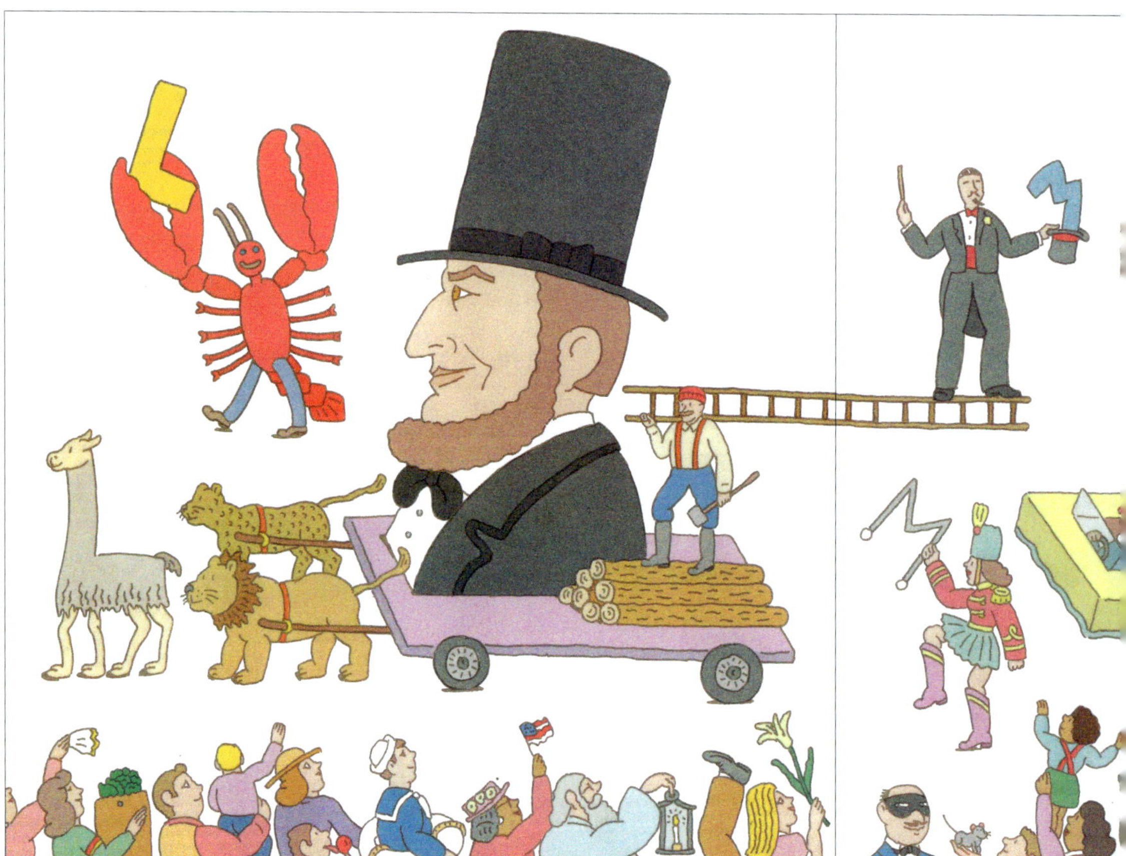
L

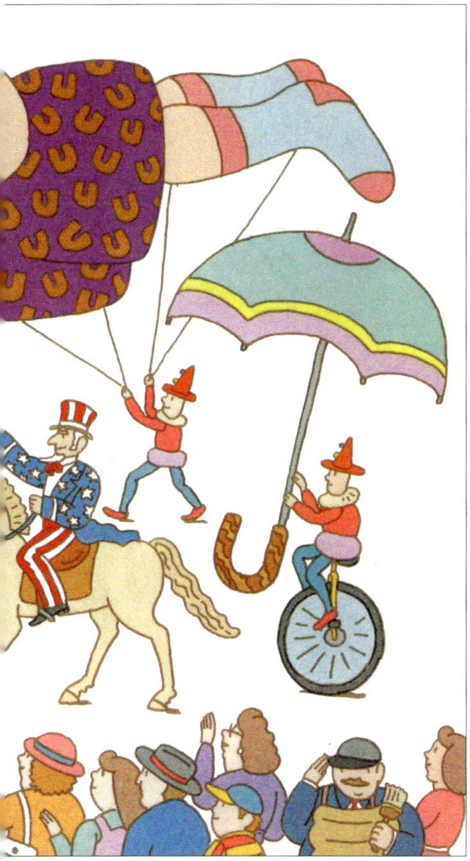

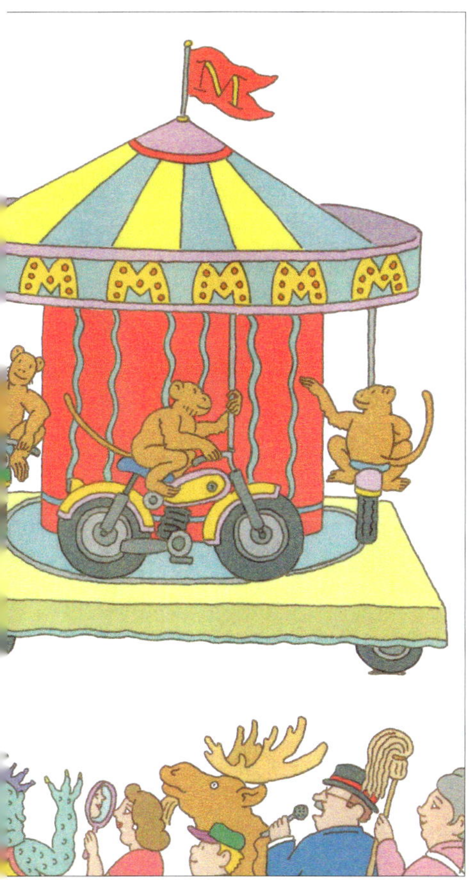

This book's "people posing as letters" concept was inspired by Karel Teige, a 1930s Bauhaus-trained graphic designer who made a figurative alphabet by photographing dancers in difficult contortions that approximate letters. Another artistic influence includes Kurt Schwitters' letterforms as people from his avant-garde children's book *The Scarecrow* (1925). Rather than duplicate Teige's or Schwitters' conceits, Chwast reinterpreted the idea using his own vocabulary of hidden graphic forms that are ultimately revealed as the pages are turned. The parade starts with a majorette tossing three batons in the air to form an A, and there is another whose batons look like an M. Virtually each parade figure displays its own letter, whether obvious or not.

The Twelve Circus Rings

A three-ring circus is commonplace fare, but Chwast exploits the chaos of many other rings in this possible homage to Dante's rings of the underworld. As Chwast explains it, the parade starts modestly with a clown and a few animals, and "more figures are added with each new ring until the craziness is seen at the end." Meanwhile, from spread to spread, the reader anticipates in wonder what will next be added to this continuous roundup of great and minor circus acts. Why did Chwast make this book? "The absurdity of the things and people that fill the 12 rings amused me," he says.

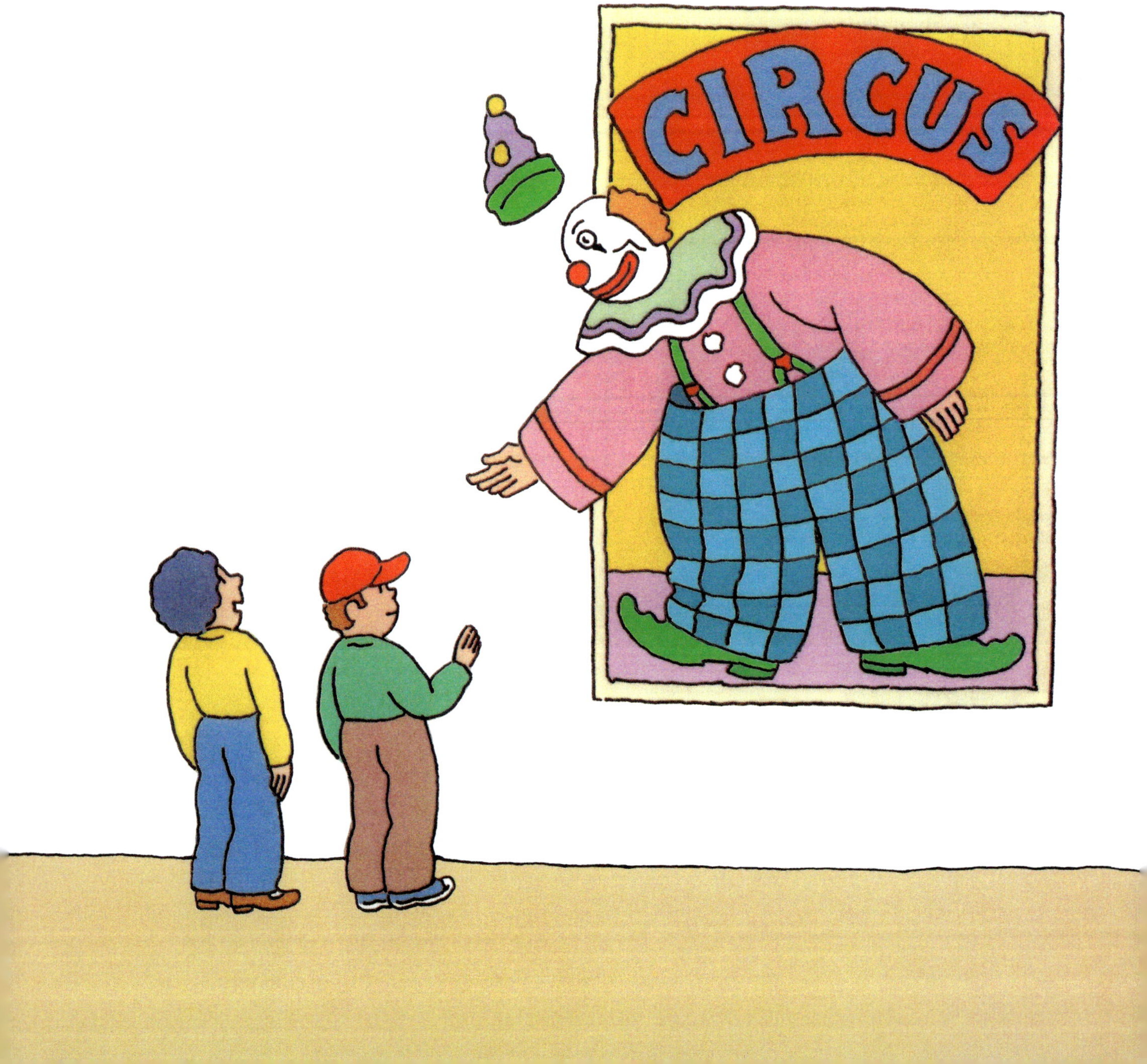

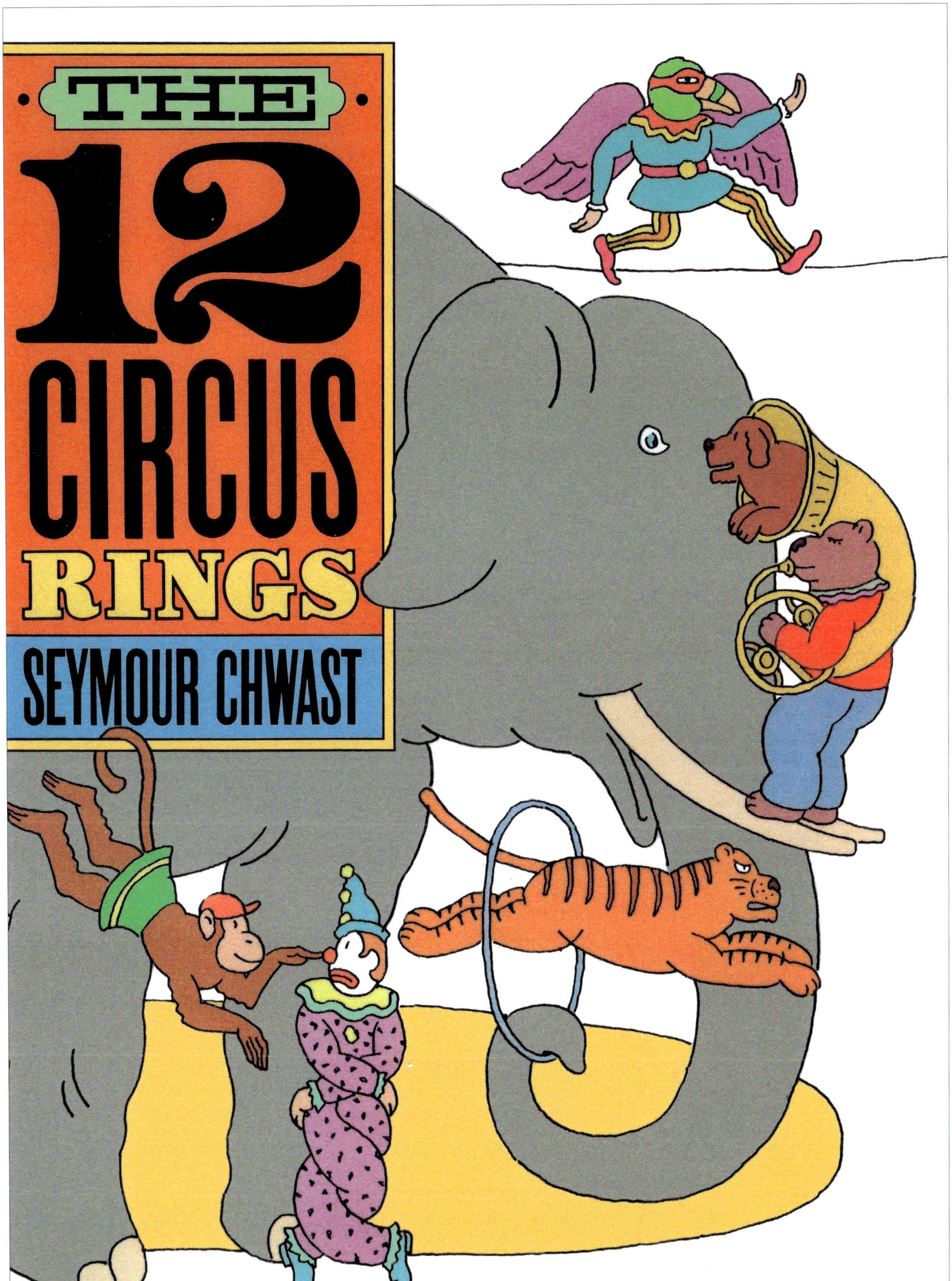

The Twelve Circus Rings, by Seymour Chwast, 1996, 9.5" × 12.75" (24.25 × 32.5 cm), 32 pages.

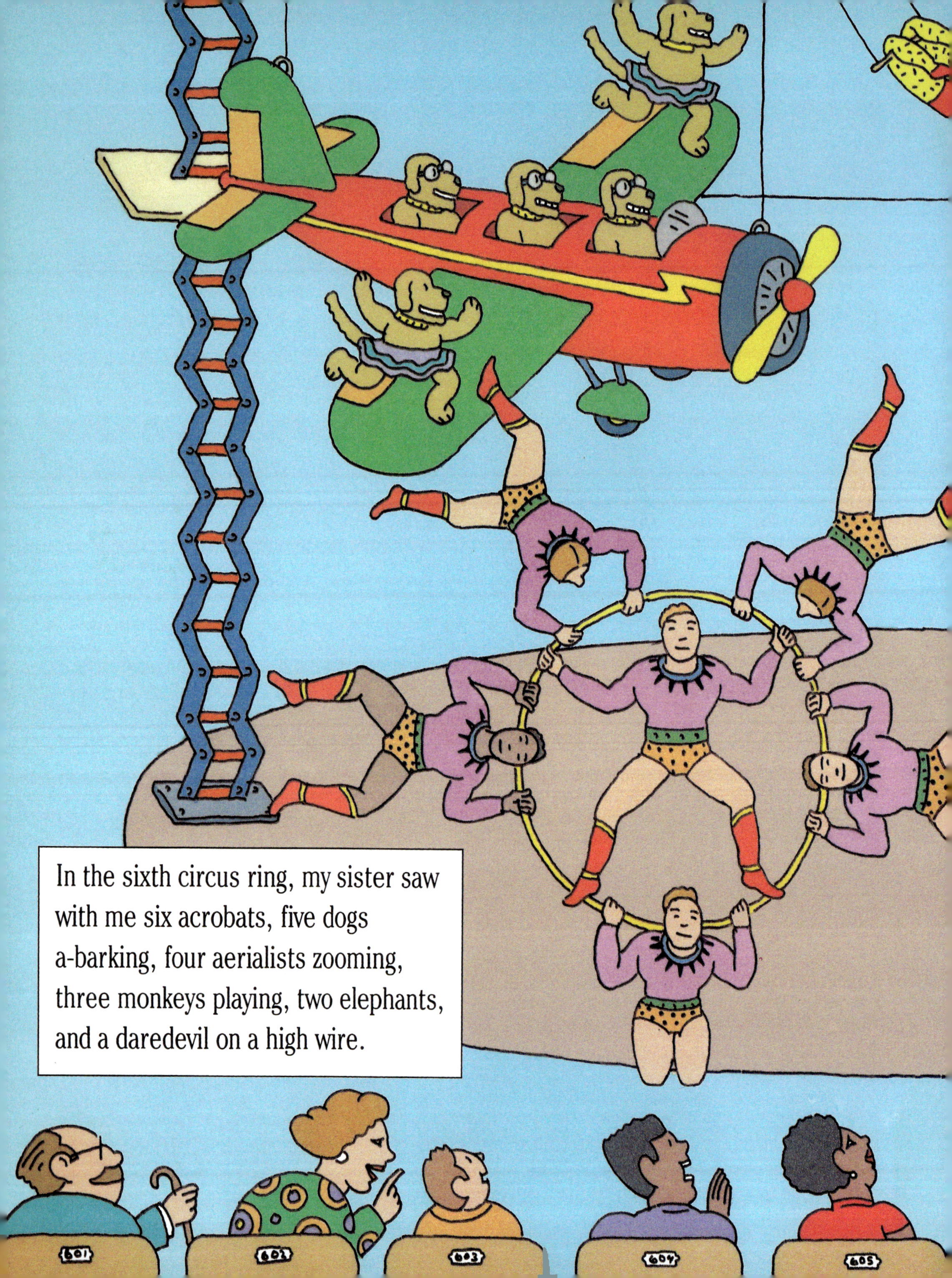

In the sixth circus ring, my sister saw with me six acrobats, five dogs a-barking, four aerialists zooming, three monkeys playing, two elephants, and a daredevil on a high wire.

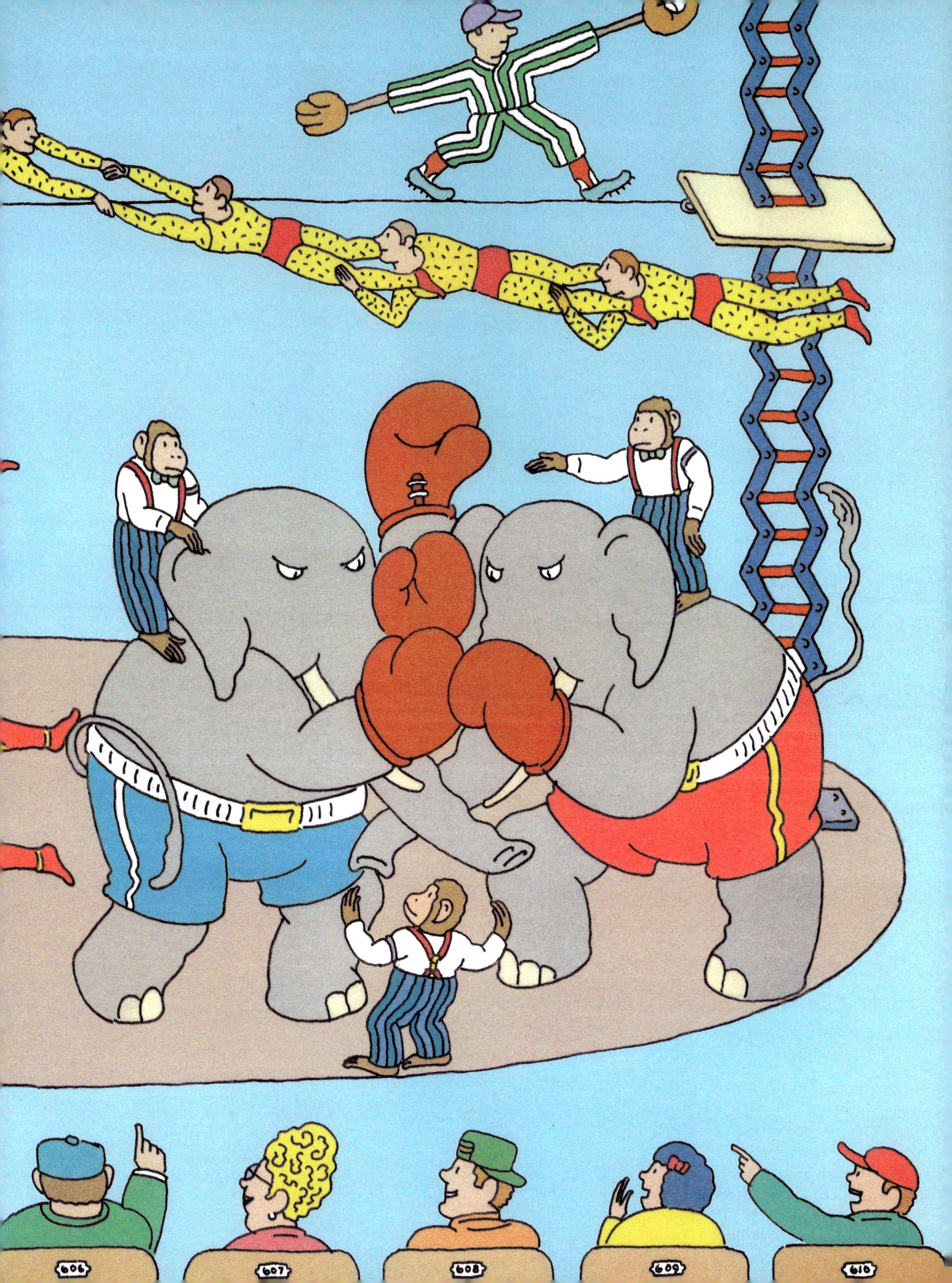
606
607
608
609
610

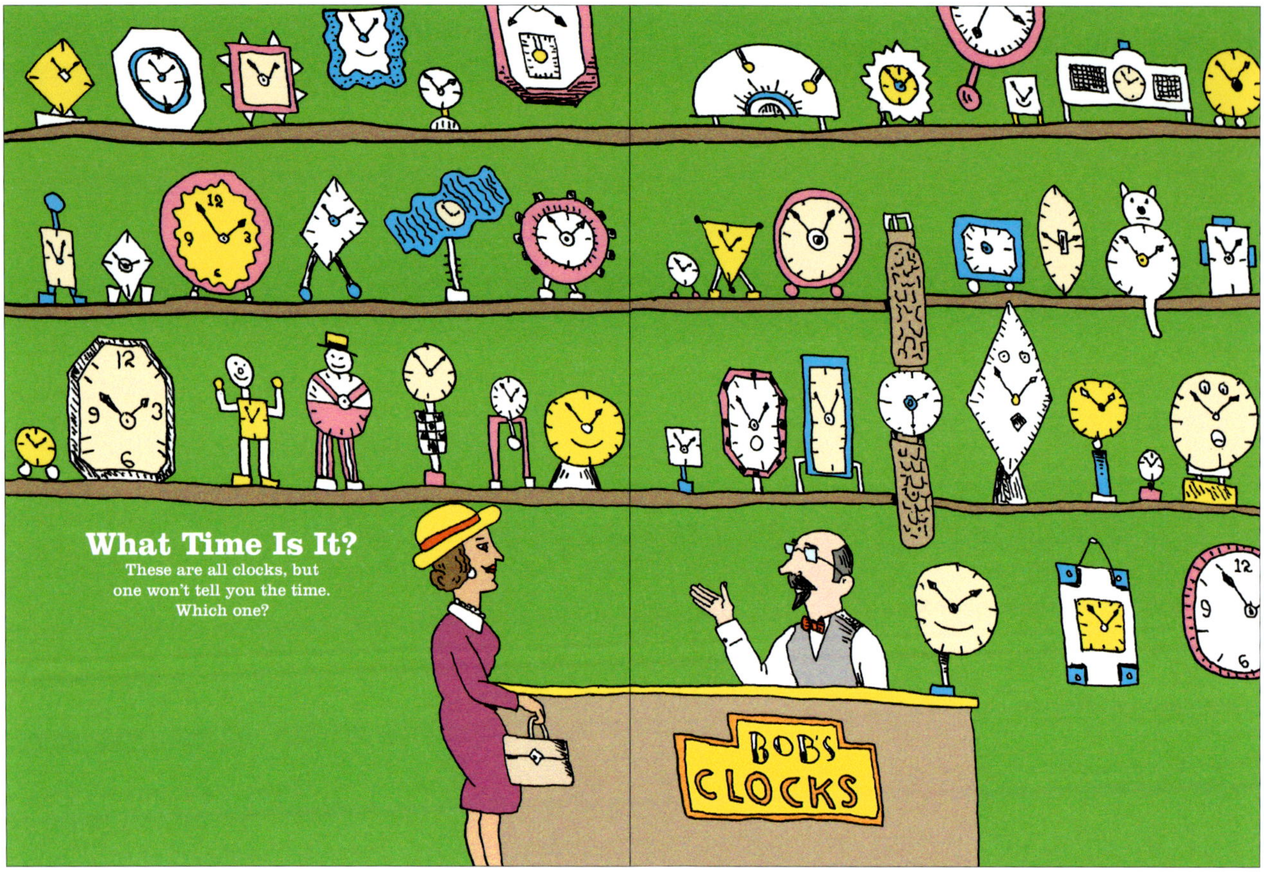

What Time Is It?

These are all clocks, but one won't tell you the time. Which one?

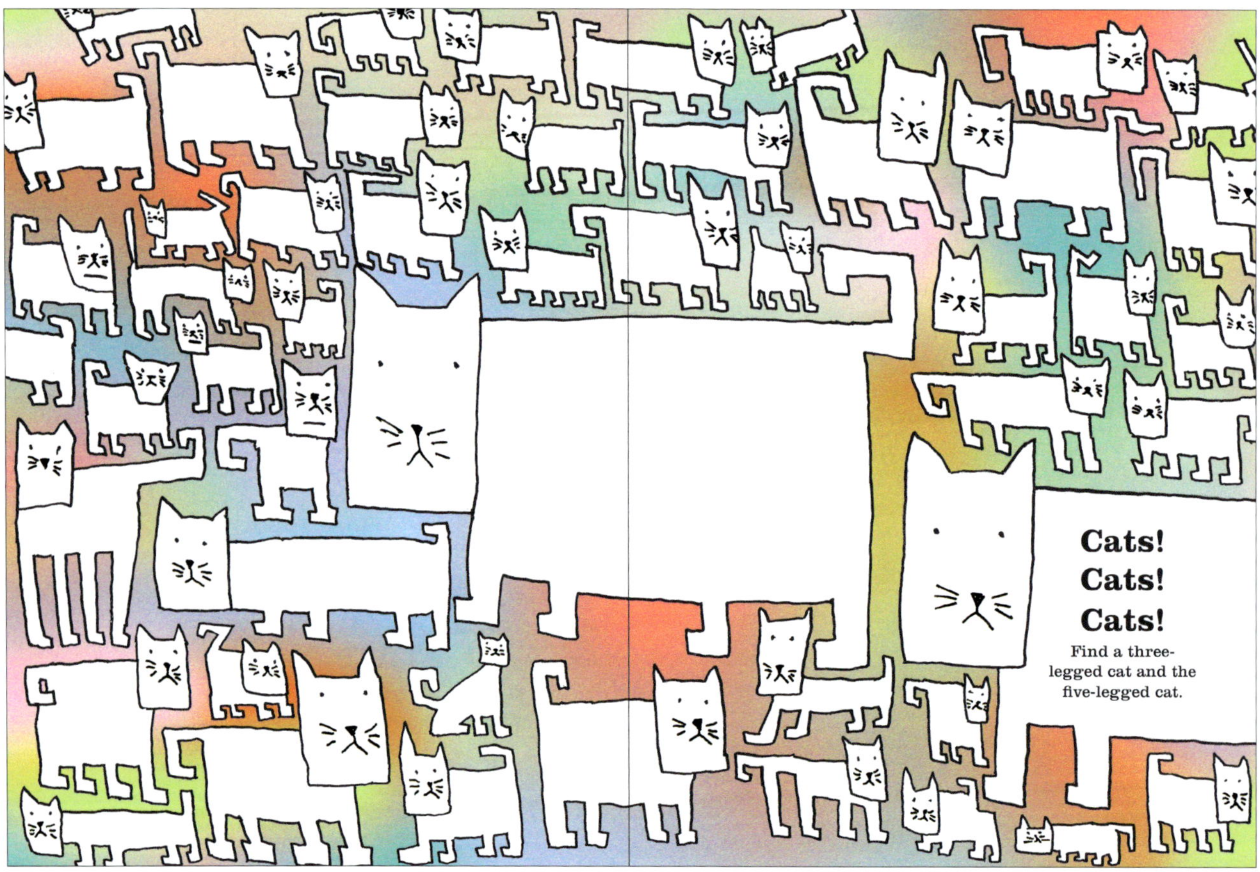

Cats! Cats! Cats!

Find a three-legged cat and the five-legged cat.

Mistakes

"What's wrong with this picture?" is a popular game genre that dates back centuries in graphic art. "What I like about this is that it satisfied my need for visual tricks," Chwast confesses. "I really enjoyed drawing the smiling mouths. I wanted to make a head with an ill-fitting hat as a mistake for the cover." For cat lovers, there's a spread devoted to finding a three-legged and a five-legged cat. At Bob's Clocks, all clocks keep the same time but one. "Another creative part," Chwast adds, "was the mistake with the spelling of the title."

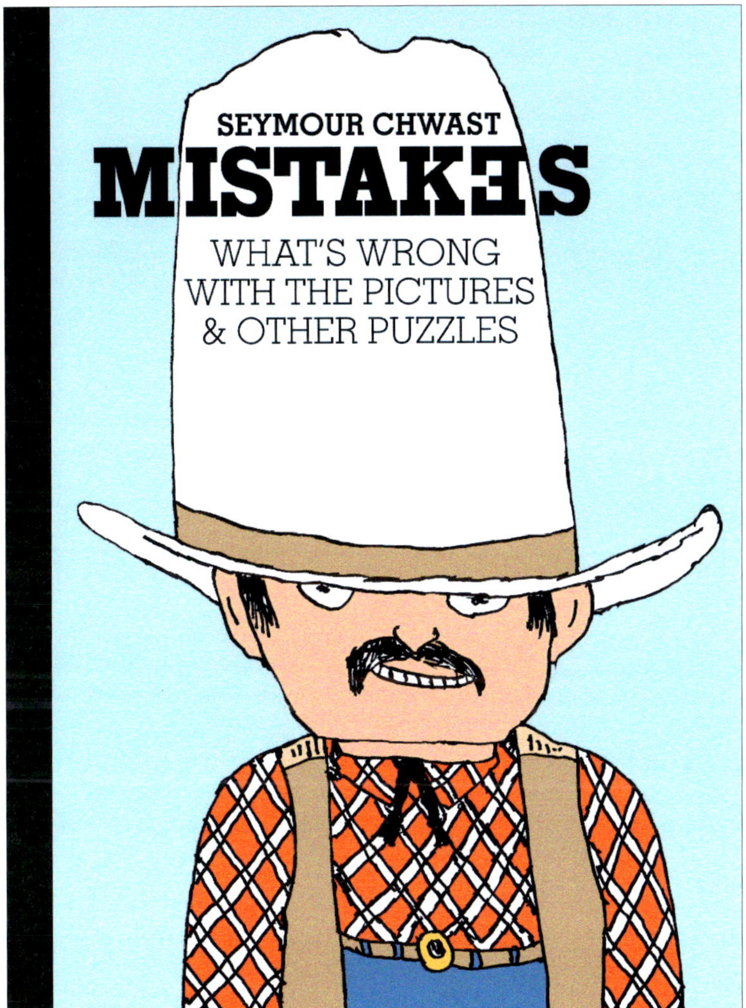

Mistakes: What's Wrong with the Pictures & Other Puzzles, by Seymour Chwast, 2023, 7.74" × 10.2" (19.75 × 26 cm), 40 pages.

MISTAKES
MISTAKES
MISTAKES
MISTAKES
MISTAKES
MISTAKES
MISTAKES

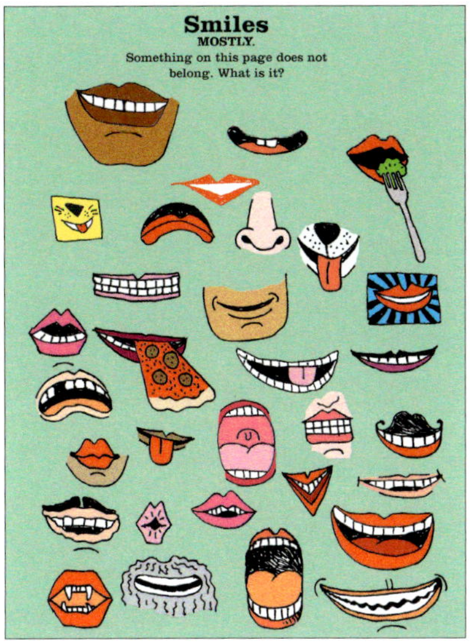
Smiles
MOSTLY.
Something on this page does not belong. What is it?

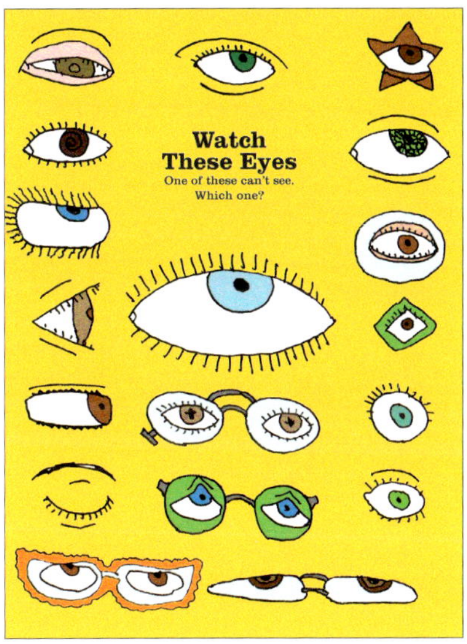
Watch These Eyes
One of these can't see. Which one?

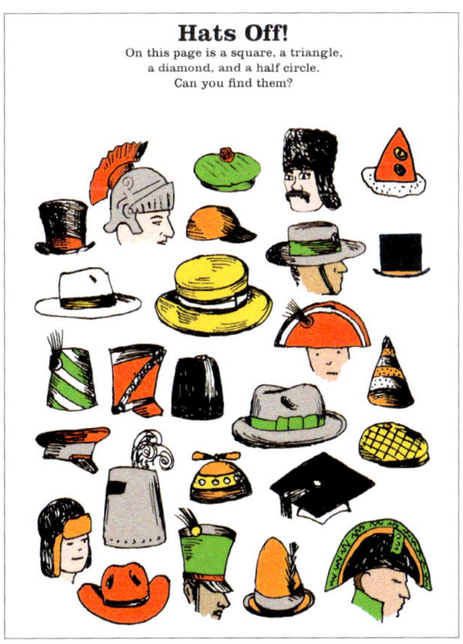
Hats Off!
On this page is a square, a triangle, a diamond, and a half circle. Can you find them?

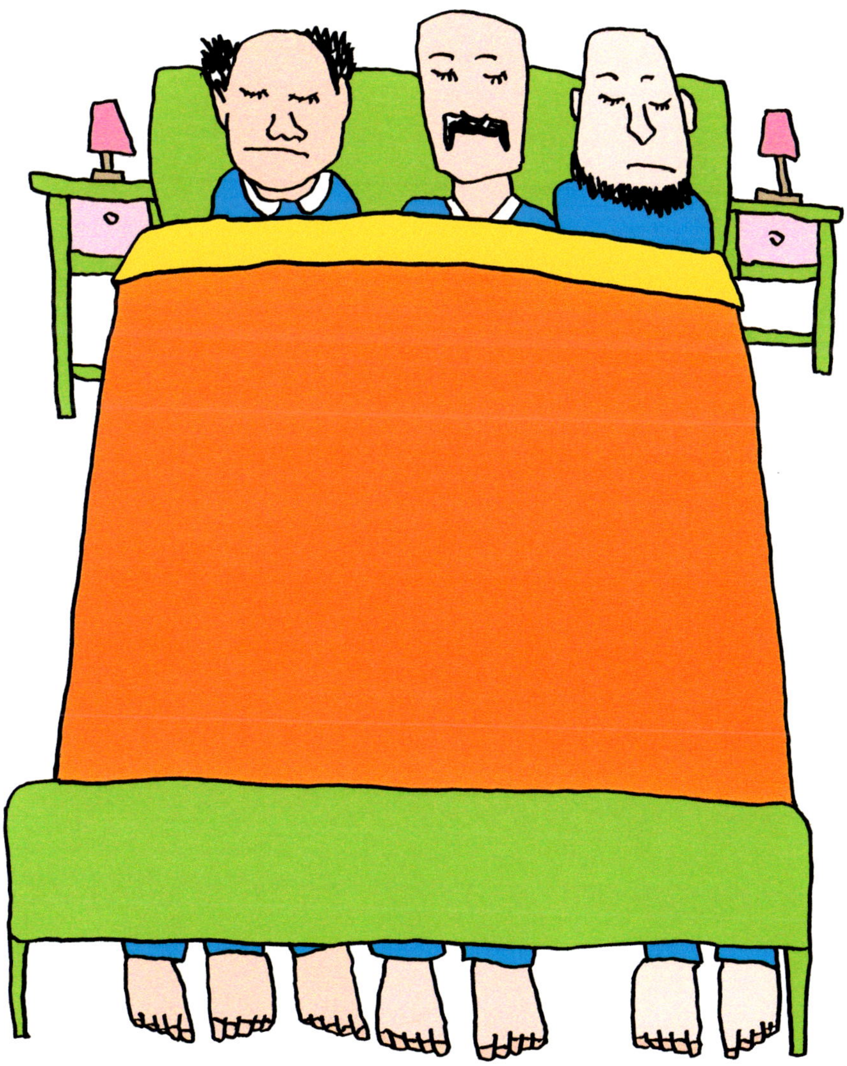

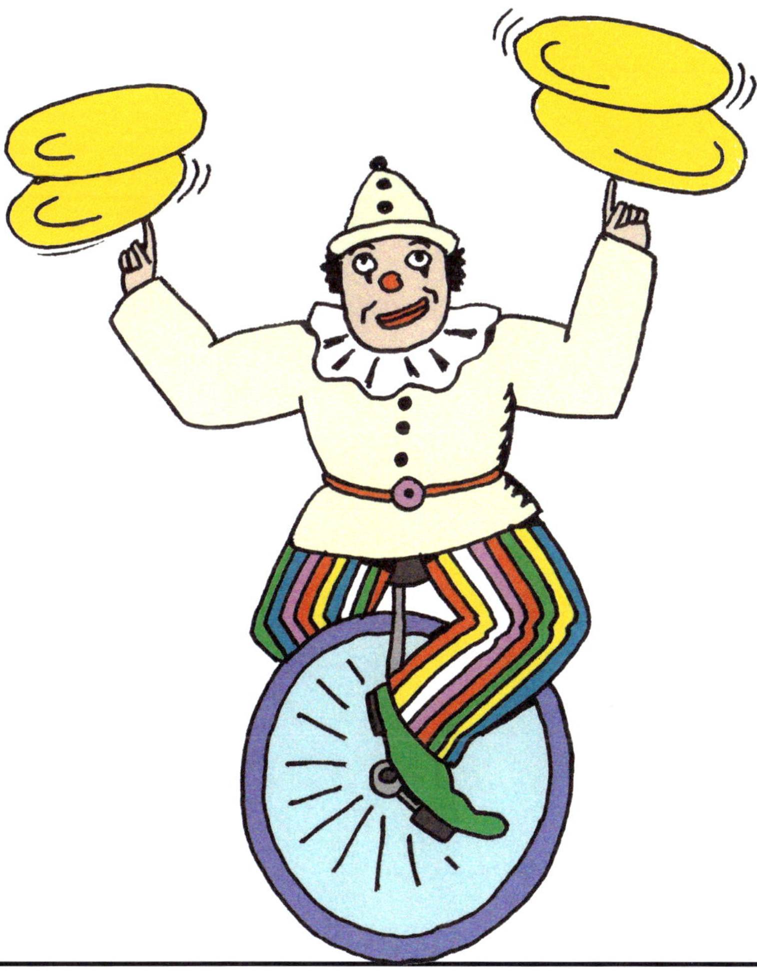

Tall City, Wide Country

What came first, the tall city or the wide country? Whichever it was, the idea to do a book that offers two physical perspectives is what drives these delightful tableaux. "I like the idea of turning a book into a toy," says Chwast. He rightly assumes the young reader will, too. This book reads from forwards or backwards. "The problem," he admits, "was finding horizontal things for the country and vertical things for the city."

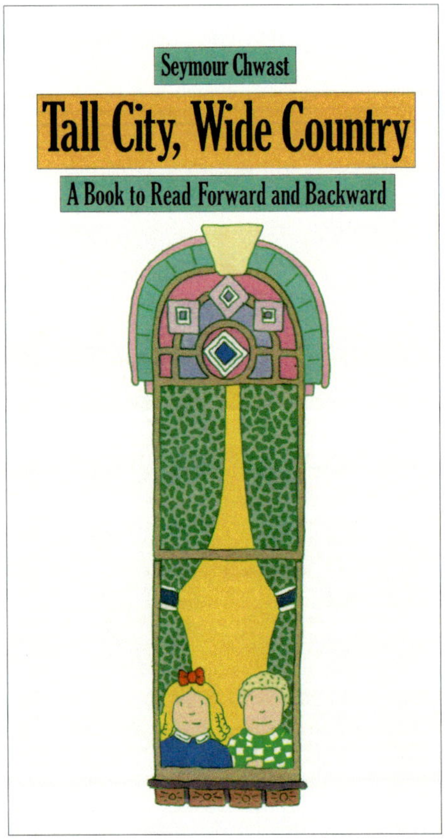

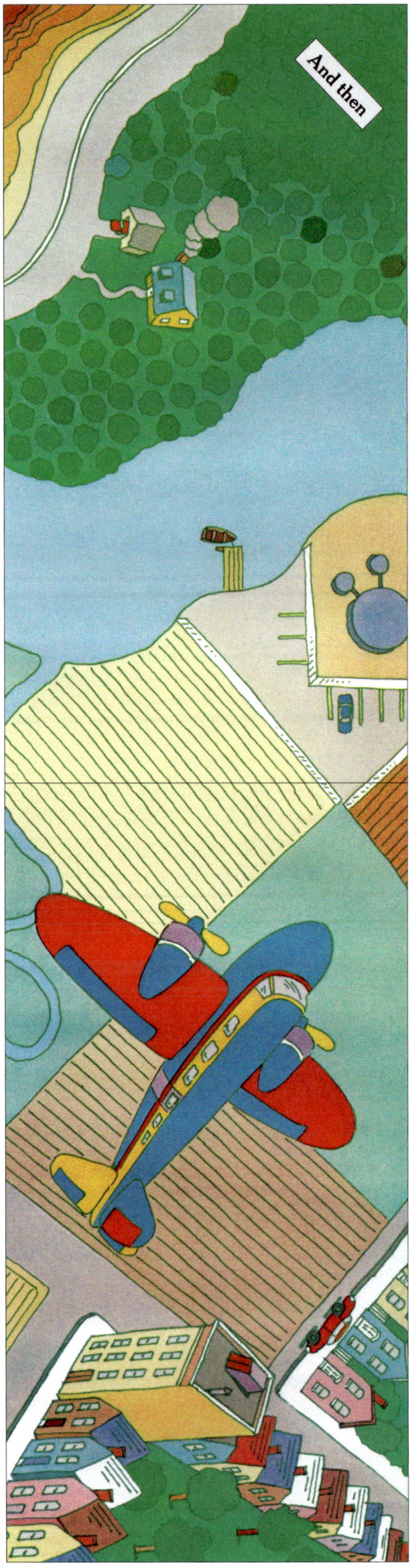

Tall City, Wide Country, by Seymour Chwast, first edition 1983, second edition 2013, 6.25" × 11.25" (16 × 28.5 cm), 32 pages.

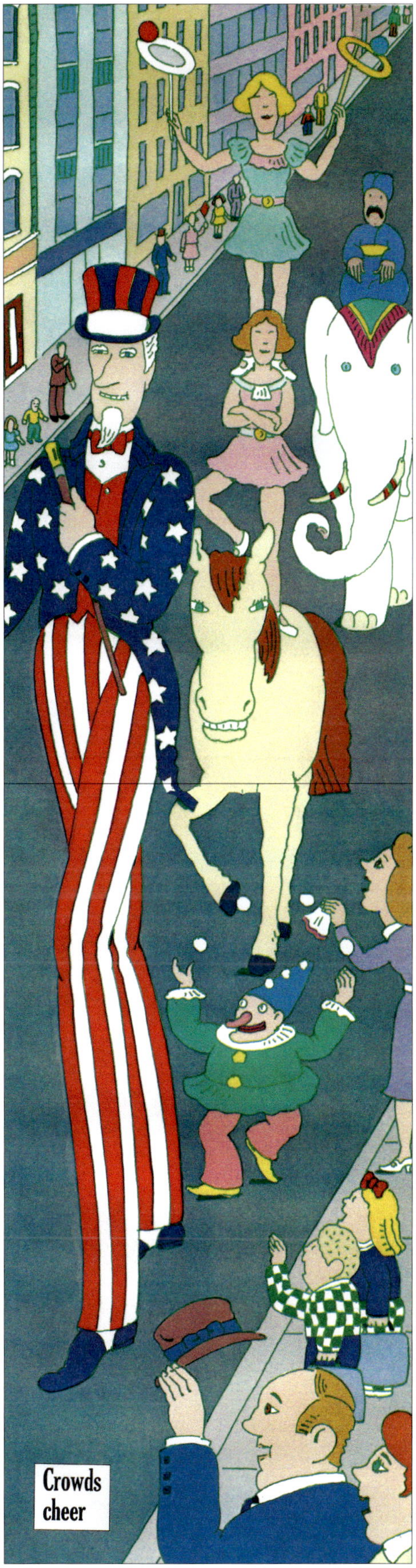
Crowds cheer

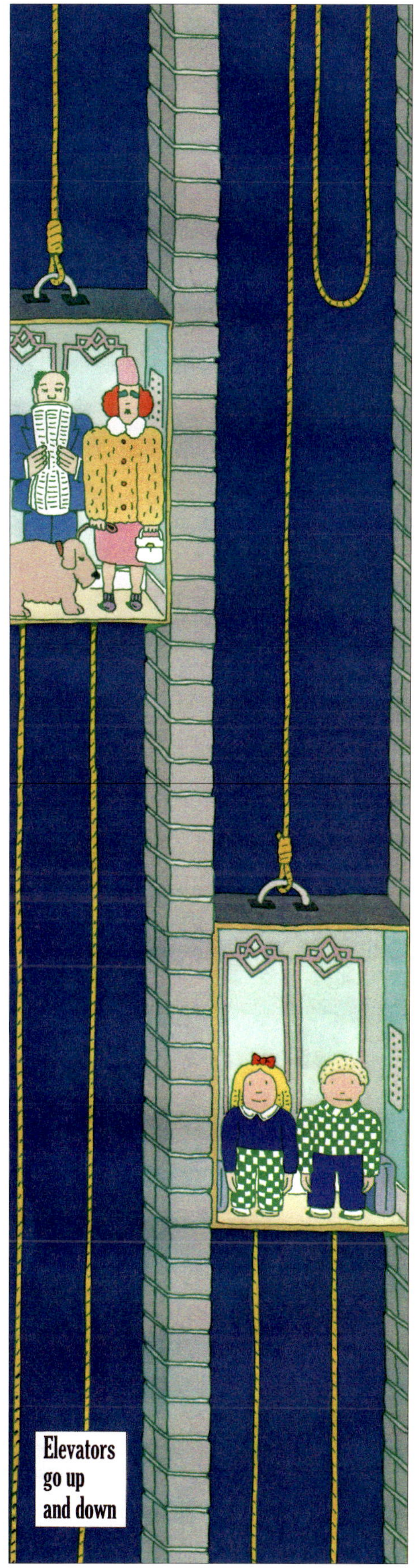
Elevators go up and down

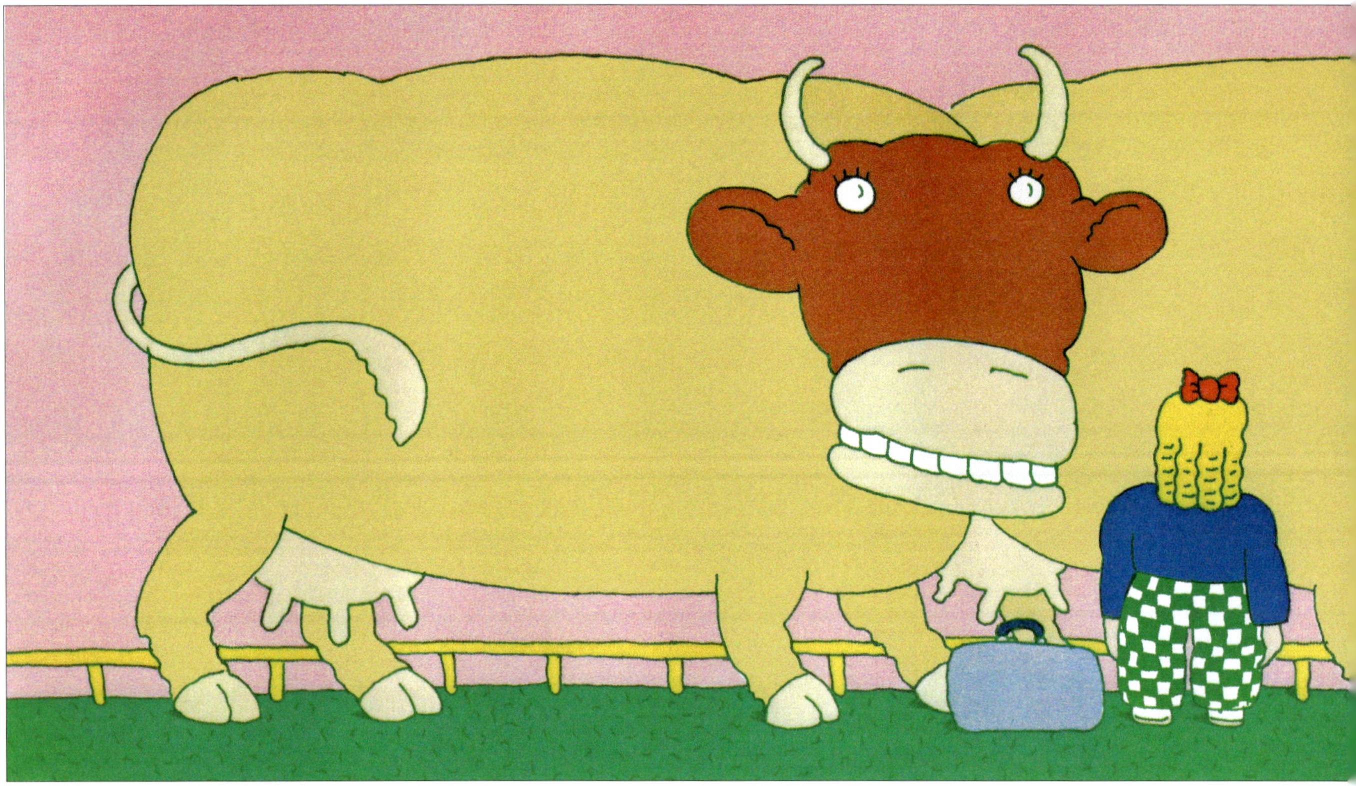

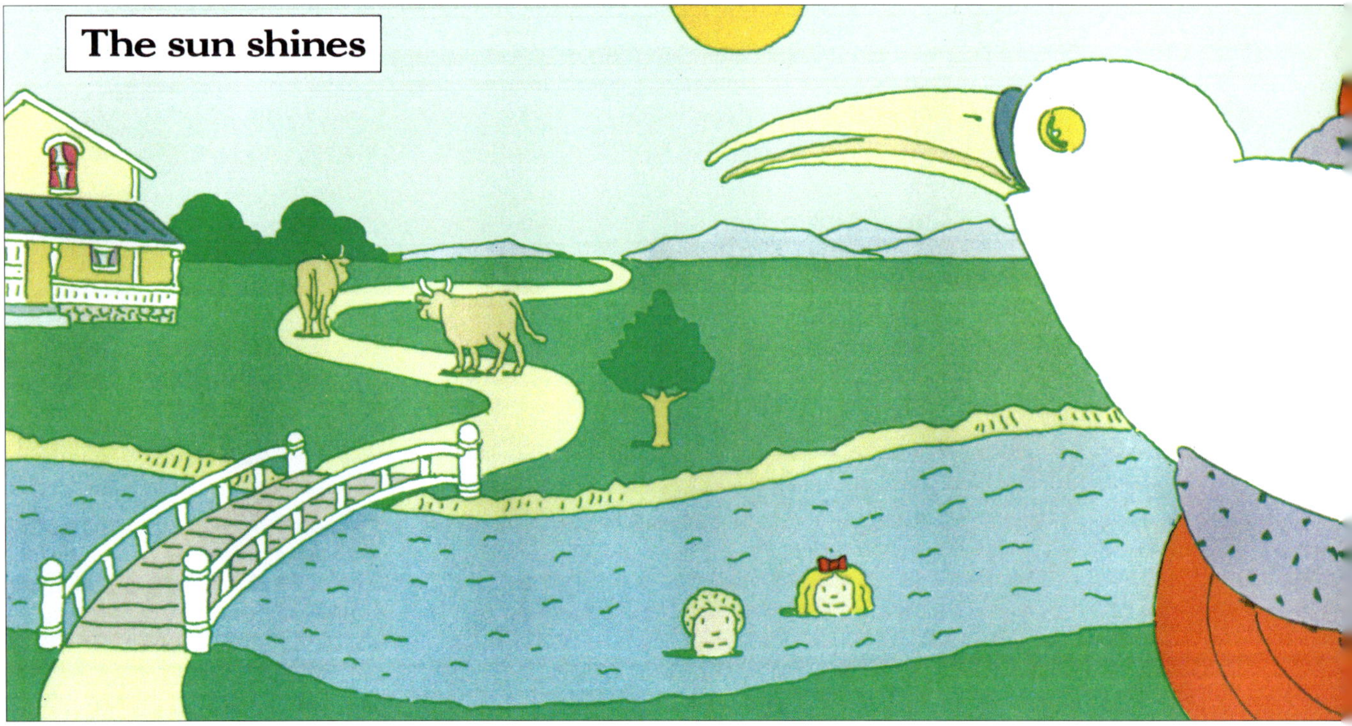
The sun shines

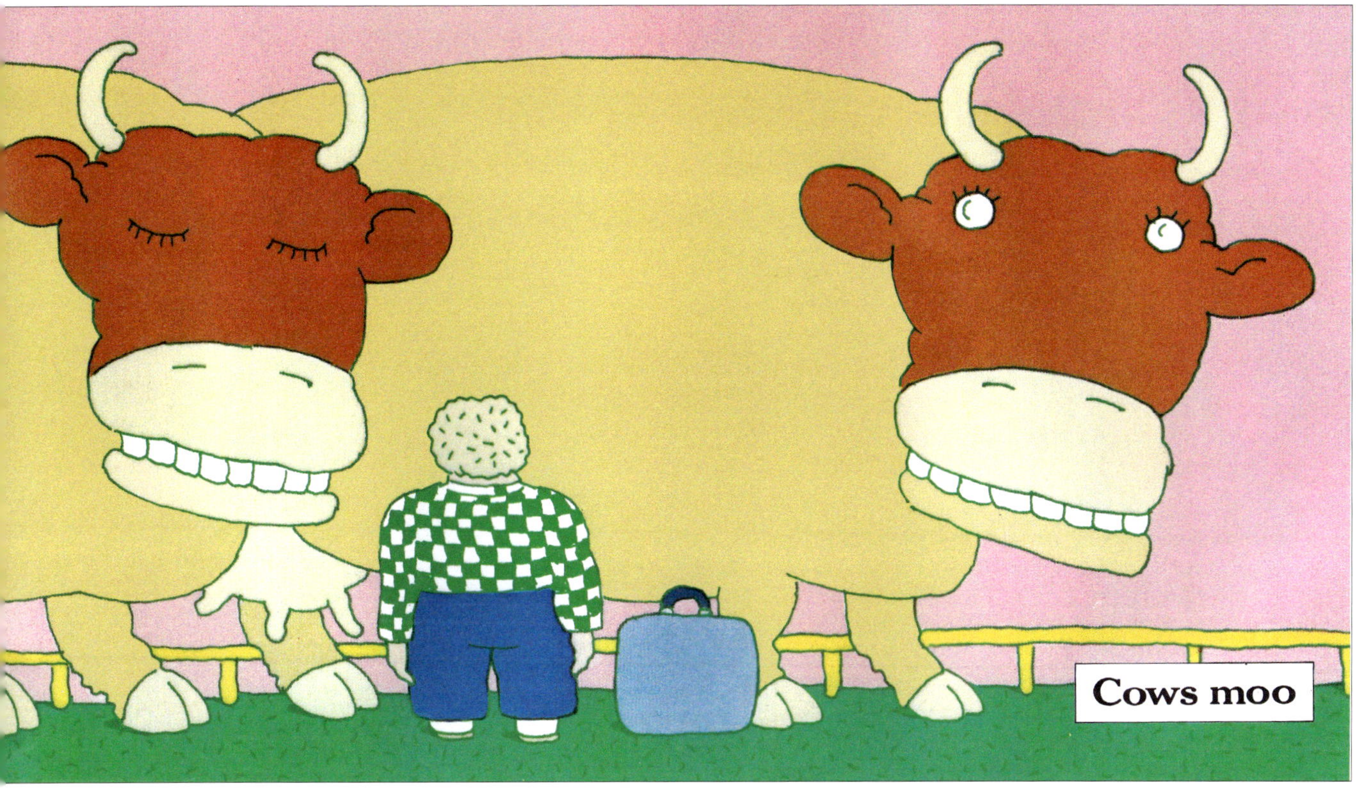
Cows moo

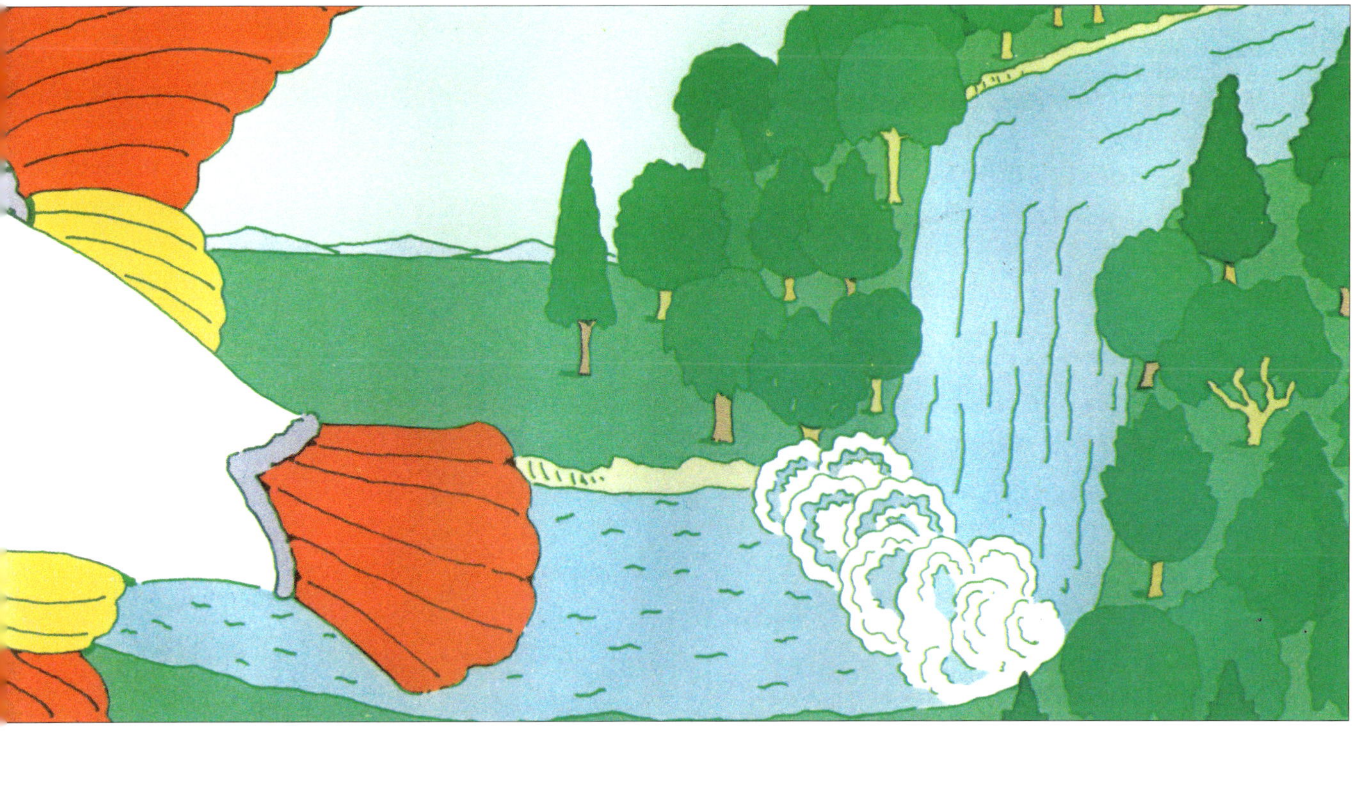

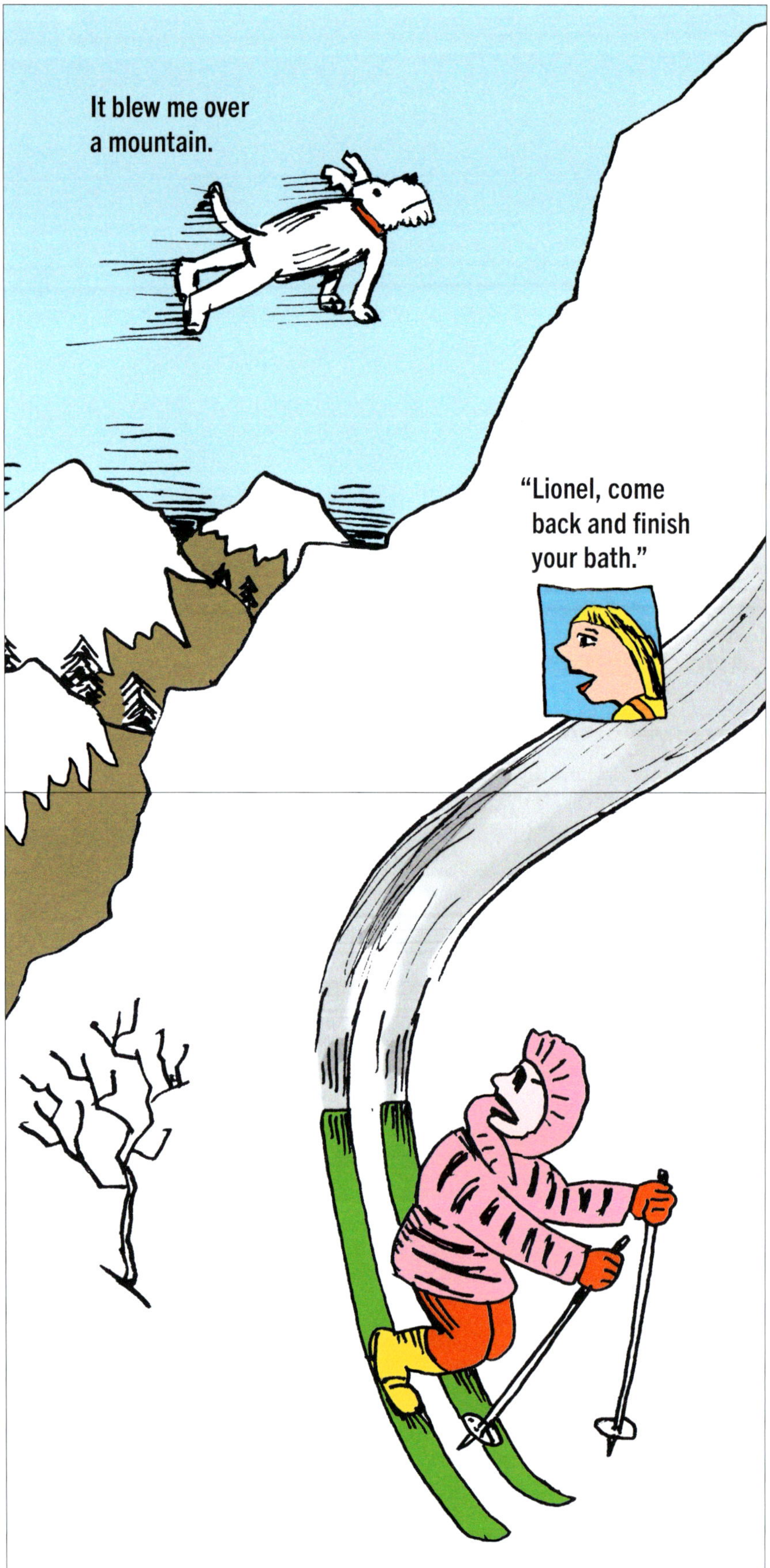
It blew me over
a mountain.
"Lionel, come
back and finish
your bath."

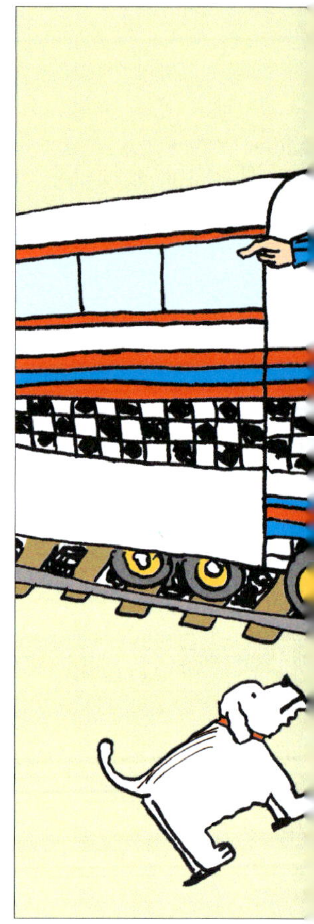

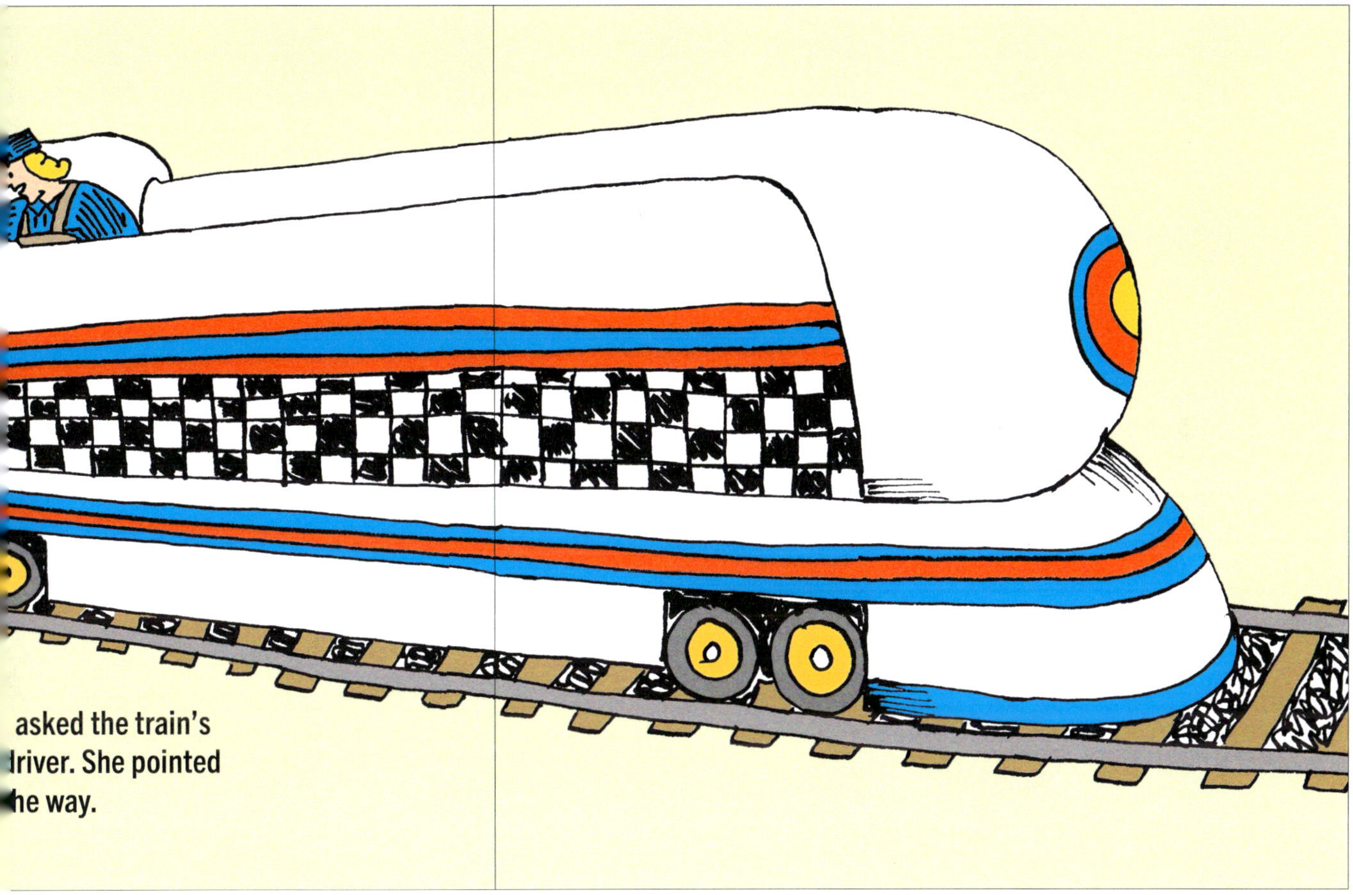

Going Home

Going Home, by Seymour Chwast, 2023, 6.25" × 6.25" (16 × 16 cm), 40 pages.

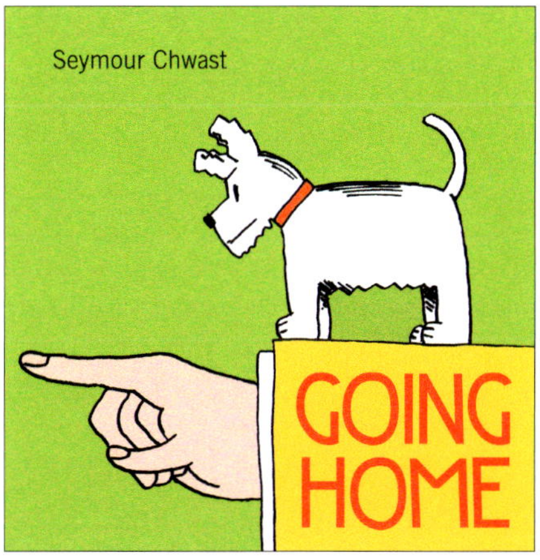

The cover of *Going Home* suggests that this is going to be a simple story for young tots. However, as it unfolds, the book's pages become populated by some of Chwast's favorite characters—a pilot, drum major, cowgirl, motorcyclist, and more. A hippo and cows, among other animals, come to play, too. And the pièce de résistance is a streamline locomotive with a woman engineer. This is *also* a toy. "It's a book that you have to turn around twice in order to read it, so it's interactive for the children," Chwast notes. But most importantly, it is a story about Lionel, a homesick dog who returns home with the help of the new friends he meets along his journey.

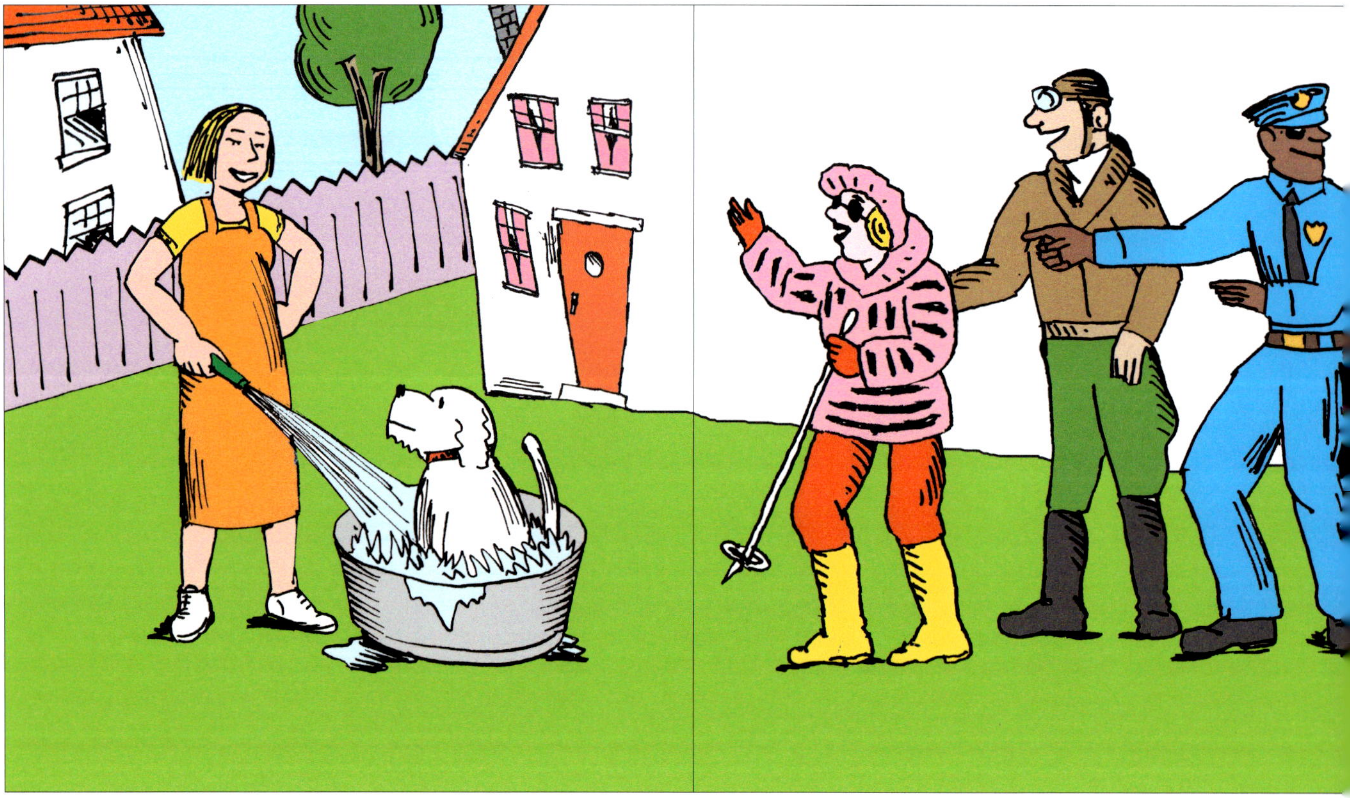

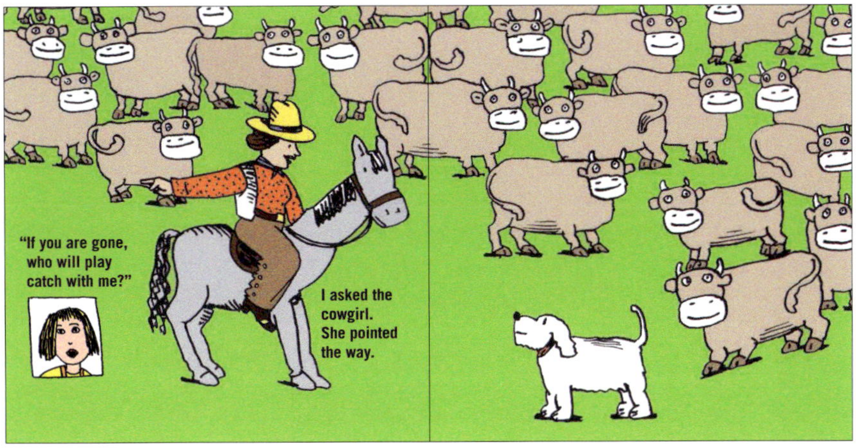
"If you are gone,
who will play
catch with me?"
I asked the
cowgirl.
She pointed
the way.

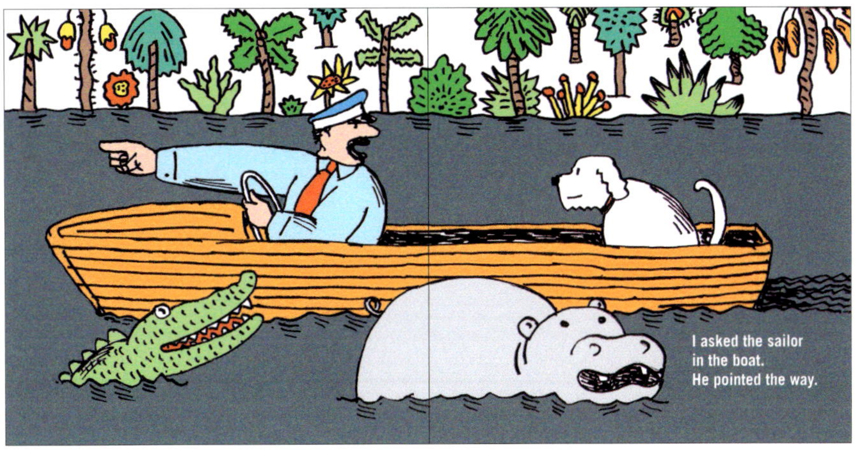
I asked the sailor
in the boat.
He pointed the way.

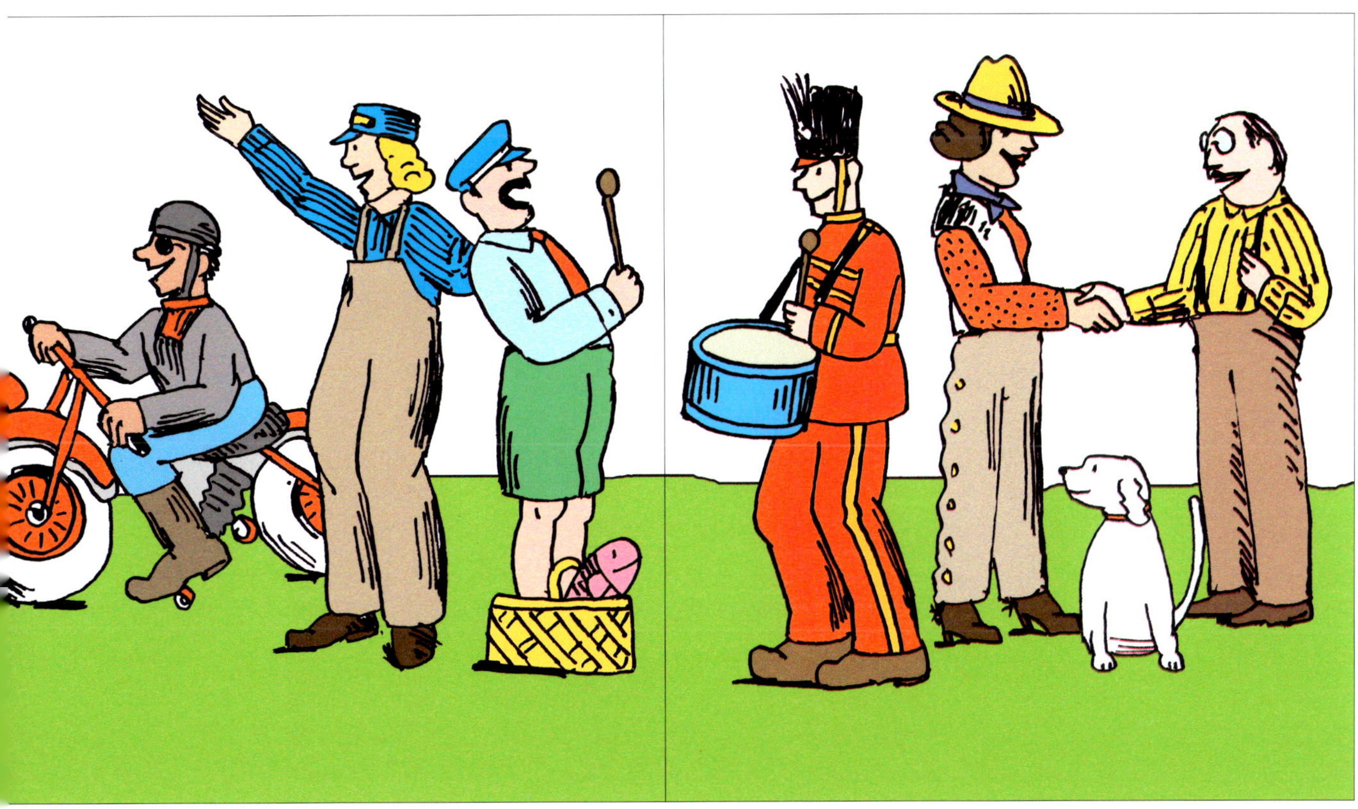

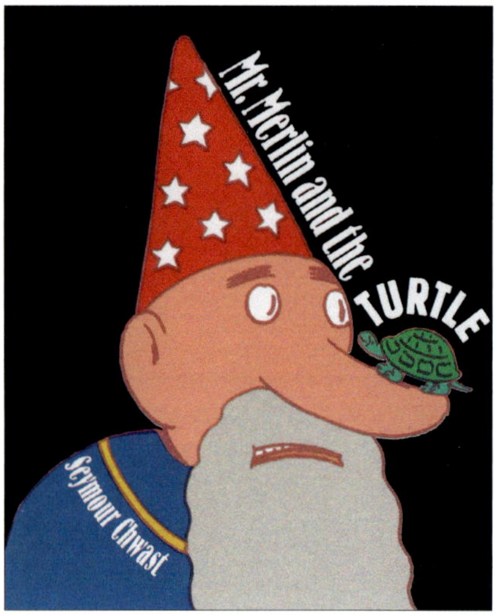

Mr. Merlin and the Turtle, by Seymour Chwast, 1996, 8" × 9.75" (20.25 × 24.75 cm), 24 pages.

Mr. Merlin and the Turtle

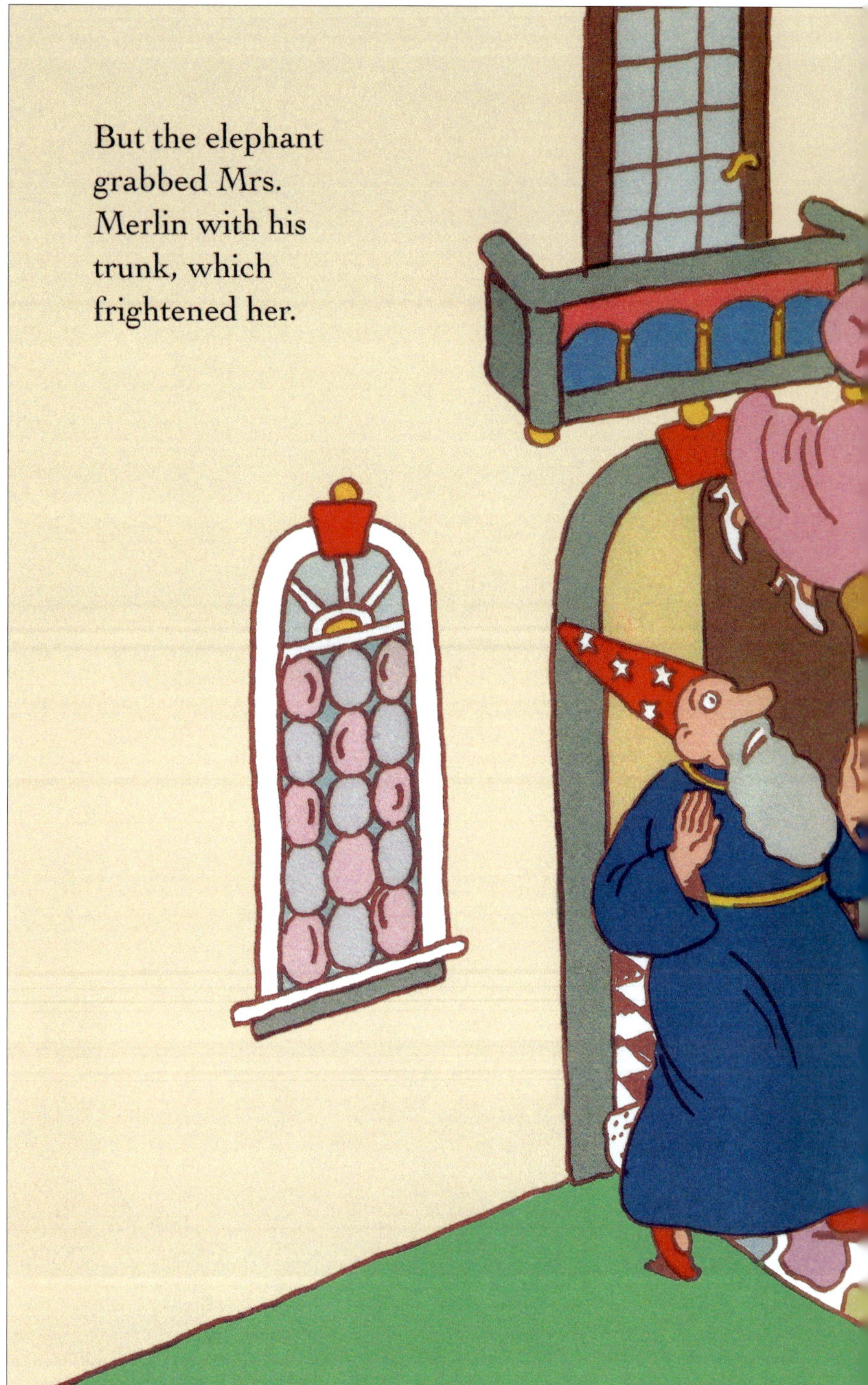

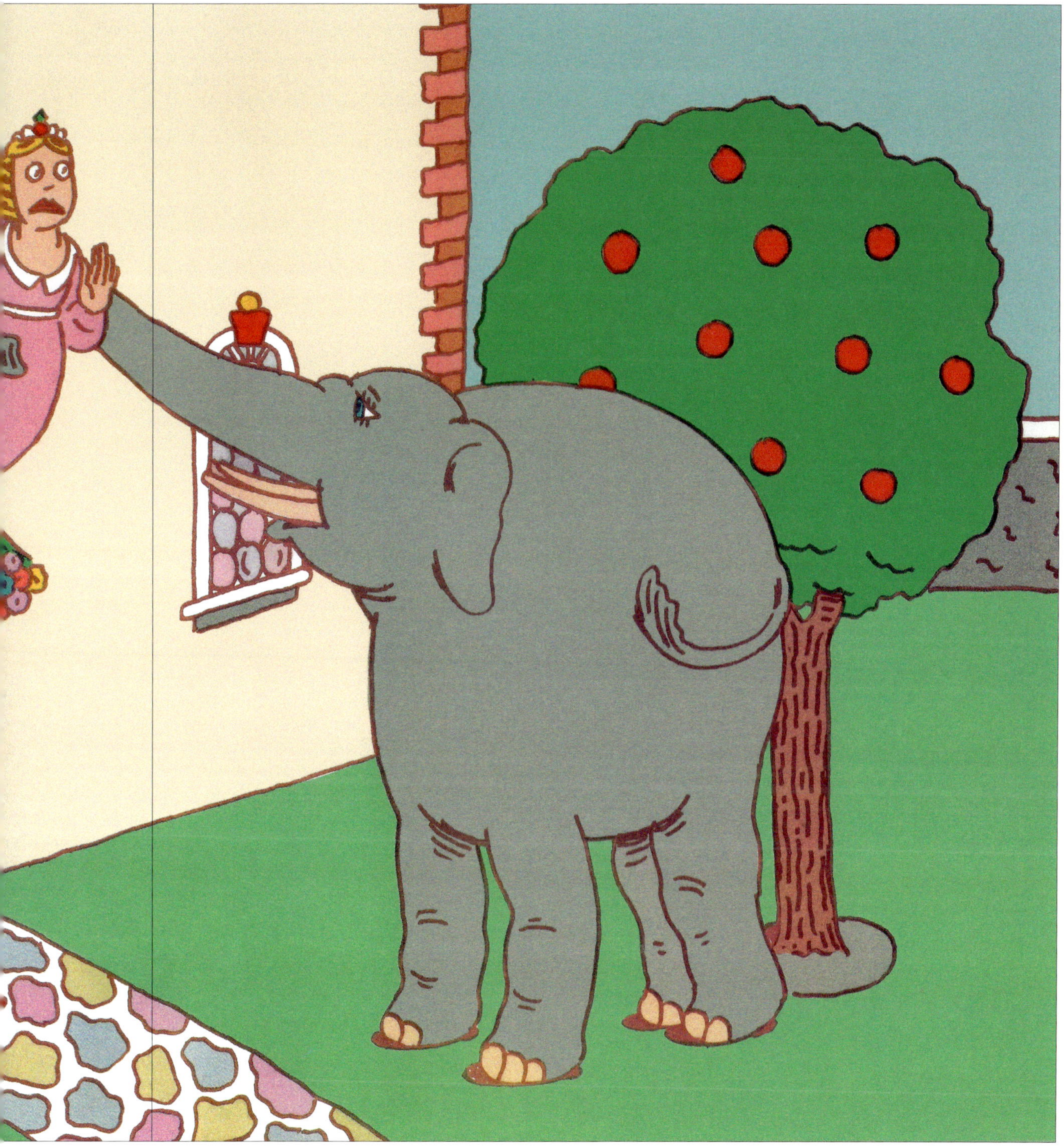

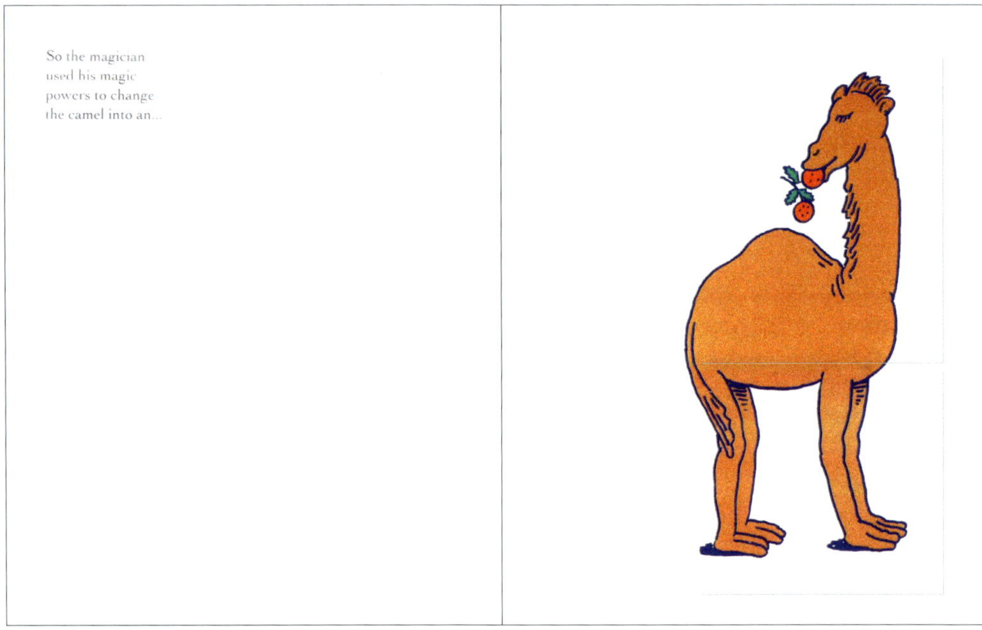

Step One: Flaps are closed.

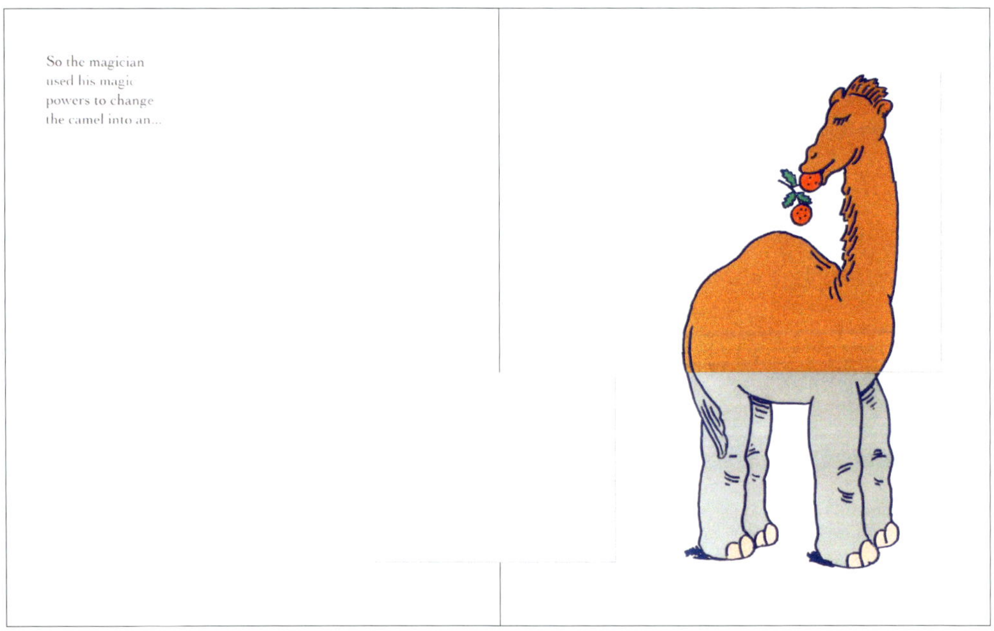

Step Two: The first flap opens.

Chwast attests that there is never too much paper engineering in books. For him, paper is the most malleable material for telling stories—and this book proves him right. With *Mr. Merlin and the Turtle,* the basic idea is "...that with folding ordinary paper you can completely change the subjects." By having a book with ever-decreasing pages folding over and atop each other, a camel could be transformed into an elephant. The artist is not limited by the dimensions of the book. And that's the challenge and joy of it, too.

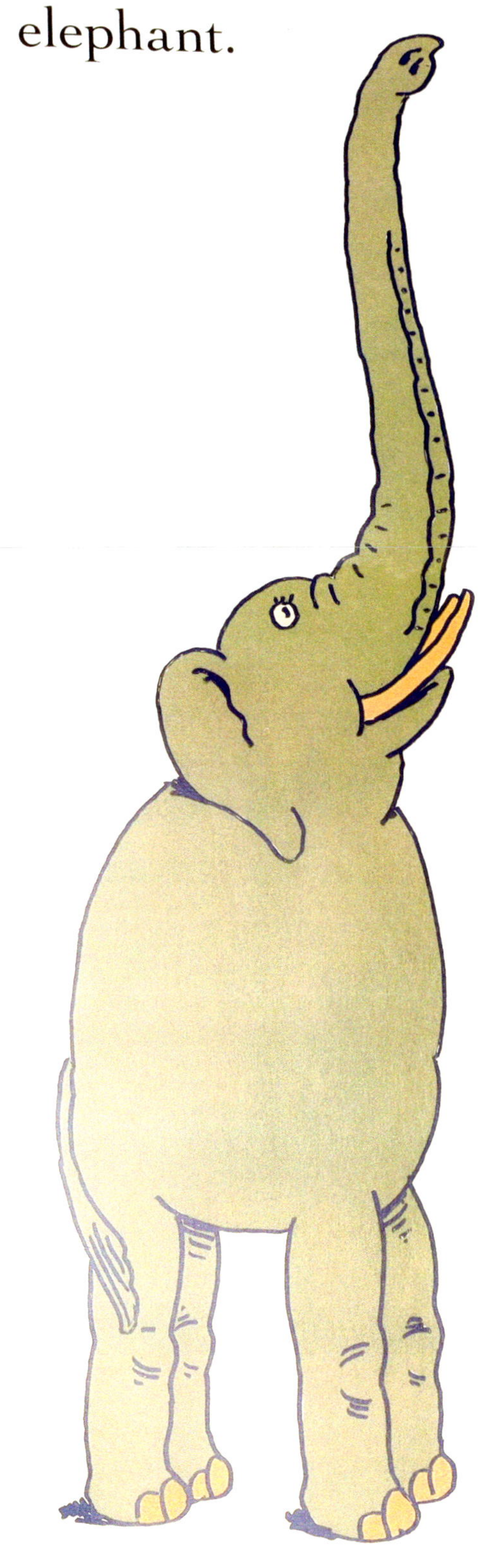

Step Three:
We see the full
transformation

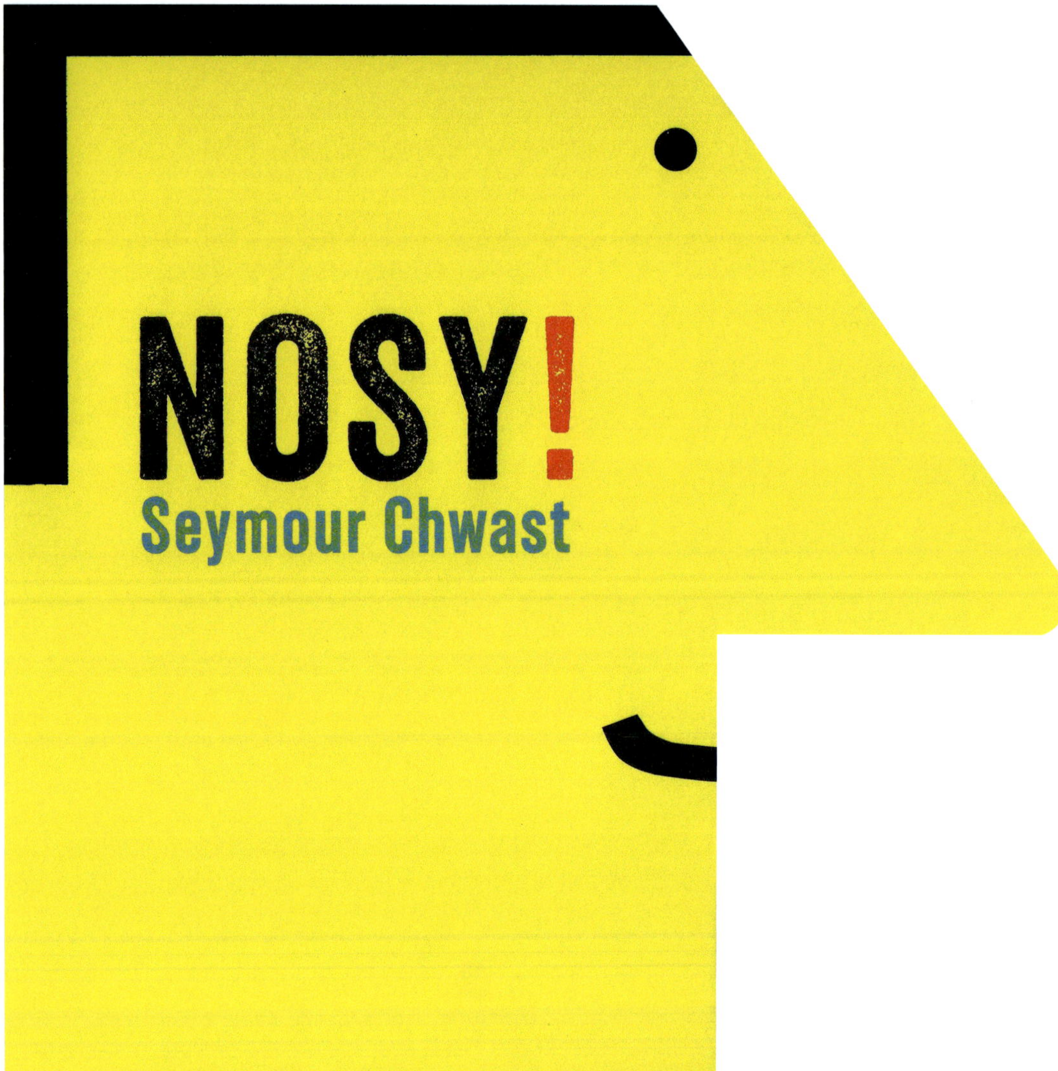

Nosy, by Seymour Chwast, 2025,
7" × 7.2" (17.75 × 18.25 cm), 22 pages.

Nosy

This is a "board book," the cover of which is made by hard cardboard, cut in the shape of a nose, and designed to celebrate a common anatomical feature. It is high on the list of Chwast's favorite picture books because the entire book-as-object is cut out in the shape of a face with a long protruding snout. Although Chwast's own nose is of average length, he uses this volume to assert that all noses, aside from being functional, are beautiful. His illustrations riff on the shapes of various animal noses and non-noses, like a bird's beak—which may not strictly be a nose, but does have nostrils.. He ends by telling the young (and old) reader to love his or her own nose. After all, he wisely notes, "It's yours!"

Birds do not have long or short noses.

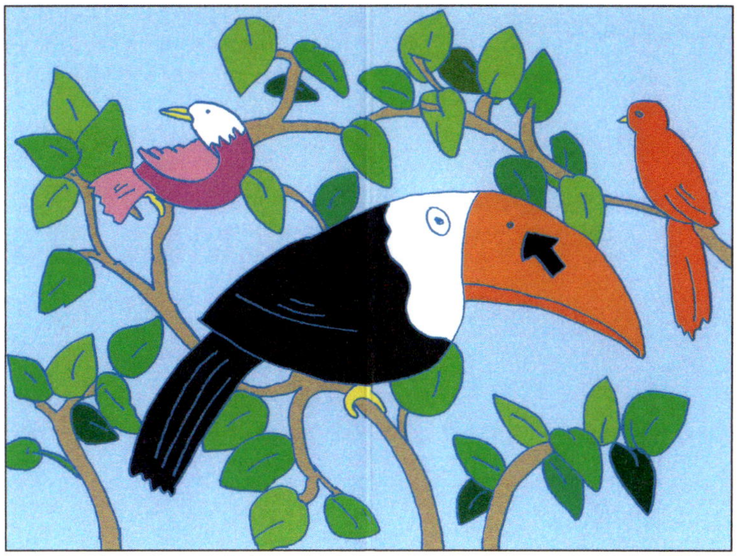

But they do have nostrils in their beaks.

Is your nose as long as a proboscis monkey's?

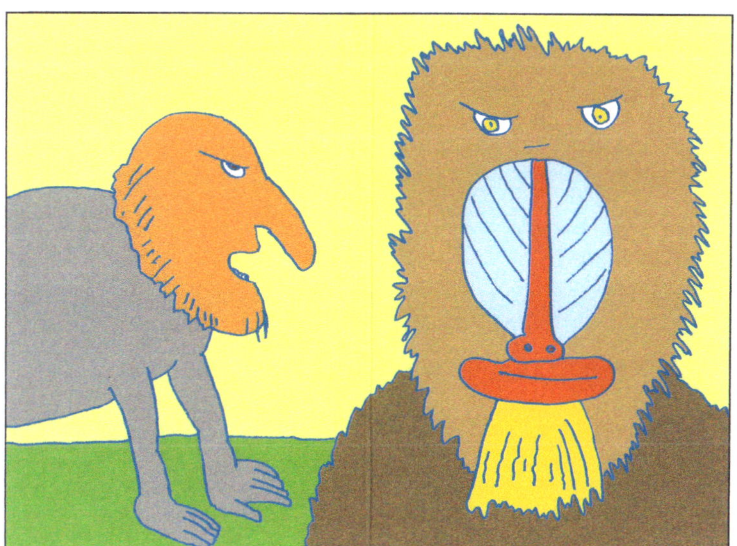

Is it as red as a mandrill's?

Noses smell
good things

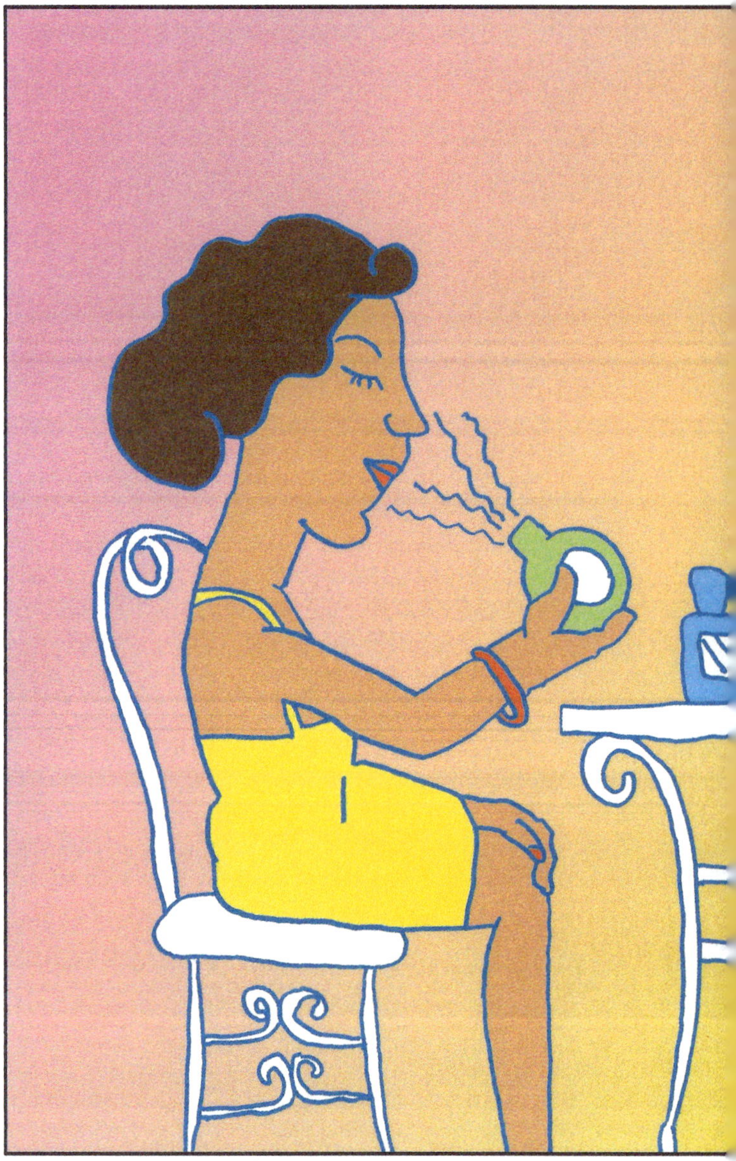

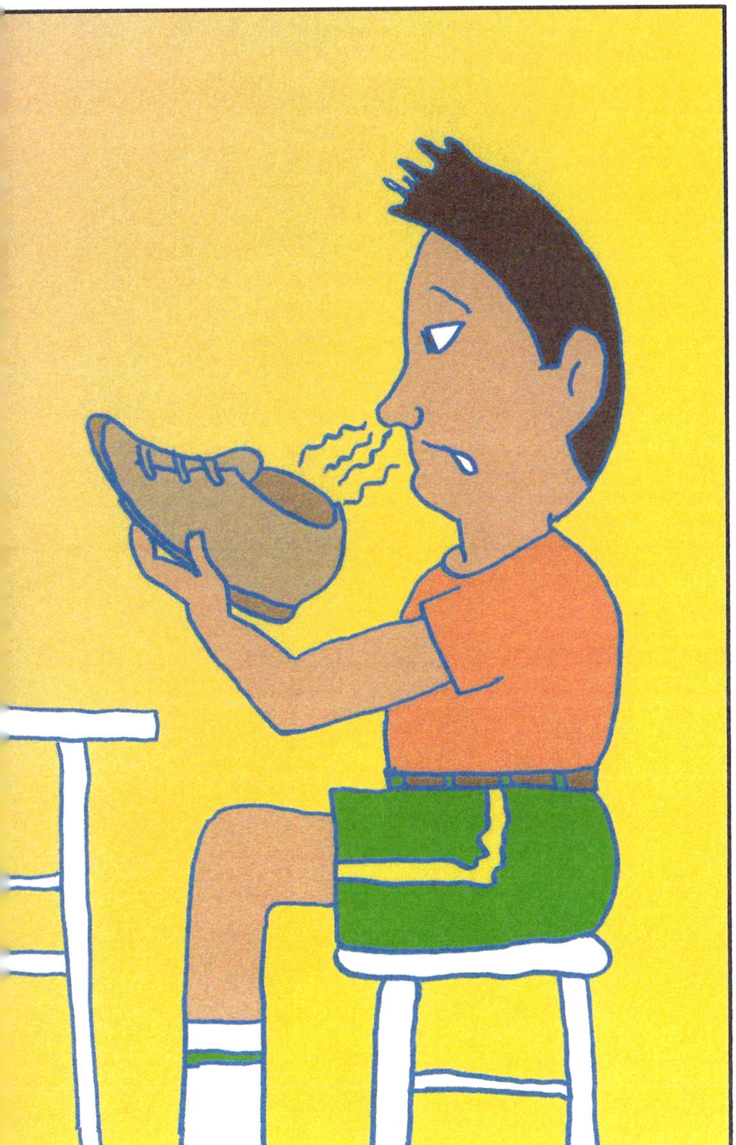

… and bad
things, too.

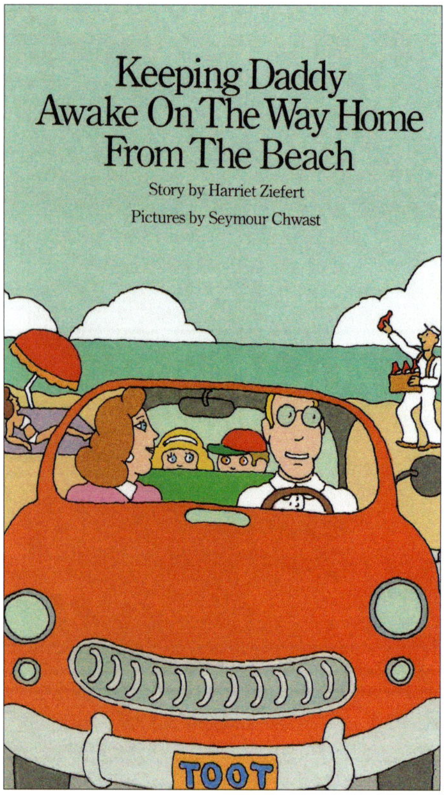

Keeping Daddy Awake On The Way Home From The Beach, by Harriet Ziefert, illustrated by Seymour Chwast, 1986, 6" × 10.25" (15.25 × 26 cm), 23 pages, folding out.

Keeping Daddy Awake On The Way Home From The Beach

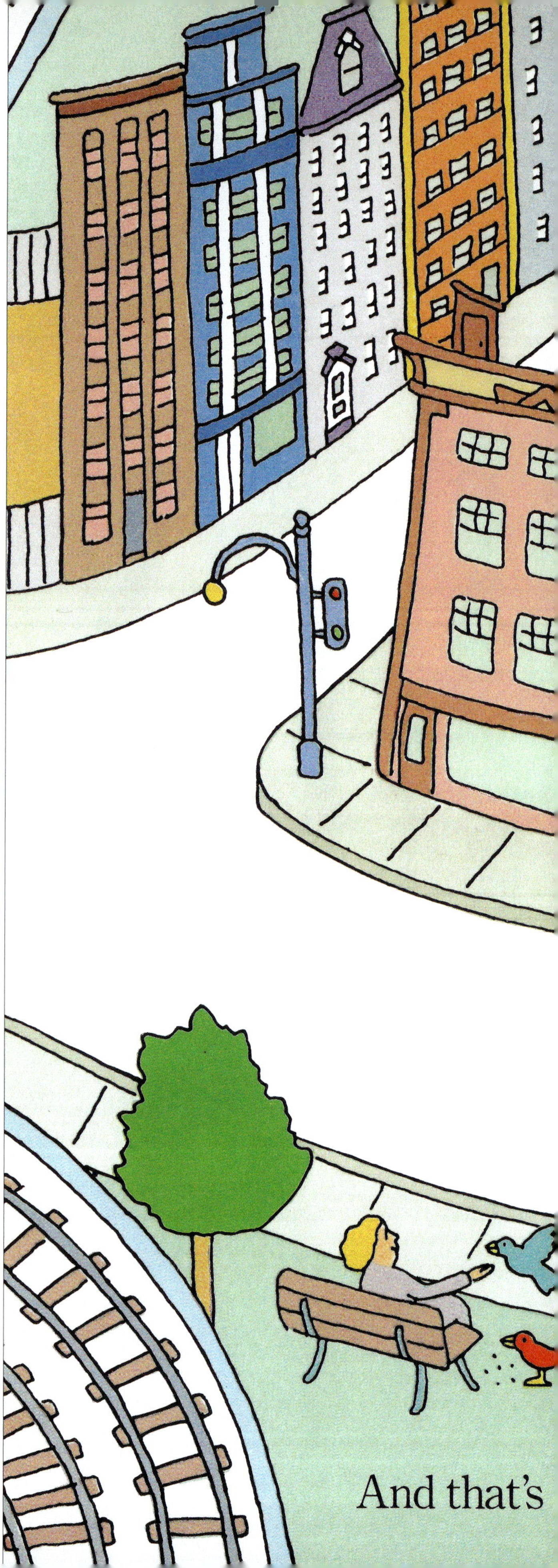

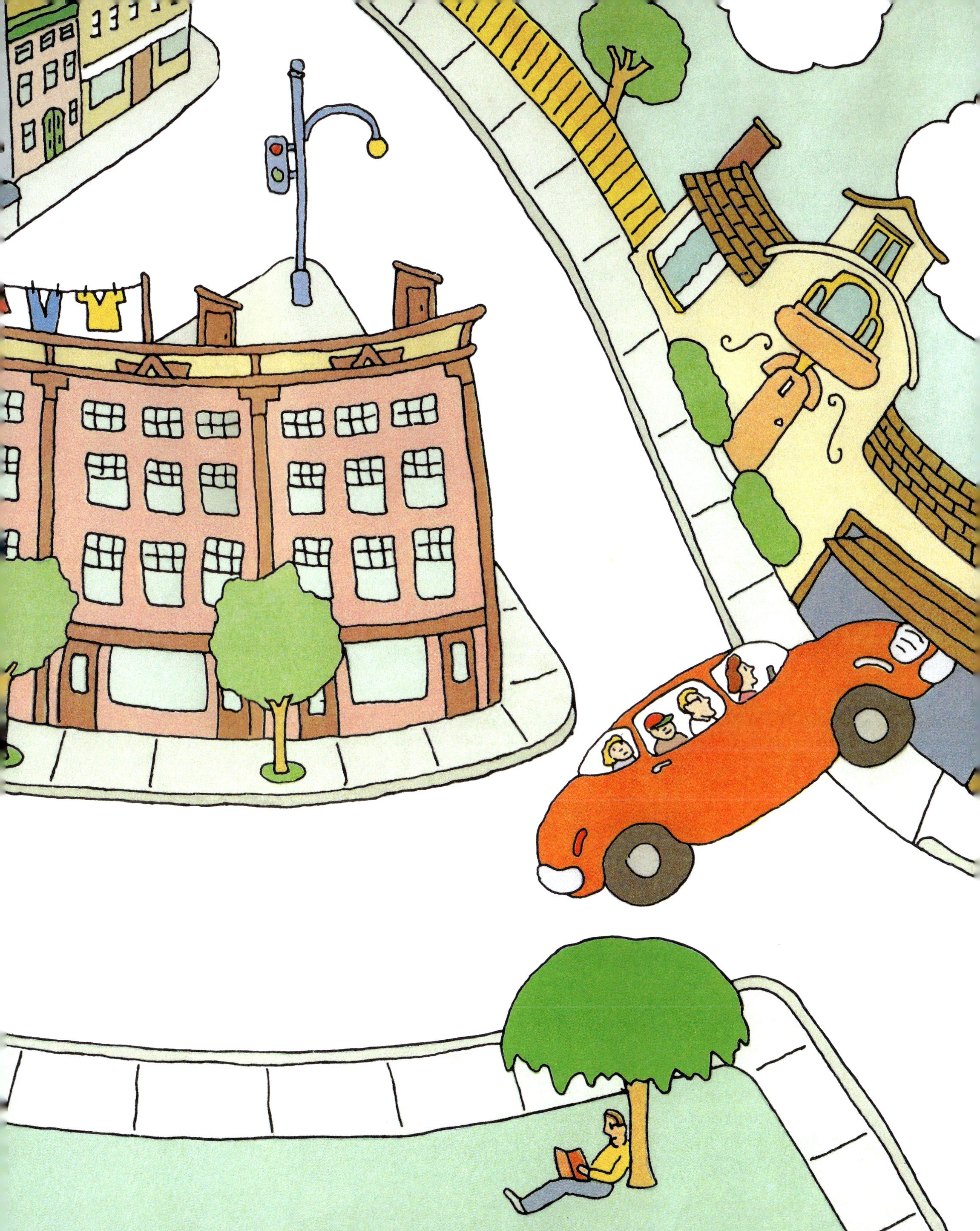

y Mom drove us all safely home. The end.

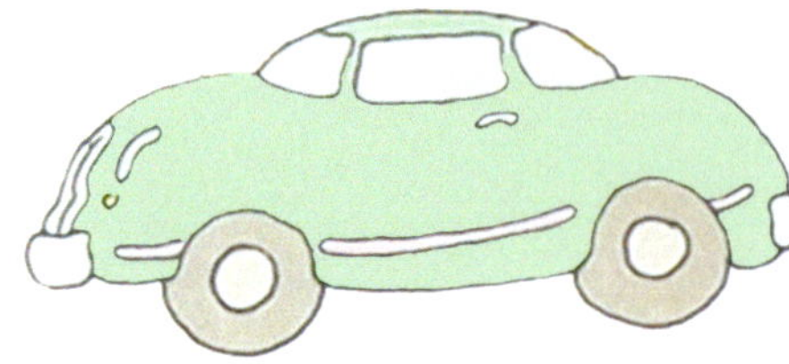

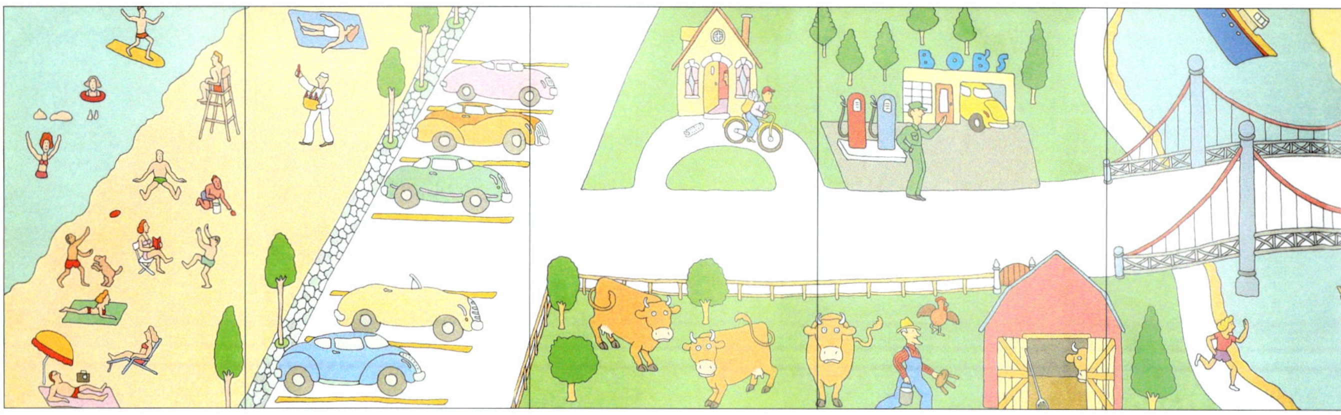
BOB'S

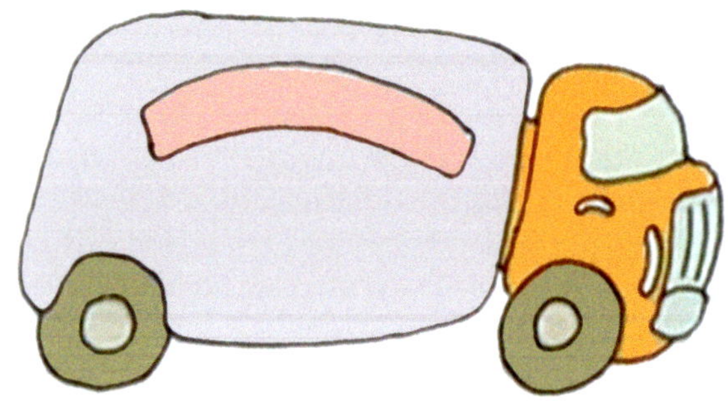

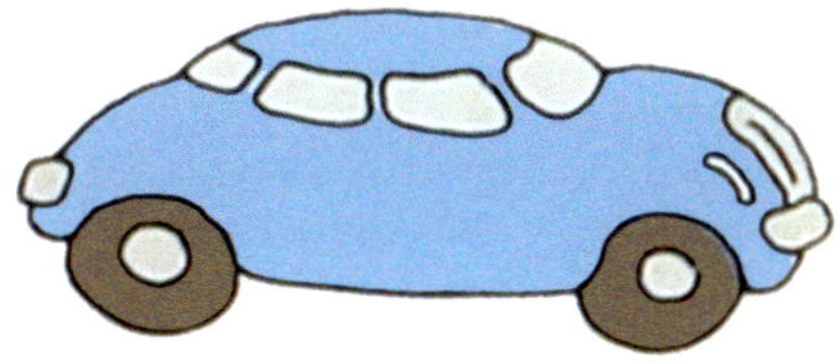

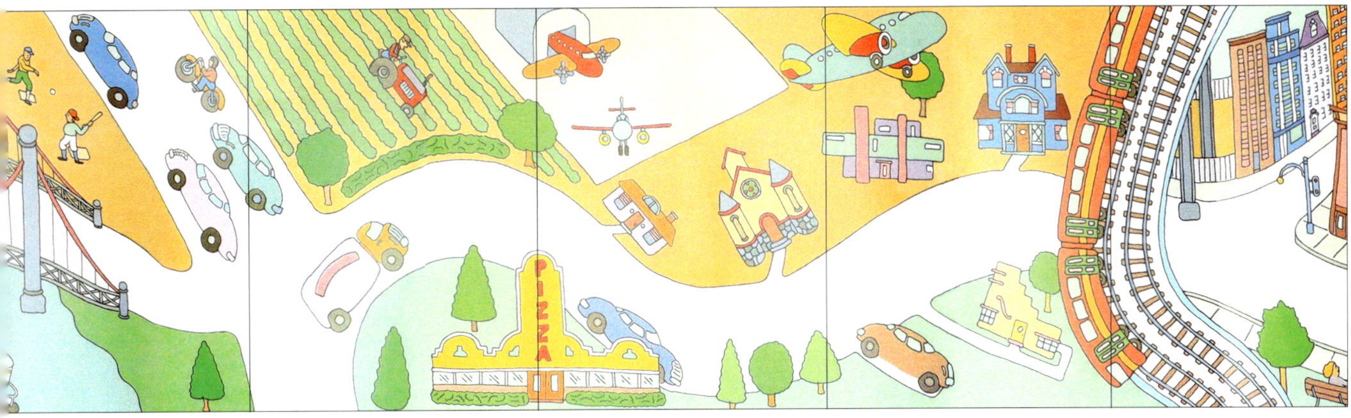

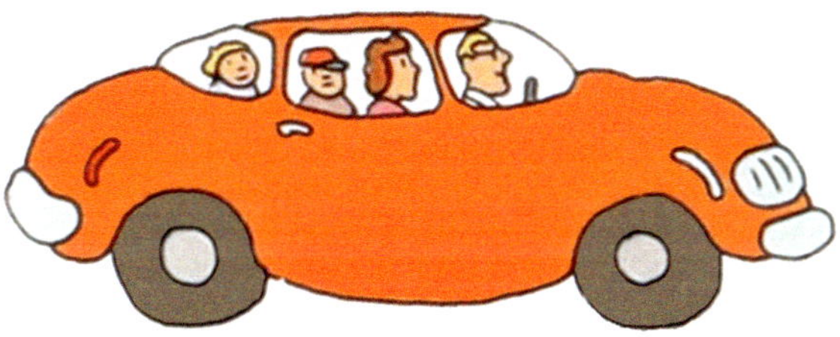

This is another one of Chwast's ingenious paper contraptions with an "scroll-style" page bound at one end of the book, which folds out into a 6-ft (1.8 m) piece of paper that can be laid out like a map. Conceived by Harriet Ziefert, the tale is about an exhausted family that drives home after an activity-packed day at the beach. Mom makes sure that the children keep Dad from falling asleep at the wheel. As the story advances, so does the book, allowing the reader to participate in the family's safe journey.

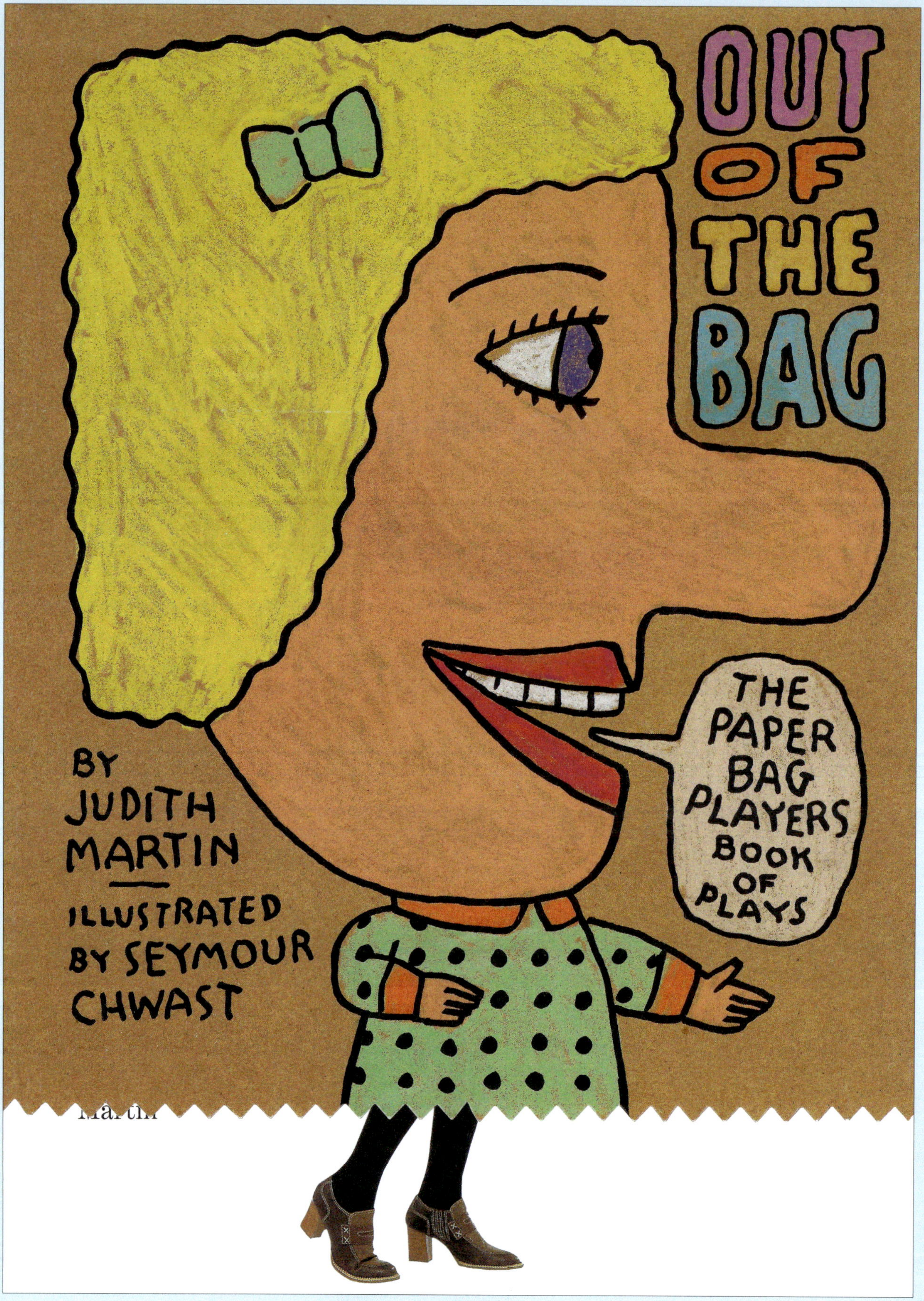
OUT OF THE BAG
THE PAPER BAG PLAYERS BOOK OF PLAYS
BY JUDITH MARTIN
ILLUSTRATED BY SEYMOUR CHWAST

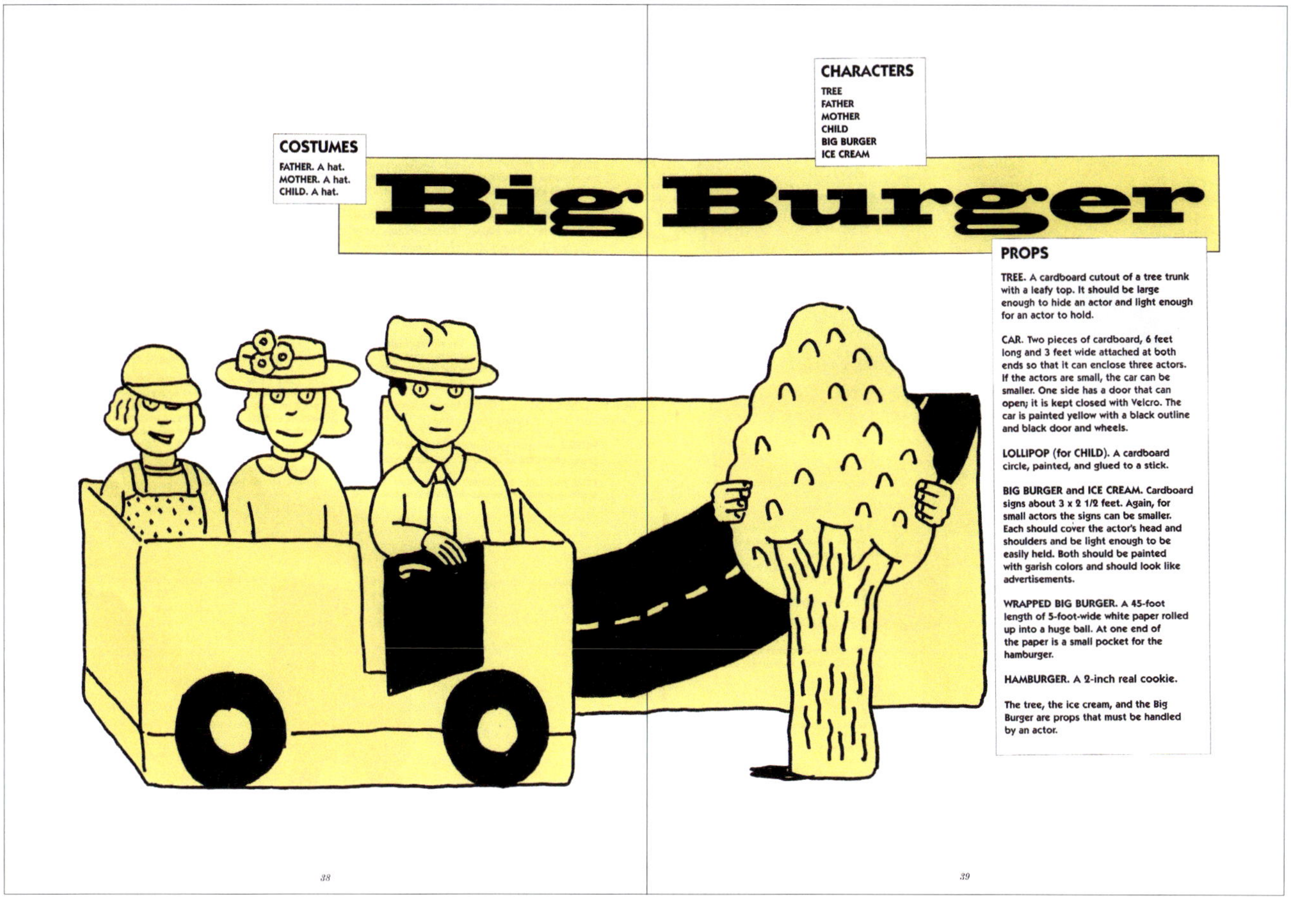

Out of the Bag

The Paper Bag Players is a famous children's theater company that is known for using everyday materials—especially paper bags and cardboard boxes—in their performances. The theater's founder, Judith Martin, wrote the book and asked Chwast to design the contents, including characters and props that children can interact with. The cover is purposely rendered roughly and without finesse, just like a childish scribble. The bag itself contains an assortment of activities that involve playing with and repurposing the paper. Scripts are included.

◂ *Out of the Bag: The Paper Bag Players Book of Plays*, by Judith Martin, illustrated by Seymour Chwast, 1997, 9" × 12" (23 × 30.5 cm), 48 pages with paper bag wrap cover.

I WON'T TAKE A BATH!

CHARACTERS

BATHTUB
SOAP
PETER
MOTHER
THE END

COSTUMES

BATHTUB. A large cardboard cutout shaped and painted to look like a bathtub. The bathtub should be about five feet long, but the size can be adjusted to accommodate a small actor.

SOAP. An oversize cardboard cutout the shape of a soap bar. It should be large enough to cover a kneeling actor with only head and shoulders showing.

PETER. An oversize painted cardboard cutout of a boy. It should be at least two feet taller than the actor who holds it. The cardboard folds at the hips and knees. The folds enable PETER to sit in the bathtub. Attached to the back is a large wooden handle. The actor behind the cutout can move the figure without ever being seen. The back of the cardboard is painted pink to look as if Peter were naked.

MOTHER. An oversize cardboard cutout, much taller than PETER and painted to look like a very large motherly woman. Probably two or more cardboard cartons opened and flattened can be put together with masking tape and braced with a wood lathe. On the back of the MOTHER are large wooden handles. Two people can get behind the MOTHER to move her. The voice of the MOTHER is best handled by an offstage microphone.

THE END. A flat, thin box such as a card table might come in. The bottom is cut out and THE END is painted on it. It is actually possible for an actor to get in it with only his legs showing. The effect is very humorous.

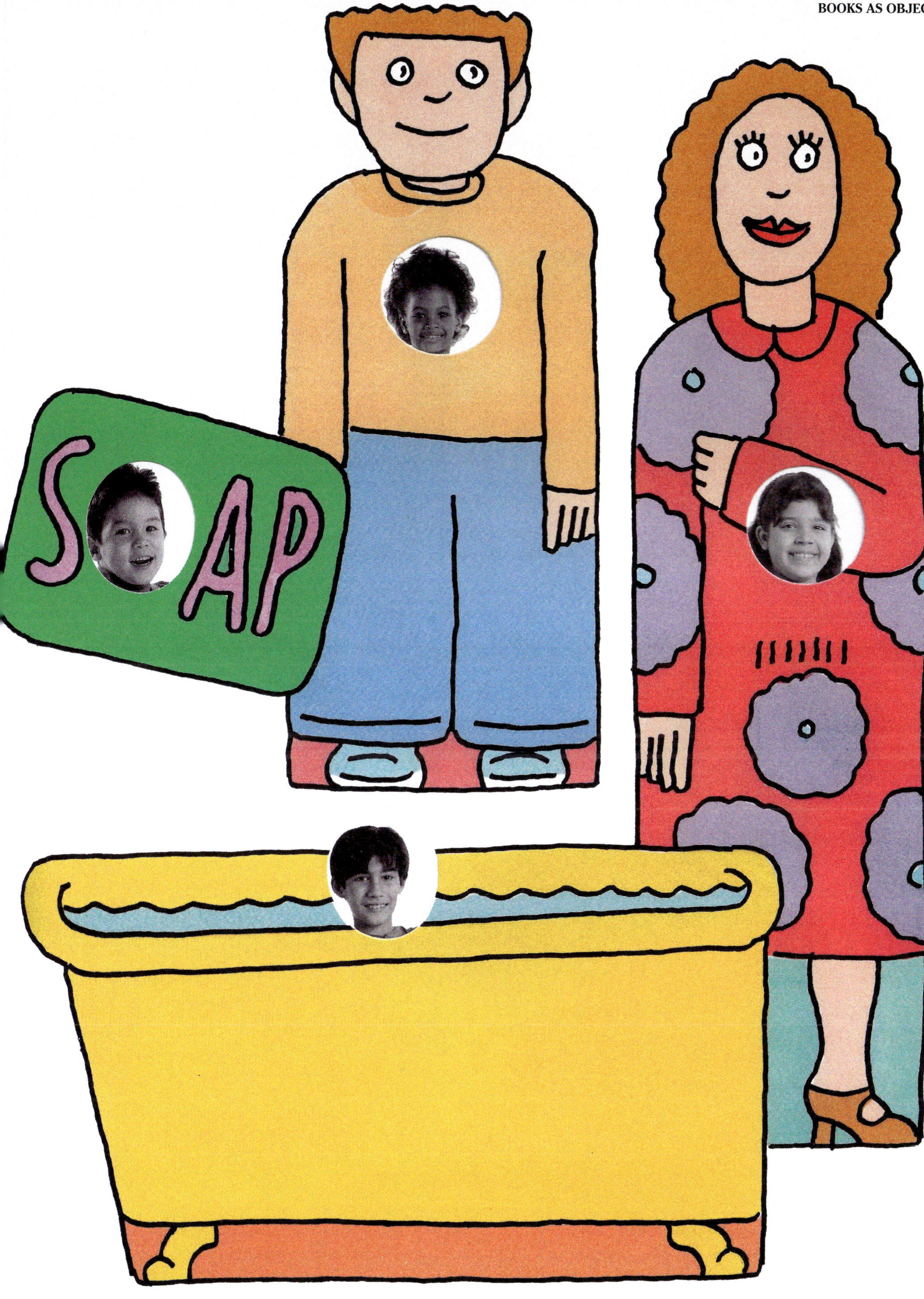
SOAP

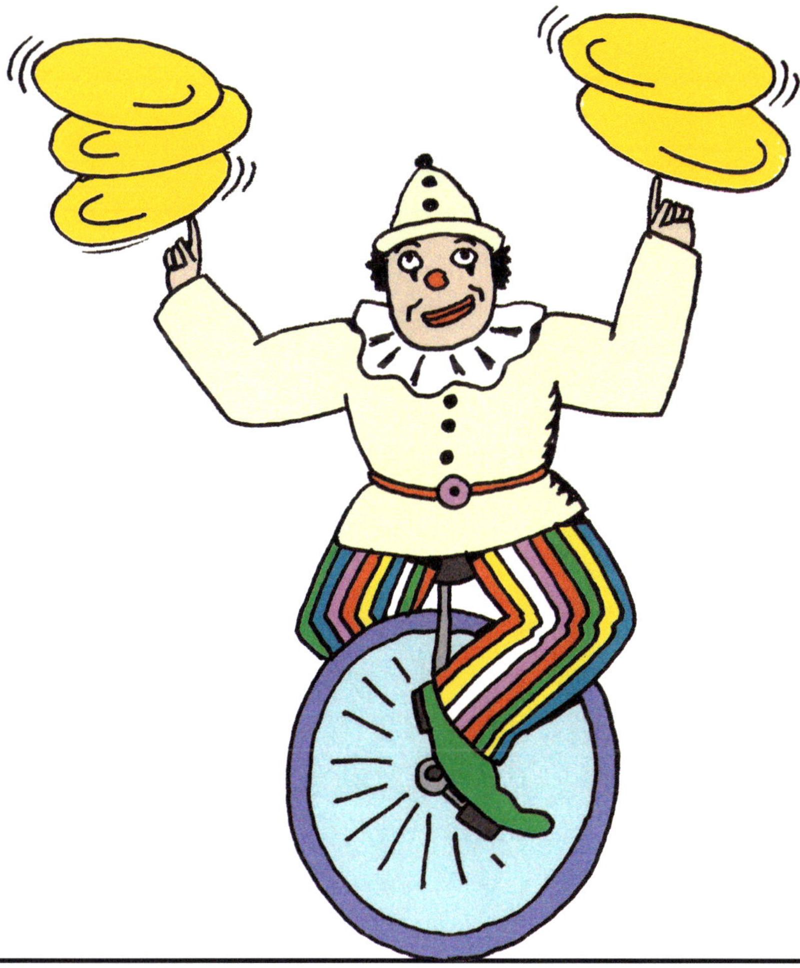

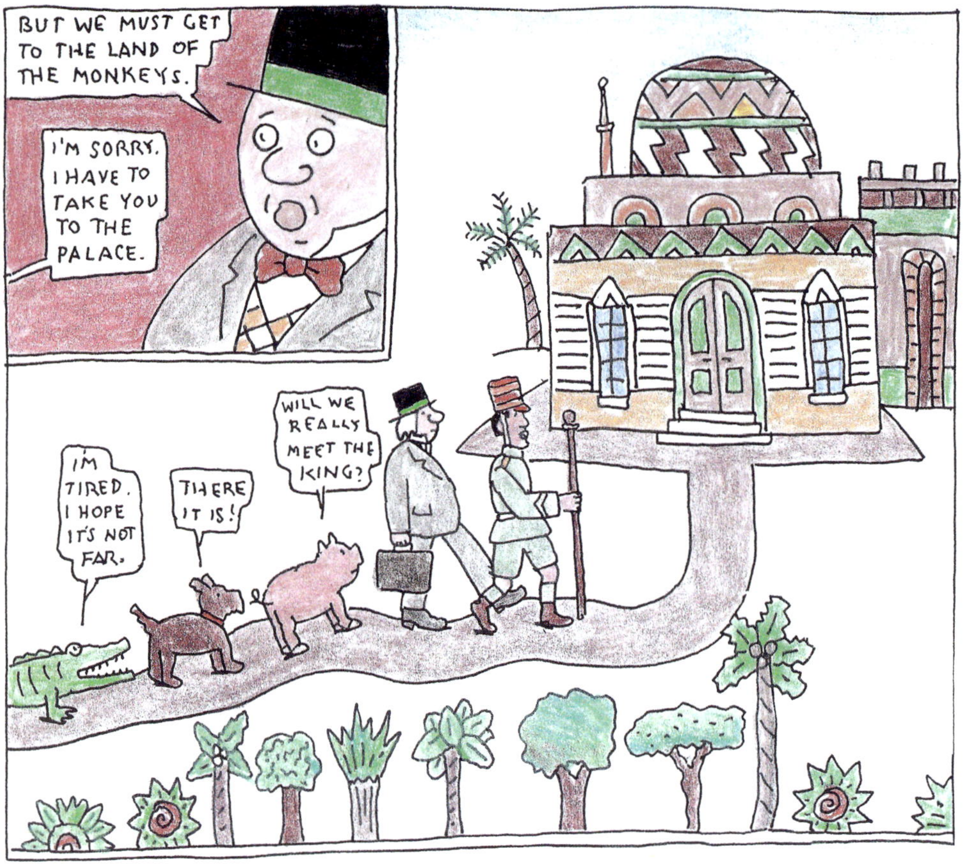
BUT WE MUST GET TO THE LAND OF THE MONKEYS.
I'M SORRY. I HAVE TO TAKE YOU TO THE PALACE.
I'M TIRED. I HOPE IT'S NOT FAR.
THERE IT IS!
WILL WE REALLY MEET THE KING?

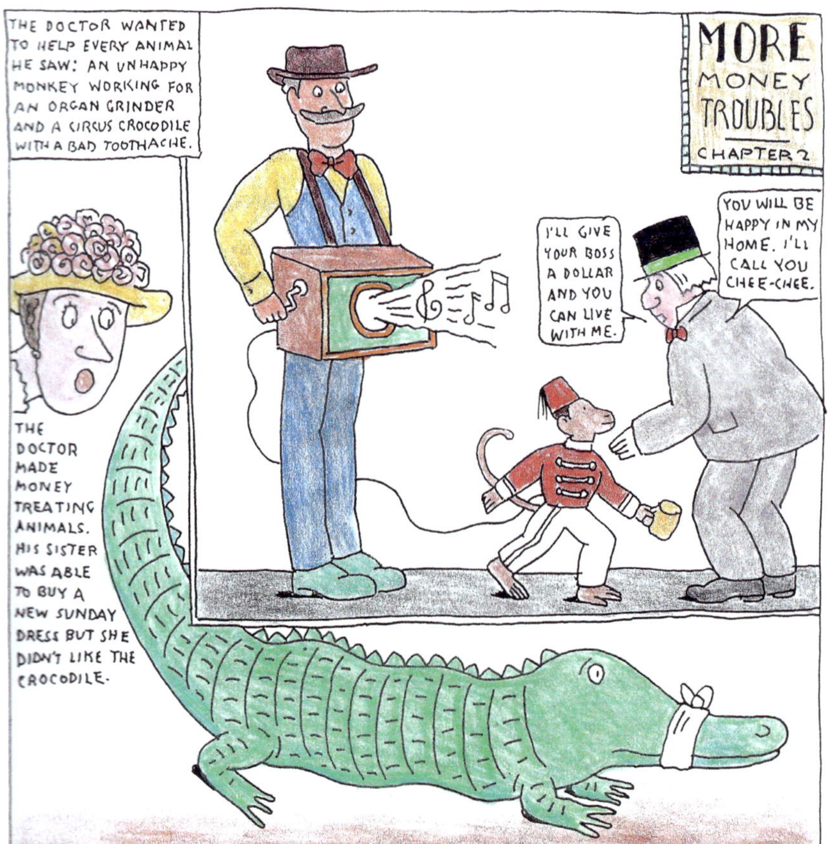
THE DOCTOR WANTED TO HELP EVERY ANIMAL HE SAW: AN UNHAPPY MONKEY WORKING FOR AN ORGAN GRINDER AND A CIRCUS CROCODILE WITH A BAD TOOTHACHE.
MORE MONEY TROUBLES
CHAPTER 2
I'LL GIVE YOUR BOSS A DOLLAR AND YOU CAN LIVE WITH ME.
YOU WILL BE HAPPY IN MY HOME. I'LL CALL YOU CHEE-CHEE.
THE DOCTOR MADE MONEY TREATING ANIMALS. HIS SISTER WAS ABLE TO BUY A NEW SUNDAY DRESS BUT SHE DIDN'T LIKE THE CROCODILE.

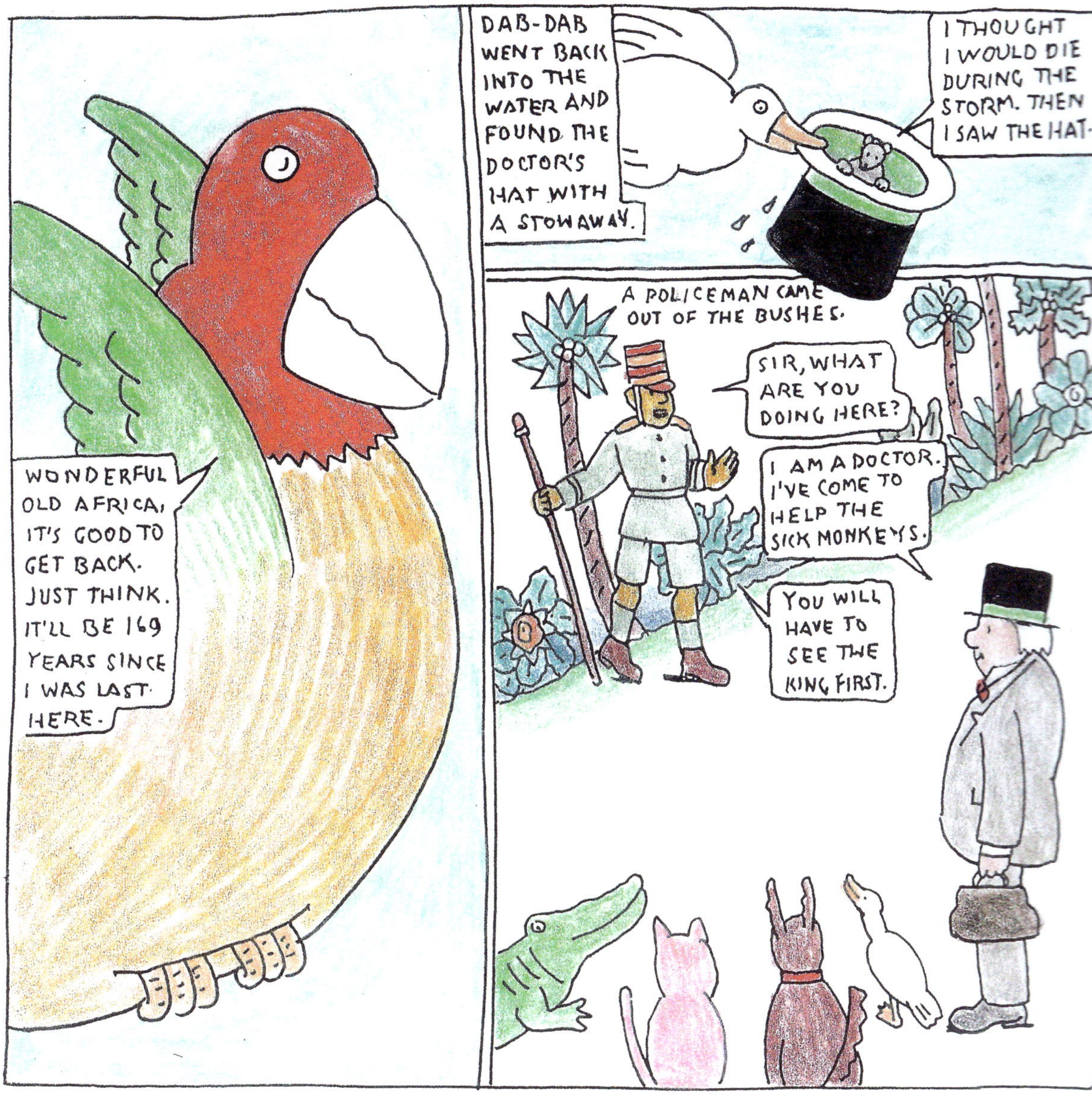

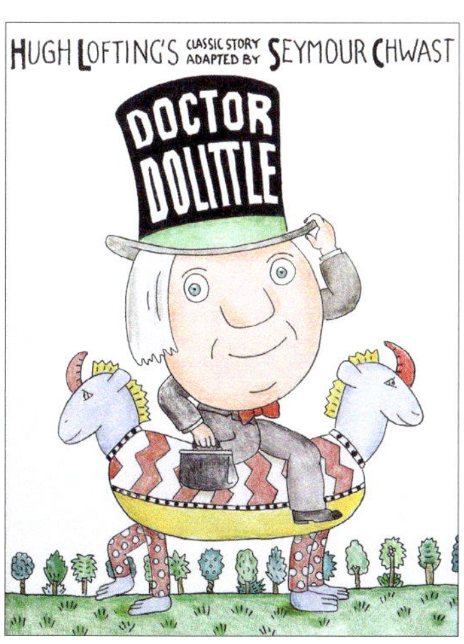

Doctor Dolittle, by Hugh Lofting, adapted and illustrated by Seymour Chwast, 2015, 9.35" × 12.3" (23.75 × 31.25 cm), 40 pages.

Doctor Dolittle

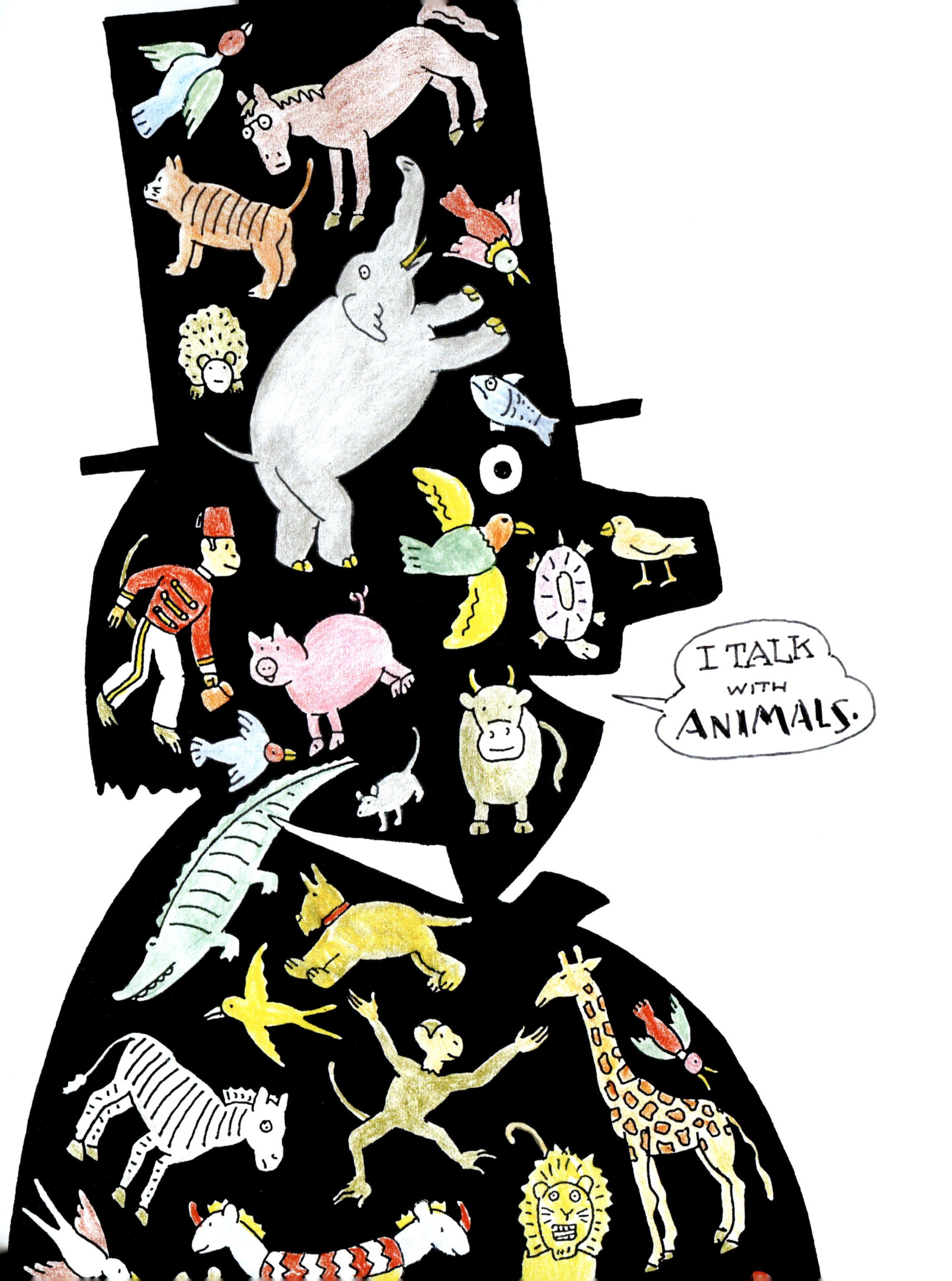
I TALK WITH ANIMALS.

Chwast grew up reading the funny pages in the Sunday newspapers, and he particularly enjoyed the classic story of Doctor Dolittle, who journeyed from Puddleby-on-the-Marsh to Africa so he could save sickly monkeys. Chwast relished the idea of reinterpreting the story as a multipanel comic book and graphic novel. In addition to being a skilled medical practitioner, Doctor Dolittle became fluent enough to speak with all the other jungle animals who returned with him to his human practice in England, where their arrival caused quite a commotion.

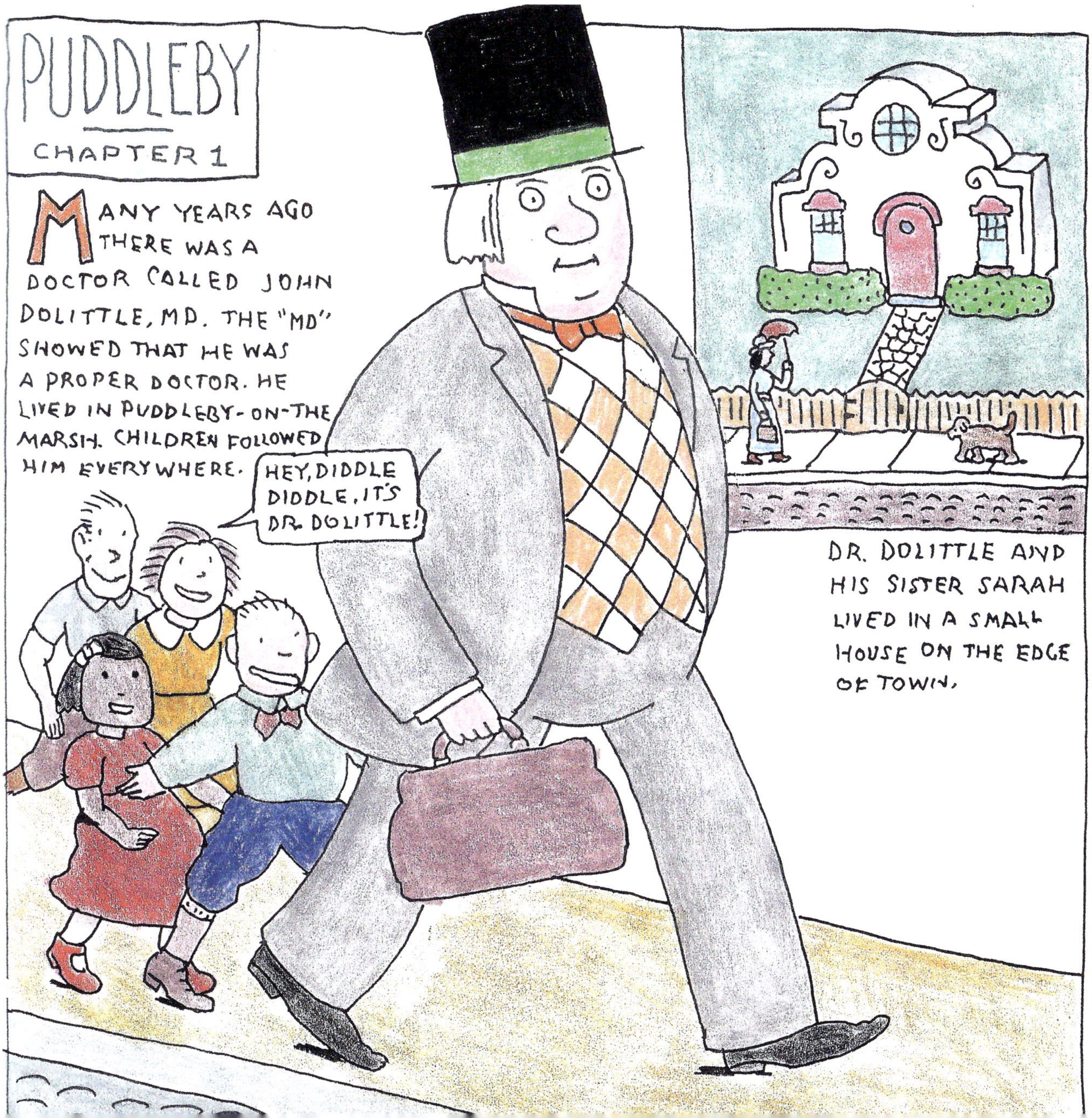

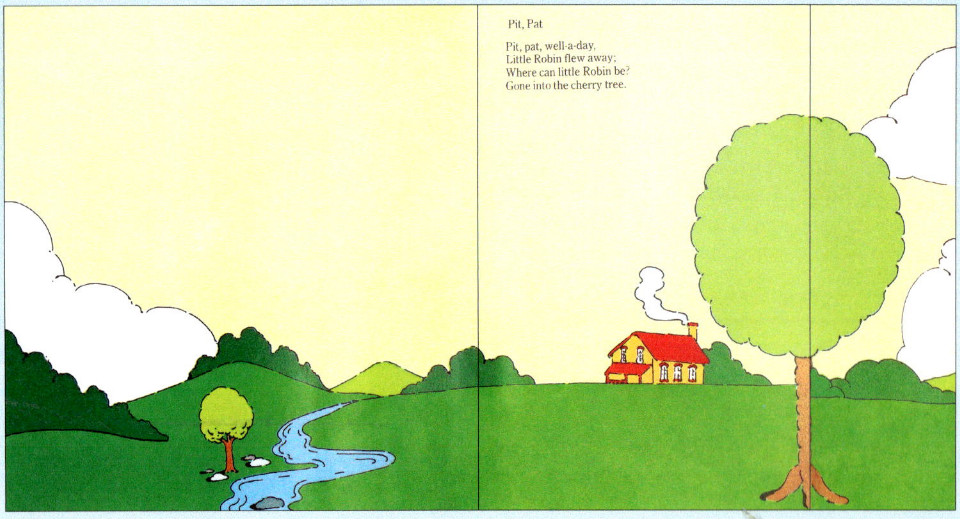

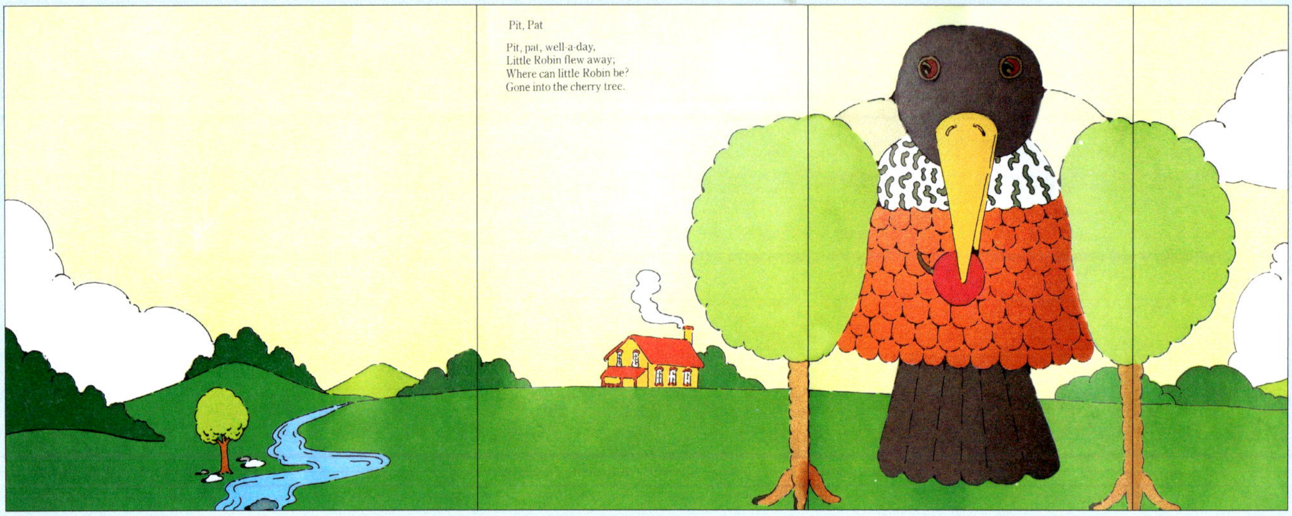

Mother Gooooooose

“It’s called a ‘flip-flap’ book because it has pages the reader can turn over,” Chwast says, as he explains how the punchlines of the nursery rhymes are revealed. This repeated flipping accounts for why there are so many letter Os in the name Mother Goose, expressively using typography to mimic the repetition of flipping pages.

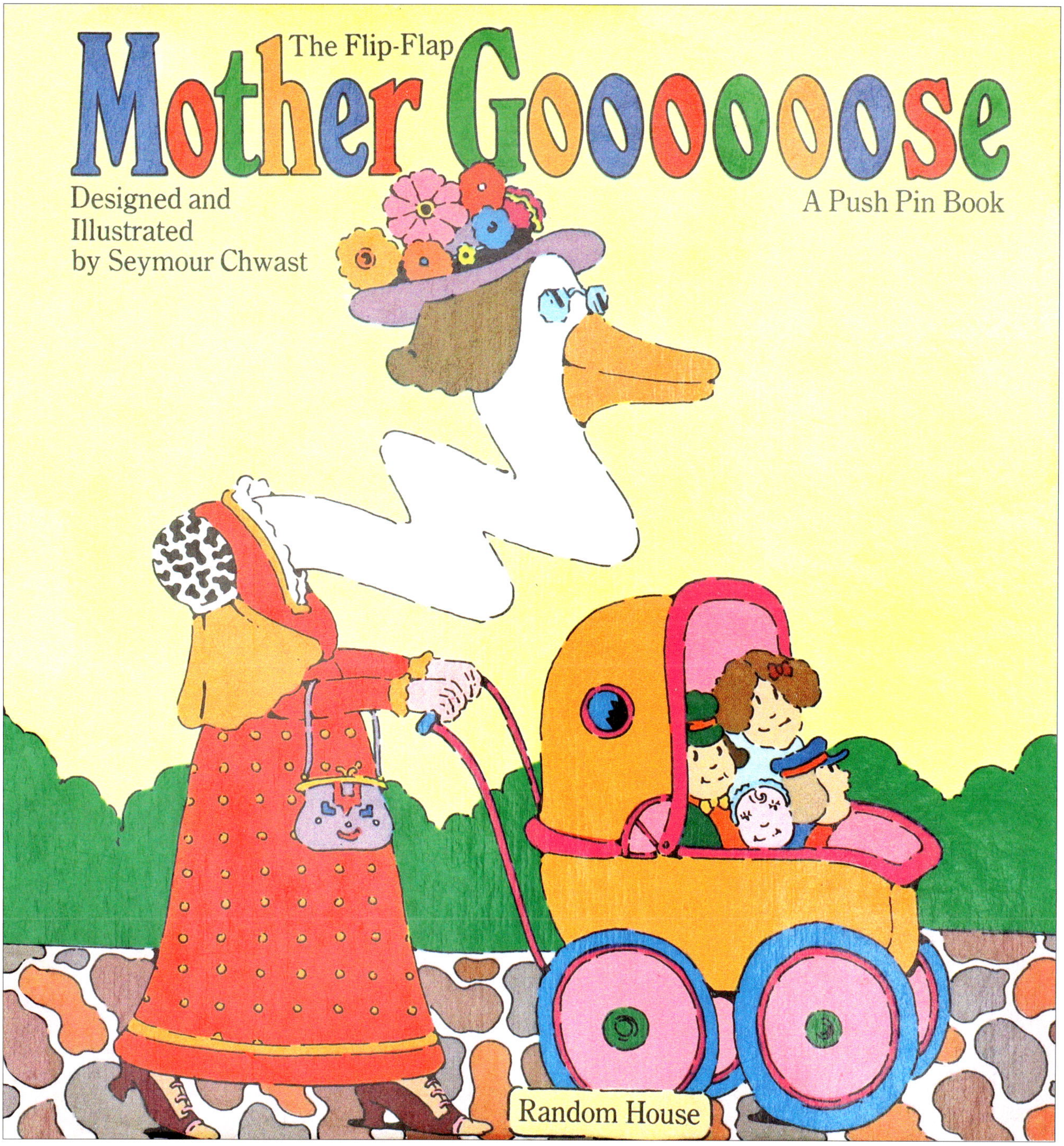

The Flip-Flap Mother Goooooose, A Push Pin Book, designed and illustrated by Seymour Chwast, 1971, 8" × 8" (20.25 × 20.25 cm), 24 pages.

Sixpence

Sing a song of sixpence,
A pocket full of rye;
Four and twenty blackbirds,
Baked in a pie.

When the pie was opened,
The birds began to sing;
Was not that a dainty dish,
To set before the king?

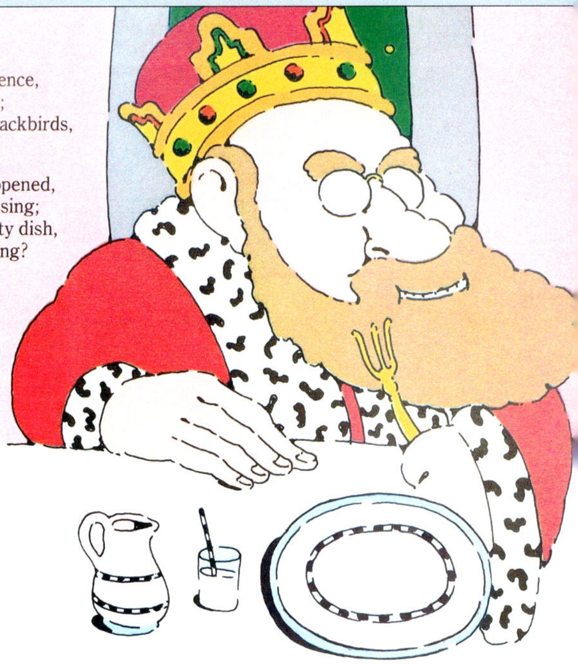

Sixpence

Sing a song of sixpence,
A pocket full of rye;
Four and twenty blackbirds,
Baked in a pie.

When the pie was opened,
The birds began to sing;
Was not that a dainty dish,
To set before the king?

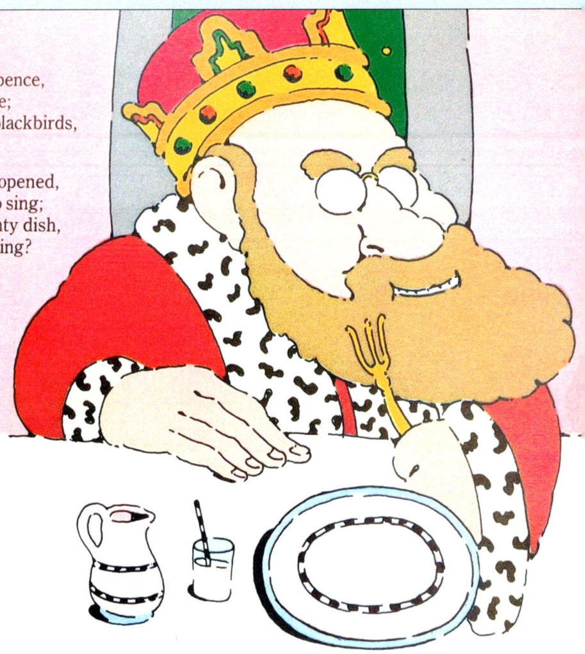

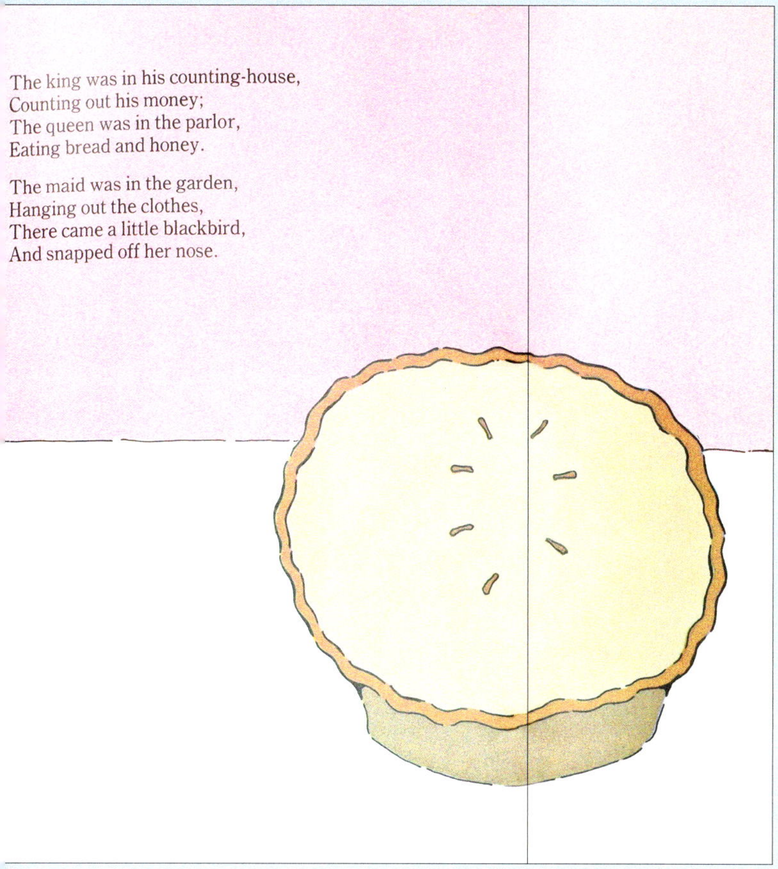
The king was in his counting-house,
Counting out his money;
The queen was in the parlor,
Eating bread and honey.

The maid was in the garden,
Hanging out the clothes,
There came a little blackbird,
And snapped off her nose.

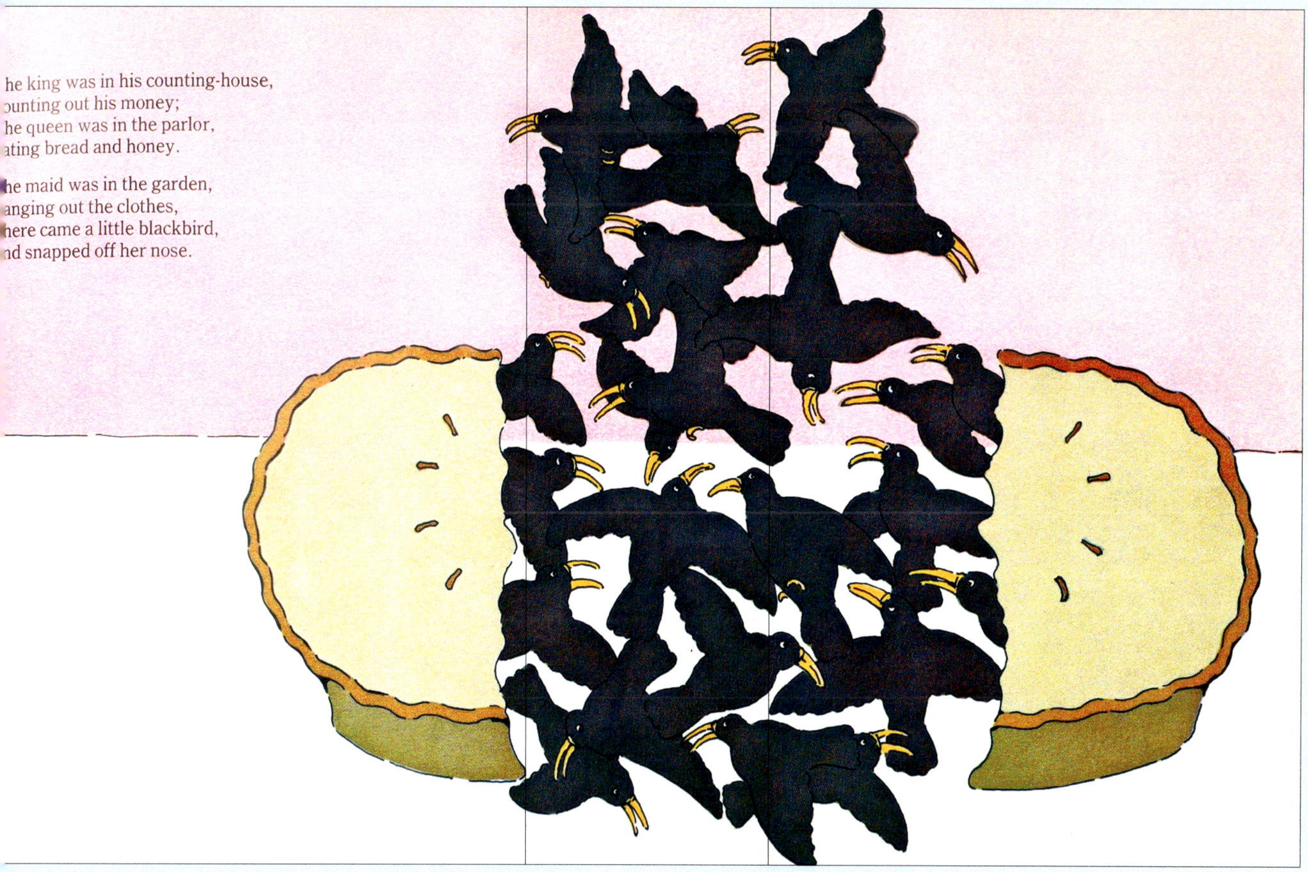
he king was in his counting-house,
ounting out his money;
he queen was in the parlor,
ating bread and honey.

he maid was in the garden,
anging out the clothes,
here came a little blackbird,
nd snapped off her nose.

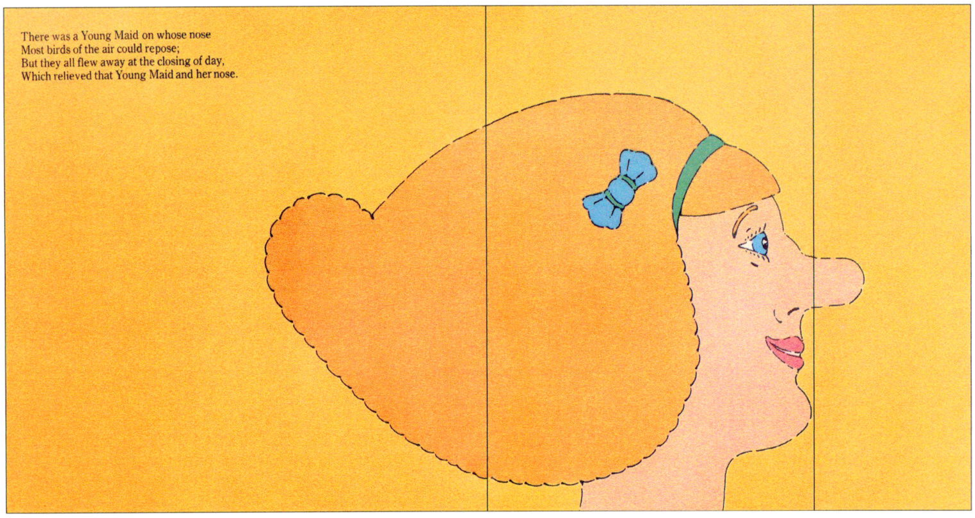

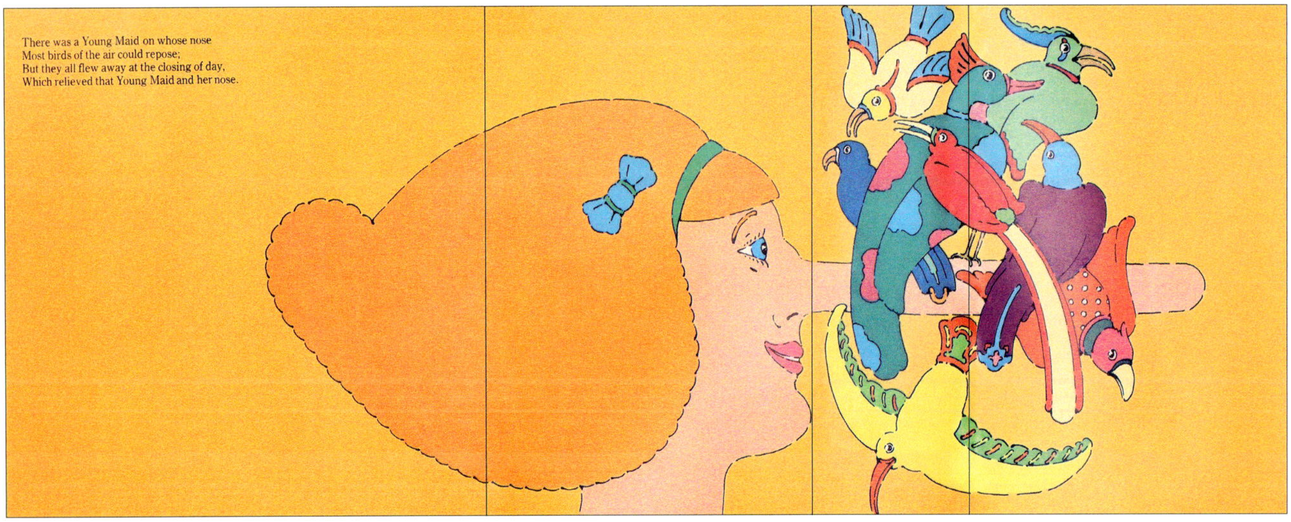

Limerickricks

The same flip-flap principle is applied to *The Flip-Flap Limerickricks* book. Some limericks tell a serious story, others tell a silly one. But all rely on the surprise visual revelation when the flaps are flipped.

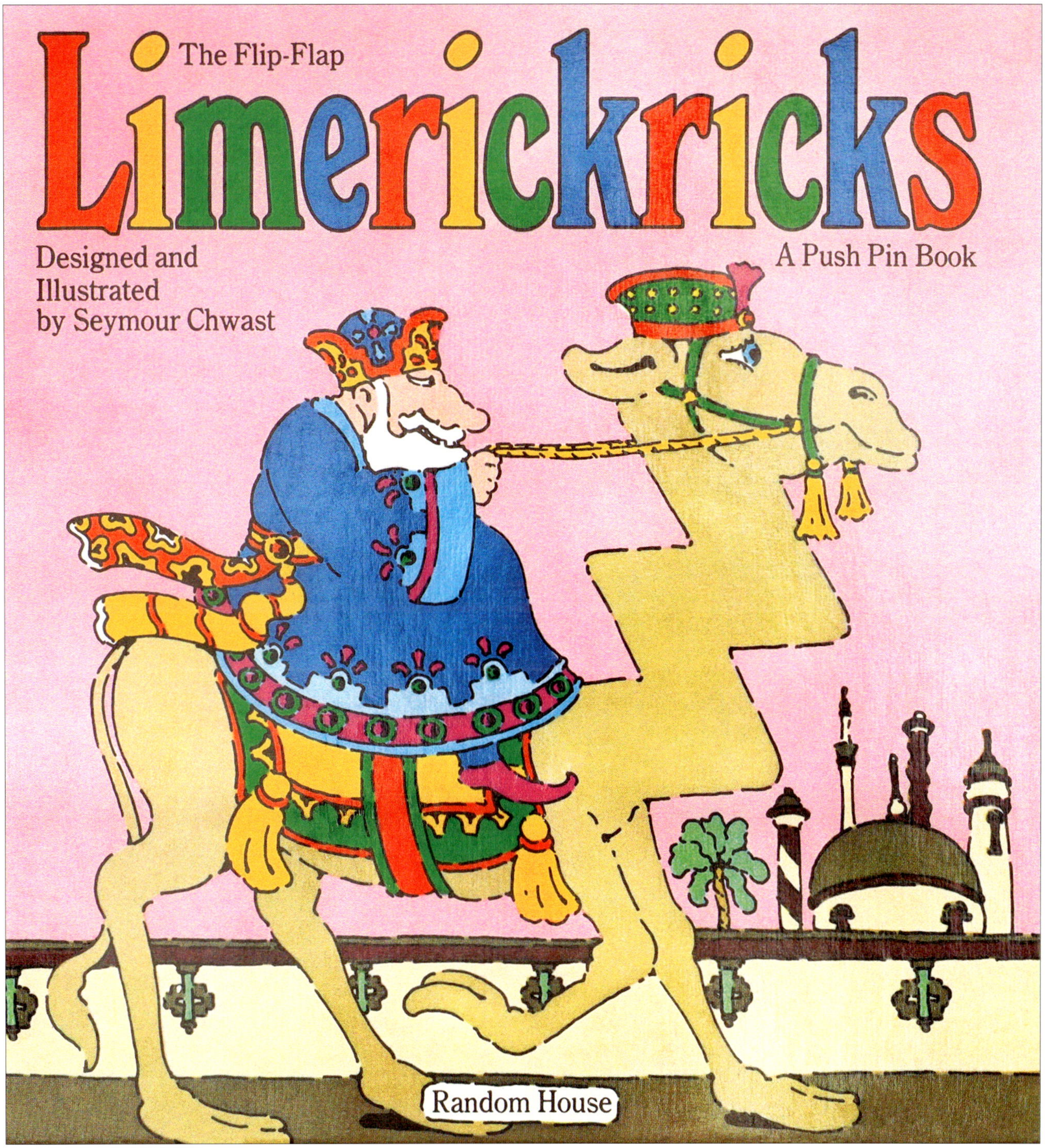

Limerickricks, A Push Pin Book, designed and illustrated by Seymour Chwast, 1972, 8" × 8" (20.25 × 20.25 cm), 24 pages.

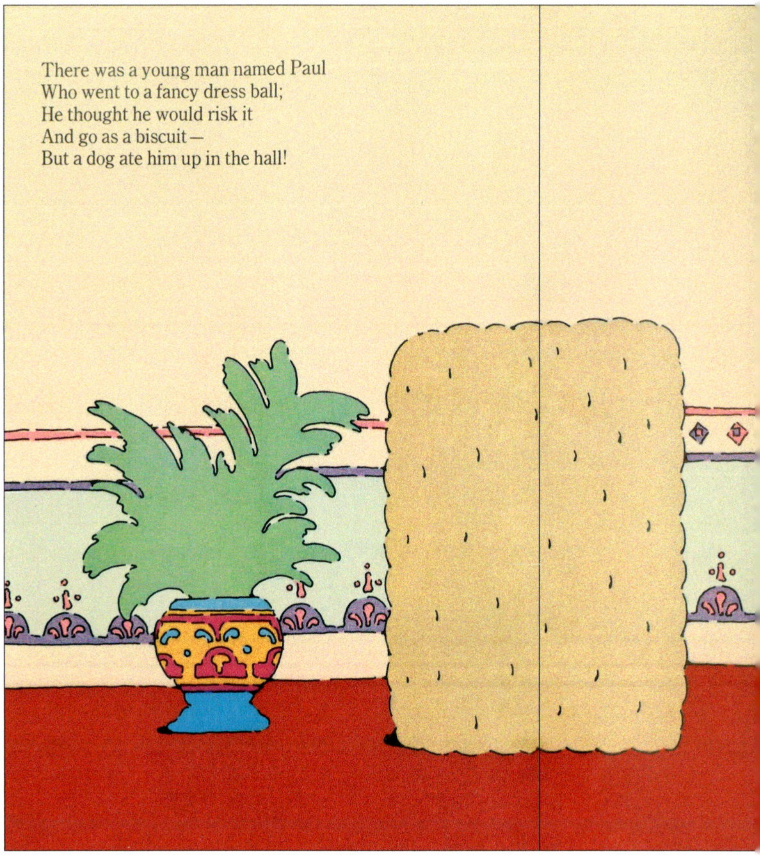
There was a young man named Paul
Who went to a fancy dress ball;
He thought he would risk it
And go as a biscuit –
But a dog ate him up in the hall!

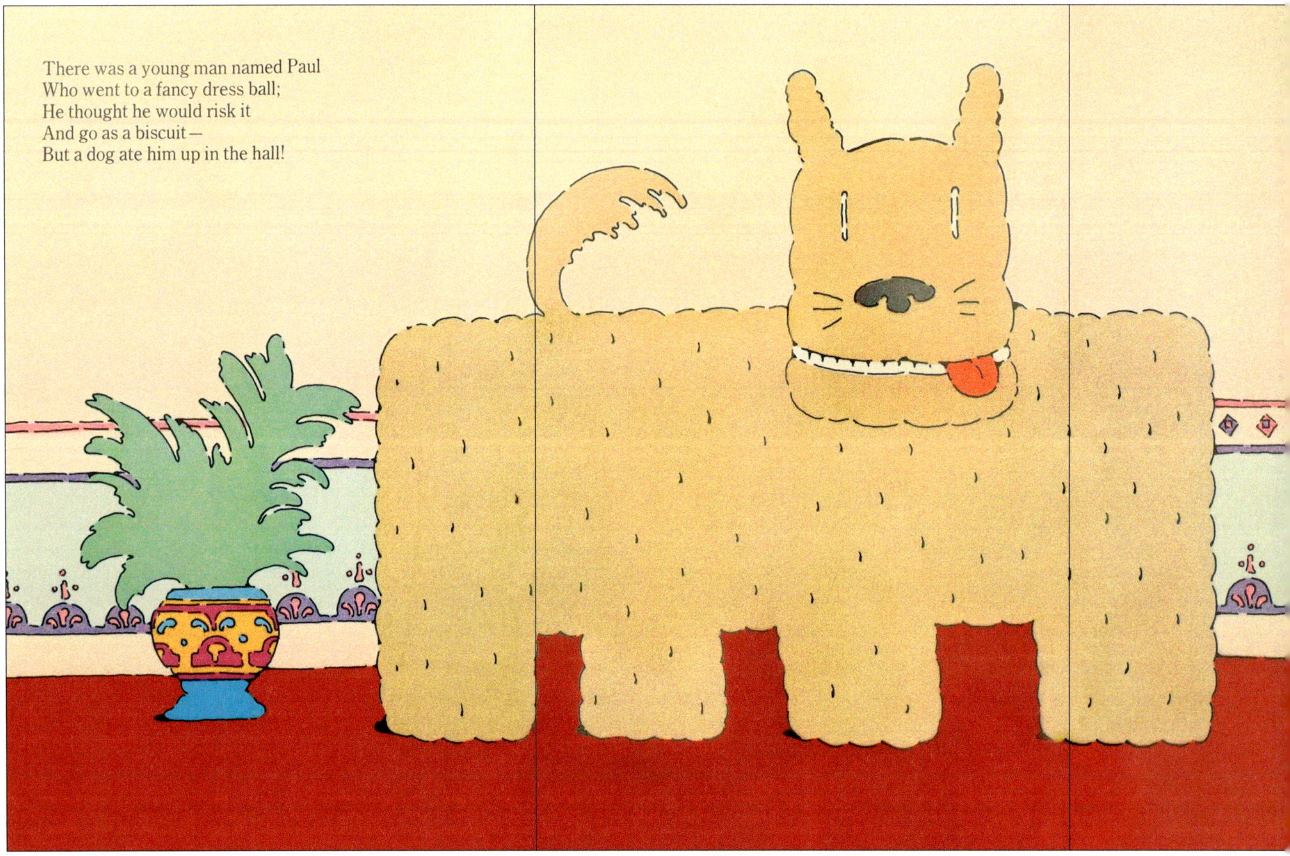
There was a young man named Paul
Who went to a fancy dress ball;
He thought he would risk it
And go as a biscuit –
But a dog ate him up in the hall!

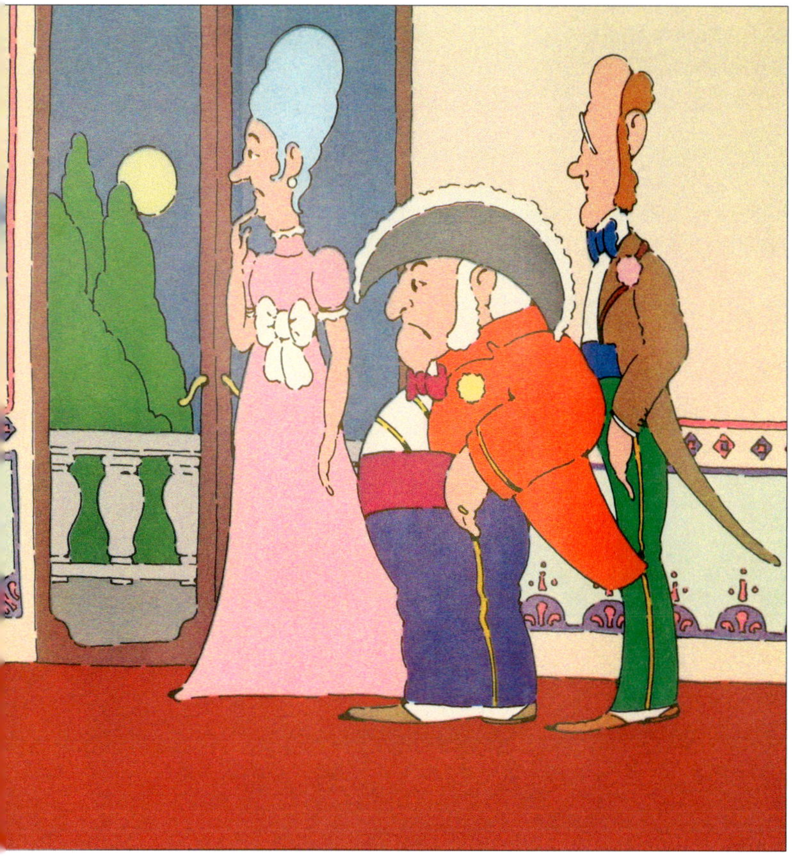

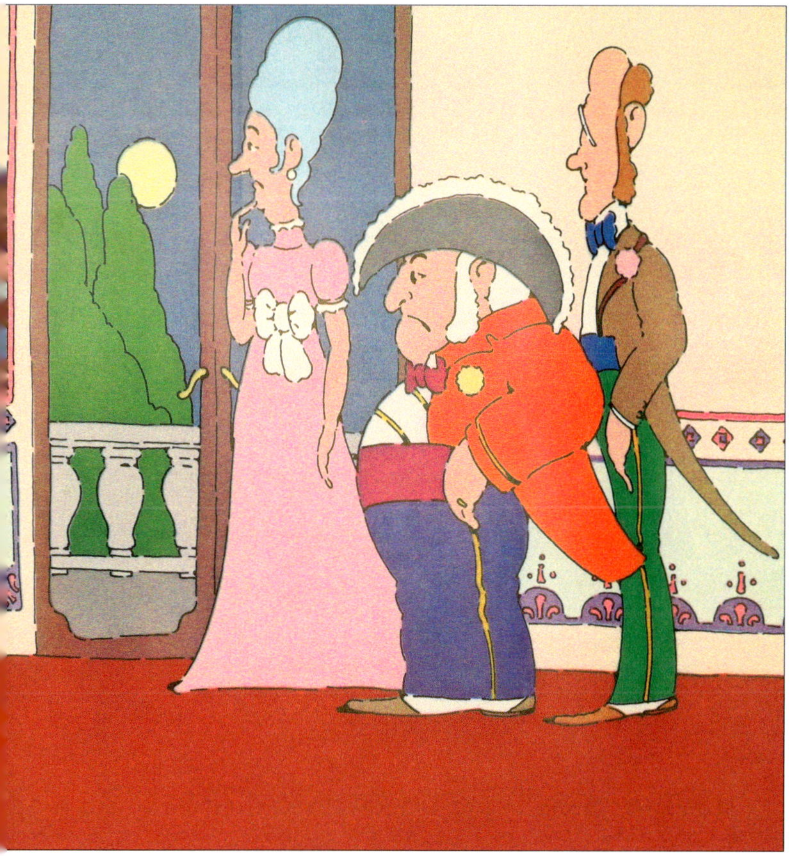

The House That Jack Built

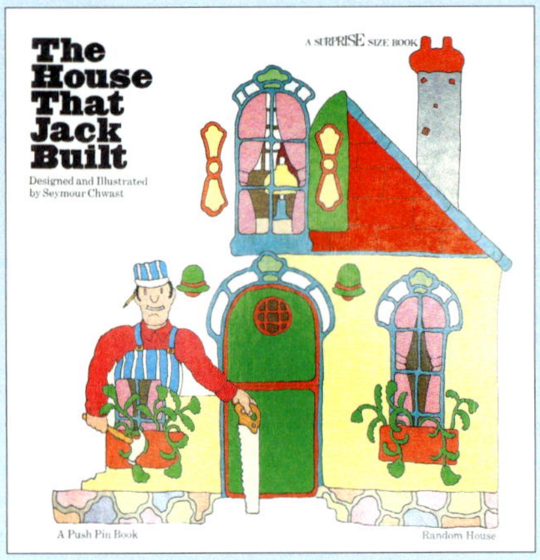

The House That Jack Built, A Push Pin Book, designed and illustrated by Seymour Chwast, 1973, 9.5" × 9.5" (24.25 × 24.25 cm), a surprise size book, 24 pages.

The flip-flap mechanism is used again in *The House That Jack Built,* this time providing the operating system as Jack builds his storied domicile. Chwast says: "The events of the famous 'cumulative' nursery rhyme are revealed pictorially to readers as they open flaps of increasing size." The physical appearance of Jack is modernized, even as the house he builds has an ornate 19th-century look about it.

This is the house
that Jack built.

This is the malt
That lay
in the house
that Jack built.

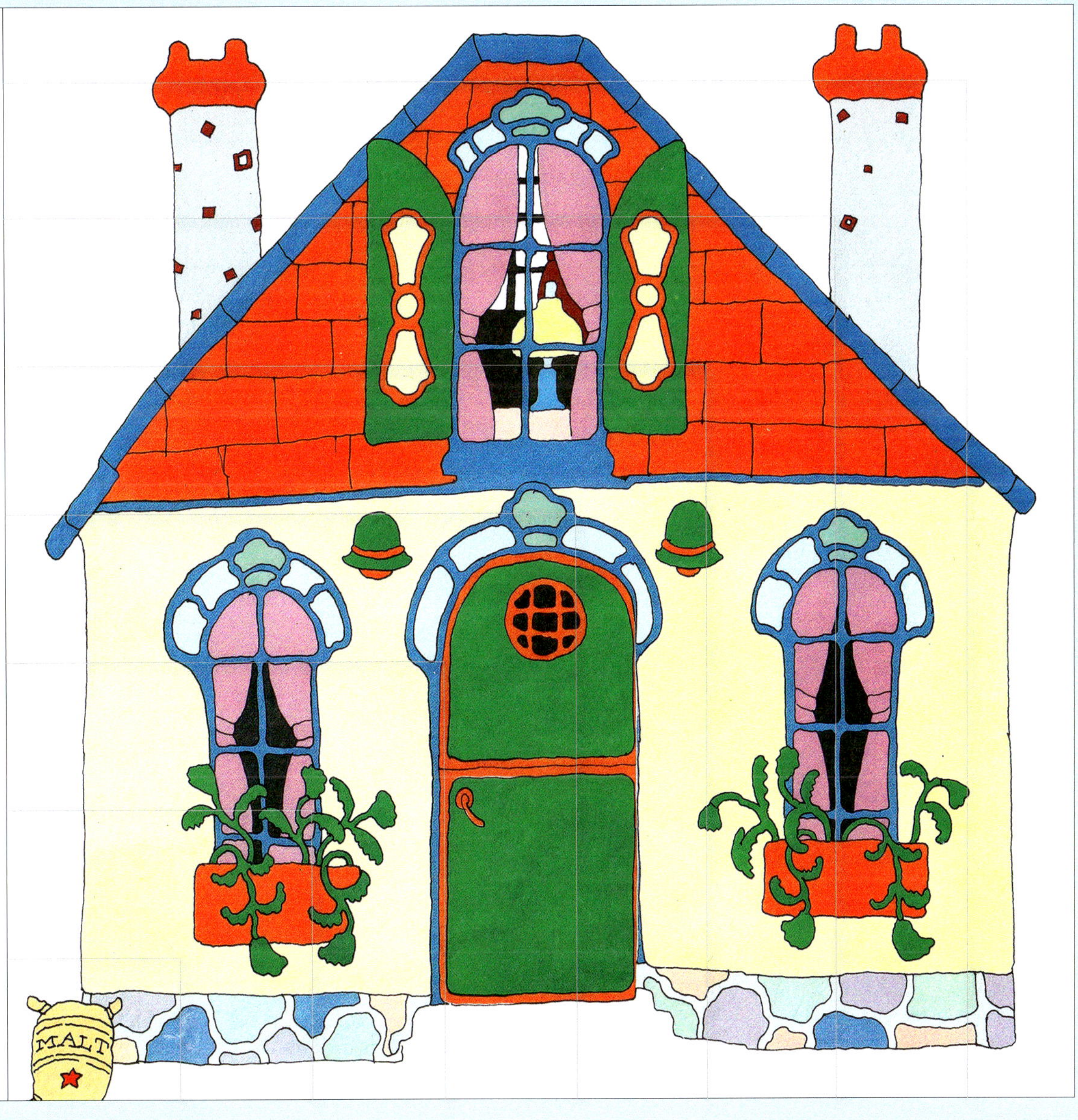

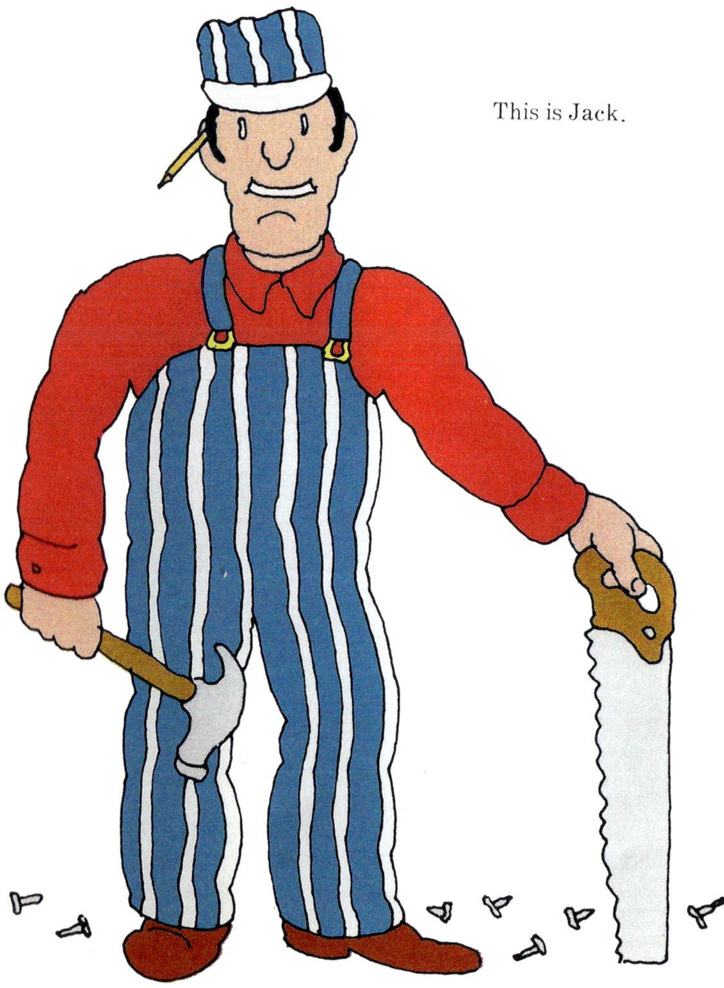

This is Jack.

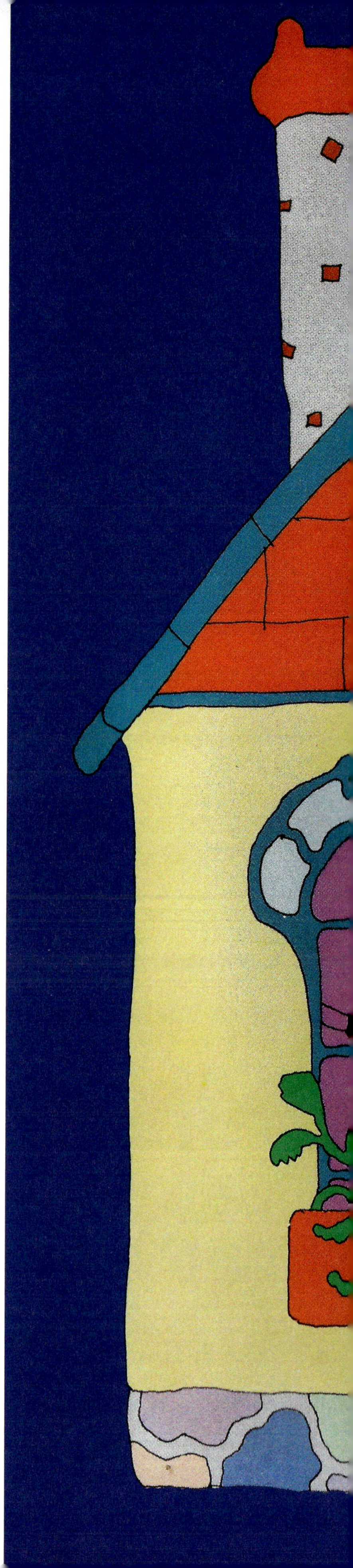

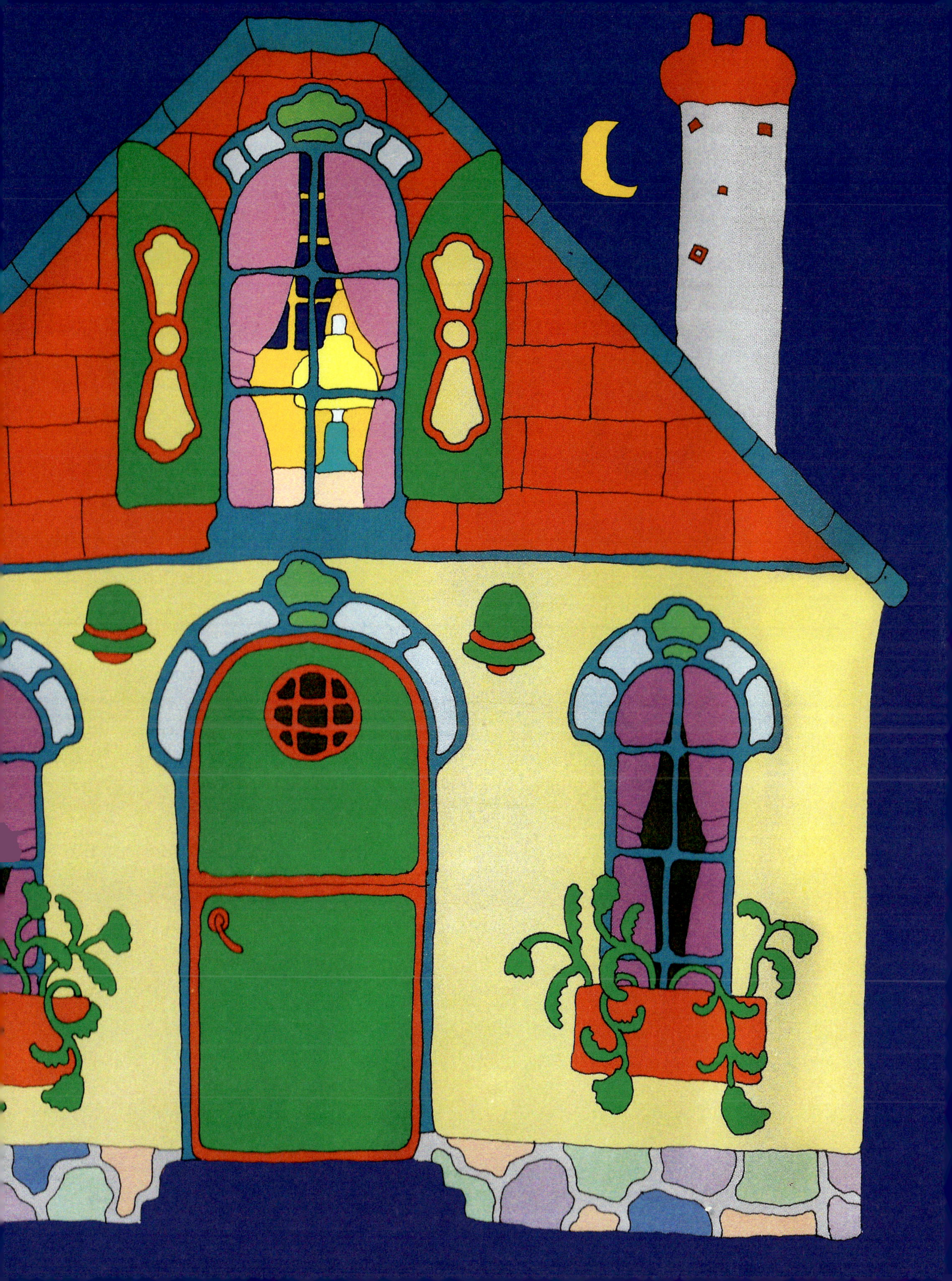

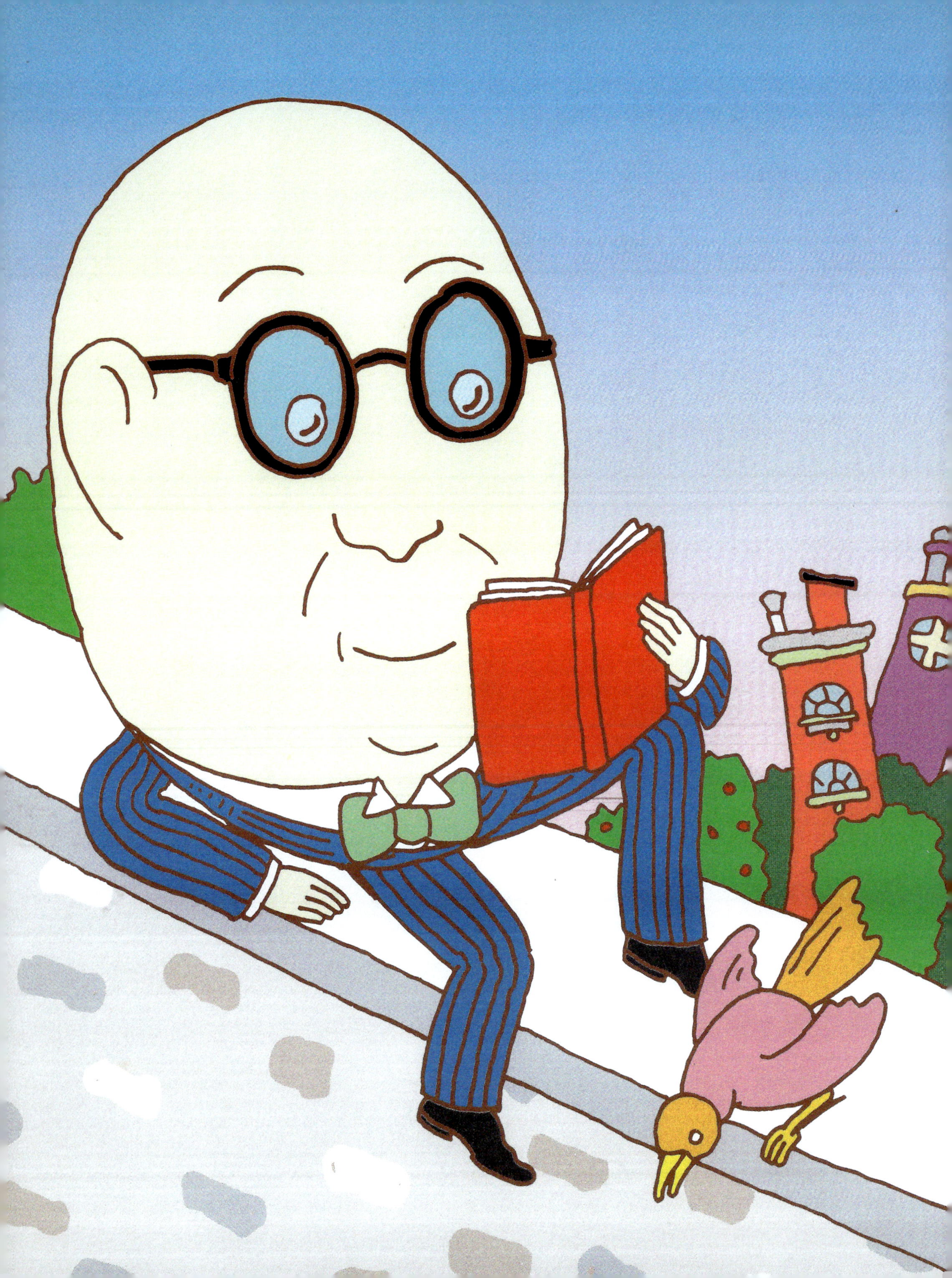

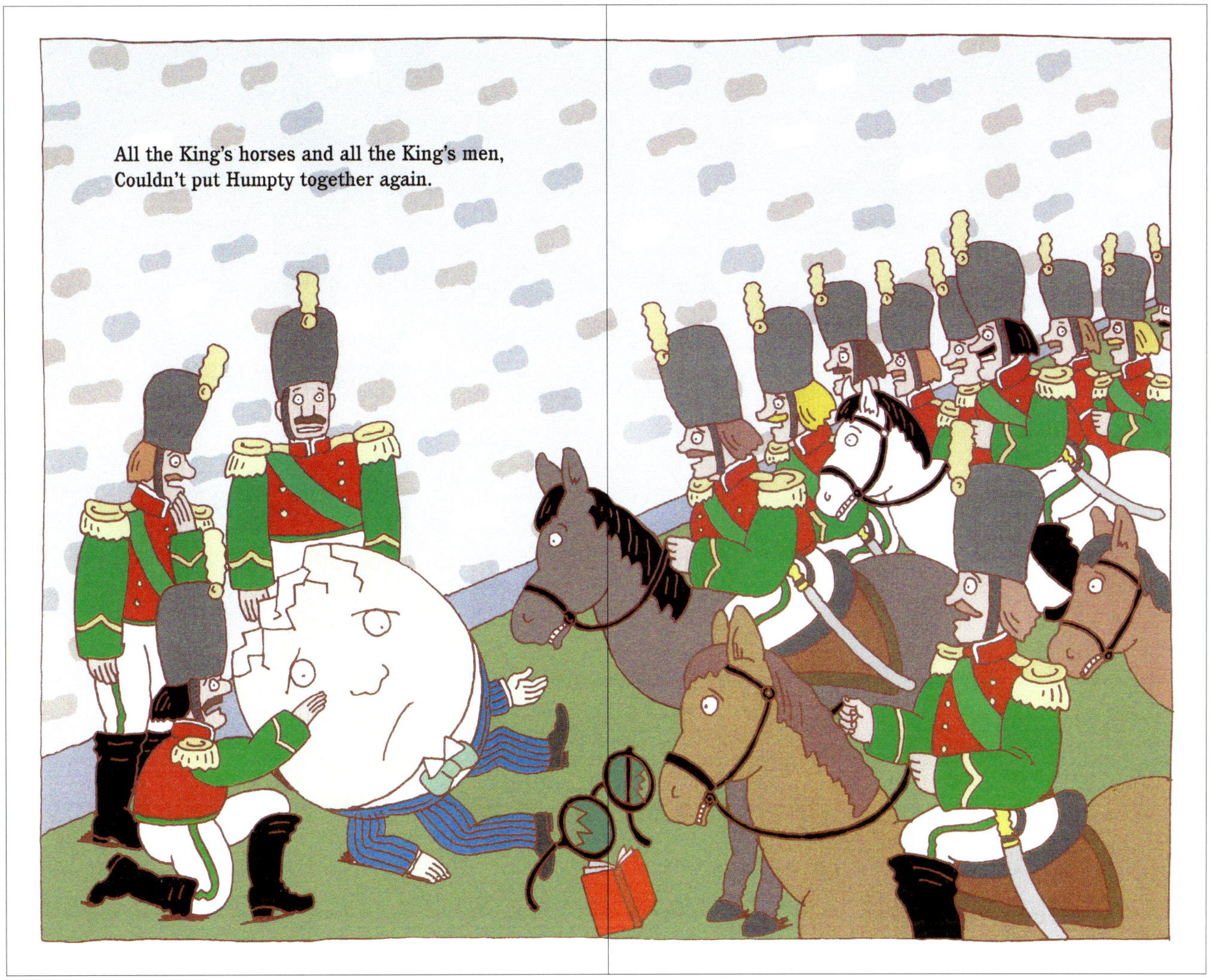

Ode to Humpty Dumpty

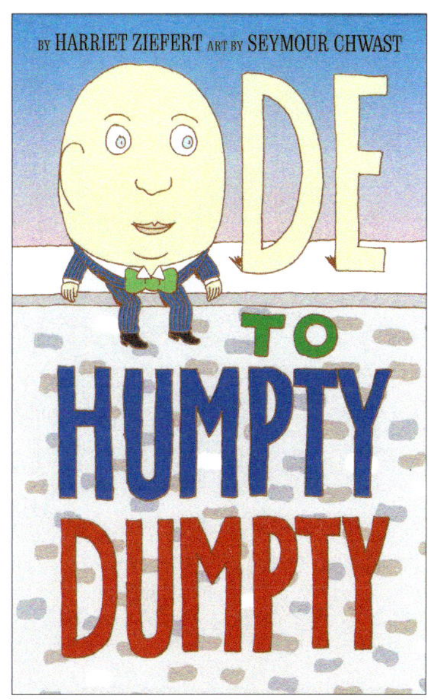

Ode to Humpty Dumpty, by Harriet Ziefert, illustrated by Seymour Chwast, 2001, 7.5" × 11.25" (19 × 28.5 cm), 32 pages.

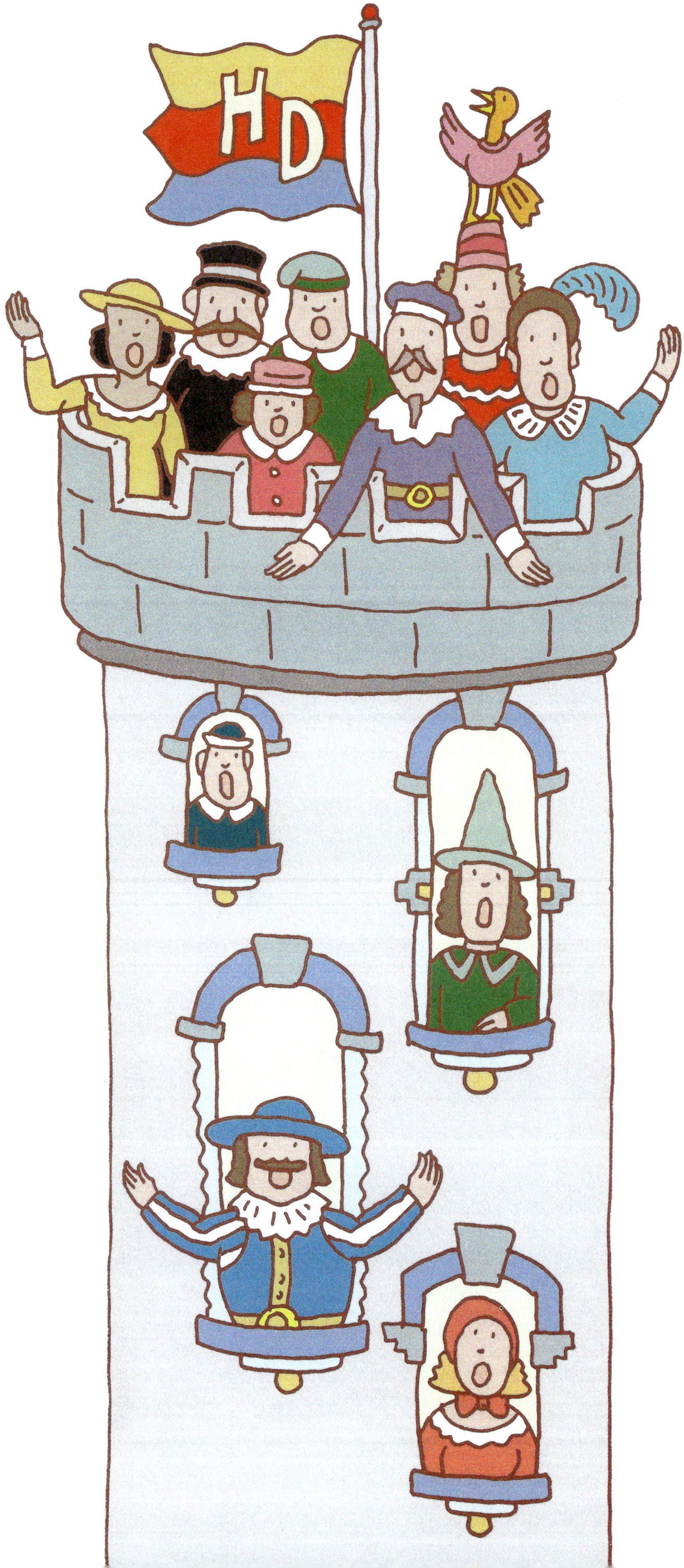

In this ode to the big egg by Harriet Ziefert, Humpty Dumpty was loved by all who knew him. So, when he fell off the wall and was unable to put himself back together again, the masses throughout the country paid homage to Humpty with statues and celebrations. Chwast took great pleasure in creating a vintage costume drama filled with ornamental flourishes that did not imitate the past but rather instilled life into old conceits.

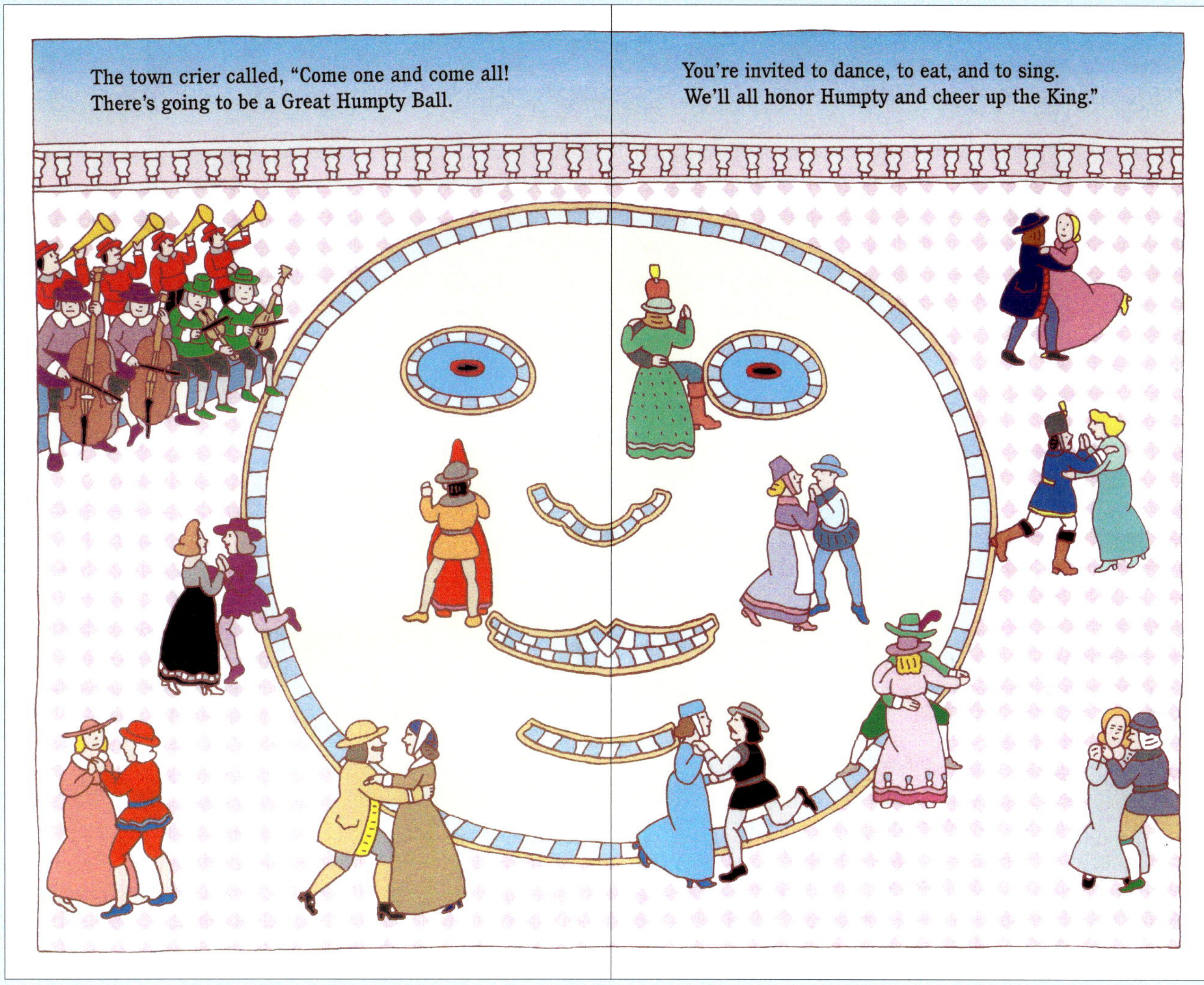
The town crier called, "Come one and come all!
There's going to be a Great Humpty Ball.
You're invited to dance, to eat, and to sing.
We'll all honor Humpty and cheer up the King."

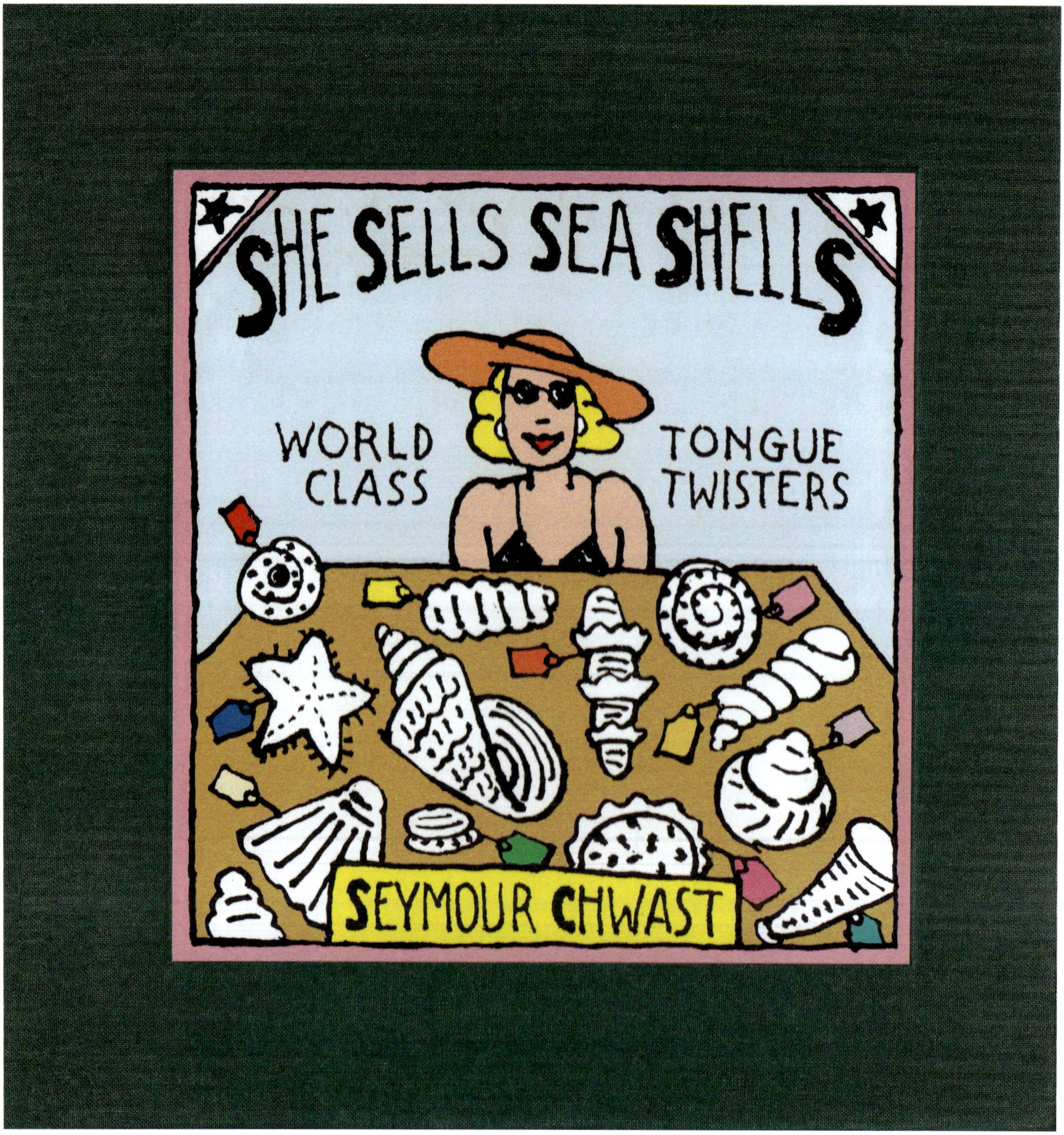

She Sells Sea Shells: World Class Tongue Twisters, by Seymour Chwast, 2008, 10" × 10" (25.5 × 25.5 cm), 64 pages.

She Sells Sea Shells

Chuck
eats cheap
Chinese.

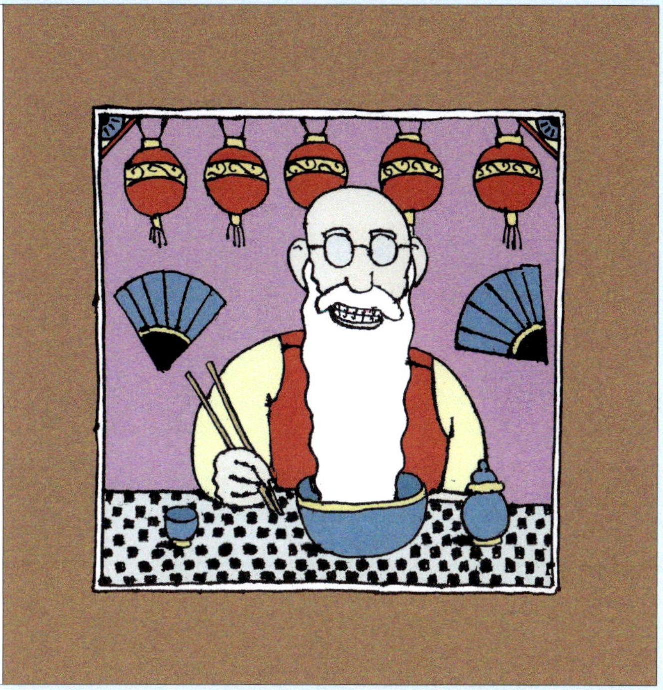

Washington
washes his britches
with dishes.

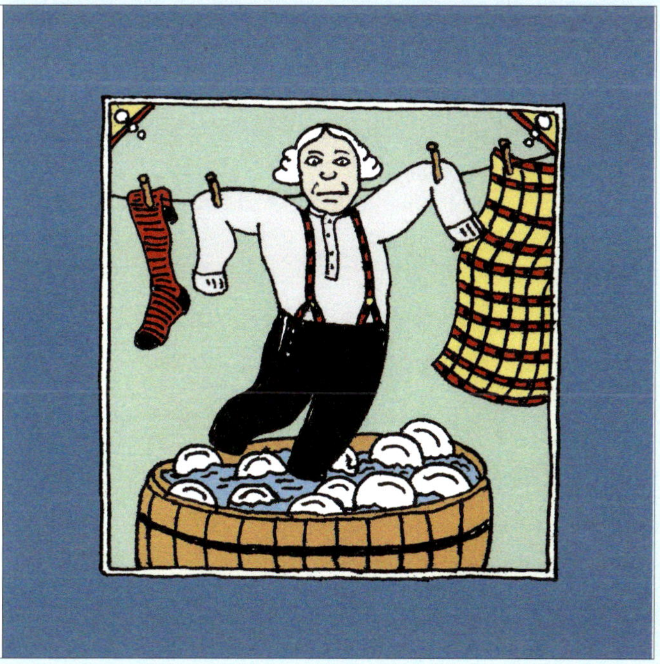

The zitherist plays his sister's zither.

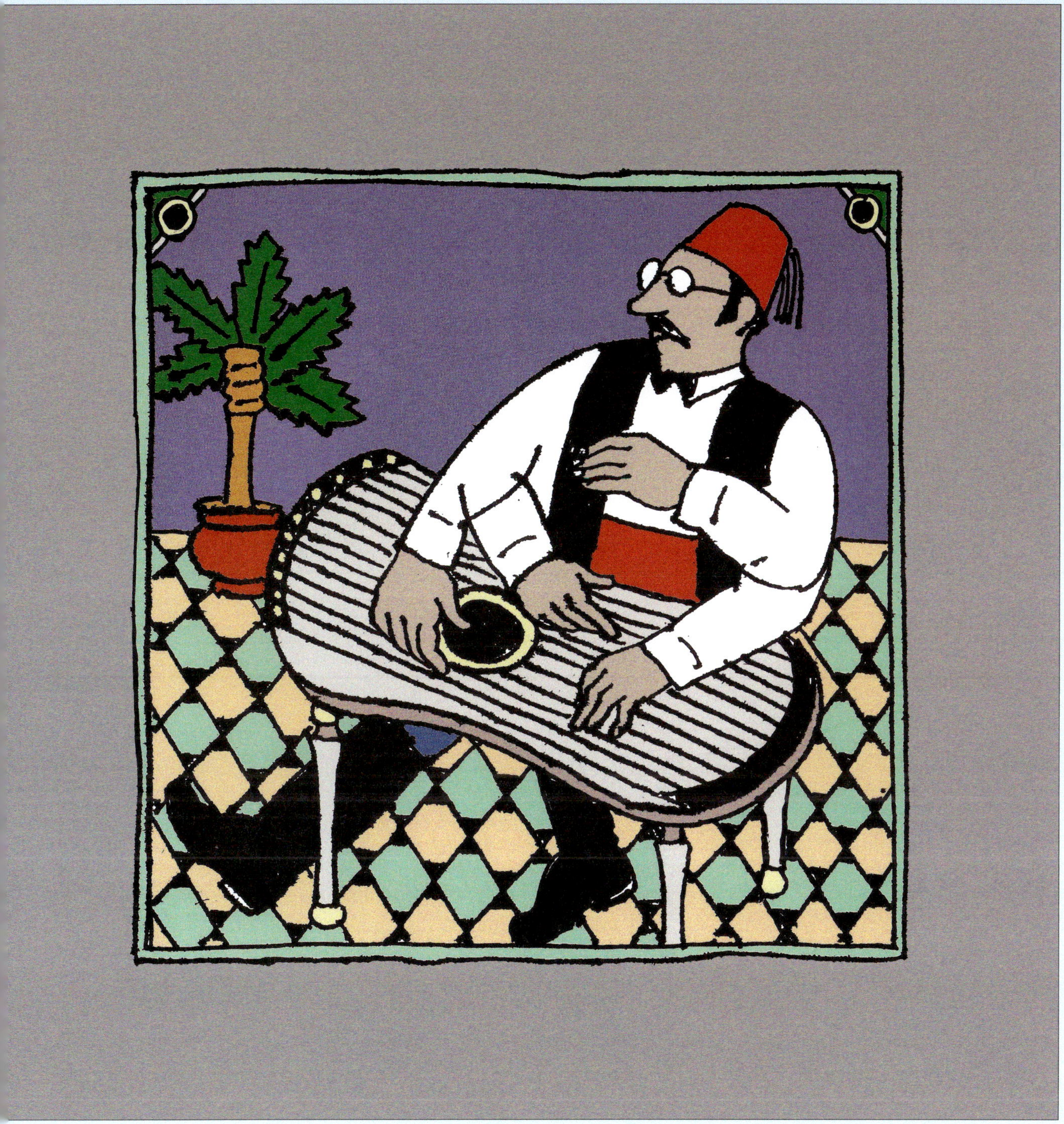

Chwast is enthralled and entertained by wordplay like "she sells sea shells." This, and the other tongue twisters in this little jewel of a book, are like mother's milk for him. The object is to pronounce the phrases as fast as possible without making a mistake; it's a perfect party game. Chwast took joy in drawing speedily as he imagined readers quickly pronouncing the words.

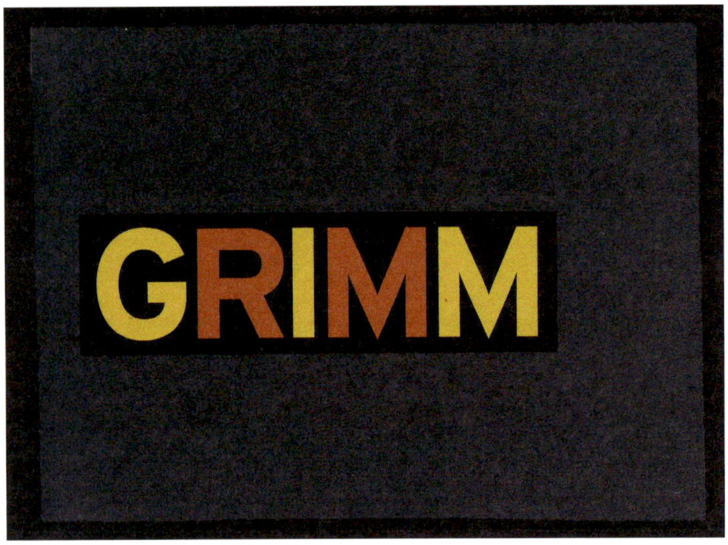

Grimm, by the Brothers Grimm, designed by Paula Scher and Lisa Mazur at Pentagram, illustrated by Seymour Chwast, 1997, 6.5" × 9" (16.5 × 23 cm), 96 pages.

Grimm

It is unclear which of the famous Grimm's fairy tales are original versions or later adaptations. The Brothers Grimm, Jacob (1785–1863) and Wilhelm (1786–1859), were famous for discovering and publishing German folk tales, including "Cinderella," "Hansel and Gretel," and "Snow White," among many more. Here, it is very clear that Chwast is the artist, however, using his faux-woodcut style and limiting the palette to three emblematic colors: black, orange, and yellow. The bold, expressive typography, designed by Paula Scher, gives the book its unique visual identity.

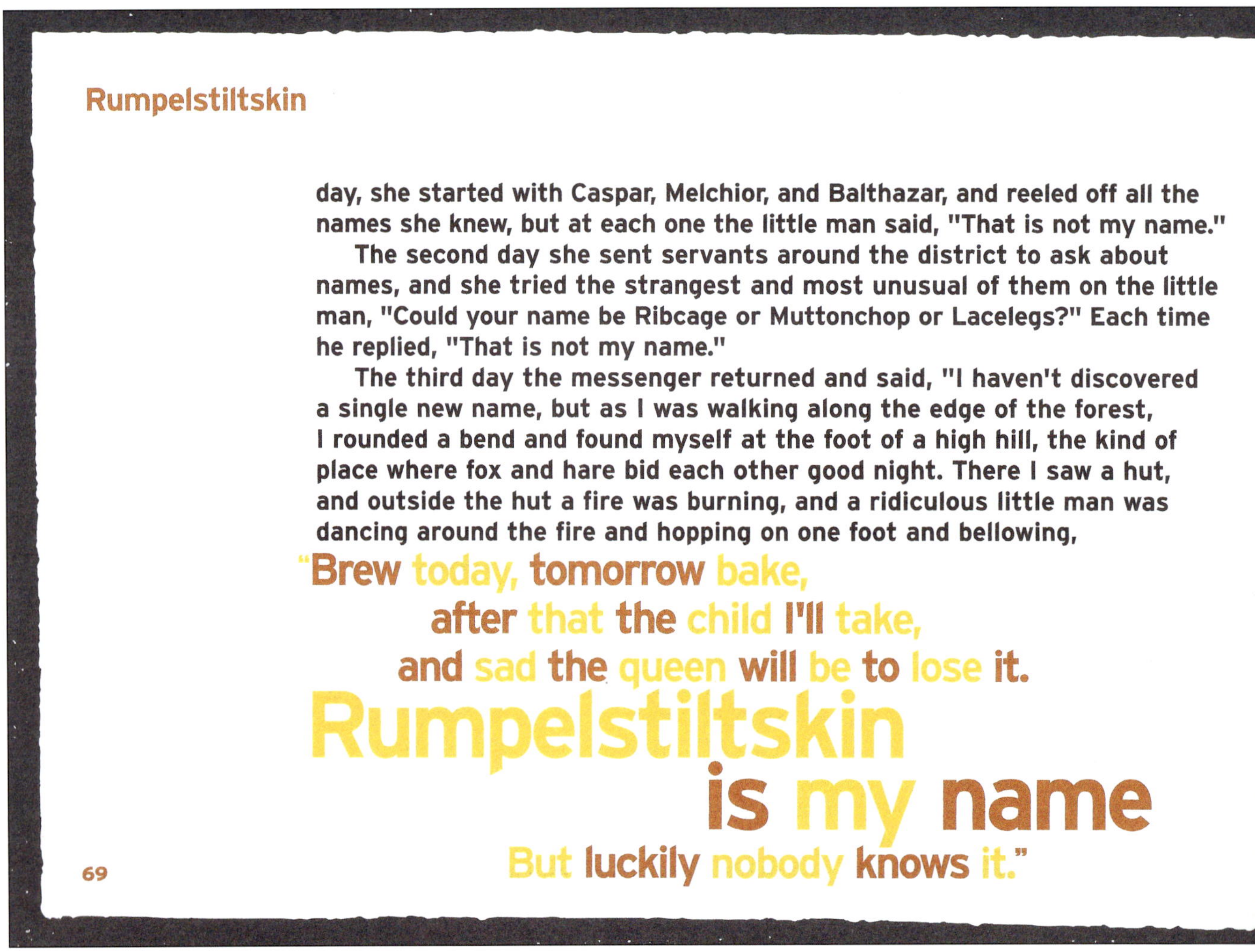
Rumpelstiltskin

day, she started with Caspar, Melchior, and Balthazar, and reeled off all the names she knew, but at each one the little man said, "That is not my name."

The second day she sent servants around the district to ask about names, and she tried the strangest and most unusual of them on the little man, "Could your name be Ribcage or Muttonchop or Lacelegs?" Each time he replied, "That is not my name."

The third day the messenger returned and said, "I haven't discovered a single new name, but as I was walking along the edge of the forest, I rounded a bend and found myself at the foot of a high hill, the kind of place where fox and hare bid each other good night. There I saw a hut, and outside the hut a fire was burning, and a ridiculous little man was dancing around the fire and hopping on one foot and bellowing,

"Brew today, tomorrow bake,
after that the child I'll take,
and sad the queen will be to lose it.
Rumpelstiltskin
is my name
But luckily nobody knows it."

69

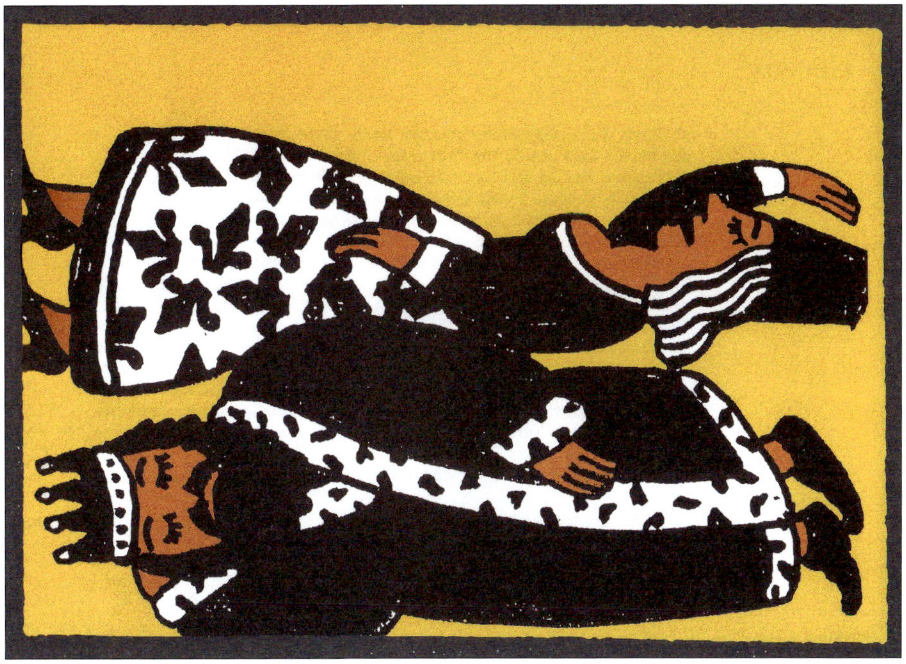

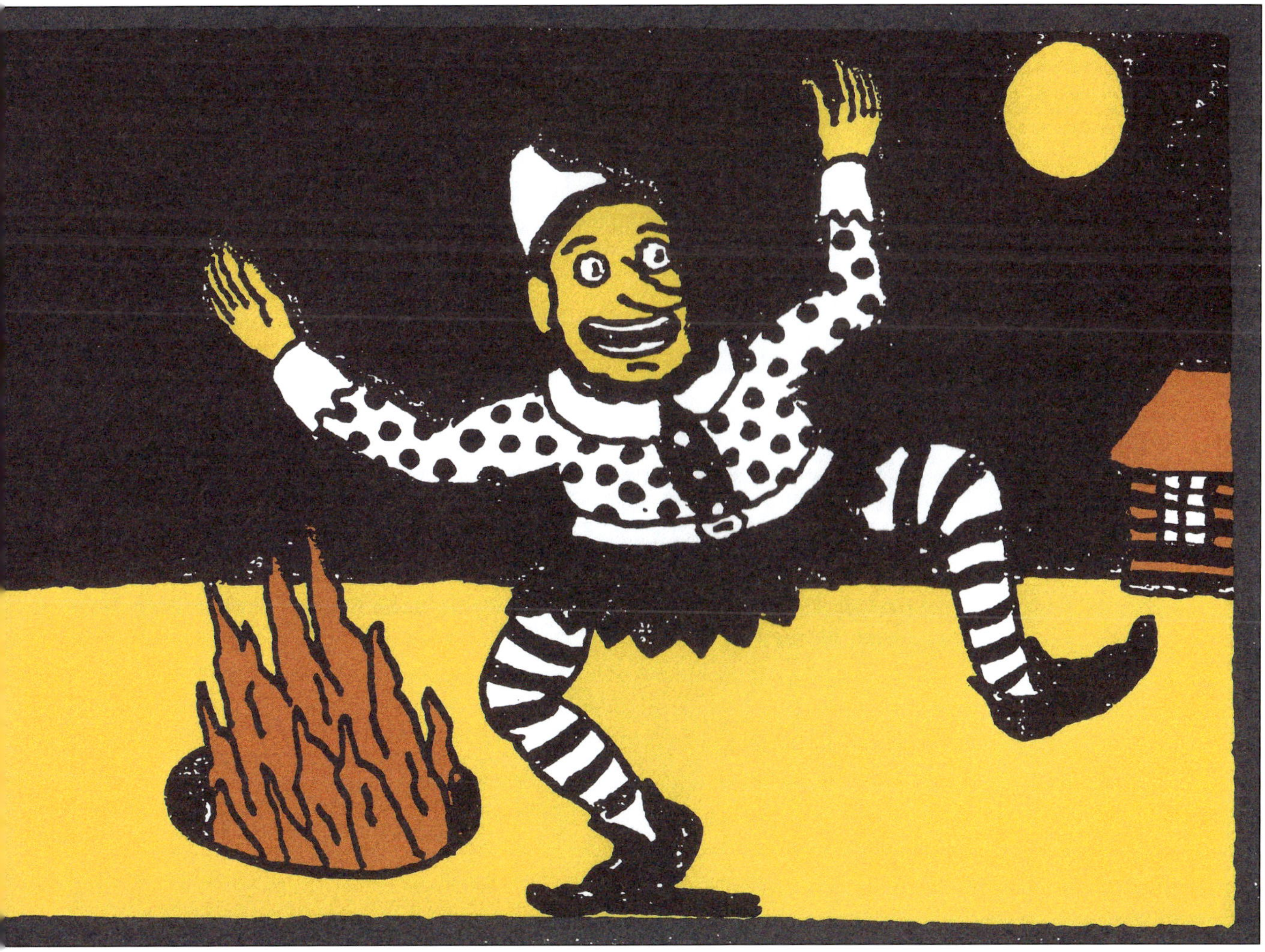

The Musicians of Bremen

tress wanted to drown me. Yes, yes I escaped, but now I'm at my wits' end—where am I to go?"

"Come to Bremen with us. You're good at serenading; you can join the band too." That appealed to the cat, and he went along.

Soon the three fugitives passed a farm. A cock was standing on the roof over the gate, crowing for all he was worth.

"Why," asked the donkey, "are you screaming like that? It's bloodcurdling."

"I'm predicting good weather," said the cock, "because it's the day Our Lady washes out the Christ Child's little shirts and hangs them up to dry. But tomorrow's Sunday. We're having company, and the farmer's wife is heartless. I heard her tell the cook she wanted to eat me tomorrow in the soup, and I'm to have my head cut off this evening. So now I'm screeching while the screeching's good."

"Redcomb," said the donkey, "don't be a fool. Why not come with us instead? We're on our way to Bremen. Whatever happens, it's sure to be better than death. You've got a fine voice, and if we all sing together, we're sure to be a hit." The cock liked the proposal and all four went on together.

But they couldn't get to Bremen in one day, and that evening they came to a forest and decided to stop for the night. The donkey and the dog lay down under a big tree, the cat climbed up on a branch and the cock flew to the very top of the tree where he felt safest. Before going to sleep, he looked around in all directions. He thought he saw a spark in the distance, and he
37 told his companions there must be a house nearby, for he'd seen a light.

Snow White

its own knife, fork, and spoon, and seven little cups. Against the wall there were seven little beds all in a row, covered with spotless white sheets. Snow White was very hungry and thirsty, but she didn't want to eat anyone's entire meal, so she ate a bit of bread and vegetables from each plate and drank a sip of wine from each cup. Then she was so tired that she lay down on one of the beds, but none of the beds quite suited her; some were too long and some were too short, but the seventh was just right. There she stayed and when she had said her prayers, she fell asleep.

When it was quite dark, the owners of the little house came home. They were seven dwarfs who went off to the mountains every day with their picks and shovels to mine silver. Once they were home, they lit their seven little candles, and when the light went up they saw someone had been there because certain things had been moved. The first said, "Who has been sitting in my chair?"

The second," Who has been eating off my plate?"

The third, "Who has taken a bite of my bread?"

The fourth, "Who has been eating some of my vegetables?"

The fifth, "Who has been using my fork?"

The sixth, "Who has been cutting with my knife?"

And the seventh, "Who has been drinking out of my cup?" The first looked around, saw a hollow in his bed and said: "Who has been lying in my bed?"

The others came running, and cried, "Somebody has been lying in my bed
55 too." But when the seventh looked at his bed, he saw Snow White lying there

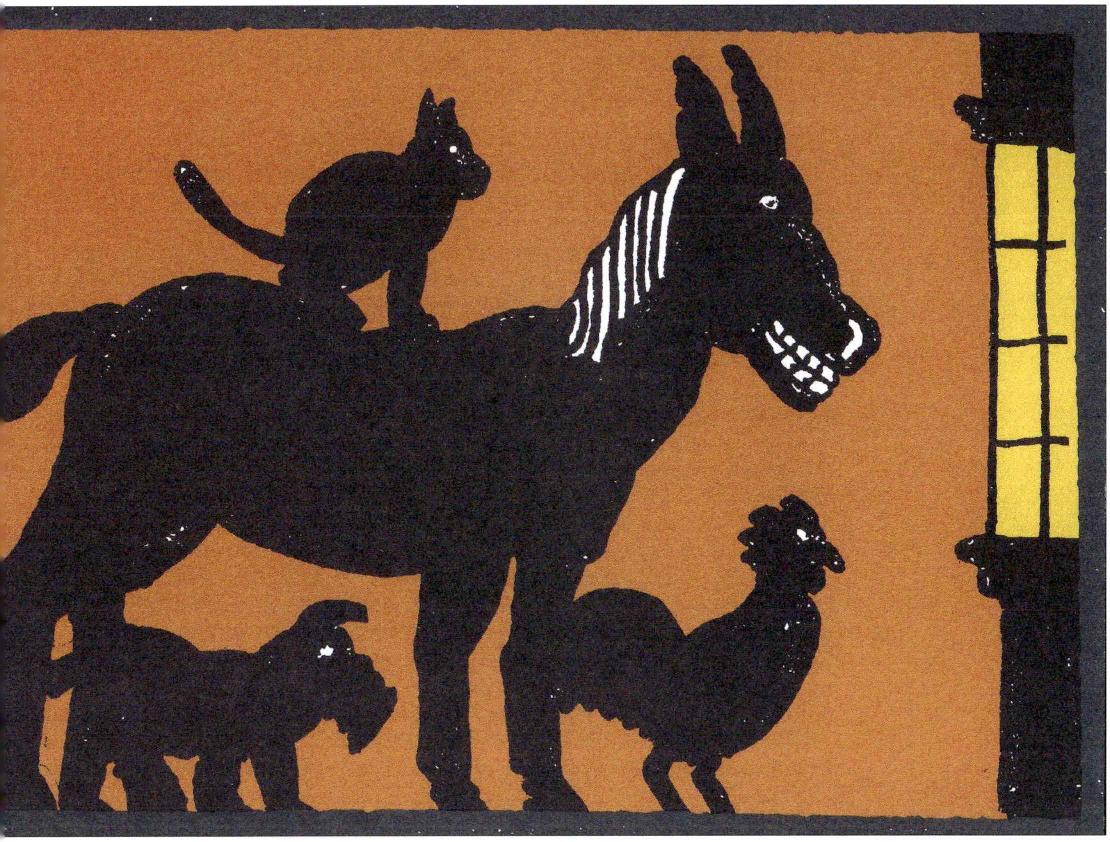

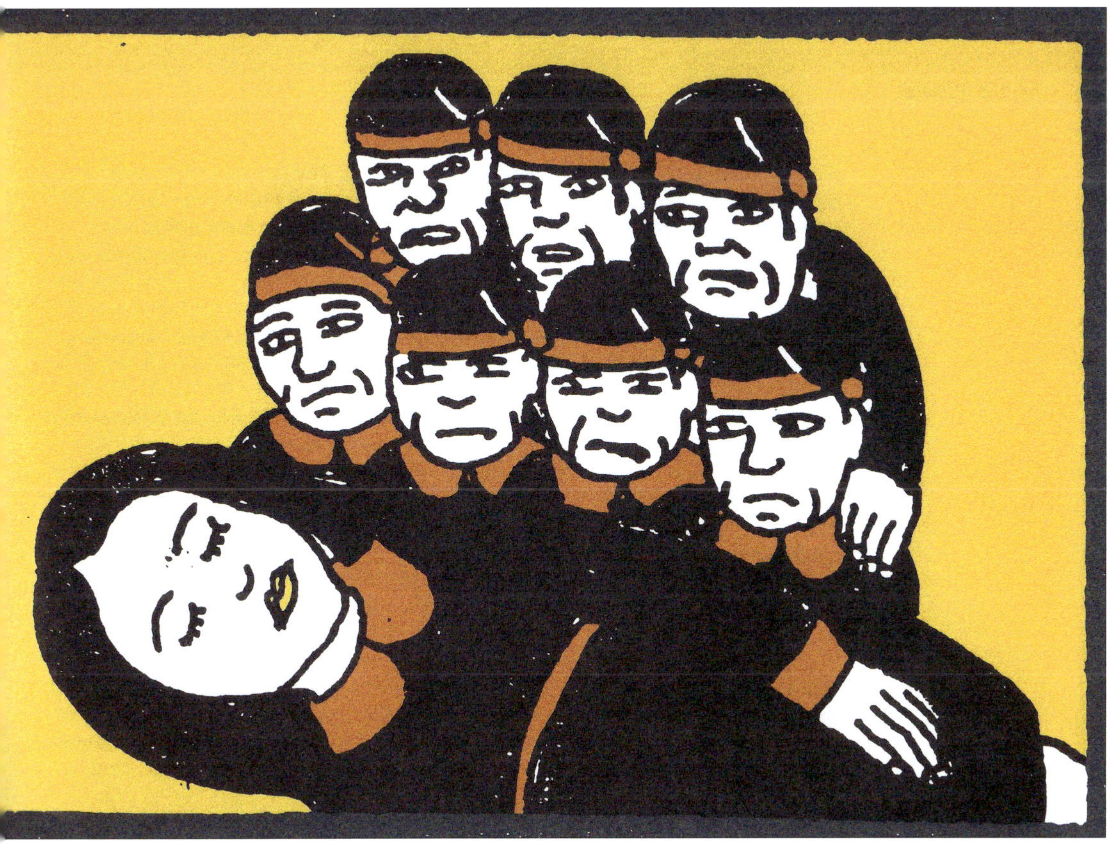

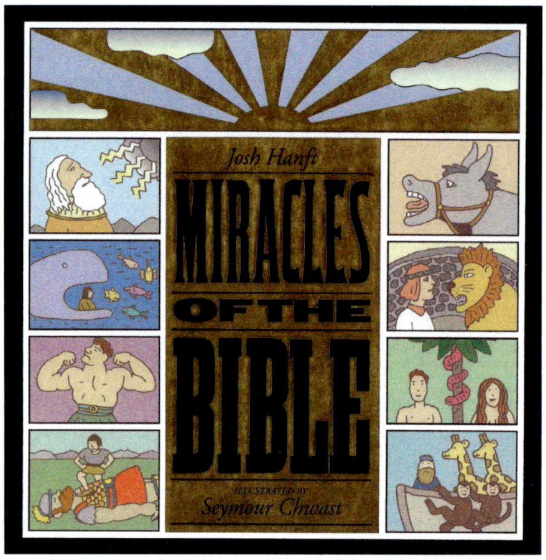

Miracles of the Bible, by Josh Hanft, illustrated by Seymour Chwast, 2007, 9.5" × 9.5" (24.25 × 24.25 cm), 32 pages.

Miracles of the Bible

Chwast employs a no-frills outline with flat color technique for this contemporary version of the Bible's miracles, interpreted by Josh Hanft. Stories such as that of David and Goliath and the parting of the Red Sea are done as tableaux consistent with their iconic appeal. When the cover flaps open, they reveal additional biblical scenes.

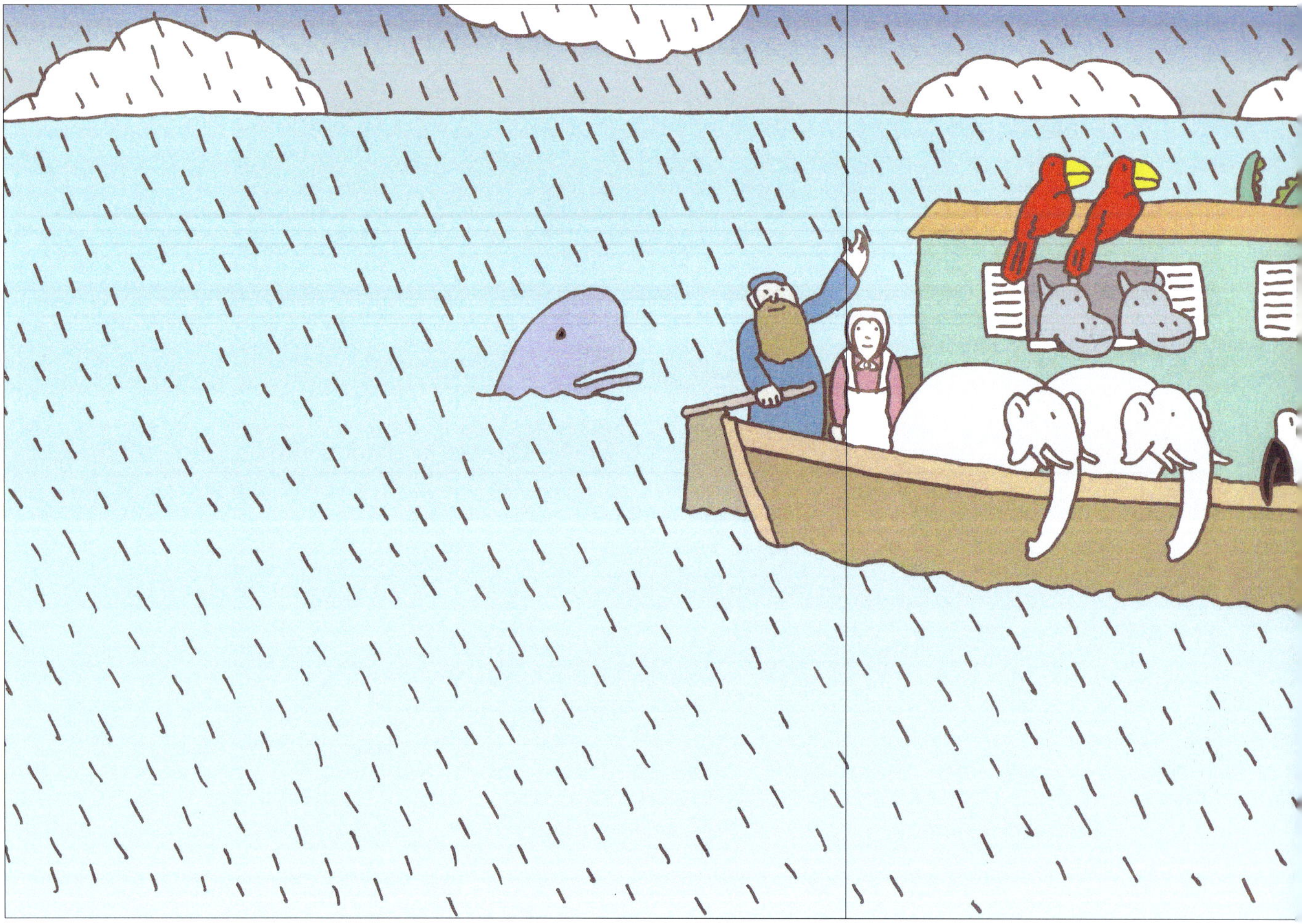

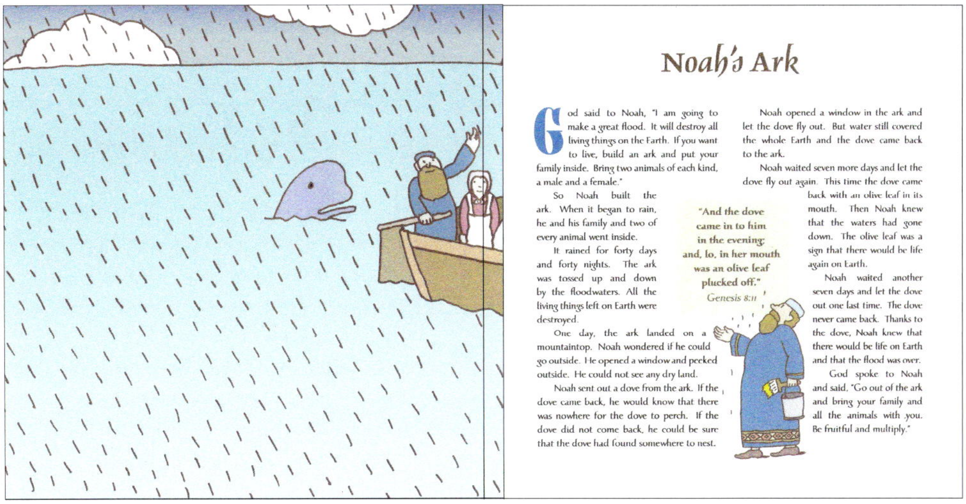

Noah's Ark

God said to Noah, "I am going to make a great flood. It will destroy all living things on the Earth. If you want to live, build an ark and put your family inside. Bring two animals of each kind, a male and a female."

So Noah built the ark. When it began to rain, he and his family and two of every animal went inside.

It rained for forty days and forty nights. The ark was tossed up and down by the floodwaters. All the living things left on Earth were destroyed.

One day, the ark landed on a mountaintop. Noah wondered if he could go outside. He opened a window and peeked outside. He could not see any dry land.

Noah sent out a dove from the ark. If the dove came back, he would know that there was nowhere for the dove to perch. If the dove did not come back, he could be sure that the dove had found somewhere to nest.

Noah opened a window in the ark and let the dove fly out. But water still covered the whole Earth and the dove came back to the ark.

Noah waited seven more days and let the dove fly out again. This time the dove came back with an olive leaf in its mouth. Then Noah knew that the waters had gone down. The olive leaf was a sign that there would be life again on Earth.

Noah waited another seven days and let the dove out one last time. The dove never came back. Thanks to the dove, Noah knew that there would be life on Earth and that the flood was over.

God spoke to Noah and said, "Go out of the ark and bring your family and all the animals with you. Be fruitful and multiply."

"And the dove came in to him in the evening; and, lo, in her mouth was an olive leaf plucked off."
Genesis 8:11

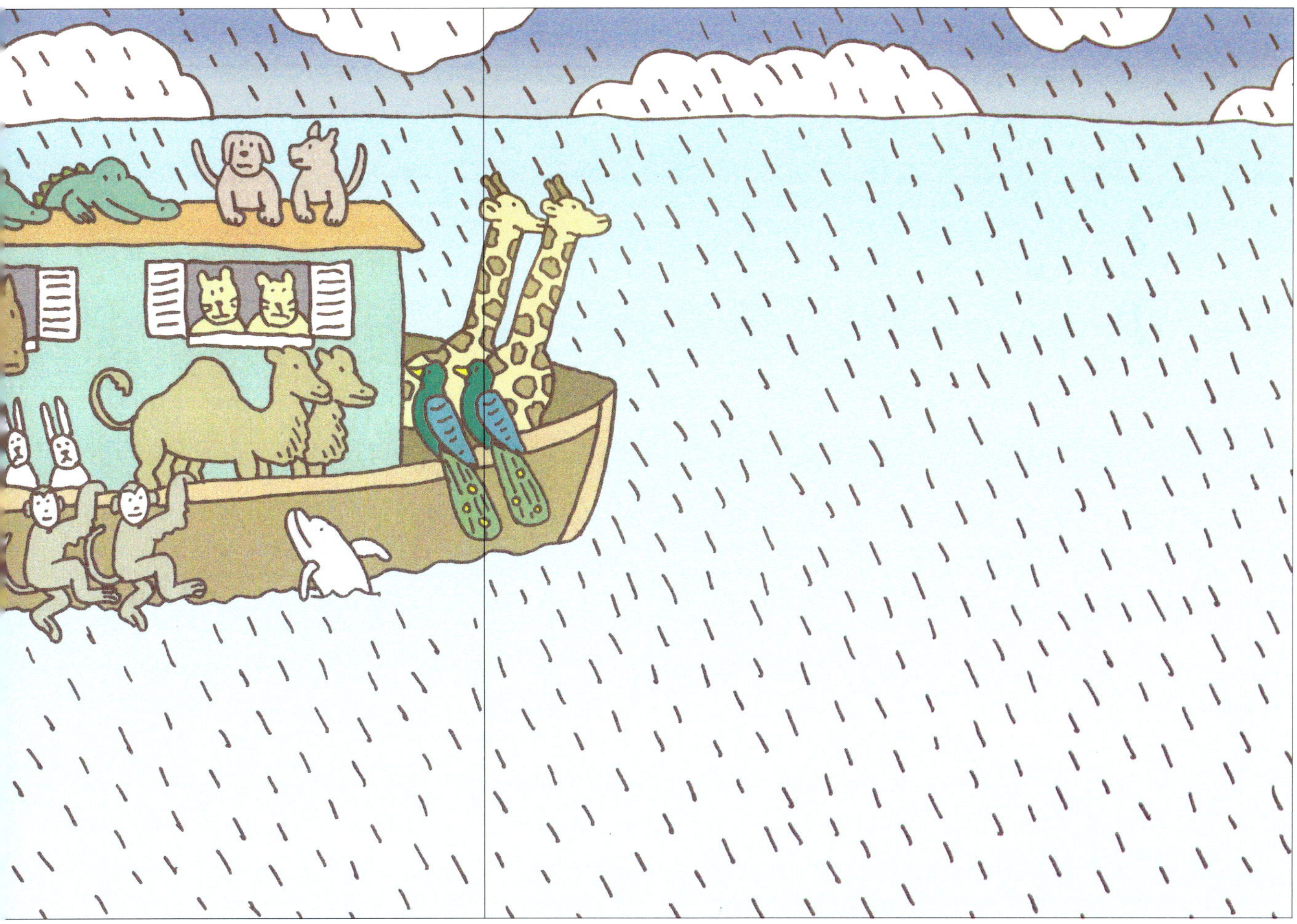

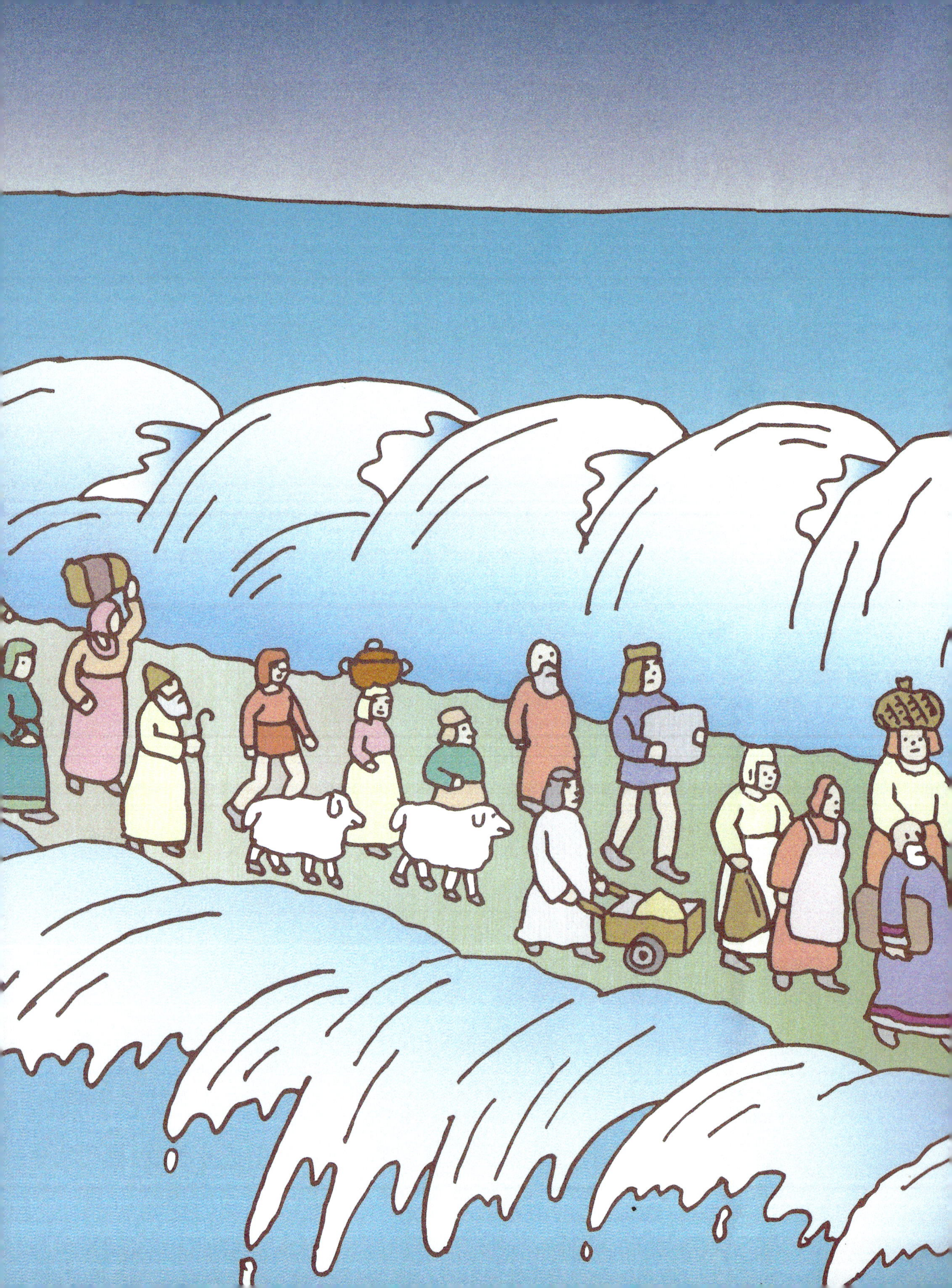

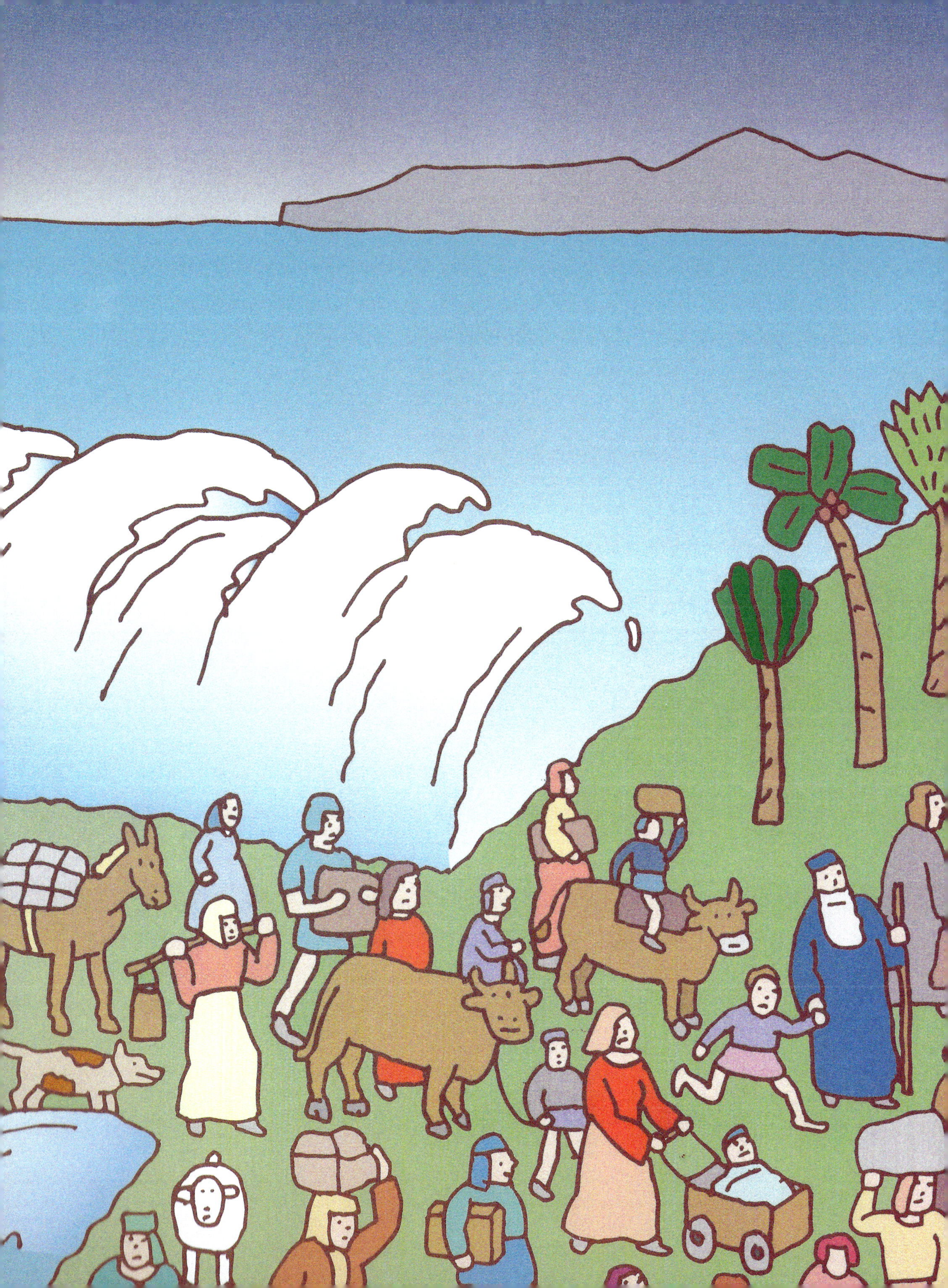

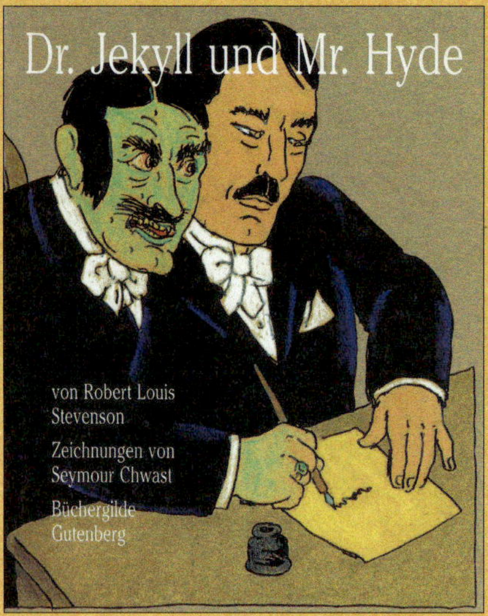

Dr. Jekyll und Mr. Hyde, by Robert Louis Stevenson, illustrated and designed by Seymour Chwast, 1995, 9.1" × 7.5" (23 × 19 cm), 96 pages.

Dr.Jekyll und Mr.Hyde

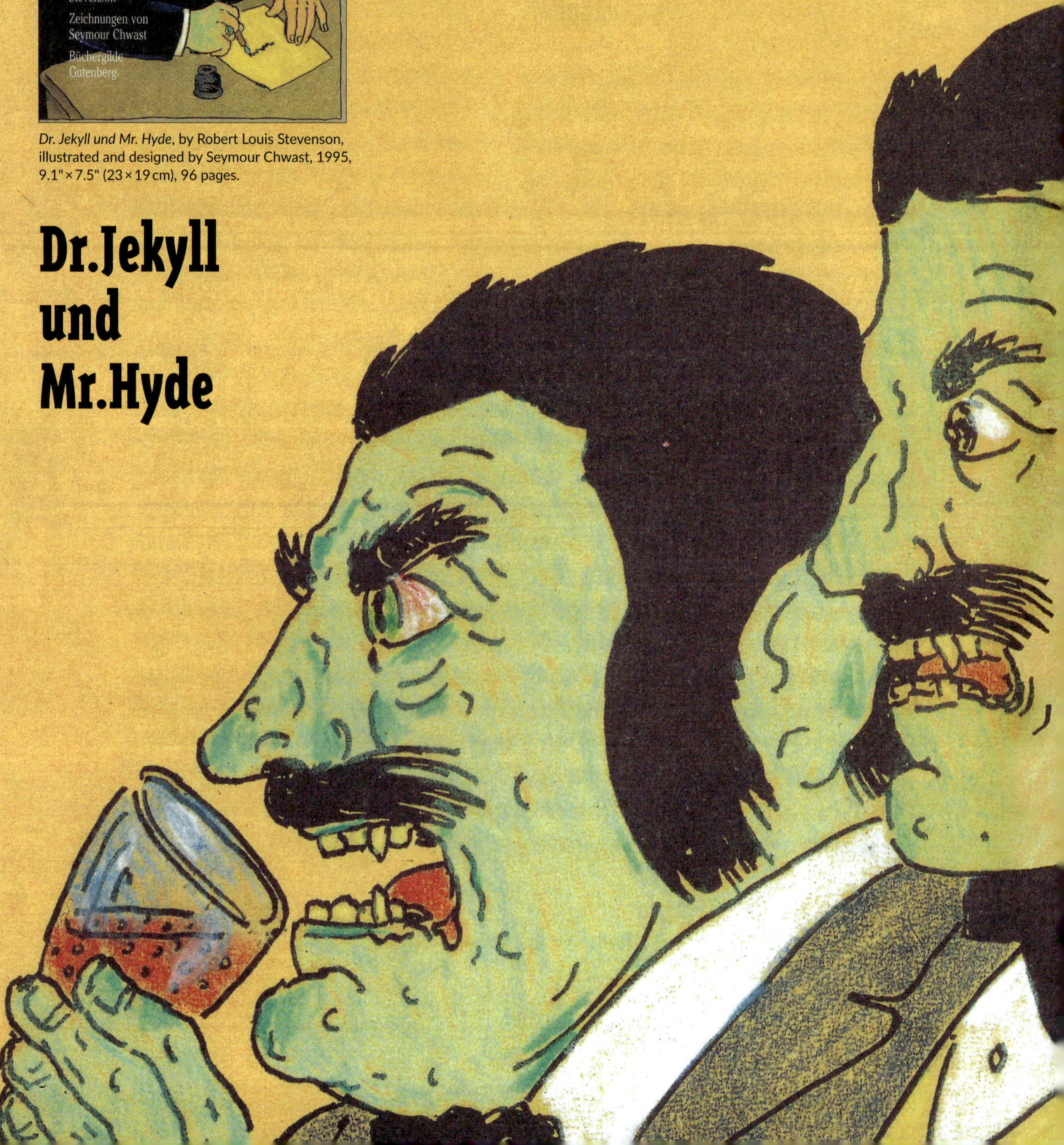

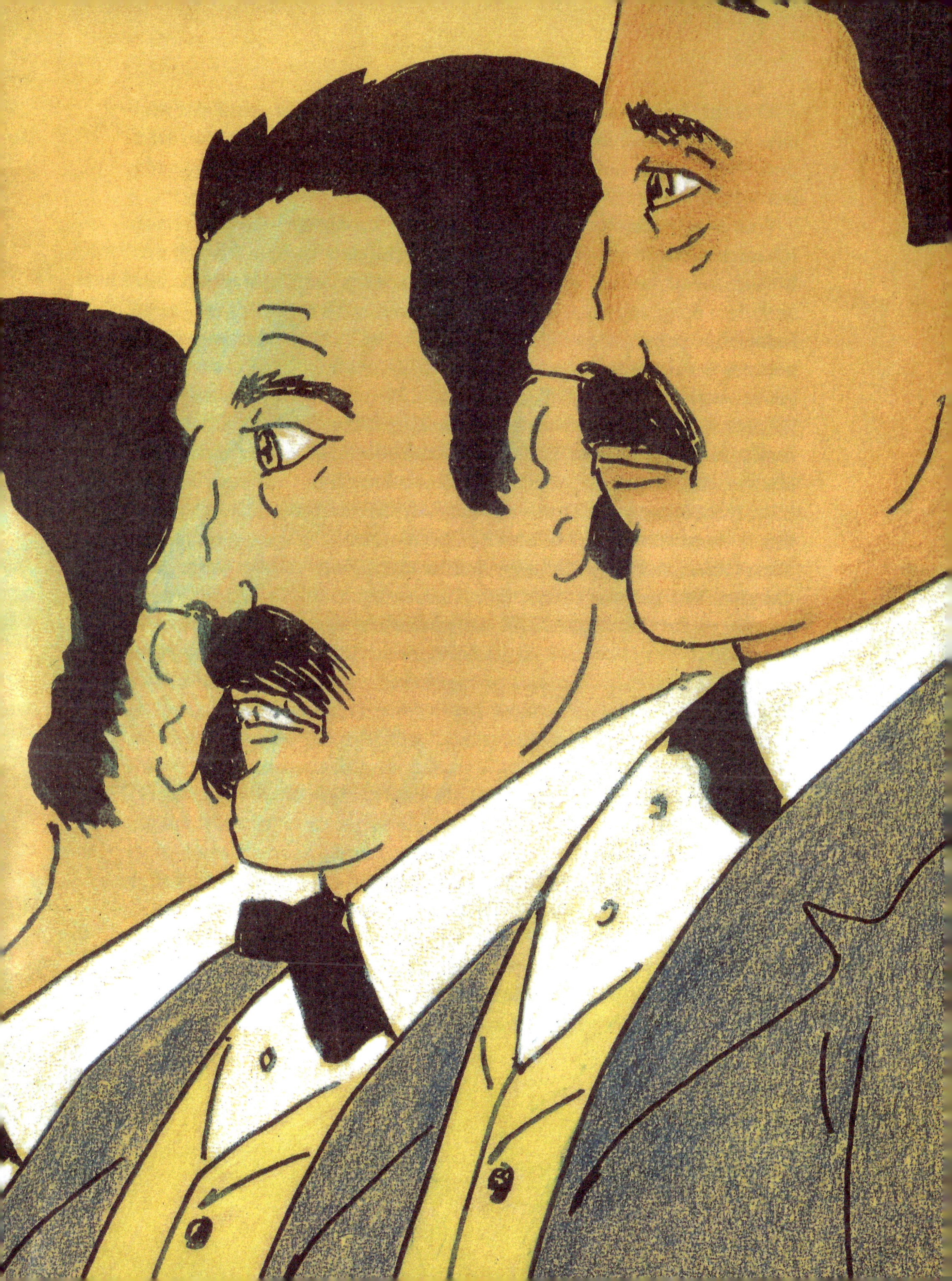

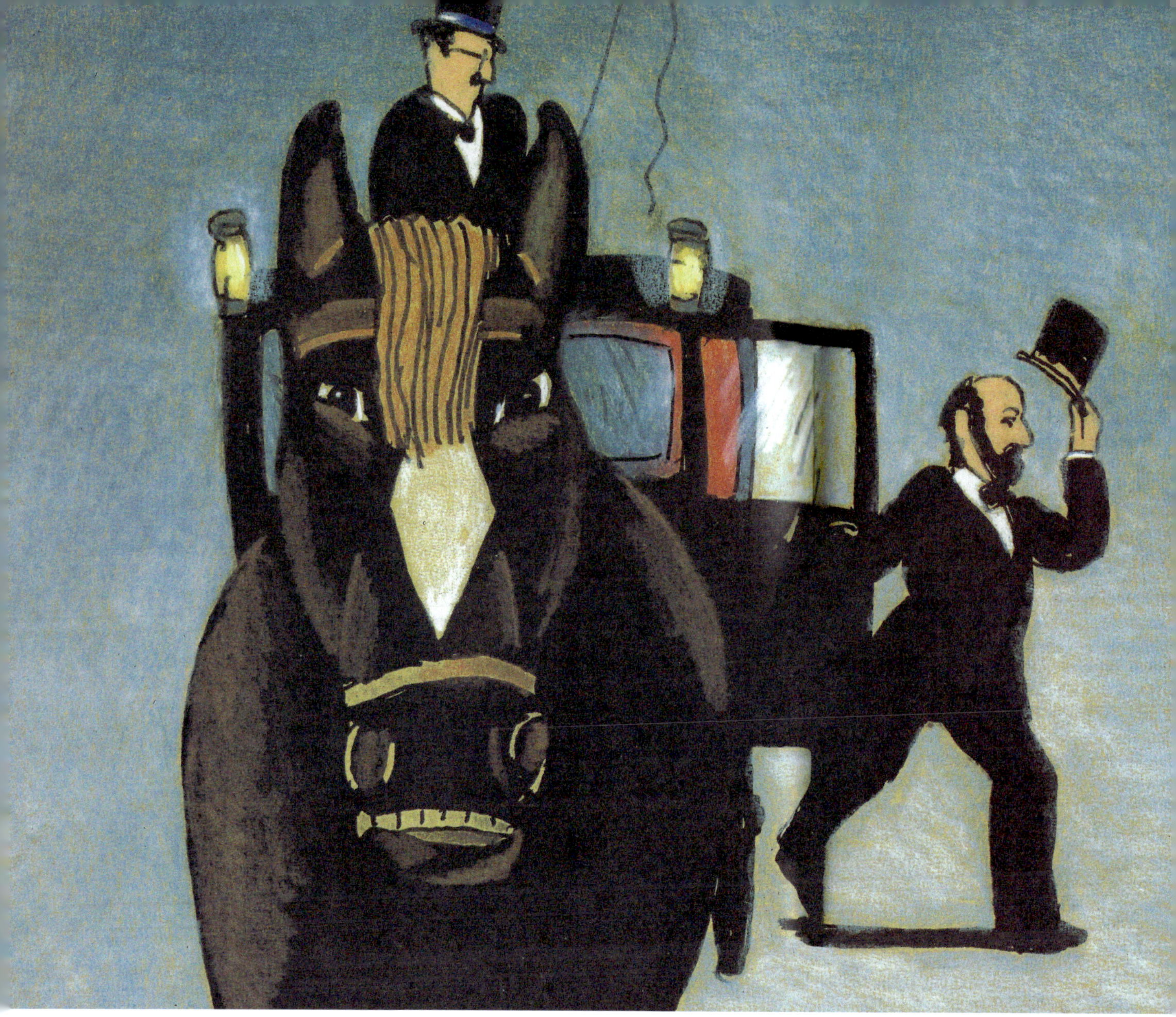

The text of the book changes in boldness to correspond with the content.

This is the first page of the text. Then, the weight gets heavier, and finally it becomes extra bold.

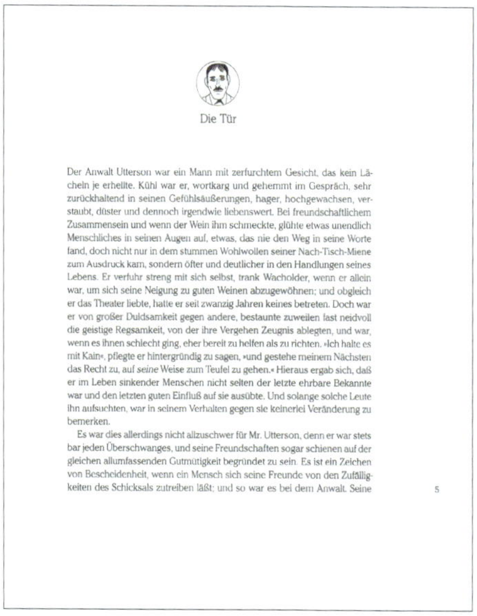

Die Tür

Der Anwalt Utterson war ein Mann mit zerfurchtem Gesicht, das kein Lächeln je erhellte. Kühl war er, wortkarg und gehemmt im Gespräch, sehr zurückhaltend in seinen Gefühlsäußerungen, hager, hochgewachsen, verstaubt, düster und dennoch irgendwie liebenswert. Bei freundschaftlichem Zusammensein und wenn der Wein ihm schmeckte, glühte etwas unendlich Menschliches in seinen Augen auf, etwas, das nie den Weg in seine Worte fand, doch nicht nur in dem stummen Wohlwollen seiner Nach-Tisch-Miene zum Ausdruck kam, sondern öfter und deutlicher in den Handlungen seines Lebens. Er verfuhr streng mit sich selbst, trank Wacholder, wenn er allein war, um sich seine Neigung zu guten Weinen abzugewöhnen; und obgleich er das Theater liebte, hatte er seit zwanzig Jahren keines betreten. Doch war er von großer Duldsamkeit gegen andere, bestaunte zuweilen fast neidvoll die geistige Regsamkeit, von der ihre Vergehen Zeugnis ablegten, und war, wenn es ihnen schlecht ging, eher bereit zu helfen als zu richten. »Ich halte es mit Kain«, pflegte er hintergründig zu sagen, »und gestehe meinem Nächsten das Recht zu, auf *seine* Weise zum Teufel zu gehen.« Hieraus ergab sich, daß er im Leben sinkender Menschen nicht selten der letzte ehrbare Bekannte war und den letzten guten Einfluß auf sie ausübte. Und solange solche Leute ihn aufsuchten, war in seinem Verhalten gegen sie keinerlei Veränderung zu bemerken.

Es war dies allerdings nicht allzuschwer für Mr. Utterson, denn er war stets bar jeden Überschwanges, und seine Freundschaften sogar schienen auf der gleichen allumfassenden Gutmütigkeit begründet zu sein. Es ist ein Zeichen von Bescheidenheit, wenn ein Mensch sich seine Freunde von den Zufälligkeiten des Schicksals zutreiben läßt; und so war es bei dem Anwalt. Seine

5

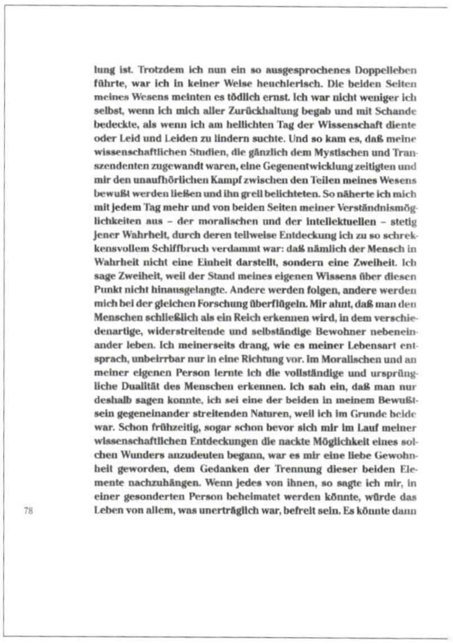

lung ist. Trotzdem ich nun ein so ausgesprochenes Doppelleben führte, war ich in keiner Weise heuchlerisch. Die beiden Seiten meines Wesens meinten es tödlich ernst. Ich war nicht weniger ich selbst, wenn ich mich aller Zurückhaltung begab und mit Schande bedeckte, als wenn ich am hellichten Tag der Wissenschaft diente oder Leid und Leiden zu lindern suchte. Und so kam es, daß meine wissenschaftlichen Studien, die gänzlich dem Mystischen und Transzendenten zugewandt waren, eine Gegenentwicklung zeitigten und mir den unaufhörlichen Kampf zwischen den Teilen meines Wesens bewußt werden ließen und ihn grell belichteten. So näherte ich mich mit jedem Tag mehr und von beiden Seiten meiner Verständnismöglichkeiten aus – der moralischen und der intellektuellen – stetig jener Wahrheit, durch deren teilweise Entdeckung ich zu so schrekkensvollem Schiffbruch verdammt war: daß nämlich der Mensch in Wahrheit nicht eine Einheit darstellt, sondern eine Zweiheit. Ich sage Zweiheit, weil der Stand meines eigenen Wissens über diesen Punkt nicht hinausgelangte. Andere werden folgen, andere werden mich bei der gleichen Forschung überflügeln. Mir ahnt, daß man den Menschen schließlich als ein Reich erkennen wird, in dem verschiedenartige, widerstreitende und selbständige Bewohner nebeneinander leben. Ich meinerseits drang, wie es meiner Lebensart entsprach, unbeirrbar nur in eine Richtung vor. Im Moralischen und an meiner eigenen Person lernte ich die vollständige und ursprüngliche Dualität des Menschen erkennen. Ich sah ein, daß man nur deshalb sagen konnte, ich sei eine der beiden in meinem Bewußtsein gegeneinander streitenden Naturen, weil ich im Grunde beide war. Schon frühzeitig, sogar schon bevor sich mir im Lauf meiner wissenschaftlichen Entdeckungen die nackte Möglichkeit eines solchen Wunders anzudeuten begann, war es mir eine liebe Gewohnheit geworden, dem Gedanken der Trennung dieser beiden Elemente nachzuhängen. Wenn jedes von ihnen, so sagte ich mir, in einer gesonderten Person beheimatet werden könnte, würde das Leben von allem, was unerträglich war, befreit sein. Es könnte dann

78

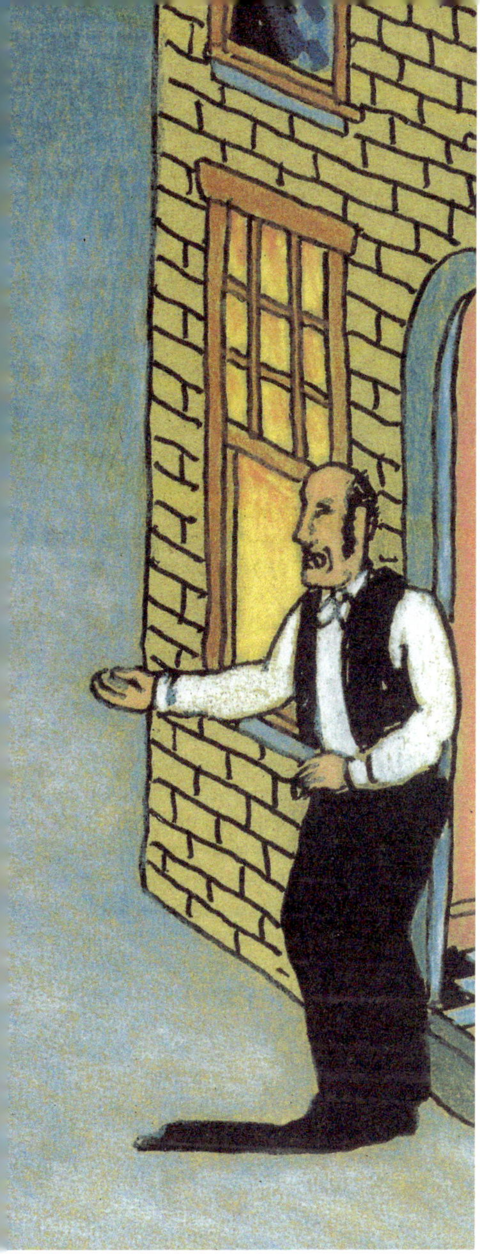

This classic from Robert Louis Stevenson has been illustrated and reimagined many times in books, film, and Classic Illustrated comic books. For a German publisher, Chwast imparts his own ghoulish expressionism to the story of a scientist who invents a serum that enables him to discover the evil side of the human condition. Most striking is the transition from the mild mannered, handsome Dr. Jekyll into the monstrous Mr. Hyde. As Chwast notes, he took license with grotesque depiction, as this is a book for older children.

der Ungerechte seinen Weg verfolgen, frei von den Sehnsüchten und der Reue seines besseren Zwillings; und der Gerechte könnte stetig und sicher seinen Pfad aufwärts verfolgen und das Gute tun, das ihm Freude einträgt, ohne der Schande und Strafe ausgesetzt zu sein durch dies ihm fremde Böse. Es war der Fluch der Menschheit, daß diese so ungleichen Reiser zusammengebündelt waren – daß im gequälten Schoß des Bewußtseins diese polar gegensätzlichen Zwillinge sich ständig befeindeten. Wie also waren sie zu trennen?

So weit war ich in meinen Erwägungen gediehen, als vom Arbeitstisch des Laboratoriums Licht fiel auf den Gegenstand meiner Forschung. Ich begann, tiefer als je ein Mensch vor mir, die bebende Unstofflichkeit, die nebelhafte Vergänglichkeit und Veränderlichkeit dieses scheinbar so festen Leibes, in den gewandet wir wandeln, wahrzunehmen. Ich fand, daß es mancherlei Mittel gab, denen die Kraft innewohnte, das fleischliche Kleid zu erschüttern und abzustreifen, wie der Wind die Vorhänge eines Zeltes aufflattern läßt. Aus zwei triftigen Gründen will ich mich nicht weiter in den wissenschaftlichen Teil meiner Beichte einlassen. Erstens, weil ich erfahren habe, daß die Schicksalsbürde unseres Daseins für immer unseren Schultern anhaftet und bei dem Versuch, sie abzuschütteln, nur drückender und qualvoller wiederkehrt. Zweitens, weil, wie es meine Erzählung nur allzu deutlich zeigen wird, meine Entdeckungen lückenhaft waren. Es genüge also zu sagen, daß ich nicht nur meinen natürlichen Leib als bloße Aura und Strahlung gewisser Kräfte, aus denen mein Geist sich zusammensetzte, erkannte, sondern daß es mir auch gelang, ein Mittel zusammenzustellen, durch welches diesen Kräften ihre bindende Übermacht genommen wurde, so daß sich eine zweite Form und Gestalt anstatt der ersten ergab, mir nicht weniger natürlich, da sie Ausdruck niederer Elemente in meiner Seele war und ihren Stempel trug.

Ich zauderte lange, ehe ich diese theoretische Erkenntnis praktisch zu erproben versuchte. Ich wußte sehr wohl, daß ich mich in Todesgefahr begab; denn ein Mittel, das so machtvoll die eigenste

79

86

anderen Bank angelegt wurde auf den Namen Edward Hydes selbst. Und als ich dann meine Handschrift verstellte, um meinem Doppelgänger auf diese Weise eine Unterschrift zu verschaffen, nahm ich an, ich sei sicher vor dem Zugriff des Schicksals.

Etwa zwei Monate vor der Ermordung Sir Danvers' war ich wieder einmal abenteuernd unterwegs gewesen und zu später Stunde heimgekehrt. Am nächsten Tag erwachte ich im Bett mit recht seltsamen Gefühlen. Vergebens suchte ich mich zurechtzufinden. Vergebens betrachtete ich die schönen Möbel und die Weiträumigkeit des Schlafzimmers meines Hauses. Vergebens erkannte ich das Muster der Bettvorhänge und die Schnitzerei an den Pfosten. Hartnäckig bestand etwas in mir darauf, daß ich mich nicht befand, wo ich war, daß ich nicht in der mich scheinbar umgebenden Umwelt erwacht sei, sondern in dem kleinen Zimmer in Soho, in dem ich zu schlafen pflegte, wenn ich Edward Hydes Gestalt angenommen hatte. Ich lachte vor mich hin und begann, da ich nun einmal psychologisch eingestellt bin, träumerisch die Ursachen dieser Täuschung zu erwägen, wobei ich unmerklich wieder in angenehmen morgendlichen Halbschlaf verfiel. Als ich in diesem Zustand einmal die Augen öffnete, fiel mein Blick auf meine Hand. Der Hand Henry Jekylls merkte man, wie Du oft gesagt hast, seinen Beruf an, sowohl der Form wie der Größe nach: Sie war kräftig, fest, weiß und gut geformt. Die Hand aber, die ich da deutlich vor mir sah, wie sie im gelben Glimmer eines Londoner Morgens halbgeschlossen auf der Bettdecke lag, war hager, sehnig, knochig, graubleich und dicht überschattet von dunklem Flaum. Es war Edward Hydes Hand.

Ich muß sie wohl sekundenlang in leerer Verwunderung angestarrt haben, ehe ein jäher Schreck meine Brust durchhallte wie das Gellen von Zimbeln. Ich sprang aus dem Bett

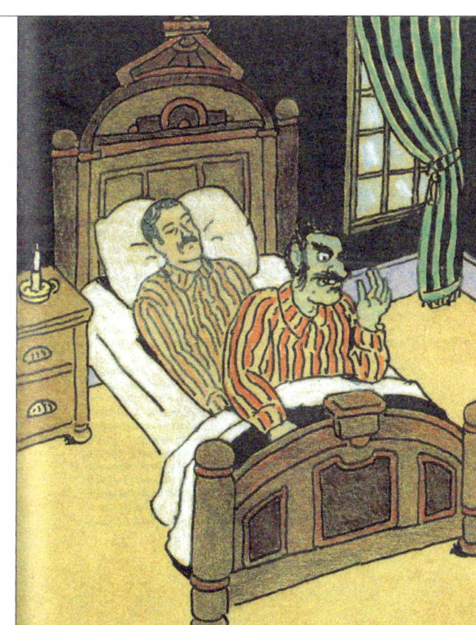

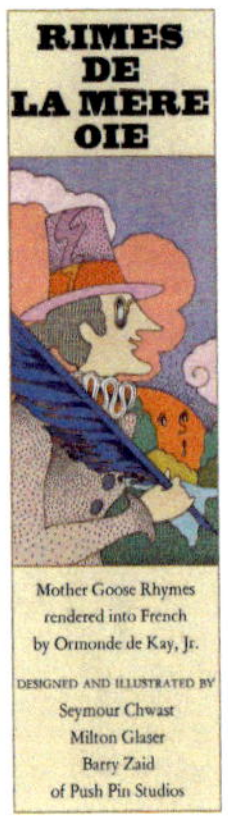

Rimes de La Mere Oie, Mother Goose Rhymes, rendered into French by Ormonde de Kay Jr., designed and illustrated by Seymour Chwast, Milton Glaser, and Barry Zaid of Push Pin Studios, 1971, 7" × 14" (17.75 × 35.5 cm), 40 pages.

Rimes de La Mere Oie

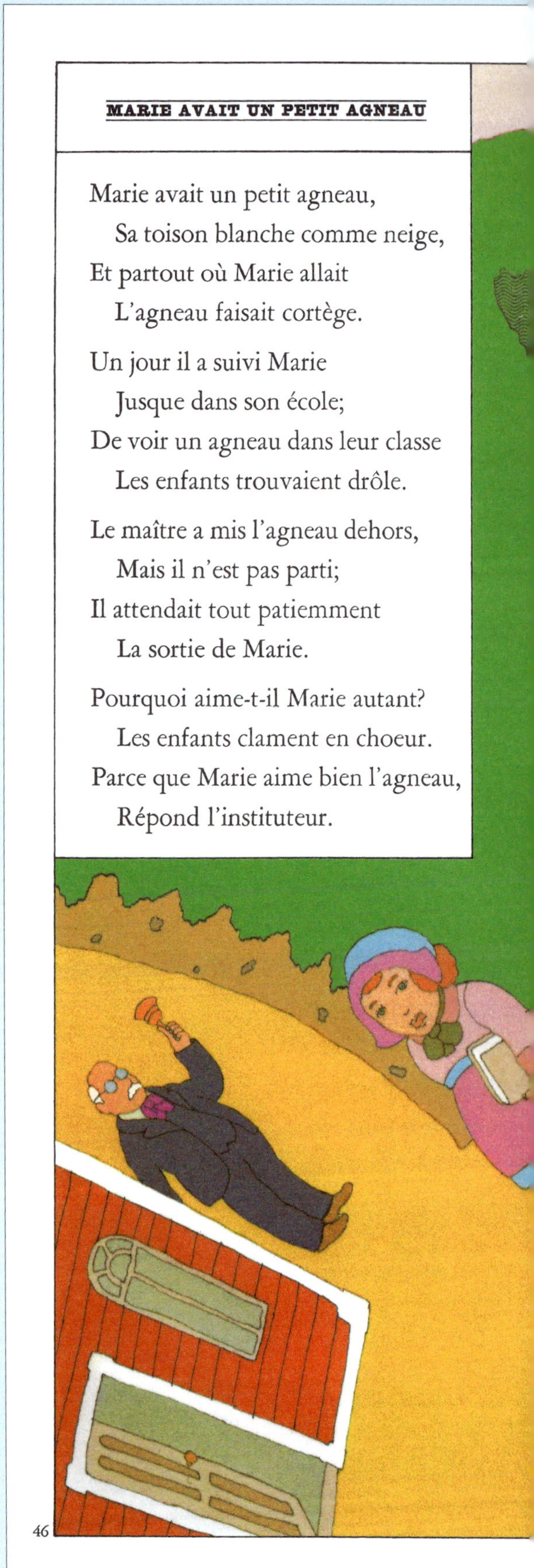

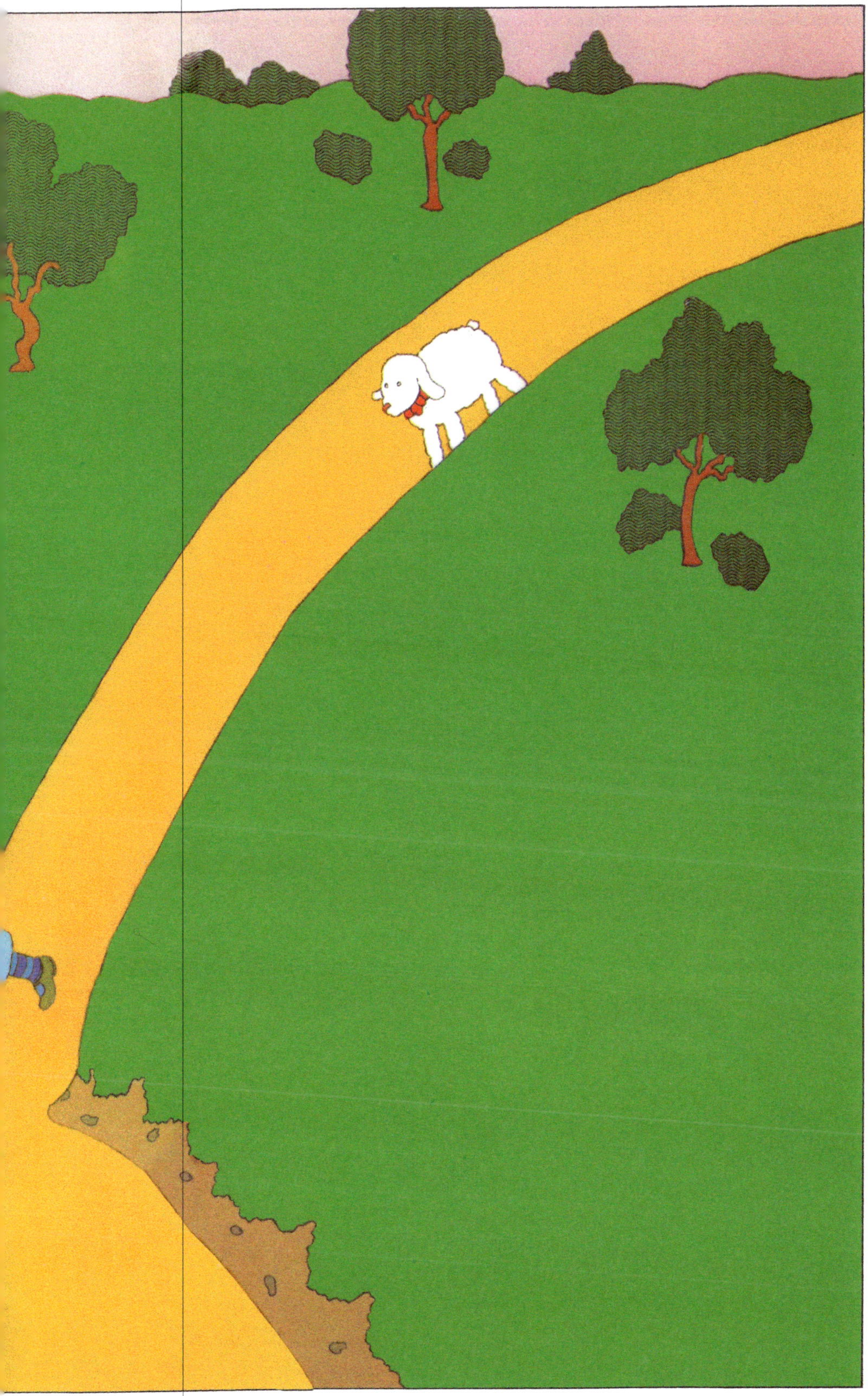

47

LA MERE GIGOGNE

La Mère Gigogne
Vit dans un soulier,
Elle a tant d'enfants
Qu'elle ne sait où tourner.

Elle leur donne du bouillon
Sans pain ni biscuit,
Les fouette tous fort
Et les envoie au lit.

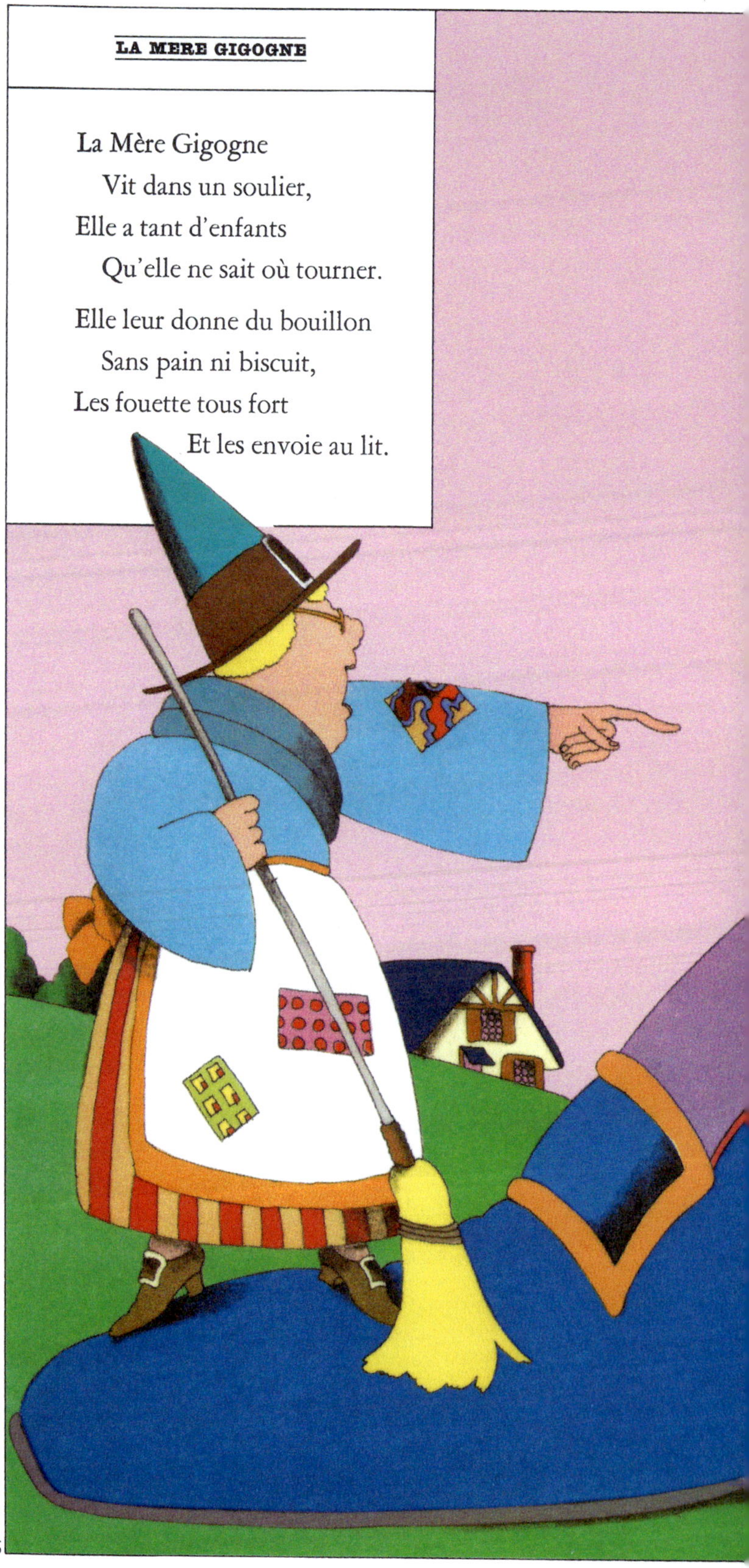

66

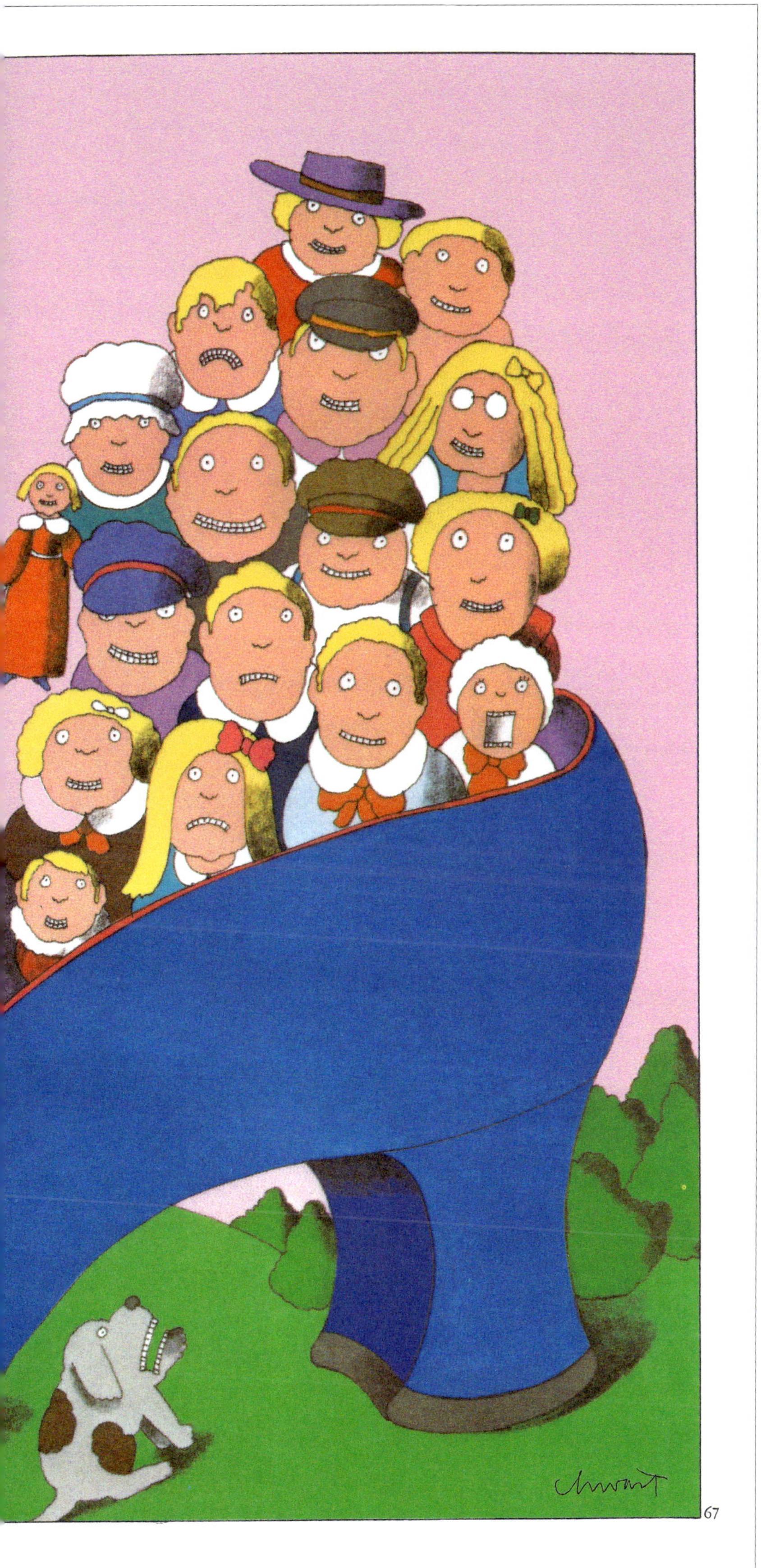

For this French version of *Mother Goose*, Chwast relies on his faithful outline and flat color style, in which he plays with perspective to provoke surreal perceptions. Working with colleagues from Push Pin Studios, Chwast contributes old favorites such as “Old Mother Hubbard” and lesser-known ones such as “Pit-a-Pat.” As in some of his other children’s books, the juxtaposition of colors suggests a psychedelic aesthetic.

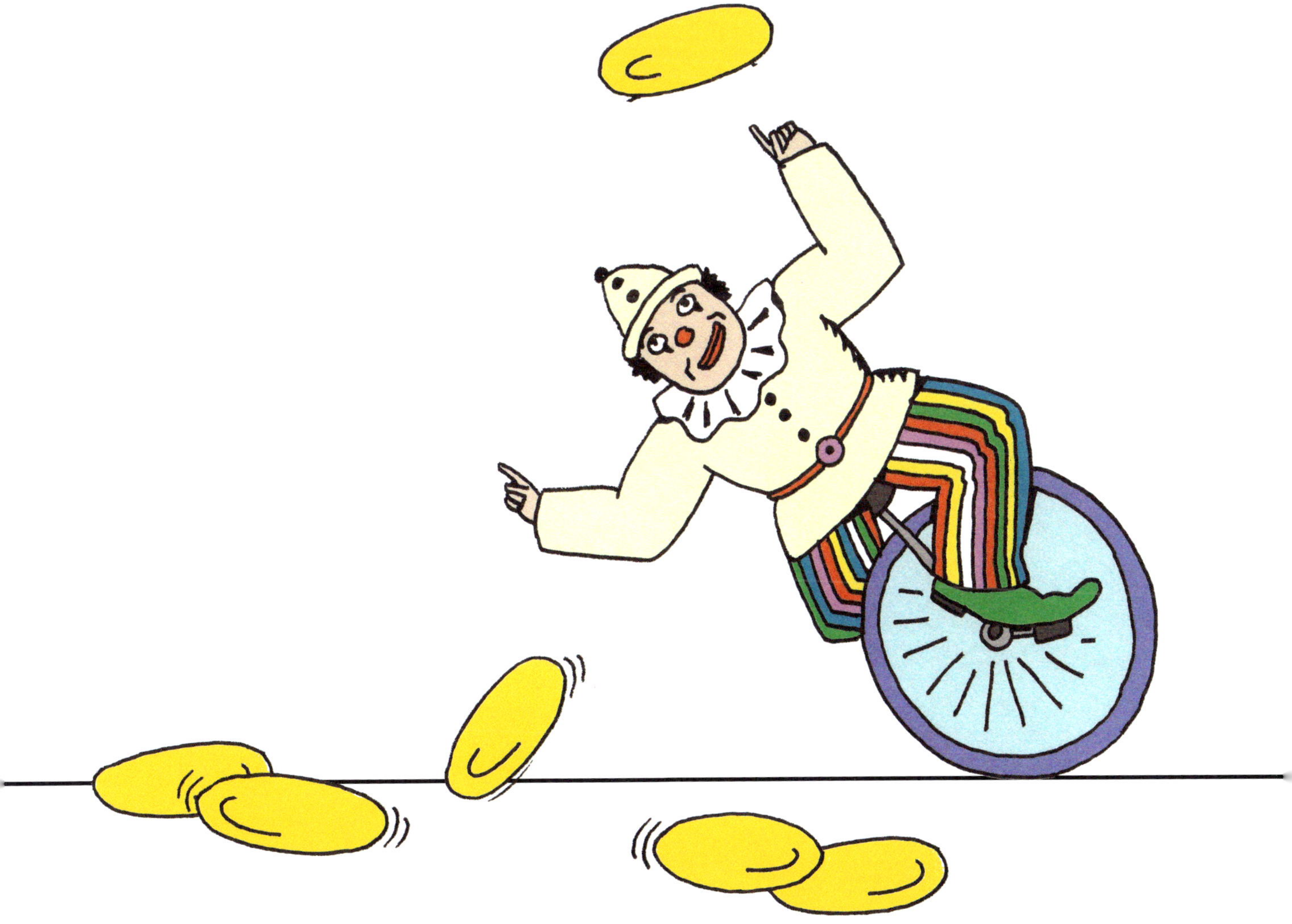

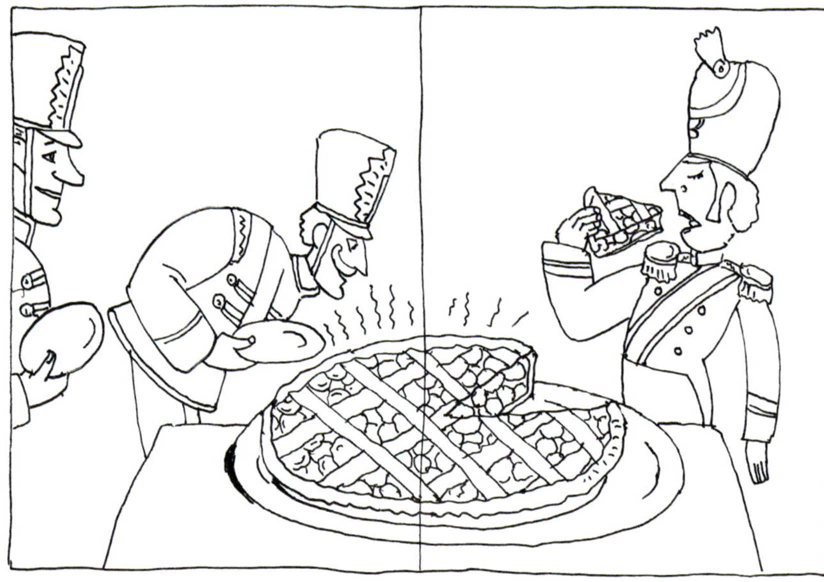

1 First-round rough sketch. Pencil on paper traced over in black pen on tracing paper. Cut out corrections placed as needed on top with white tape and scanned to begin with. The sketch is made to the trim size of the book.

How to Create a Children's Book

BY CAMILLE MURPHY

CAMILLE MURPHY is a designer and visual storyteller with a career spanning Penguin Putnam Books for Young Readers, Marvel Comics, and Simon & Schuster. For the past 12 years, she has collaborated closely with Seymour Chwast at the Pushpin Group as a designer in the studio, and her long partnership with Chwast gives her a unique perspective on what makes his stories and illustrations so enduring.

Seymour Chwast approaches children's bookmaking with the same combination of intuition, discipline, and restless curiosity that has defined his entire career. Ideas often arrive in the early morning. "Waking up in the morning, I think about it and make a note to myself," he explains. What matters is not the initial spark but its endurance; if the idea still feels promising a few hours later, only then is it worth pursuing. This simple ritual of reflection and reassessment is Chwast's first editorial pass, a self-imposed filter that protects him from the fleeting and the flimsy. Once the idea is in place, the development of a book can take several months to a few years, depending on the complexity of the project and other variables.

To illustrate this process, we can look at the making of *The Man in the Moon*, published by Corraini in 2019. The initial concept focused on an island inhabited by two distinct groups: people who grow fruit and people who bake. When an earthquake strikes, each group blames the other and conflict arises. A visitor, the man in the moon, arrives to help resolve the dispute and ultimately guides the community to understand that the solution is to treat one another with kindness.

From this starting point, Seymour begins sketching. His first round of drawings is usually done in pencil on tracing paper, a material that allows him to create overlays and make adjustments as the narrative and visual ideas develop.

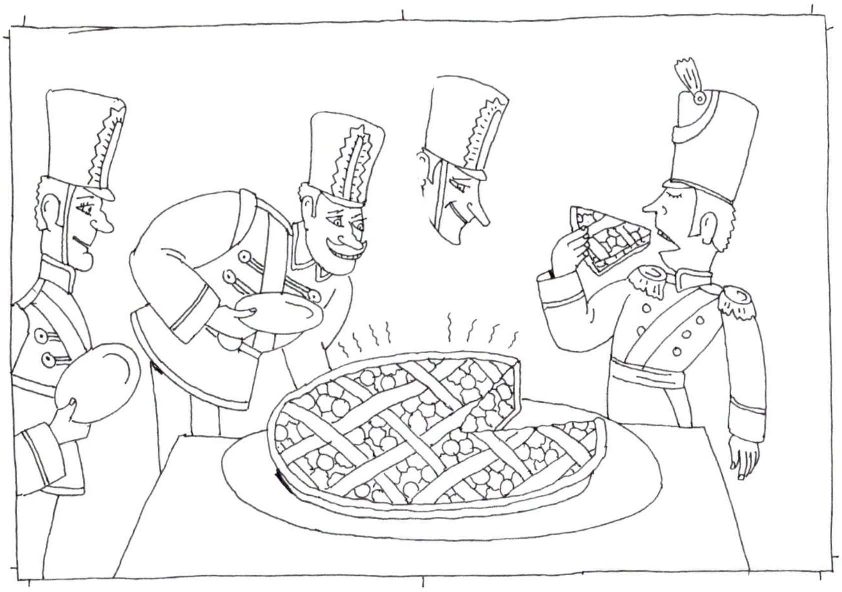

2 Second-round sketch. This is the tighter line art second-round sketch, sometimes also called the Tight Sketch or "The Finish." This sketch is then scanned in at 600 or 1200 dpi and imported into Adobe Photoshop. We always scan at a higher resolution than needed (typically most books are published at 300 dpi) in case we want to scale the art and not lose resolution later or in case we decide to use the work for larger marketing outcomes, like a poster.

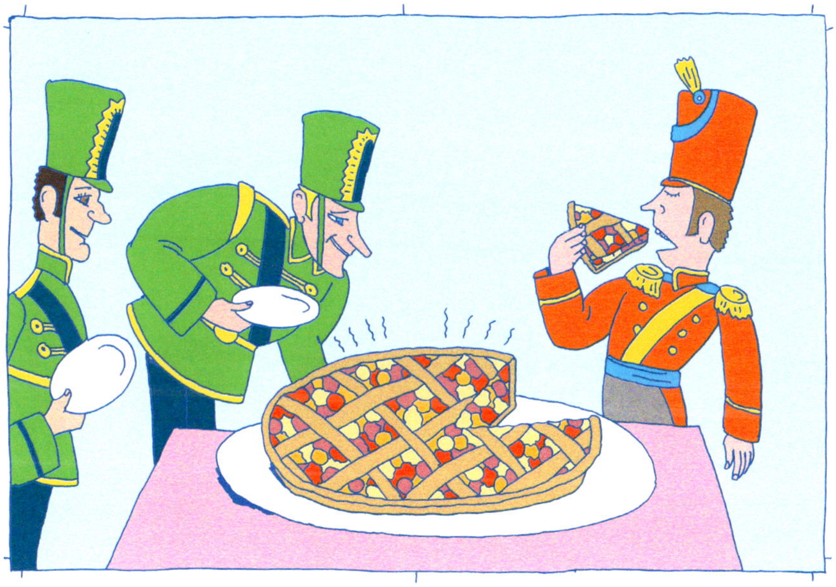

3 Third-round color. The refined second-round sketch is placed on a background layer in Photoshop. An adjustment layer is added to increase the contrast, followed by an edit layer for any small corrections. Color is then applied on the top layer. Seymour's preferred red is C0M80Y100K0, and his preferred yellow is C0M10Y100K0 (shown here).

Pro tip: We created a custom "Seymour Brush" in Photoshop so that retouching can have the same line quality as his line art.

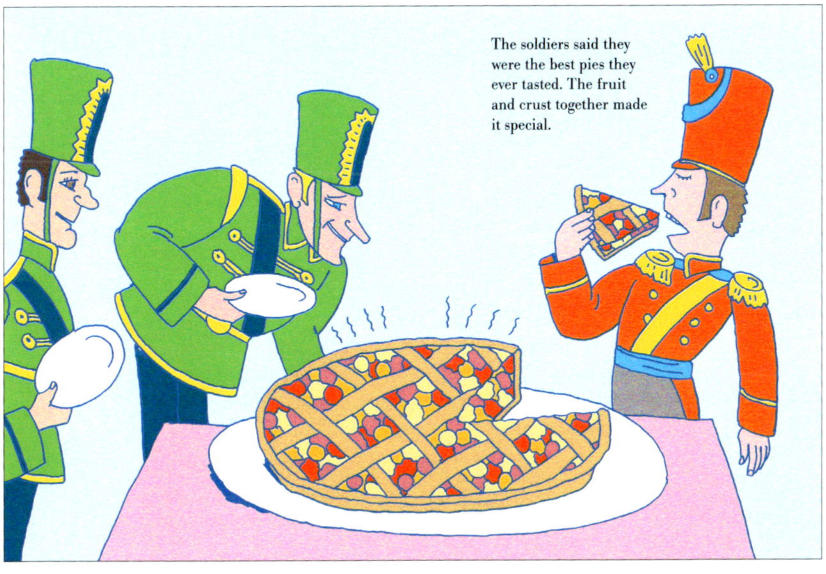

4 Final art. The final Photoshop file is then placed into the book mechanical in Adobe InDesign, where the text is added.

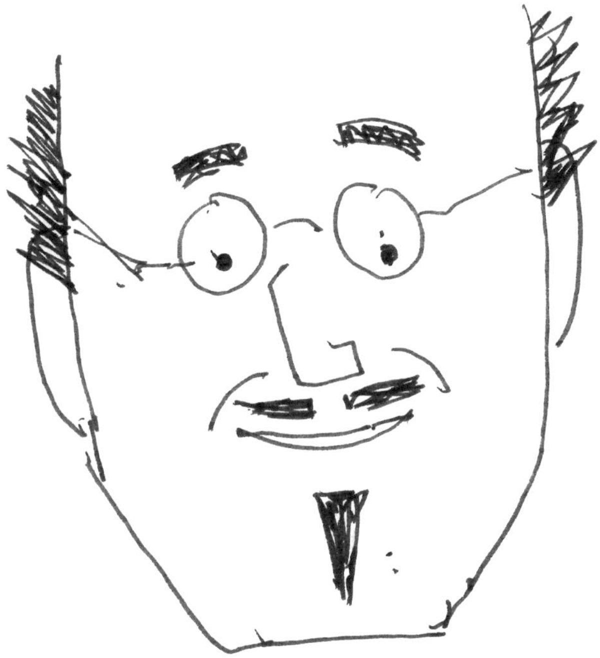

1 Cover art initial sketch. To develop the character and cover art, Chwast begins with sketches. Here are a few initial character sketches for the cover art.

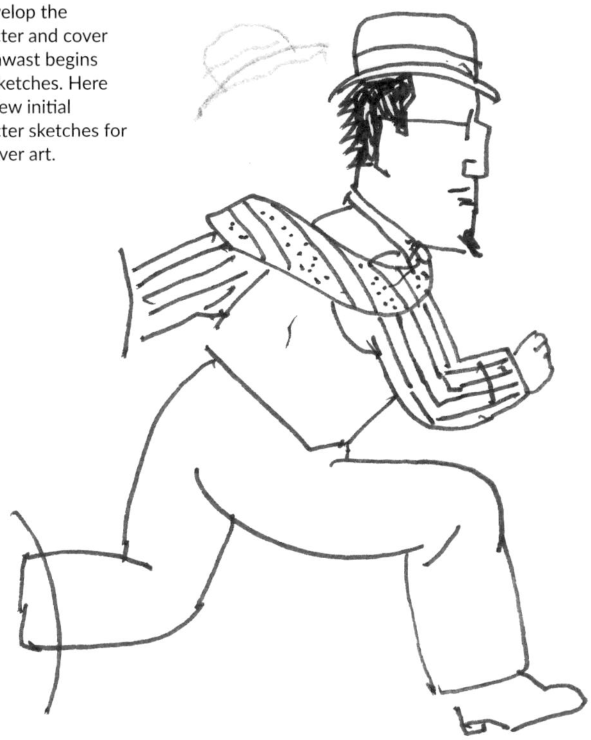

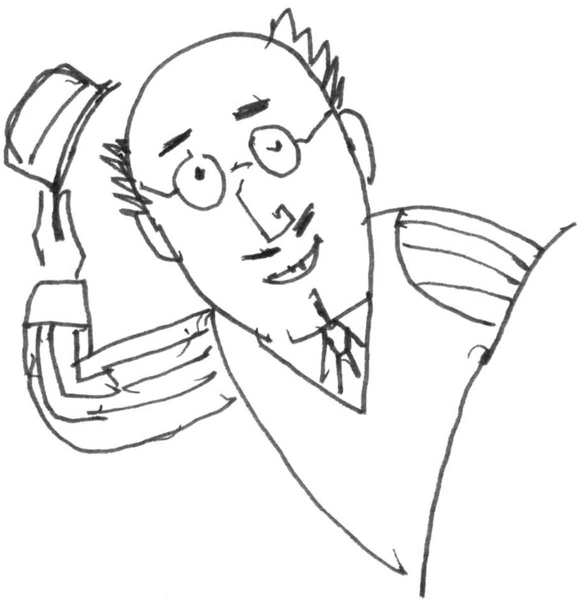

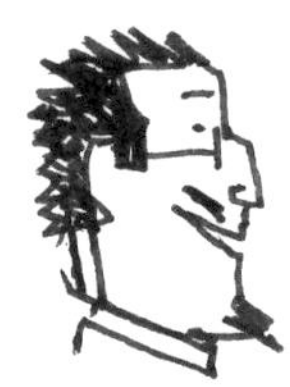

STRUCTURAL DESIGN AND SECOND-ROUND SKETCHES

After the initial exploratory sketches, Chwast turns to the structural design of the book with his characteristic precision. One of his first deliberate decisions is the trim size—an element that functions as a creative constraint rather than merely a production specification. Scale directs pacing, proportion, and the balance between text and image. Once the dimensions are fixed, he drafts a bounding area to indicate where images and text will appear. This framework becomes the underlying architecture for the project. At this time, the page count and written text are developed. It is important to note that most children's books are printed in page counts divisible by eight, a result of the signature-based structure of offset printing. Consequently, narratives are generally developed to fit standard formats, most commonly 32 or 40 pages.

Working within these parameters, Chwast develops a second, more resolved set of sketches at full size. These drawings clarify composition, character placement, and the visual rhythm of the book. Tracing paper remains central, allowing Chwast to layer corrections and refinements without losing the energy of earlier sketches. A black Pilot Razor Point pen remains his preferred tool, and revisions are applied judiciously using tape and white-out, preserving both the immediacy and the history of the drawing.

2 Cover Art rough sketch. This is the original first rough sketch for the cover of *The Man in the Moon*.

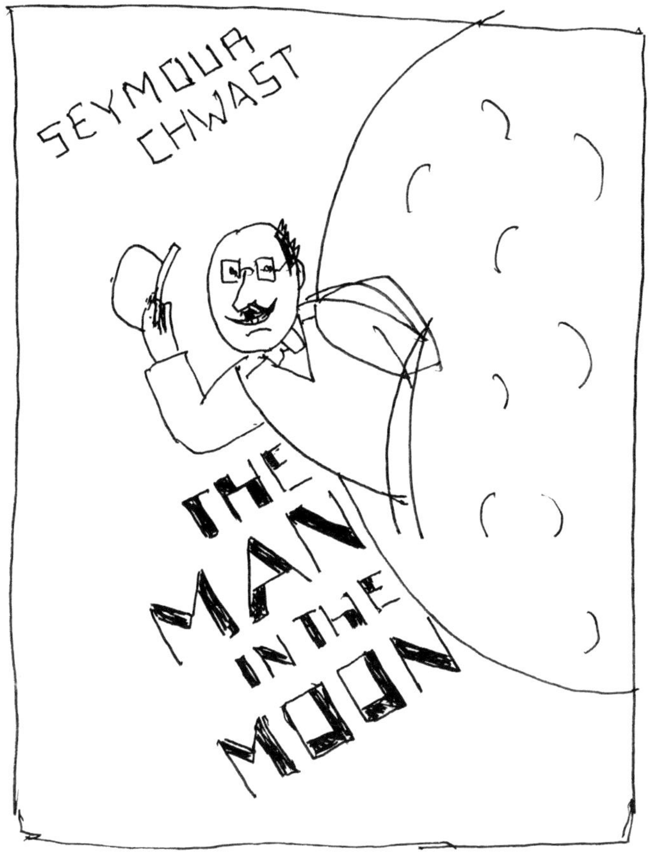

3 Cover art tight sketch. The character is refined and detail is added.

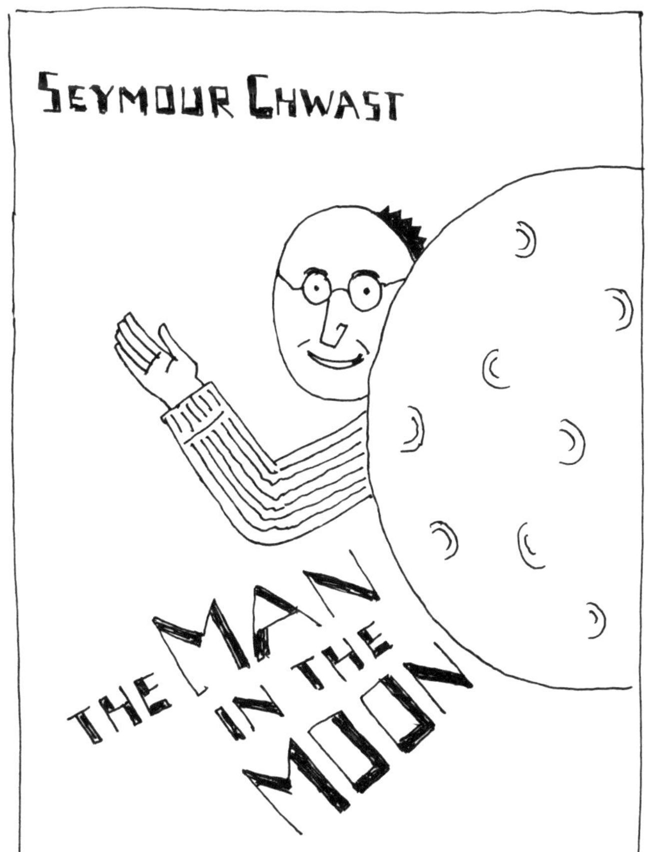

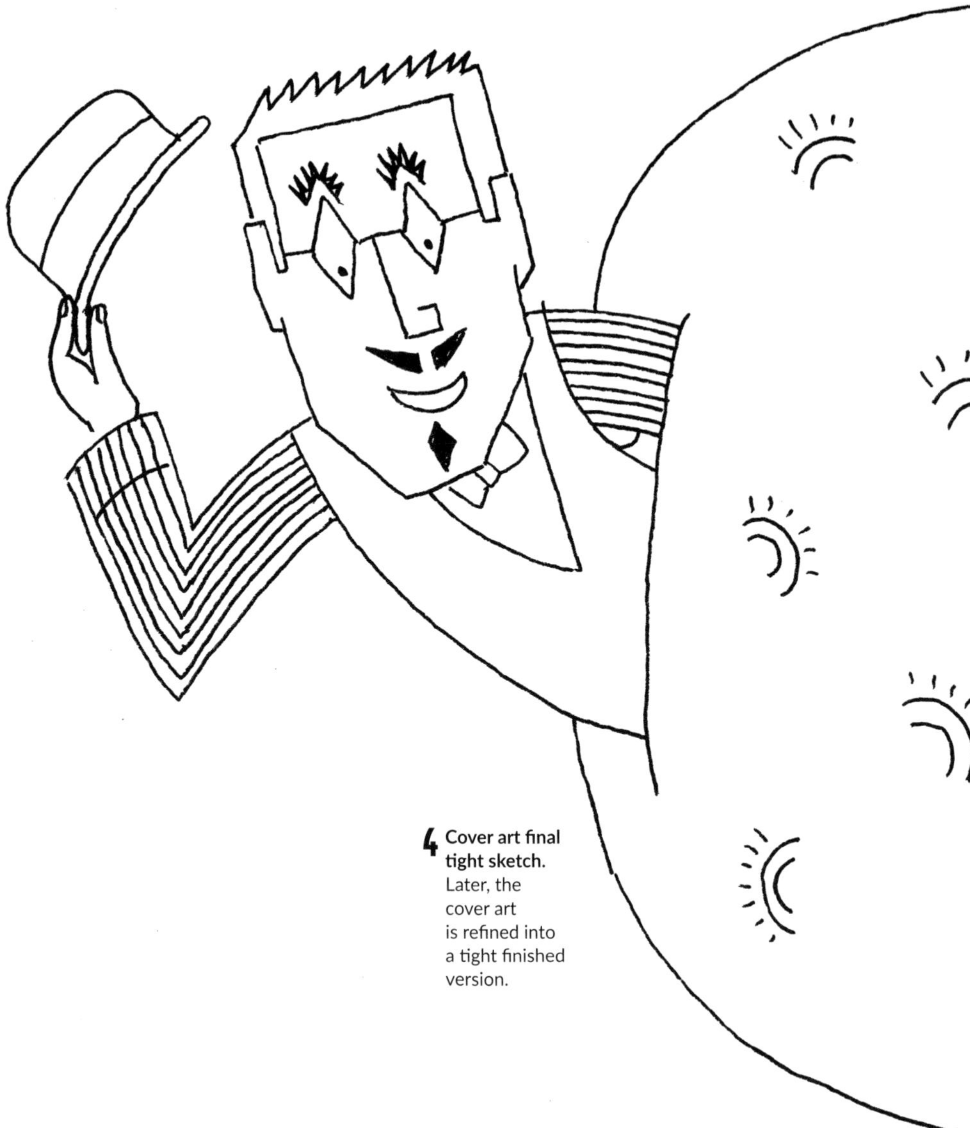

4 Cover art final tight sketch. Later, the cover art is refined into a tight finished version.

FINAL ART AND DIGITIZATION

For *The Man in the Moon*, Chwast's final line drawings were created in pen on tracing paper and then digitized using a flatbed scanner. Scans are made at 600 to 1200 dpi, a resolution that allows for enlargement while retaining the necessary sharpness for 300 dpi print. Digitization preserves the handmade qualities while enabling integration into a digital workflow. In Photoshop, color is applied in layers, often beginning with an adjustment layer to enhance line contrast. The palette is deliberate: Chwast favors a warm red (C0M80Y100K0) and a warm yellow (C0M10Y100K0), recurring hues that lend clarity and warmth to the printed pages. A custom "Seymour Brush" was created in Photoshop to ensure retouching preserves the quality and character of his line work.

Once the artwork is complete, the pages are assembled into the book's mechanical in Adobe InDesign. Images and text are integrated, and covers may be designed as independent files or as parent pages within the document, depending on the project. Additional production elements such as endpapers, die-cuts, or foldouts are also incorporated at this stage to ensure the physical book aligns with its conceptual design.

SUBMISSION, PUBLICATION, AND MARKETING

To present a project to publishers, Chwast prepares a submission package for his agent, Ann Tanenbaum. This typically includes a descriptive cover sheet and selected spreads, though fully paginated dummies are sometimes provided. The agent advises on refinements, identifies suitable publishers, and negotiates contracts, receiving a commission in accordance with trade practice.

After a publisher acquires the book, Chwast delivers final files and collaborates on production adjustments as needed. Proofs serve as the final checkpoint before printing. Once approved, the book proceeds to press and distribution.

As publication nears, Chwast provides promotional materials, such as a biography, headshot, social media accounts, and marketing information. Authors may participate in events, signings, or readings, though the scope of these activities varies. Compensation typically includes an advance against royalties, with rates falling within standard industry ranges.

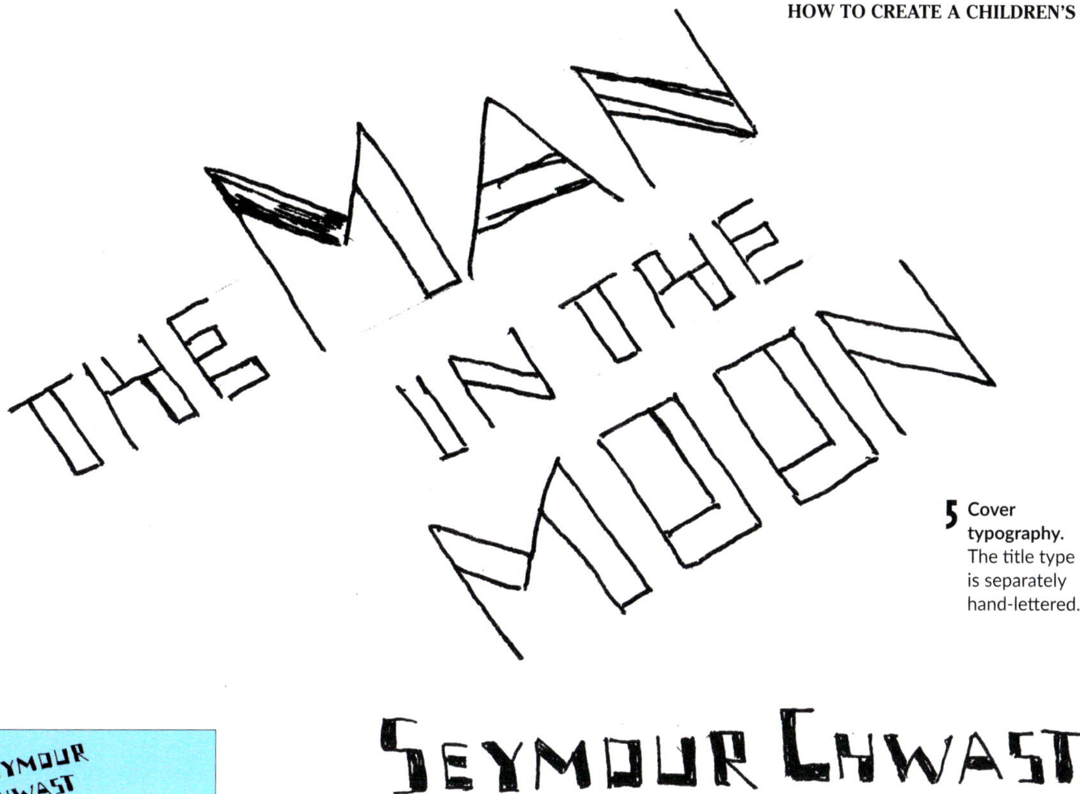

5 Cover typography. The title type is separately hand-lettered.

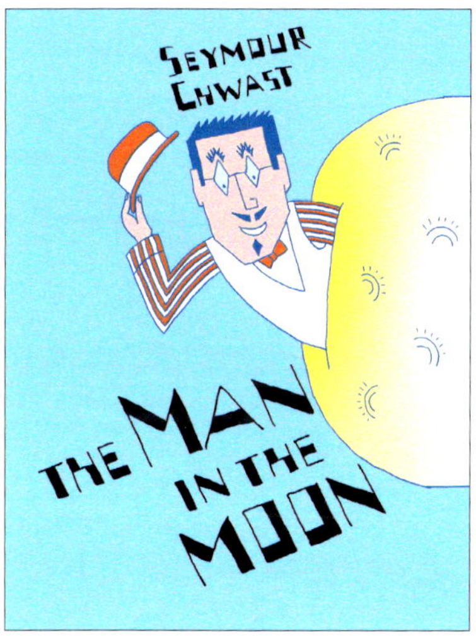

6 First pass of cover design. The tight cover art is colored in Adobe Photoshop. Then the layout is made in Adobe Indesign.

A DISTINCTIVE PROCESS

From initial concept to printed book, Chwast's approach combines intuition, craft, and personal methodology. His mixture of analog drawing, layered refinement, and digital adaptation forms a system uniquely his own, demonstrating how a disciplined yet experimental workflow can transform a simple idea into enduring children's literature.

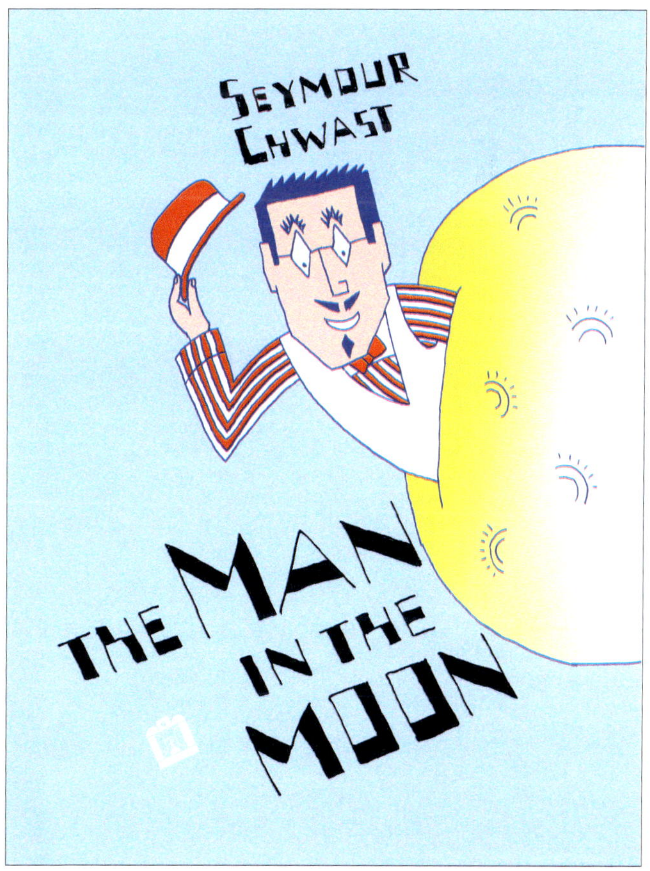

The finished art for the cover! Final cover of *The Man in the Moon*

Steven Heller

The Picture Book Book

The Art of Seymour Chwast

For Eve, Pamela, Jacob, Brian, and Kyle.

This book was edited by gestalten.

Edited by Friederike Christoph and Iris Hempelmann

Text and preface by Steven Heller

Illustrations Seymour Chwast

Text How to Create a Children's Book by Camille Murphy

Design & layout by Seymour Chwast

Associate design by Camille Murphy

Book photography by Todd Cooper Barnes

Production management by Martin Bretschneider

Typefaces by Łukasz Dziedzic (Lato), Zuzana Licko (Triplex),
Tony Stan (Cheltenham), Joel Kaden and Tony Stan (American Typewriter),
Seymour Chwast (Baseball)

Printed by Printer Trento S. p. A., Trento

Made in Italy

Published by gestalten, Berlin 2026

ISBN 978-3-96704-239-9

1st printing, 2026

For more information and to order books, please visit www.gestalten.com

Die Gestalten Verlag GmbH & Co. KG
Mariannenstrasse 9–10
10999 Berlin, Germany
hello@gestalten.com

Bibliographic information published by the Deutsche Nationalbibliothek

The Deutsche Nationalbibliothek lists this publication in the Deutsche Nationalbibliografie;

detailed bibliographic data is available online at www.dnb.de

None of the content in this book was published in exchange for payment by commercial parties or designers; the inclusion of all work is based solely on its artistic merit.

This book was printed on paper certified according to the standards of the FSC®.

FSC www.fsc.org MIX Paper | Supporting responsible forestry FSC® C015829